THE AGE OF JACKSON AND THE
ART OF AMERICAN POWER, 1815–1848

Also by William Nester

The Revolutionary Years, 1775–1789:
The Art of American Power During the Early Republic

The Hamiltonian Vision, 1789–1800:
The Art of American Power During the Early Republic

The Jeffersonian Vision, 1801–1815:
The Art of American Power During the Early Republic

THE AGE OF JACKSON

AND THE ART OF AMERICAN POWER,

1815–1848

WILLIAM NESTER

Potomac Books
An imprint of the University of Nebraska Press

Potomac Books is an imprint of the
University of Nebraska Press.
Maps by Jay Karamales.

Library of Congress
Cataloging-in-Publication Data
Nester, William R., 1956–
The age of Jackson and the art of American
power, 1815–1848 / William Nester. — First
edition.
pages cm
Includes bibliographical references and index.
ISBN 978-1-61234-605-2 (hardcover: acid-free
paper) — ISBN 978-1-61234-606-9 (electronic)
1. Jackson, Andrew, 1767–1845. 2. Presidents—
United States—Biography. 3. United States—
Politics and government—1815–1861. I. Title.
E382.N47 2013
973.5'6092—dc23
[B]
2013011714

First Edition

CONTENTS

ACKNOWLEDGMENTS

As always, I want to express my deep gratitude to Elizabeth Demers, the former senior editor at Potomac Books, first for wanting to publish my Art of American Power series, then for carefully editing each book. I am also very grateful to Julie Kimmel for her own very meticulous copyediting. Finally, I want to thank Kathryn Owens, the production editor, for expertly and swiftly guiding my book through the process. It is such a great pleasure to work with such wonderful people and outstanding professionals as Elizabeth, Julie, and Kathryn.

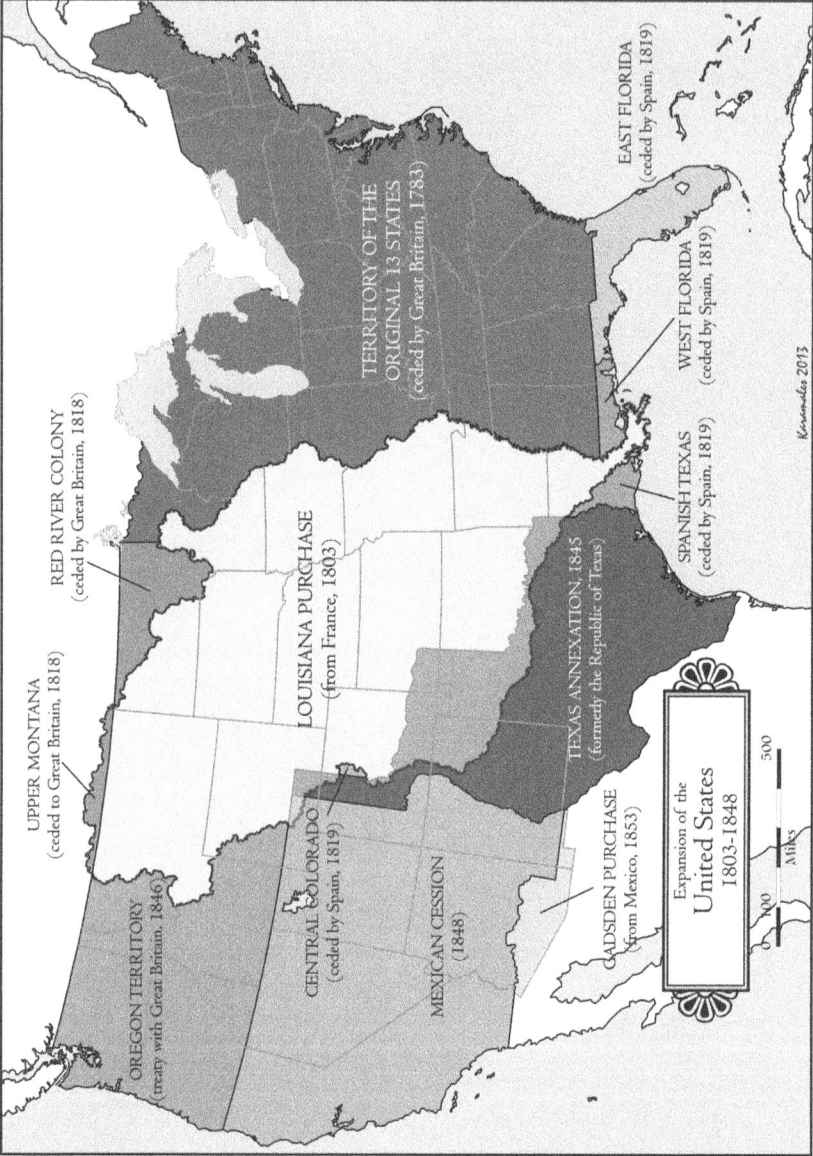

UPPER MONTANA
(ceded to Great Britain, 1818)

RED RIVER COLONY
(ceded by Great Britain, 1818)

OREGON TERRITORY
(treaty with Great Britain, 1846)

CENTRAL COLORADO
(ceded by Spain, 1819)

MEXICAN CESSION
(1848)

GADSDEN PURCHASE
(from Mexico, 1853)

LOUISIANA PURCHASE
(from France, 1803)

TERRITORY OF THE
ORIGINAL 13 STATES
(ceded by Great Britain, 1783)

TEXAS ANNEXATION: 1845
(formerly the Republic of Texas)

SPANISH TEXAS
(ceded by Spain, 1819)

WEST FLORIDA
(ceded by Spain, 1819)

EAST FLORIDA
(ceded by Spain, 1819)

Expansion of the
United States
1803-1848

100   500
Miles

Karawahla 2013

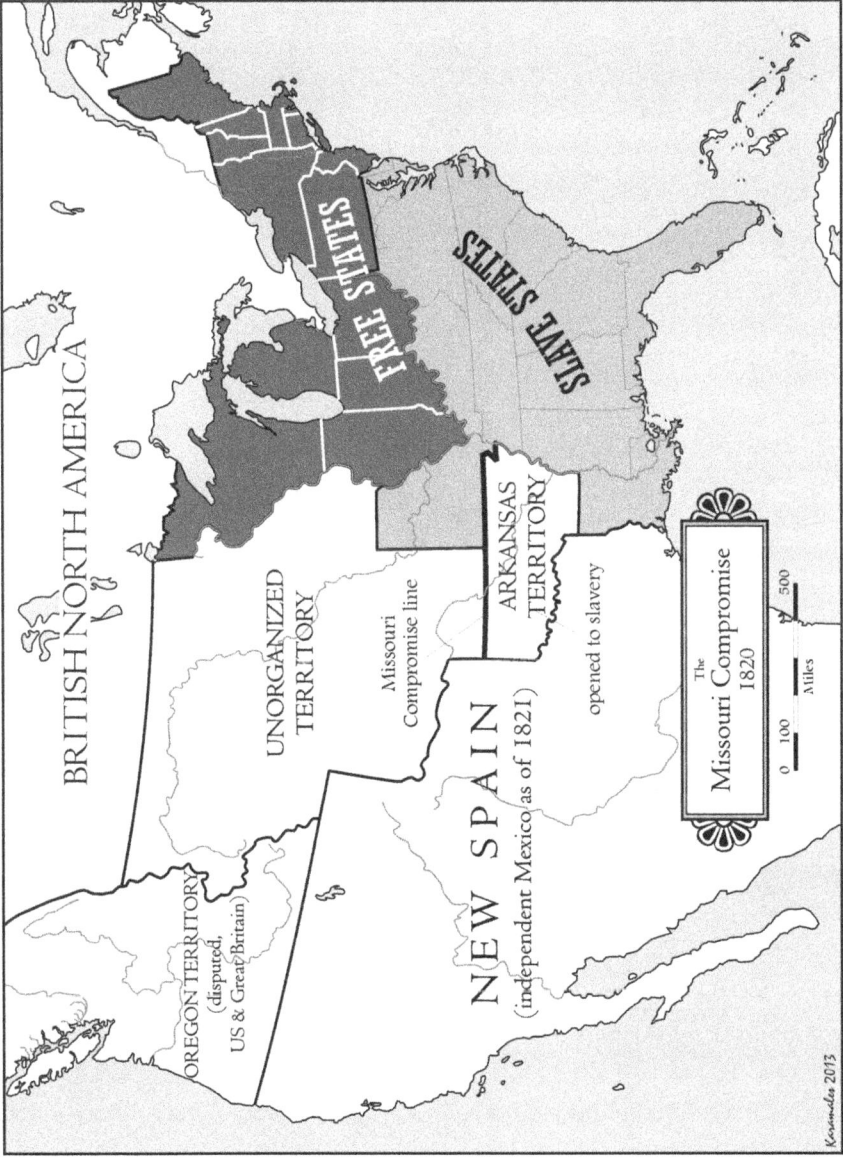

BRITISH NORTH AMERICA

FREE STATES

SLAVE STATES

OREGON TERRITORY
(disputed,
US & Great Britain)

UNORGANIZED
TERRITORY

Missouri
Compromise line

ARKANSAS
TERRITORY

opened to slavery

NEW SPAIN
(independent Mexico as of 1821)

The
Missouri Compromise
1820

0   100   500
         Miles

Kosmerdee 2013

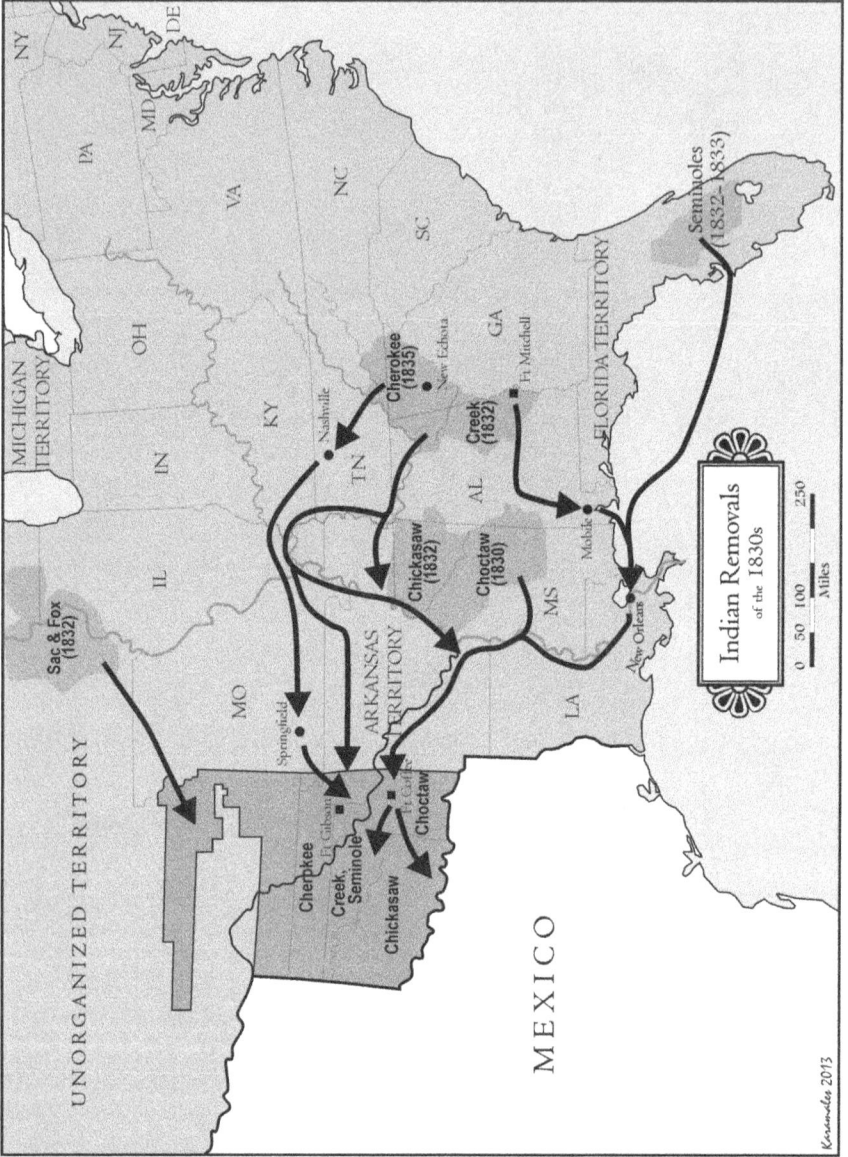

Indian Removals
of the 1830s

0 50 100   250
            Miles

Korsmeder 2013

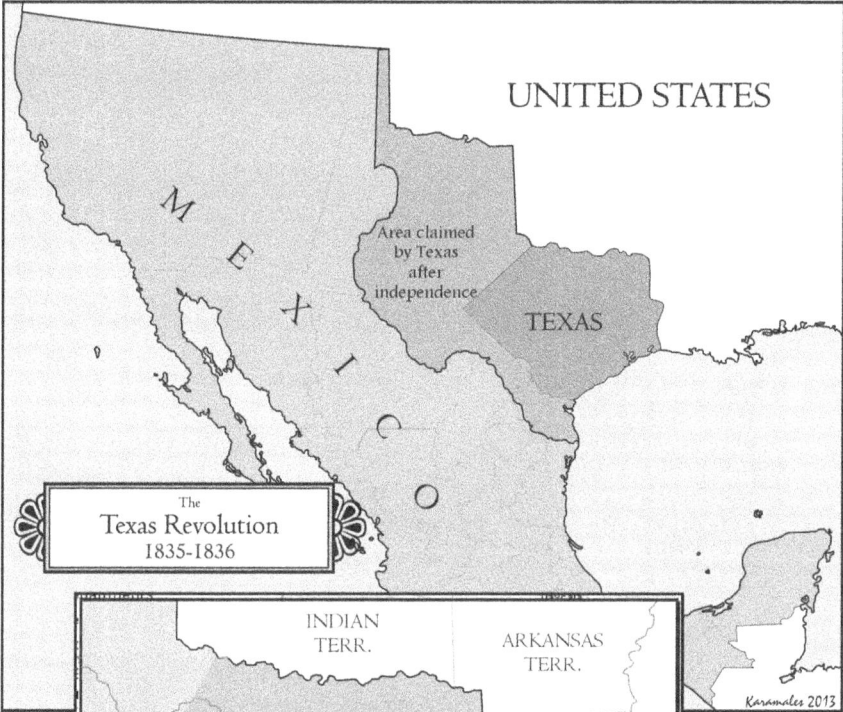

UNITED STATES

Area claimed
by Texas
after
independence

TEXAS

The
Texas Revolution
1835-1836

Karamales 2013

INDIAN
TERR.

ARKANSAS
TERR.

REPUBLIC OF TEXAS

LA

Mississippi

Brazos

Disputed area

Nueces

Alamo
6 Mar 1836

San Jacinto
21 Apr 1836

San Antonio
10 Dec 1835

Gonzales
2 Oct 1835

Goliad
20 Mar 1836

Refugio
14 Mar 1836

☆ Mexican victory
☆ Texan victory

MEXICO

Rio Grande

0   100   200

Miles

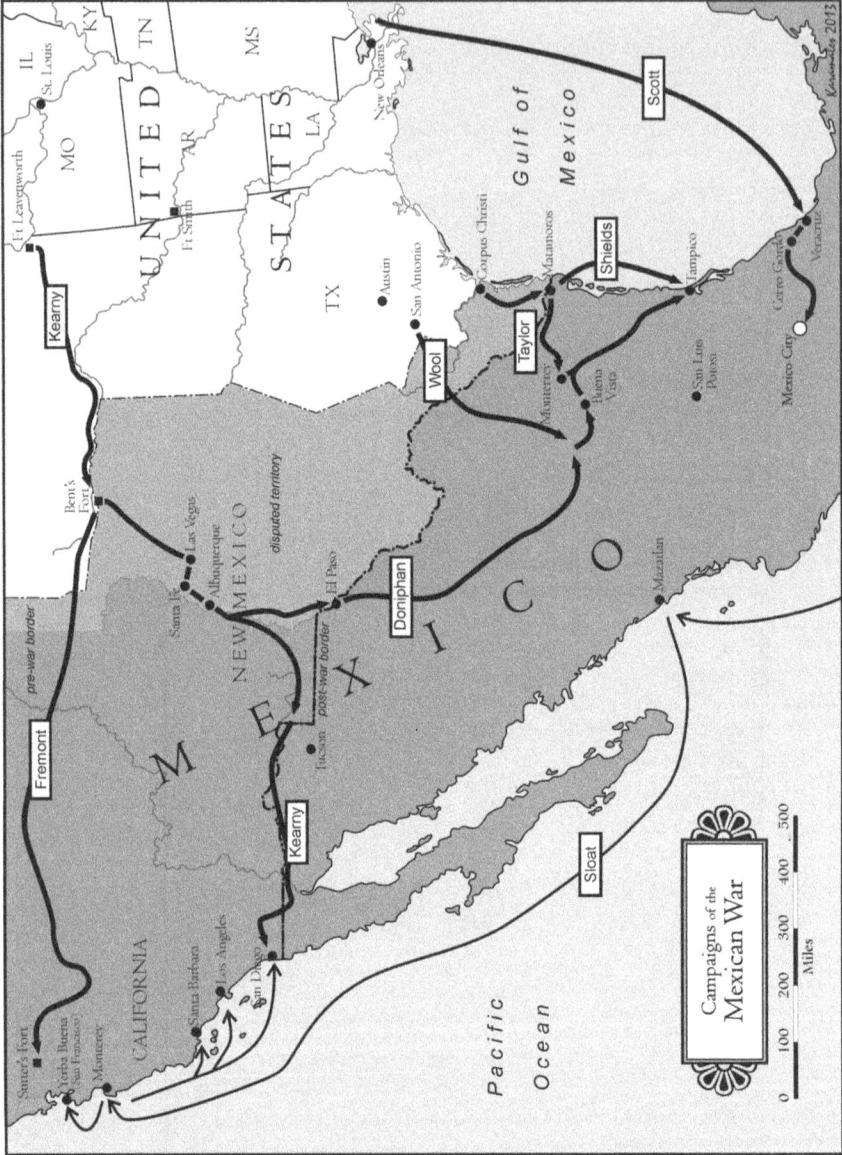

Campaigns of the
Mexican War

THE AGE OF JACKSON AND THE
ART OF AMERICAN POWER, 1815–1848

Introduction

The Art of Jacksonian Power

The great object of the institution of civil government
is the improvement of the condition of those
who are parties to the social compact.

JOHN QUINCY ADAMS

The government that governs least, governs best.

THOMAS JEFFERSON

Then we will have peace for then we will be prepared for war.
Every man with a gun in his hand, all Europe combined cannot hurt us. And all the world will be anxious to be on
friendly terms with us because all the world will see we wish
peace with all but are prepared for defense against those
who would wantonly infringe our national rights.

ANDREW JACKSON

Experience has taught me two lessons: first, that things are seen plainer
after the events have occurred; second, that the most confident critics
are generally those who know the least about the matter criticized.

ULYSSES S. GRANT

Andrew Jackson is among the more immediately recognizable of the presidents, and not just because his portrait is engraved on the twenty dollar bill. His physical appearance was as extraordinary as his deeds. At six feet tall, he loomed over most other men of his era. In his early manhood he was all lean muscle, but diseases and gunshot wounds gradually emaciated him until he was cadaverous skin and bones and rendered his gaunt, horselike face even longer. The thick, unruly dark red mane of his younger decades turned steel gray by his forties and snowy white by the time he entered the White House. Yet he is more than a striking national icon—he inspired an era.

It takes quite a leader to personify an age. Andrew Jackson was the titan of the thirty-three years that spanned 1815 to 1848.[1] During this time, his image, character, beliefs, and acts dominated American politics. This was no easy task as he squared off against such powerful political foes as Henry Clay, John Quincy Adams, John Calhoun, Daniel Webster, and John Marshall. Although in March 1837, after eight years as president, Jackson returned to his Tennessee plantation, he continued to overshadow American politics. Two of his protégés, Martin Van Buren, "the Magician," and James Polk, "Young Hickory," followed him to the White House and carried on his agenda.

Jackson dominated his age for many reasons but ultimately because he had mastered the art of power. This art includes getting what he wanted, getting others to do what they would otherwise not do, preventing others from doing what they would otherwise do, and taking from others what they would otherwise keep. Jackson excelled at all of these.

Two key events bracketed the age of Jackson—the Battle of New Orleans, fought on January 8, 1815, and the Treaty of Guadeloupe Hidalgo, signed on February 2, 1848. The battle was Jackson's greatest military victory. The treaty, which won for the United States uncontested title to Texas, New Mexico, and California, was the greatest political victory for Jackson's disciple James Polk. Each win epitomized Jackson's version of the art of power—the assertion of overwhelming, brute force. In any conflict, he demanded that all involved either stand with him or against him. He warred mercilessly against his enemies by massing all the available physical and emotional sources of power until they were utterly crushed. To this end, he made no more compromises and took no more prisoners than were necessary.

Jackson's art of power was not all hard coercion but had a soft, persuasive side as well. A vital portion of his success as a general and politician came from his ability to epitomize how most American men wanted to see themselves—as fearless, principled, and patriotic. He inspired others to emulate and follow him. Even his political foes, who castigated Jackson for repeatedly violating the Constitution and derailing their progressive agenda, could not dispute, and quite likely envied, his natural virility.

Hatred can be a source of power, and Jackson was a great hater. Indeed his hatreds were so volcanic that they appear to have exceeded even those of more recent presidents such as Richard Nixon and George W. Bush, who were notorious for projecting their own inner demons onto their opponents. Some of Jackson's foes returned his hatred. It is unsurprising that Jackson was both the first president to be assaulted and the first to be targeted for assassination.

Yet another critical dimension of Jackson's ability to dominate the age was his brilliance in innovating old and inventing new ways to wield power. He carried existing political practices to unprecedented heights. All six presidents before him had only nine vetoes among them and justified each by arguing that the bill was unconstitutional. By contrast, Jackson defended his twelve vetoes by asserting that the bills would damage the nation. He either initiated or provoked such other firsts in American political history as firing a cabinet secretary, pocketing a veto, and being censured by the Senate. This "man of the people" was the first to deploy federal troops to crush a labor strike. Jackson's administration was the first to experience a sex scandal, and the adultery charges that erupted shortly after he entered the White House revealed unique insights about him and the nature of power in his era. During the age of Jackson, new terms and practices, including "spoils system," "kitchen cabinet," "dark-horse candidate," and "political convention," entered the lexicon.

Although Jackson himself was not venal, his policies inadvertently unleashed corruption on a massive national scale that dwarfed all the combined, and usually unfounded, accusations against the administrations of his half-dozen predecessors. He and his followers either pioneered or proliferated the seamier side of American politics, including party machines, payback to allies, and a highly emotional, volatile populism that eviscerated any foes. Indeed, Jackson was often compared to Coriolanus, the tyrant who ruled partly by inciting the mob against those who opposed him.

For better or worse, Andrew Jackson radically changed both the style and substance of power in America forever. Ever since, countless politicians have emulated his art of power, either reluctantly or zealously. Yet adherents of two additional, alternative visions of American power have jostled with each other since before Jackson's era and with Jacksonism from then through today.[2]

One is Hamiltonism.[3] None of the founders was more gifted with refined intellect and raw courage than Alexander Hamilton. During the War for Independence, he fought valiantly at the front and served as George Washington's most trusted aide. After the war, he was a leading force behind the convention that, during the long, hot summer of 1787, hammered out the Constitution. Then, to explain the new document and justify its ratification, he enlisted John Jay and James Madison to help him write the brilliant series of essays known as the Federalist Papers; he penned fifty-five of those eighty-five essays himself. As the nation's first treasury secretary, he converted a vicious cycle of low national growth and high debt, joblessness, and wildly fluctuating prices into a virtuous cycle of economic expansion, exports, innovations, and prosperity. He did so by consolidating the state and national debts; establishing the First Bank of the United States to finance that debt and foster critical investments; creating a national mint to produce the silver dollar; promoting internal improvements, including the building of roads, ports, and canals; and setting a tariff that raised revenues and protected infant industries. Tragically his life was cut short when Aaron Burr killed him in a duel in 1804.

Hamilton's art of power revolutionized all aspects of American life, enabling the United States to surpass Britain and become the world's most powerful nation. Hamiltonism's bottom line is the reality that the more diversified a nation's economy, the more wealth it creates and distributes, and thus the more it empowers the nation to resist recessions and win trade or military wars. To this end, Hamilton advocated a muscular, problem-solving national government that nurtured the creation and distribution of wealth through critical investments in infrastructure, industry, innovation, and education. He promoted a professional army and navy strong enough to deter or defeat any genuine foreign or domestic military threats. He continuously defended his policies on constitutional grounds, arguing that the Constitution's explicit and implicit powers not only permitted, but required, the federal government to engage in these activities for the welfare of the state and its citizens.

Each generation or so, a president has asserted this Hamiltonian version of the art of power. The most prominent of these presidents have been George Washington, John Quincy Adams, Abraham Lincoln, Theodore Roosevelt, Franklin Roosevelt, Richard Nixon, Bill Clinton, and Barack Obama. Adams, the son of the second president, succinctly expressed Hamilton's vision: "The great object of the institution of civil government is the improvement of the condition of those who are parties to the social compact."[4]

Jeffersonism is the other alternative to Jacksonism.[5] Thomas Jefferson is best known for expressing the American mind by penning the Declaration of Independence. This revolutionary document was the apex of an astonishing political career that included stints as a Virginia assemblyman, congressman, and governor; ambassador to France; secretary of state; vice president; and, finally, president from 1801 to 1809. In contrast to Hamilton, Jefferson's record at managing American power was starkly mixed. His greatest long-term contribution to the nation's development was the Louisiana Purchase in 1803. But Jefferson devastated the economy with his 1807 embargo, which kept American ships from engaging in trade with foreign countries.

Jefferson's maxim "the government that governs least, governs best" epitomizes his art of power. Bare-bones authority should be decentralized from the federal government toward the state and local levels. To his dying day, he clung to the sentimental notion that farmers "are the chosen people of God" and thus should be the backbone of both the economy and the republic. He was content to let other countries excel in industry, trade, and finance while Americans concentrated on raising crops and livestock. Worried that a standing army threatened liberty, he insisted that the nation was best defended by village militia companies and by small gunboats anchored in local ports.[6]

Jeffersonism's descendants in the White House include James Madison, John Tyler, Millard Fillmore, Franklin Pierce, James Buchanan,

Andrew Johnson, Warren Harding, Calvin Coolidge, and Herbert Hoover. In an increasingly globalization-driven, interdependent world, Jefferson's vision of a puny national government, agrarianism, and isolationism is practically impossible. Yet despite, or more likely because of this, his vision remains emotionally and politically appealing. The Tea Party movement is the most recent popular expression of Jeffersonism.

Jacksonism combines elements of Hamiltonism and Jeffersonism but asserts behaviors and values abhorred by these rival approaches to the art of power. Like Jefferson, Jackson espoused agrarianism and states' rights. He departed from Jefferson in two areas—the army and the law. Jackson worshiped the military as much as Jefferson disdained and feared it. Jackson was contemptuous of the law and even the Constitution when it forbade his intended actions. In contrast, Jefferson agonized whether his policies corresponded with his cramped interpretation of the Constitution. Although Hamilton and Jackson both believed in a strong executive, they differed on one crucial point. For Hamilton, presidential and all other institutional powers must always adhere to those powers explicitly or implicitly articulated in the Constitution. Jackson contemptuously trampled such legal restraints. In his mind, a president's power should be as great as his ambitions and the challenges facing the nation. No president better epitomized Andrew Jackson's philosophy in action, if not his character, than George W. Bush and, to a lesser extent, James Polk and Ronald Reagan. Neoconservatism epitomizes Jacksonism.

Andrew Jackson provoked firestorms of political passions throughout his era. Far more people loved than hated him, but the fervor was just as pitched either way. Although the passions have subsided, the debate lingers. Historians are split over Jackson's legacy. Some extol him as among America's greatest presidents, citing his championing of the common man, holding the country together during the nullification crisis, and eliminating the national debt.[7] Others excoriate him as a mean-spirited despot who shredded the Constitution and damaged the nation's development by destroying the Second Bank of the United States, defying the Supreme Court, grossly worsening political corruption through his spoils system, and expelling tens of thousands of eastern Indians from their homes on a Trail of Tears that led far west of the Mississippi River and left thousands buried along the way. Although he was touted as "a man of the people," Jackson's policies shamelessly enriched speculators, slave masters, and corrupt officials.[8]

This book provides new insights and perspectives in this old debate and in the very nature of power itself. It does so guided by some time-less wisdom from Ulysses S. Grant, who fought as a lieutenant in the Mexican War: "Experience has taught me two lessons: first, that things are seen plainer after the events have occurred; second, that the most confident critics are generally those who know the least about the matter criticized."[9]

1

The Precedents,
1769–1829

I

The Making of the Man

Who are we? And for what are we going to fight?

ANDREW JACKSON

Those who are not with us are against us,
and will be dealt with accordingly.

ANDREW JACKSON

What a country God has given us! How thankful
we ought to be. . . . We have the best country
and the best institutions in the world.

ANDREW JACKSON

What makes a man? Like everyone, Andrew Jackson reflected the time
and place in which he lived. Unlike most people, he as much shaped
as was shaped by his age.

Tragedy, violence, suffering, and deprivation tormented Jackson's
boyhood. He was born into poverty in the Waxhaws region of South
Carolina on March 15, 1767. His parents were Scotch-Irish immigrants,
two of a quarter million who disembarked in America during the eigh-

teenth century. Like other immigrant groups, the Scotch-Irish tended to settle among those who came before them. More than most groups, they were characterized by their clannishness, quick tempers, and hard-as-nails toughness.

Jackson never knew his father and namesake, who died from exhaustion and illness before he was born. He adored his mother, Elizabeth, whose essential sweetness softened her Presbyterian piety, stern moral code, and steely courage. After her husband's death, Elizabeth and her three young boys moved in with her sister Jane; her husband, James Crawford; and their eight children. With all these playmates, Jackson enjoyed a rowdy childhood that came to an abrupt and tragic end.

Andrew Jackson hated the British from his early teens until the day he died. This hatred was well-founded. The British invaded the Carolinas in 1779, and for the next two years they and their local Tory allies rampaged through the region, pillaging, raping, murdering, and burning virtually everywhere they marched or camped.

Andrew and his older brothers, Hugh and Robert, joined the Patriot cause. Only Andrew survived the war. Disease killed Hugh after he fought at Stono Ferry in June 1779. In their militia company, Robert was a private, and thirteen-year-old Jackson was a courier and scout.

British dragoons routed their militia company. The survivors scattered. Jackson holed up with his brother and several others at a nearby cousin's home. The dragoons surrounded and captured them and pillaged the home. Jackson could not stifle his rage at the depredation. When an officer ordered him to blacken his boots, Jackson defiantly refused. The officer drew his sword and slashed the boy's skull, face, and upheld hand. To his dying day, Jackson was reminded of British brutality every time he glanced at the scar across his hand or down the gaunt face staring back from a mirror.

The dragoons herded their prisoners to Camden and packed them with 250 others in a barn. Smallpox broke out and sickened and killed many captives. Learning of her sons' fate, Elizabeth hurried to Camden and convinced the commander to release them. Smallpox afflicted the brothers. Robert died soon after reaching home. Andrew gradually recovered.

Satisfied that her last child would survive, Elizabeth journeyed from her home to Charleston, 150 miles away, to care for and try to free other family members imprisoned there. Instead, she died of cholera. When he learned of his mother's death, Jackson "at first could not believe it," but "when I finally realized the truth I was utterly alone, and tried to recall her last words to me."[1]

Then, a four-hundred-pound-sterling inheritance from his paternal grandfather in Ireland offered Jackson a chance to escape from poverty. He hurried to Charleston to collect the money and visit his mother's grave. Then he proceeded to gamble away his newfound wealth in a few weeks of riotous living. He returned to the Waxhaws as poor as he had left, and apparently none the wiser. He tried teaching school but lasted no more than a few weeks in the classroom. Whether he quit or was dismissed is unknown, but regardless, this restless, hormone-addled, barely literate teenager was hardly suited for the profession.

Jackson turned his back on the Waxhaws in December 1784 and strode to Salisbury, North Carolina, where he sought a mentor with whom to learn law. During his years there, he became renowned far more for hell-raising than for studying. Nonetheless, he passed the bar in September 1787 and spent another half year in Salisbury trying to drum up clients. Word that a public prosecutor's office had opened in Jonesborough, Tennessee, inspired him to head west in the spring of 1788.

Most folks in Salisbury could not wait to see the last of him, although apparently none dared say so within earshot of the young hothead. Two surviving stories reveal some of the antics of his law school years. He provoked a scandal when he invited two local prostitutes—a mother and daughter—to the town ball. One drunken night he and his cohorts started smashing their glasses after each shot. When they ran out of glasses, they took turns gulping from the jug, breaking up the furniture, and feeding the pieces to the fire.

Jackson cut a striking figure. One woman later vividly recalled that he was

> always dressed neat and tidy and carried himself as if he was a rich man's son. The day he was licensed he had on a new suit, with broadcloth coat, ruffled shirt, and other garments in the best of fashion. The style of powdering the hair was still in vogue then; but he had his abundant . . . dark red hair combed carefully back from his forehead . . . and . . . made to lay down sooth with bear's oil. He

was full six feet tall and very slender, but yet of such straightness of form and such produce and graceful carriage as to make him look well-proportioned. In feature he was by no means good-looking. His face was long and narrow, his features sharp and angular, and his complexion yellow and freckled. But his eyes . . . were very large, a kind of steel-blue, and when he talked to you he always looked straight into your eyes. . . . When he was calm he talked slowly and with very good selected language. But if animated by anything, then he would talk in with a very marked North-Irish brogue. . . . But either calm or animated there was always something about him I cannot describe except to say it was a presence, or a kind of majesty I never saw in any other young man.[2]

Jackson was only twenty-one when he arrived in Jonesborough to serve as the district prosecutor. He soon violated at least one of the very laws he had pledged to uphold. A twisted sense of pride provoked him to issue his first challenge to a duel. His opponent was the defense attorney for a suspect he had prosecuted. Jackson accused the attorney of sullying his honor by besting him in the courtroom. Fortunately, like many duels, this one ended without bloodshed as their seconds prearranged for both to fire into the air. Most of Jackson's future duels would not be resolved so civilly.

Although he had defended his honor, the humiliating sting of his bumbling courtroom performances persisted. He resigned his post and headed west through 230 miles of wilderness to Nashville, where he could start fresh. Not long after he arrived in October 1788, he set up a law practice, was named the district's public prosecutor, and got into trouble, this time with another man's wife.

Rachel Donelson Robards was the love of Andrew Jackson's life. She was vivacious, passionate, pretty, and plump. Physically she was said to resemble his beloved mother. Their mutual attraction deepened. One obstacle stymied their relationship—Rachel was married. Her husband, Lewis Robards, was frequently drunk, jealous, and abusive. The three could not avoid each other. Rachel and Robards lived in her mother's home, where Jackson boarded. One day Jackson squared off with Robards after he vented his rage on Rachel. Robards backed down, vowed to get a divorce, and fled to his family's home in Kentucky.

Once again Jackson's behavior had kicked up an acrid small-town cloud of gossip. Many folks condemned him for stealing another man's wife. Of course, for the same reason many a man envied him. Regardless, the scandal choked his legal practice and social standing. In the autumn of 1790 Jackson and Rachel escaped Nashville's moral censure by journeying down the 440-mile Natchez Trace to Spanish territory.[3]

Jackson was already familiar with Natchez. During a previous visit in July 1789, he had sworn allegiance to the Spanish king. Anyone who wanted to live and work in the Spanish empire was legally required to take the oath. Although Jackson soon returned to Nashville, being a Spanish citizen made it easier to resettle in Natchez with Rachel.

Word reached them that Robards had obtained a divorce. Actually, he had only filed for divorce with Virginia's legislature, which at that time still governed Kentucky. Jackson and Rachel were apparently ignorant of that fact when they married in Natchez. The newlyweds returned to Nashville, where Jackson resumed his law practice.

Meanwhile, Tennessee had become part of the Southwest Territory with its capital at Nashville. The governor was William Blount, who, like Jackson, became a lawyer after fighting in the Revolutionary War. Jackson wangled an interview with the governor, who was won over by the brash, bright, energetic young man with his striking appearance. It was not just charisma that impressed Blount. Jackson's legal training, experience, and skills may have been meager, but they were in great demand on this still raw frontier.

With Blount as his patron, Jackson rose rapidly in the region's economic, social, and political ranks. He became the attorney general and a trustee of Davidson Academy in 1791. His wealth grew not just from practicing law but from buying and selling merchandise, slaves, and land.

Then came the bombshell in late 1793 that Robards had only recently obtained a divorce. The Jacksons had been living happily together, oblivious that they were bigamists. On January 18, 1794, they again exchanged wedding vows, this time before a local justice of the peace. To their relief, the inevitable gossip eventually dissipated. Jackson was no longer an outsider but had become part of Tennessee's elite.

He and the other local movers and shakers were determined to transform Tennessee from a territory into a state. A census in November 1795 counted 77,362 inhabitants of the territory, with 65,776 whites,

10,613 slaves, and 973 free blacks, a number well above the minimum population of 60,000 needed for statehood. Because of high property requirements, only a fraction of Tennesseans were considered citizens and even fewer exercised their right to vote. In the plebiscite, 6,504 favored and 2,562 opposed statehood.[4]

Jackson was elected a delegate to Tennessee's constitutional convention at Knoxville, which met from January 11 to February 6, 1796. The delegates drafted a constitution and sent it to Philadelphia, the nation's capital from 1790 to 1800, for Congress's approval. Tennessee officially became the sixteenth state on June 1, 1796, when President George Washington signed the enabling bill and state constitution into law.

Meanwhile, Jackson sought to realize his greatest dream—becoming a military leader. He first ran for election as the major general of Tennessee's militia in November 1796. His rival John Conway was backed by Governor Jack Sevier, Tennessee's first governor and a hero of the Revolutionary War and of local campaigns against the Cherokees. To ensure that his candidate won, Sevier issued commissions for promises of support. When Jackson criticized this practice, Sevier dismissed him as "a poor pitiful pettifogging lawyer" suitable for nothing but "contempt."[5] Jackson obtained a copy of the letter and returned it to the governor along with a challenge to a duel. Sevier dismissed the challenge as inappropriate from one so low to one so high. For now, Jackson could only fume, enraged as he suffered an election loss atop the insult. But one day he would avenge himself.

William Blount consoled his fiery protégé with an opportunity to climb the next rung of Tennessee's political ladder, this one possibly leading to national renown and power, if Jackson played his cards right. Why not serve as Tennessee's first representative to Congress? Jackson eagerly agreed and, with Blount pulling the political levers behind the scenes, was elected in October 1796. Blount accompanied Jackson to Philadelphia, having been elected one of Tennessee's two senators by the assembly.

Neither man held his seat for long. A Senate investigation found damning evidence that Blount had grossly abused his powers as territorial governor. He was accused of corruption and conspiring with the Spanish. A majority of senators voted to expel him without trial. His supporters greeted him as a hero when he returned to Tennessee. Blount lined up enough votes in the assembly to tap Representative Jackson to take his place in the Senate.

Lacking the necessary intellectual and emotional depth, Jackson made no lasting contribution in either house. For the first time in his life, he was intimidated. Most of his colleagues, especially in the Senate, disdained him for his uncouth frontier mannerisms and ignorance of history, philosophy, and national issues. He felt equally out of place when he stepped beyond Congress. Philadelphia was too sophisticated and expensive for Jackson's tastes and pocketbook.[6]

As a representative, Jackson did kick up some political dust. He was one of only four representatives who voted against a resolution extravagantly thanking George Washington for his service to the nation as he prepared to retire to Mount Vernon. In doing so, Jackson showed the courage to stand on his political convictions, unlike virtually all other Jeffersonians, who held their noses and voted for the measure even as they privately disparaged the first executive.

Jackson resigned in April 1798, when Governor Sevier enticed him to return to Tennessee to be a justice on the state's supreme court. The offer was motivated by Sevier's hope to free the Senate seat from the lackluster Jackson and hand it to one of his cronies, while perhaps converting a political enemy in the process. Alas, Jackson was no more suited to interpreting laws than to writing them. He rooted his judgments on gut feelings rather than on an understanding of the complexities of the laws or cases before him. Yet it was on the court that Jackson showed his true character in a remarkable act of bravery.[7]

The town bully was summoned to face charges. Brandishing a pistol and knife, he threatened to kill anyone who tried to bring him to justice. The sheriff backed off from apprehending him. Jackson asked for volunteers whom he would deputize to arrest the miscreant. No one stepped forward. Finally, Jackson ordered the sheriff to deputize him and lend him a pistol. Then Jackson strode from the court and down the street where the bully was ranting threats and boasts. Locking eyes with the man, Jackson commanded, "Surrender you infernal villain this very instant or I'll blow you through."

The brute meekly did as he was told. He later explained, "When he came up, I looked him in the eye and I saw shoot. There wasn't shoot in nary any other eye in the crowd. So I says to myself, says I: Hoss, it's about time to sing small and so I did."

Facing down the occasional bad man was not the only stress of being a judge. The position conferred status and income, but at the cost of being away from home for months each year while riding the circuit. Jackson capitalized on these journeys by cutting business deals along the way. He also organized and led a lodge of Freemasons. When William Blount died in March 1800, Jackson asserted control over the political machine he left behind.

Jackson never abandoned his dream to be the state's militia general. When the post opened in 1802, he mobilized support for his candidacy. This time he faced Jack Sevier himself, who had been forced to step down as governor after reaching the three consecutive term limit. The result was a tie. When Sevier proposed a second vote, Jackson refused, arguing that the state constitution empowered the governor to break any ties. The governor, Archibald Roane, was a friend of Jackson's. Roane swore in Jackson as Tennessee's militia general on April 1, 1802. The military neophyte had beaten a genuine American military hero.

Sevier's resentment led to another duel.[8] That year Sevier beat Roane in a gubernatorial election in which each candidate and his supporters hurled incendiary accusations at the other. A chance meeting between Jackson and Sevier in Knoxville led to fighting words. Sevier ridiculed Jackson's achievements as the triumph of patronage over ability. When Jackson tried to defend his public service, Sevier cut him short.

"Services? I know of no great service you rendered the country except taking a trip to Natchez with another man's wife."

"Great God!" Jackson sputtered. "Do you mention her sacred name?"

Each man men drew his flintlock pistol and fired. The balls whizzed past the duelists; one grazed a spectator. Bystanders rushed to separate the two as they lunged at each other. The following day Jackson issued a formal challenge. Sevier accepted only if they met in a neighboring state to avoid violating Tennessee's antidueling law. Although theoretically everyone was equal before the law, it might especially damage public order if the governor and militia general blatantly defied state law, let alone killed each other.

The dueling ground was several days' riding from Knoxville to Virginia's southwestern tip. Jackson and his second arrived early, waited impatiently for several hours, and then headed back. They met Sevier and his son along the way. The result was another semicomic brawl rather than a formal duel at ten or so paces. Pistols were drawn by all four and pointed at one another. Had they all fired at once the next passersby might have viewed the odd spectacle of four dead men in a loose circle. Fortunately, no one squeezed his trigger. Someone reckoned that they had satisfied honor. The others agreed. They lowered their guns, mounted their horses, and rode back together to Knoxville.

Jackson's 1806 duel was tragic rather than comic.[9] As before, a false sense of honor was the cause. Jackson won a large bet from Charles Dickinson over a horse race. Dickinson made disparaging remarks about Jackson and Rachel. Jackson issued a challenge. They met on May 30. Any bets on the outcome would have favored Dickinson, who was a crack shot. This did not deter Jackson, who was fearless. He announced that he would blow Dickinson's brains out. This troubled Dickinson. At twenty-four paces between them, each raised his pistol and fired. Jackson's pistol did not discharge as it was at half cock. Dickinson's bullet ploughed into Jackson's chest, missing his heart by an inch. Jackson grimaced at the impact but did not drop or even mutter an audible groan. Instead he coolly pulled back the hammer, aimed, and fired. The ball struck Dickinson in the stomach, severed an artery, and killed him from massive internal bleeding later that day.

Given Jackson's ornery disposition and political status, it was perhaps inevitable that he allied himself with the most notorious duelist in American history.[10] Aaron Burr was as politically cunning as he was amoral, ambitious, and ruthless. In the 1790s he latched onto Thomas Jefferson's Republican Party as a better path to power than Alexander Hamilton's Federalist Party. By 1800 he had amassed enough political capital to be tapped as Jefferson's unofficial running mate. In those days there were no party tickets; the runner-up became vice president. Jefferson and Burr each received seventy-three electoral votes. Rather than gracefully concede, Burr tried to elbow Jefferson aside for the presidency. The decision shifted to the House of Representatives, where each state had one vote. For thirty-four rounds the result was a tie, until Delaware's lone representative shifted his vote to Jefferson. By 1804, recognizing that Jefferson would easily win a second term, Burr sought the governorship of New York. Hamilton condemned the candidacy of the man he viewed as a danger to the American republic. Burr challenged Hamilton to a duel. The two met on the early morning of July

12, 1804. Hamilton shot high, to preserve honor; Burr shot to kill. In destroying Hamilton's life, Burr destroyed his own political career. But he concocted another means of gaining ultimate power. And this path brought him to Andrew Jackson.

People living west of the Appalachian Mountains felt either neglected or exploited by easterners.[11] Bitter resentment lingered despite the resolution of the worst western complaint—the severance of their access to the sea. From 1783 to 1795 the Spanish forbade American merchants from floating boatloads of goods down the Mississippi River in their territory; merchants who violated the decree suffered the confiscation of their cargoes and jail time. The policy stunted the West's economic development. But this issue largely disappeared with the 1795 Pinckney Treaty, which opened the Mississippi River to navigation and thus opened New Orleans to American goods. The 1803 Louisiana Purchase included not only New Orleans but the entire western Mississippi River watershed to the Rocky Mountains.

Yet westerners still scapegoated easterners for their own unresolved political, economic, and social animosities. Aaron Burr sought to exploit this anger by provoking a western revolt that would create an independent country with himself as dictator. He targeted Andrew Jackson as among the region's most important leaders to enlist in his scheme. When Burr first visited Nashville in May 1805, Jackson helped throw a celebratory dinner for him with prominent Tennesseans and then hosted him at his home for several days. Burr concealed his true ambition within a scheme to conquer Mexico. Jackson promised to help scrape up money, men, and supplies for the expedition when Burr gave the word to proceed. The order, and $3,500, came in October 1806. Jackson dutifully issued a proclamation calling on volunteers to gather and began buying boats and supplies. The following month Burr visited Jackson in his second circuit through the West to prepare his campaign.

The conspiracy soon unraveled. Earlier in the year, President Jefferson had received and dismissed several warnings from patriotic Americans whom Burr had approached as part of his treasonous plot. However, the president could not ignore a letter from Gen. James Wilkinson, the southern district's commander. Wilkinson was actually Burr's second in command, but he got cold feet when he realized the plan would most likely not succeed and he would be hanged for treason. He betrayed

Burr to the president without revealing his own part in the plot. Jefferson issued warrants for the arrest of Burr and his confederates. Federal and state officials began rolling up the operation; eventually Burr was nabbed and taken to Richmond, Virginia for trial.

Jackson and most of Burr's web of supporters across the region were genuinely shocked when they learned the charges. Jackson was one of scores of witnesses subpoenaed to testify at Burr's treason trial. The evidence against Burr was voluminous but circumstantial. Burr had kept his cards close to his vest, apparently only revealing the plot's true goal to Wilkinson, who would have incriminated himself had he revealed his knowledge during his testimony. In the end, the court dismissed the case and Burr walked free.

Jackson's involvement in both the duels and the Burr conspiracy obscures the reality that the threat or use of violence in his early life was actually quite rare. His duties as a peacetime militia general were virtually nil. He spent most of his time speculating in land, slaves, and merchandise, and after 1804 he began developing a plantation named the Hermitage, a dozen miles east of Nashville. His happiest moments were with his beloved Rachel. Yet, the couple could not conceive a child, probably because the smallpox that Jackson suffered during the Revolution left him sterile. So, in December 1809, when they were both forty-one, they adopted a twin son of Rachel's brother and wife and named him Andrew Jackson Jr.

Jackson was now entering middle age as a devoted family man and prosperous, powerful member of Tennessee's elite. But there was a void in his life. He was a natural warrior chief in search of a clan to lead. At age forty-five, he finally got the war he had longed for nearly all his life.[12]

Beliefs and behavior are inseparable for most people, with each shaping and reflecting the other. For Andrew Jackson, nothing animated his behavior and beliefs more than rage. At a young age, he had experienced the devastating loss of his family and many relatives and friends amid the horrors of a vicious war. Deep insecurities lurked beneath the aggressive stance and moral certainty that Jackson displayed throughout his life. The tragedies he suffered left him scarred by persecution and savior complexes. He constantly felt that evil was out to get him because he represented all that was good in nature, particularly honor, the virtues of the common man, and the promise and character of the American nation.

Moreover, chronic health problems exacerbated his pathologies. Smallpox had nearly killed him when he was thirteen years old; later he appeared to have contracted malaria, parasites, and hepatitis. Lead slowly and insidiously poisoned him from the ball embedded in his chest from his duel with Dickinson. His shattered shoulder from another duel never healed properly and remained painful and stiff all his life. Each wound left a chronic low-grade infection that often flared under stress or other illness. The mercury- and lead-based medicines that he took to alleviate his ailments worsened them. A sparrowlike appetite and persistent diarrhea left him bone-thin and malnourished. At times he was so feeble that he was bedridden for days or weeks. More often he was arthritic to the point that he needed help to mount a horse, put his arms through the sleeves of a shirt or jacket, write a letter, or lift a spoon to his mouth. All these afflictions would have frustrated anyone but were especially enraging for Jackson, given his fiery disposition.[13] The only surprise is that he lasted as long as he did, a feat perhaps best attributed to his indomitable will.

When Jackson fixed his mind on doing or believing something, nothing could convince him otherwise. Indeed, quite likely no president was more hardheaded than Jackson—although a recent successor may be a serious contender for the dubious title. For Jackson, other like-minded folks, and their supporters, "staying the course" with moral certainty reflects deep character. For their critics, such people exist in moral and intellectual vacuums. People able to think outside ideological and emotional boxes deplore the triumph of blind belief over hard reason in anyone. Acting on beliefs disdainful of objective reality is dangerous; the danger of hurting others along with oneself rises with one's power. The presidency, even its weaker nineteenth-century version, has given its holders enormous power to do both good and evil.

Honor dominated Jackson's beliefs and behavior. A gentleman defended his own honor and that of esteemed others to death. This code was a godsend for Jackson. He had a hair-trigger temper that the slightest real or imagined affront could ignite. Boiling with rage, Jackson either had to frequently vent or risk self-destruction.

Jackson's advice to an acquaintance facing a duel provides insight into his own character: "Charge your friend to preserve his fire, keeping his teeth firmly clenched, and his fingers in a position that if fired on and hit, his fire may not be extorted. . . . Charge your friend to preserve his fire until he shoots his antagonist through the brain, for if he fires and does not kill his antagonist, he leaves himself fully in his power."[14]

Jackson used his rage to conquer his fears on the dueling as well as the battleground. Having mastered fear within himself, he wielded it to master others. Although he rarely lost complete self-control, at times he feigned doing so to bully others into bowing to his will. The ultimate assertion of power is getting others to desist resisting in the first place. He used his notoriety for having a vicious temper to coax others to tiptoe around him, fearful that they might somehow set him off.

Ruthlessly crushing those who do resist can deter others from daring to do the same. This was how Jackson waged war. Against the Creeks, he left a trail of burned villages, littered with hundreds of dead, in his army's wake. To prevent foreign arms, munitions, and other aid from getting to the Seminoles, he had one British agent hanged and another shot. To keep order in his own army's ranks, he presided over the swift trial, conviction, and execution of a sentry guilty of nothing more serious than talking back to an officer.

Jackson had no trouble finding enemies. From his youth through middle age, he squared off in a series of battles to the death with villains who offended his sense of honor, Indian "savages," and British redcoats. He largely set aside violence after he reentered national politics in the 1820s, although he hated his opponents as fiercely as ever. He demonized individual enemies such as Henry Clay, John Quincy Adams, John Calhoun, Nicholas Biddle, and John Marshall; groups such as eastern financiers, abolitionists, and nullifiers; and institutions such as the Second Bank of the United States.

In his teens and early twenties, Jackson's rage was exacerbated by hormones and adrenaline. He vented his roiling passions through hell-raising and boisterous pranks. Before he fell in love with Rachel, horse racing, crap shooting, cock fighting, binge drinking, and whoremongering were his favorite releases. Afterward, he curbed all these vices but horse racing.

Jackson's power to transform his behavior reveals that he was more than a tangle of rage, paranoia, and aggression. He had a gentle, affectionate, and nurturing side. He loved Rachel so much that there is no evidence that he ever dallied with another woman. She was plain-faced and grew fatter with age. But she was the only one who could calm his rants with her gentle voice, reason, and perhaps most important, her resemblance to his mother.[15]

Jackson also loved horses and children, and he seems to have passed his happiest times frolicking with each. History does not record him siring his own child. He sought compensation through substitutes. He plucked an Indian boy from the mangled bodies and smoldering ruins of a Creek village his troops had devastated and adopted him. He happily served as a father figure to a dozen or so young devotees in search of guidance, meaning, and a hero to emulate.

Andrew Jackson was, moreover, quite bright. He best revealed his intelligence through his pen rather than his tongue. Many of his letters are vividly written models of logical arguments. In contrast, he was not known for his oratory. His passions tended to tangle his syntax, and he was always worked up into a lather about something. He wielded his brain not so much to reason his way to a decision as to rationalize a decision that his emotions and prejudices had already conceived.

As for his political beliefs, Jackson early in life embraced the outlook of Thomas Jefferson, who championed states' rights and the common man. Other than owning plantations worked by scores of slaves, the two men shared little beyond these two values. Jefferson personified decorum, learning, reserve, and reason; Jackson was often blustering and bullying, and he scorned study and reflection. Yet Jackson admired not just Jefferson's thought but his persona.

The feeling was hardly mutual. Jackson's violations of the Constitution and law appalled Jefferson. He confided to Daniel Webster, "I feel much alarmed at the prospect of seeing General Jackson president. He is one of the most unfit men I know of for such a place. He has very little respect for law or constitutions. . . . He is a dangerous man."[16]

Jackson repeatedly realized Jefferson's fears. His reaction to the antiwar Hartford Convention of New England delegates during the War of 1812 epitomized his contempt for Americans who exercised their First Amendment rights by expressing opinions contrary to his own: "Had I commanded the military department where the Hartford Convention met . . . I should have hung up the three principal leaders of the party."[17]

For Jackson, politics, like all other dimensions of life, was an incessant Darwinian survival of the fittest. One survived and ideally thrived by being more ruthless than one's enemies. Might makes right was his key belief. Laws and even the Constitution itself could be cherry-picked for the excerpts that bolstered his cause but ultimately were worth nothing more that the paper they were printed on. In Jackson's mind, the framers had not constructed a political system with a division of labor among the branches whose duty was rational governance; they had created a war of all against all: "The Congress, the Executive, and the Court must each for himself be guided by his own opinion of the Constitution. . . . The opinion of the judges has no more authority over Congress than the opinion of Congress has over the judges, and on that point the President is Independent of both."[18]

Jackson held firmly to a double standard whereby he and his allies were above the strict rules of legal, professional, moral, and rational behavior that he reserved for his enemies. He did so blind to his own hypocrisy. He never gave the slightest sign that he was even aware of his glaring double standard, let alone that it gave him the least twinge of unease.

He projected onto others his own worst characteristics. For instance, he condemned President Washington for "grasping after power . . . that he was not constitutionally invested with." He later lectured newly elected President James Monroe on his duty to adhere to pure nonpartisanship in federal appointments: "In every selection, party and party feeling ought to be laid out of view . . . by selecting those the most honest, processing capacity, virtue, and firmness. By this course you steer the national ship to honor and preferment."[19] Yet when Jackson took power, he shamelessly packed his administration, the bureaucracy, and the courts with political partisans, countless of whom were inept and corrupt, while asserting "power he was not constitutionally invested with."[20]

For Jackson, power ultimately rested in a gun barrel: "Then we will have peace for then we will be prepared for war. Every man with a gun in his hand, all Europe combined cannot hurt us. And all the world will be anxious to be on friendly terms with us, because all the world will see we wish peace with all but are prepared for defense against those who would wantonly infringe our national rights."[21]

Andrew Jackson was the first "western" president. Although he was born in the Carolinas, as a young man he migrated west of the Appalachian Mountains and thereafter claimed Tennessee as his home. As long as America has had a West, most folks from the region have seen life differently from most easterners. Vital issues appear much more like simplistic choices of good versus evil on the frontier. But Jackson was also a proud southern planter with more than a hundred slaves under his thumb. This too warped his vision. Slavery was the poison pill in American power. Slavery figuratively shackled America as well as millions of blacks. The notion that to spare the lash would spoil the slave could be applied to other realms of politics. Yet, to his credit, Jackson was an American first and a southerner second.

To Jackson, American unity and liberty were inseparable: "There is nothing that I shudder at more than the idea of a separation of the Union. Should such an event ever happen . . . from that date, I view our liberty done." Upholding the union and liberty was a balance of power among the federal government, the state governments, and the American people. Of the three, he had the most "confidence in the virtue of the majority of the people."[22]

Jackson's love for America was profound. During a presidential steamboat trip up the Hudson River, he was moved to exclaim, "What a country God has given us! How thankful we ought to be that God has given us such a country to live in. We have the best country and the best institutions in the world."[23]

His evocation of God reveals the depth of his feelings. When it came to religion, Jackson was refreshingly open-minded. Although he called himself a Christian, he was no regular churchgoer. His beloved mother and Rachel were devout Presbyterians who failed to inspire in him their fervor. He once described himself as "no sectarian, though a lover of the Christian religion, I do not believe that any who shall be so fortunate as to be received into heaven will be asked" their denomination. He added, "All Christians are brethren. . . . A true Christian loves all, immaterial to what sect or church he belongs." He best expressed his ecumenism by observing, "Charity is the real basis of all true religion."[24]

Jackson believed that he was destined for greatness. His strongest evidence for this was somehow surviving numerous duels and battles long before he became president, as well as two assassination attempts after he entered the White House. This convinced him that God wanted him to survive. And God's will included everything in which Jackson believed and for which he fought.

Had Andrew Jackson been nothing more than a brawler and blus-terer, he would not have risen to the summit of American power. His belief that God was on his side bolstered a natural inclination (figura-tively and at times literally) to cut with a sword an impassible line in the ground between himself and his enemies, in every conflict. The last sentence of Jackson's declaration of martial law on the eve of the British invasion of New Orleans summed up his approach to politics: "Those who are not with us are against us, and will be dealt with accordingly."[25]

2

The Battle of New Orleans

I owe Britain a debt of retaliatory vengeance; should
our forces meet I trust I shall pay the debt.

ANDREW JACKSON

We shot them like dogs.

DAVID CROCKETT

An Eye for an Eye, Tooth for Tooth, and Scalp for Scalp.

ANDREW JACKSON

The only question was whether the Law should bend
to the General or the General to the Law.

JUDGE DOMINICK HALL

The War of 1812 was among the most controversial and disastrous in
American history.[1] Opponents condemned it as "Mr. Madison's War,"
but if one man epitomized the passions, assertions, and ambitions that
stampeded the nation into that conflagration, it was not the mild-
mannered President Madison.

Andrew Jackson had been among the most fervent "War Hawk"

voices demanding that the United States square off with Britain. The War Hawk ranks, volume, and vitriol swelled until they smothered all voices of prudence and proportion. Jackson admitted as much in his address to the Tennessee militia: "Your government has at last yielded to the impulse of the Nation."[2]

For Jackson, war for vengeance, honor, and character filled an existential void for the entire nation. He famously asked his soldiers to ponder eternal questions: "Who are we? And for what are we going to fight?" He then provided the answer: "The hour of vengeance is at hand. . . . We are the free born sons of America. . . . We are going to fight for the reestablishment of our national character."[3]

Genuine issues fueled this explosive cocktail of rage and hubris. Many Americans believed that their nation could not avoid the war that had begun in Europe two decades earlier. The French Revolution that erupted in 1789 imperiled all the crowned heads of Europe. Rulers feared that the same volatile mix of abysmal and worsening economic conditions for most people, liberal ideals, and charismatic revolutionary leaders might ignite their own realms. France's revolutionary regime became increasingly radical and declared war against the Austrians and Prussians in April 1792, against Britain and the Netherlands in February 1793, and against Spain in May 1793.

President George Washington declared American neutrality in April 1793, and he and his successors largely maintained this policy for the next nineteen years. The United States prospered for most of this time as American merchants expanded their sales into markets suddenly denied to countries at war. The belligerents at once vied for American trade and sought to sever that same trade with their enemies. The British and French governments authorized their warships and privateers to seize American merchant ships filled with "contraband," or war products sailing to the other side. The British reduced their depredations after the Jay Treaty with the United States was ratified in 1796. But French confiscations persisted to the point that President John Adams convinced Congress to approve a naval Quasi-War with France from 1798 to 1800. Napoleon Bonaparte ended this war in 1800 by negotiating the Treaty of Mortefontaine and curbing the confiscations of American merchant ships. The Louisiana Purchase three years later further strengthened American relations with France.

Meanwhile, the British became more aggressive and predatory. They did so because they were increasingly desperate and powerful. The war dragged on as the French defeated one British-led coalition after another. The cost to Britain in blood and treasure soared. The British reasoned that if they and their allies were incapable of defeating the French revolutionary forces and then the Napoleonic armies on land, they could at least make the most of their naval superiority. And this meant sweeping the seas of any vessels, enemy or neutral, whose cargoes might enrich France and its allies. British naval power culminated in the Battle of Trafalgar in October 1805, which largely destroyed a combined French and Spanish fleet. This left His Majesty's warships free to confiscate more American vessels with contraband cargoes and to impress any "British" citizens aboard. Ruined merchants and shipowners implored the federal government to resist British depredations and seek compensation for the loss of goods and seamen. The British did not just threaten American national security at sea. British agents supplied Indians in the Northwest and Southwest Territories against advancing American settlers, traders, and officials, even though these lands were technically within the United States.

The naked belligerence of British policies culminated in June 1807, when the HMS *Leopard* blasted three broadsides into the USS *Chesapeake*, killing three and wounding eighteen Americans. The British captain ordered his gunners to fire after the American captain refused to permit royal marines to search his ship for British deserters. The American captain struck the colors of his crippled frigate. British marines barged aboard, searched the ship, and dragged away four sailors whom they claimed were deserters.

This atrocity might have led to war. President Thomas Jefferson, however, was desperate to keep the peace. Although he was outraged by the attack, he knew that the nation was totally unprepared to fight. He demanded and eventually received an apology and compensation, although the British did so belatedly, grudgingly, and stingily.

Jefferson was right. The United States simply lacked the power to deter British depredations let alone fight a war against that mighty empire. The president and his followers championed market over military power. They believed that they could bring Britain to its knees by denying its merchants access to American consumers or producers.

To this end, in December 1807 Jefferson signed the Embargo Act, which forbade American ships and goods from leaving port, although foreign ships could drop anchor and sell goods in the United States. Jefferson naively believed that this law would force the British to compromise. The result was economic disaster. American exports plummeted from $108 million in 1807 to $22 million in 1808. Ports became ghost towns with vessels rotting at anchor, warehouses packed with unsold goods, rows of empty stores, and streets filled with jobless men desperate for work. Government revenues plunged and debt soared. The economic depression spread across the country.

Jefferson refused to deviate from his policy despite evidence that it was ruining the country and despite pressure from business. Congressional majorities eventually responded to these realities by replacing the embargo with the Non-Intercourse Act of March 1809. This permitted trade with all countries except Britain and France, although volume remained only a fraction of what it had been before the embargo because most trade was with these two nations. Interest groups increased their pressure. Congress relented again, this time with Macon Bill Number 2, which President James Madison signed into law in May 1810. This bill permitted free trade with France and Britain—with a catch. If either power ended its depredations, the United States would continue trading with that nation and sever trade with the continuing belligerent. After Napoleon announced in 1810 that he would rescind his policy of preying on American ships, Madison promptly ended trade with Britain. This did not, however, force the British to make any concessions.[4]

This disastrous series of policies was rooted in how Jefferson conceived the "art of power." Jeffersonians believed in a weak central government, states' rights, an agrarian-based economy, minimal international trade, and use of only militia and gunboats for defense. The "Revolution of 1800" that brought Jefferson to the presidency and his Republican Party to majorities in both houses of Congress appeared to repudiate Alexander Hamilton's previous, bolder version of the art of power.

Hamiltonism advocated a muscular, problem-solving government that worked with the private sector to develop the nation's infrastructure, industries, innovations, trade, finance, and schools. The result would be a dynamic, prosperous, diversified economy that would eventually surpass Britain and all other countries. The economy would generate greater revenues, which would be both reinvested and devoted to maintaining a small but professional army and navy to deter or, if need be, defeat any aggressor.

Jeffersonism's abject failures atop Hamiltonism's political demise provided the opening for a third version of the art of power. Jacksonism's attitudes and assertions existed long before it became a movement with a label. Indeed, Jacksonism's core attitudes are as old as America. The slogans "might makes right," "shoot first and don't ask questions later," and "my nation, right or wrong," to cite some of the more prominent, appeal to those who are ignorant, angry, and fearful facing challenges to the nation that are rooted in the real world's complexities, laws, paradoxes, and outright contradictions. For Jacksonians, greed reinforced and reflected creed. Beneath all the flag-waving was the drive to seize ancestral lands from the Indians, to take Canada from Britain, and to pry Florida from Spain. Jacksonians insisted that acquiring these lands by force rather than diplomacy would allow land agents, farmers, and merchants to develop them sooner.

Jeffersonians and Hamiltonians alike opposed going to war with Britain, but by 1812 the Jacksonians had surpassed each in political power. Jacksonians dominated Jefferson's Republican Party, which held 75 percent of the House seats and 82 percent of the Senate seats. War Hawks such as Henry Clay, John Calhoun, Felix Grundy, Peter Porter, George Troup, Langdon Cleves, and William Lowndes beat the drum for war with ever more frenzy during the first half of 1812.[5]

Swelling numbers of congressmen, newspaper editors, and other influential Americans identified themselves as War Hawks who were committed to settling the issue with force. They insisted that the United States could defeat the British Empire by swiftly conquering Canada. Then they could either wield Canada as a bargaining chip in negotiations for British concessions or simply attach the vast territory and its natural resources to the United States.

Historians have long debated why President Madison submitted a war message to Congress on June 1, 1812. Jefferson's most devout protégé let the War Hawks bully him into calling for a war that he himself opposed. Solid congressional majorities enthusiastically approved going to war, with votes of 79 to 49 in the House and 19 to 13 in the Senate. Madison signed the bill declaring war against Britain on June 18, 1812.

He did not ask Congress to call off the war after he learned in August that Britain had rescinded its policy of confiscating American merchant vessels and cargoes two months earlier. Much more was at stake than money and lives—the War Hawk vision of American honor, along with political expediency, demanded that Madison stay the course.

The War Hawks promised the nation a swift and glorious victory over the British by capturing Canada and forcing the enemy to yield to all American demands. What they delivered instead was a series of utter disasters. The war went badly from the start. Gen. William Hull surrendered an army at Detroit to a British and Indian force fielding half as many fighters. Elsewhere the redcoats repeatedly trounced American attempts to invade Canada via the Niagara River, the St. Lawrence, and Lake Champlain valleys. The most humiliating defeat of all came in August 1814, when a British expedition routed a more numerous American army at the Battle of Bladensburg and then marched on to sack an undefended Washington City. The body count and national debt soared.

The Americans did win some limited victories. Cdre. Oliver Perry led a flotilla that battered and captured a superior British fleet at Put-in-Bay on Lake Erie. Gen. William Henry Harrison's army retook Detroit, crossed over into Canada, and routed a British and Indian army at the Battle of the Thames, killing the famous Shawnee leader Tecumseh. The Americans repelled British attacks at Baltimore, Maryland, and Plattsburg, New York. On the high seas American frigates outfought and captured British frigates in most duels between them. But Andrew Jackson's army ultimately inflicted the most devastating defeat against British forces.

All this lay ahead. For the first few months of the war, soldier Andrew Jackson fumed on the sidelines. He was under the command of Maj. Gen. James Wilkinson, who directed the Southwest Military District from his headquarters at New Orleans. This district was a sleepy backwater until October 1812, when intelligence reached Wilkinson of a pending British invasion. He called on Jackson to gather his men.

Jackson eventually mustered 2,071 troops, of whom 1,400 were split into two infantry regiments commanded by Col. William Hall and Col. Thomas Hart Benton. Most of the rest were cavalry commanded by Col. John Coffee. Jackson led his army from Nashville on the 440-mile march down the Natchez Trace on January 7, 1813. From Natchez, the army would be transported by boat to New Orleans. Shortly after they reached Natchez, Jackson received devastating news from War Secretary John Armstrong: "The causes embodying and marching to New Orleans the Corps under your command having ceased to exist, you will . . . consider it dismissed from service and take measures to have delivered over to Major General Wilkinson all articles of public property which may have been put into its possession. You will accept for yourself and the Corps the thanks of the President of the United States."[6]

Jackson had no choice but to about-face his men and head back to Nashville. It was on this grueling march that he earned his sobriquet "Old Hickory." He gave up his own horse to one of the couple of hundred sick soldiers who straggled along with the army. He ate the same bland ration of cornmeal and salt pork as his men. Most visibly, he was constantly circulating among his troops, whether on the march or in camp, trying to buck up their spirits. Although he inwardly boiled with rage at Armstrong and Wilkinson for having sent him and two thousand Tennesseans on a wasteful, exhausting wild goose chase, he expressed only solicitude for his "boys." He dismissed them at Nashville with deep gratitude for their service and warned them to be prepared to come back.

Unfortunately, despite the firm command that he displayed on the aborted campaign, Jackson could not quell petty jealousies among his officers. One such dispute between William Carroll and Little Johnston led to the latter's challenge. Carroll haughtily spurned the call with the excuse that no gentleman issued it. Johnston asked Jesse Benton, Thomas's brother, to stand for him. Benton agreed and Carroll had no choice but to accept. Jackson reluctantly accepted Carroll's request to act as his second.

It was a classic duel in which the men stood back to back, strode ten paces, and then turned to fire. As they faced each other with lowered pistols, Carroll stood erect and Benton squatted. Benton's ball seared Carroll's hand. Carroll's ball, perhaps appropriately, struck Benton's buttocks. Thus was Carroll's honor preserved and Benton's subjected to ridicule.

Thomas Benton tried to retrieve some of his brother's honor by firing off a letter to Jackson castigating him for organizing an "unequal, base, and unfair" duel.[7] These accusations made Benton and Jackson mortal enemies. In a growing but still small town like Nashville, it was only a matter of time before they encountered each other. On September 4, 1813, the Benton brothers were lounging on the City Hotel's veranda when Jackson and Coffee strode up.

Jesse Benton and Andrew Jackson locked hate-filled eyes and drew their pistols; Jesse was faster and fired first. The ball staggered Jackson as it plowed into his shoulder; he squeezed his trigger but the ball missed. Thomas Benton apparently dodged, lost his footing, and stumbled down the steps. Jesse pulled a second pistol and fired; the ball grazed Jackson, who collapsed. By chance, two of Rachel's relatives, Stockley Hays and Alexander Donelson, were passing when the gunshots rang out. Seeing Jackson imperiled, each pulled a knife and rushed the Bentons. Other bystanders pulled apart the combatants.

Coffee apparently was unarmed and stood frozen in disbelief as the battle broke out and was broken up in a matter of seconds. Jackson was bleeding profusely as Coffee and others carried him to the Nashville Inn. The doctor's verdict was more painful to Jackson than his wounds—he could choose to lose either his arm or his life. Jackson gasped that he would keep his arm to his grave. For weeks Jackson lay near death. Then word arrived of an event that forced him to rise to his feet and lead his soldiers into the field.

For years the possibility of war had brewed hotter between the Americans and a Creek faction called the Red Sticks for the color they painted their war clubs.[8] Leading the Red Sticks was Red Eagle, also known as William Weatherford, the son of a Creek woman and white trader. War became all but a matter of time starting in 1811, when the Red Sticks hosted Tecumseh, the brilliant Shawnee leader. Tecumseh called on them to join an alliance among all the western Indians that one day would drive the Americans back across the Appalachians. Groups of Red Sticks journeyed to Pensacola, Spanish West Florida's capital, where British agents armed them with muskets, gunpowder, and admonitions to emulate their red brothers under Tecumseh far to the north and prepare to destroy the whites in their midst.

The Red Stick War broke out at Burnt Corn Creek on July 27, 1813, when a militia company opened fire on a Red Stick group returning from Pensacola with horses packed with war supplies. The Indians fled. The militia captured their horses and supplies. The Red Sticks soon reaped a bloody vengeance for their humiliation.

Fort Mims stood on the Alabama River about forty miles north of Mobile. It was garrisoned by 120 militia commanded by Maj. Daniel Beasley and further crowded with several hundred refugees who had fled there, fearful of Red Stick war preparations. Yet, Beasley did nothing to prepare his men for an attack. If any sentries were posted on August 30, 1813, they were not paying attention when as many as a thousand Red Sticks burst from the surrounding woods, rushed the fort, swarmed through the open gate, and massacred nearly everyone, by one account all but 13 of 533 soldiers and civilians.[9]

Jackson was bedridden and stricken by pain when word arrived of the Fort Mims massacre. His indomitable will enabled him to stagger to his feet, push his arm through his ruffled shirt and his swallow-tailed heavy-wool blue coat, and call his officers to council. He issued an order for the militia to assemble at Fayetteville, eighty miles south of Nashville. His aides helped him mount his horse. Every hoof step must have been sheer agony, but he set his jaw and rode on. He finally had a genuine military campaign to lead.

The plan was for four armies, three of militia and one of regulars, to converge on the heart of Red Stick power in central Alabama. Jackson would join Maj. Gen. John Cocke midway up the Coosa River and then attack the Red Stick villages in the northern region. Meanwhile, Gen. John Floyd's militia and Brig. Gen. Ferdinand Claiborne's regulars would march west from Georgia to attack the central and southern Red Stick villages.

It was a good plan. The trouble was that only Jackson carried it out. The other expeditions faltered from lack of will and supplies and withdrew before inflicting any significant defeats on the enemy. The political consequences were enormous. Jackson did not have to share any of the glory, and he alone imposed a crushing peace on not just his vanquished foes, but also on his Creek allies in the Treaty of Fort Jackson. This alone made him a national hero. Yet he would surpass all that in the popular imagination with his victory over the British at New Orleans.

Around two thousand men, twelve hundred infantry and eight hundred cavalry, joined Jackson at Fayetteville. Among these troops were two who, like Jackson, would become American heroes, David Crockett and Sam Houston. On October 7, 1813, Jackson led his army to the Tennessee River, where he established Fort Deposit. There a few hundred Creek and Cherokee warriors met Jackson, who had them wear white plumes or deer tails in their hair to distinguish them from hostile Indians.

Jackson led his men south along the trail sixty miles to the Coosa River, where they built Fort Strother. After vainly waiting for General Cocke's army to appear, Jackson ordered General Coffee and his cavalry to wipe out the Red Stick town of Tallushatchee, defended by a couple of hundred warriors thirteen miles east. After encircling the town on November 3, 1813, the frontiersmen slaughtered every man and many women and children in the village, 186 altogether, and captured eighty-four women and children, with the loss of only five killed and forty-one wounded.[10] They then triumphantly brought their scalps, loot, and captives back to parade before Jackson.

Among the survivors was a ten-month-old boy whose family was wiped out in the attack. When Jackson asked the Indian women to care for the child, they refused, saying he was better off dead. Suddenly, the horrifying moral dilemmas of war struck Jackson with full force. He adopted the toddler and sent him to Rachel to raise as their own.

There was an even bloodier battle at Talladega, a village of friendly Creeks thirty miles south of Fort Strother. When word reached Jackson that Red Eagle and his warriors were besieging Talladega, he hurried to the rescue. They surprised the Red Sticks on the morning of November 9 and killed around three hundred while suffering only fifteen dead and eighty-five wounded.[11]

After Jackson withdrew his army to Fort Strother to prepare a knockout blow against the Red Sticks, he faced two daunting obstacles— most of his troops' enlistments and supplies ran out. When a brigade threatened to march home on December 10, the day its enlistment expired, Jackson deployed troops with longer enlistments across the road and ordered them to load their muskets and cannons. He then tersely explained the choice to those who intended to leave. Reinforcements were on the way. Until they arrived, no one could leave camp, and anyone who tried would be executed for desertion. The choice was clear: "You must now determine whether you will go or peacefully remain."[12] The would-be returnees headed sullenly back to camp, undoubtedly cursing under their breath.

Two days later General Cocke and fifteen hundred militia finally straggled into Fort Strother. This forced Jackson to fulfill his promise to release the men whose enlistments had expired. A few days after he did so, Cocke informed him that his own men's duty had ended, and he would lead them home. Yet another blow came when Jackson learned that most of Cocke's cavalry had also cantered off. Jackson was left with less than half of his command. He lost nearly all of them when their enlistments ended on January 4, 1814.

Jackson faced the absurd prospect of defiantly defending Fort Strother with a handful of followers against a thousand or more Red Sticks, eager for vengeance. This daunting possibility disappeared when eight hundred fresh militia and supplies appeared on January 14. A few days later he led his new troops south against the Red Stick stronghold of Tohopeka at Horseshoe Bend, where the Tallapoosa River enclosed a hundred acres near its confluence with the Coosa River.

Red Eagle and about a thousand warriors were at Horseshoe Bend when Jackson and his men appeared on January 21. Rather than wait to be attacked, the Red Sticks surged out against the Tennesseans. The fighting was desperate as the Red Sticks struck from different directions and tried to encircle their foes. With his ammunition and other supplies nearly exhausted, Jackson ordered a withdrawal. He had lost around twenty dead and eighty wounded, while the Red Sticks may have suffered as many as two hundred dead. Although the Red Sticks drove off the enemy, their victory was purely Pyrrhic. They had lost many of their bravest warriors and had expended most of their ammunition. Red Eagle and a delegation departed on a long journey to recruit more followers and supplies.

At Fort Strother, Jackson massed more men and equipment for another thrust against Horseshoe Bend. It was also essential to train and instill discipline in his raw recruits. More men slipped away at night despite knowing that they could be executed for desertion if they were caught. Jackson needed to make a harsh example of one or more miscreants to deter the rest.

Pvt. John Woods became that example. He had spent a frigid night on sentry duty and had been released by an officer to return to camp. On his way back, he encountered another officer who demanded to know why he was not at his post. Rather than simply explain that he had received permission, Woods grew indignant. They exchanged angry words. When the officer ordered his arrest, Woods briefly threatened to shoot anyone who tried but finally gave up. Word of the incident enraged Jackson, who shouted, "Which is the damned rascal. Shoot him! Shoot him! Blow ten balls through the damned villain's body."[13]

Jackson ordered a court-martial to convene immediately, hear the evidence, and reach a verdict. The court found Woods guilty of mutiny and ordered his execution. Jackson wrote a farewell statement to Woods, to be read just before his execution, to explain why it was necessary:

The offenses of which you have been found guilty are such as cannot be permitted to pass unpunished in an army but at the hazard of its ruin. An army cannot exist where order and subordination are wholly disregarded. . . . This is an important crisis in which if we act as becomes us, every thing is to be hoped for towards the accomplishment of the objects of our government; if otherwise, every thing to be feared. How it becomes us to act, we all know, and what our punishment shall be if we act otherwise, must be known also.[14]

This summed up a crucial element of Jackson's political philosophy. Yet he had a double standard when it came to questions of authority, orders, and obedience. He asserted his principles strictly with others but behaved as if he himself were beholden to no one, including, eventually, the president, Congress, the Constitution, and international law.

Jackson soon buried this grim incident in his mind. Reinforcements swelled his ranks to four thousand men. He left 450 troops at Fort Strother and advanced down the Coosa River valley. Thirty miles downstream, he established Fort William, garrisoned it with several hundred troops, and marched on.

Jackson and his army reached Horseshoe Bend on the morning of March 26, 1814. Upon listening to his scouts' reports on the town's fortifications and defenders, he swiftly devised a plan. His Tennesseans would attack the breastwork across the peninsula directly while his Indian allies lined the woods on the riverbank to cut off any retreat. He had the crews of his two cannons, a six-pounder and a three-pounder, open fire to breach the wall. Although the shot was too light and the walls were too thick, the effort did force the Red Sticks to keep their heads down. This gave Jackson's Indian allies a chance to ensure that the besieged could not retreat. They swam across, climbed into the canoes lining the muddy shore around the village, and paddled them to the river's far side.

Jackson ordered his troops to charge. The Red Sticks repulsed the first attack. After briefly resting his men, Jackson asked for volunteers to lead a second assault. A few men stepped forward and were followed by hundreds more. This time the Tennesseans swarmed over the wall and slaughtered nearly everyone in the town. They counted the bodies of 557 Indians and estimated that perhaps another 300 had been drowned or killed trying to cross the river. Count was kept by cutting off each dead Indian's nose tip. That victory was costly—the Tennesseans lost 47 dead and 159 wounded, and their Indian allies lost 23 killed and 47 wounded.[15]

The Battle of Horseshoe Bend, like all other engagements of the Red Stick War, was fought mercilessly. David Crockett, then a militia private, recalled,

> We shot them like dogs and then set the house on fire, and burned it up with forty-six warriors in it. Many of the carcasses of the Indians were still to be seen. They looked very awful, for the burning had not entirely consumed them. . . . It was . . . found out that the house had a potato cellar under it. . . . We were all hungry as wolves . . . and hunger compelled us to eat them, though I had rather not if I could have helped it, for the oil of the Indians had run down on them and they looked as if they had been stewed with fat meat.[16]

Among the grievously wounded was Sam Houston.[17] He was an adventurer and romantic, inspired by such literary works as George Gordon, Lord Byron's poetry and Alexander Pope's translation of Homer's *The Iliad*. At age thirteen, he ran away from a domineering father and five brothers to join the Cherokees. Chief Oolooteka adopted him and named him the Raven. During his initial three years with the Cherokees, he became fluent in their language and ways and, most important, found true affection and support.

Houston returned to his original family with the idea to set up his own school for the area's children. He spent only six months trying to inspire students to love literature and learning when the War of 1812 erupted. He joined the army as a private but soon earned promotions to ensign and lieutenant. This swift ascent up the ranks was attributable to his intelligence, charisma, and appearance—he was tall, broad-shouldered, and as tough as he was bright and self-assured. At Horseshoe Bend he first inspired Jackson's friendship for a warrior as fierce as himself.

Houston was dead set to be the first into the enemy town. He dashed forward and scrambled atop the breastwork. An arrow sliced deep into his thigh. He was dragged back to the Tennessee lines by the soldiers who survived the assault. He gritted his teeth at the excruciating pain as his comrades held him down, pulled out the arrow, and bandaged his leg. He heard Jackson's call for volunteers to lead a second assault. He hobbled over and was among those who charged ahead of the others. Once again he pulled himself atop the wall. A bullet struck him in the shoulder and knocked him back. He eventually recovered and, with Jackson's support, joined and rose through Tennessee's elite.

Jackson marched his troops to the confluence of the Coosa and Tallapoosa Rivers, where they erected Fort Jackson upon the ruins of old French Fort Toulouse. There he gathered more supplies for one last campaign to wipe out the remaining Red Sticks. He sent word to the Creeks that he would generously award anyone who brought in Red Eagle alive.

Red Eagle was away when the Tennesseans destroyed Tohopeka and slaughtered his people. This so demoralized him that he decided to surrender. He arrived alone at Fort Jackson and was escorted to Jackson. Col. William Carroll recalled that the chief "was solemn in manner and seemed greatly depressed by the forlorn condition of his people, though he did not seem to care for his own fate."[18]

Red Eagle's courage deeply impressed Jackson, who remarked, "I had directed that you should be brought to me confined. Had you appeared in this way, I should have known how to have treated you."

"I am in your power," the chief replied. "Do with me as you please. I have done the white people all the harm I could. . . . My people are now all gone. I can now do no more than weep over the misfortunes of my nation."

Jackson shook hands with Red Eagle and let him go. Later in the same year he would not let off the Creeks so easy, not just the Red Sticks but also the allies who had fought alongside him.

The Madison administration rewarded Jackson for his victory by offering him a brigadier general's commission in the regular army and command of the Seventh Military District, which included Louisiana, the Mississippi Territory, and Tennessee. Jackson at first angrily rejected the offer as an insult. He expected no less than a major general's commission. But he accepted after Secretary Armstrong explained that Congress had legally designated only a few major generalships and for now they were all taken. With patience and continued victories, Jackson would undoubtedly be promoted.[19] The president also named Jackson, along with Benjamin Hawkins and Thomas Pinckney, as a commissioner to negotiate a peace treaty with the Creeks.

Jackson sent out runners to all the Creek villages with word to attend a peace council to open on August 1 at Fort Jackson. After the Red Stick and Creek chiefs convened, he sternly asserted the terms of peace. The Creek people, friend and foe alike, would pay for the Red Stick War. The Creeks needed to permit military roads and trading posts to be established throughout their remaining territory. In addition, they needed to end all their trade, aid, and diplomatic relations with Spanish Florida. Finally, the boundary would now run down the Coosa River to the Big Falls, eight miles north of Fort Jackson, then due east to Georgia. The Creeks would cede the vast triangle of land east and north of that line, amounting to 23 million acres, to the United States. The chiefs gasped in dismay. The Creek allies were stunned that Jackson betrayed their loyalty by confiscating their ancestral lands. Jackson would not yield an acre. Render all that now, he coldly stated, or be prepared to lose far more in the next war. The chiefs reluctantly signed the Treaty of Fort Jackson on August 9, 1814, and returned to their villages with the devastating news.

Although the Battle of Horseshoe Bend and the Treaty of Fort Jackson decisively crushed Creek power in the heart of the old Southwest Territory, these events did not end the region's Indian war. The remnants of the Red Sticks gathered with other Indian renegades and hundreds of runaway slaves in villages in Spanish Florida, a mingling of peoples who became known as the Seminoles. From their refuge, the Seminoles raided the American frontier.

The power of first the Red Sticks and then the Seminoles to wage war ultimately depended on British agents with who supplied them with shiploads of arms and munitions at Pensacola and their access to smaller ports and river mouths in Spanish Florida. Jackson sought to sever their British supply line.

Jackson marched with a portion of his army to Mobile. After arriving on August 22, he fired off a letter to Mateo González Manrique, Pensacola's commandant. He condemned González for permitting the British "to land within the territory of Spain 25,000 stand of arms with 300 barrels of ammunition for the avowed purpose of enabling the vanquished Creeks to renew a sanguinary war with the United States."[20] British major Edward Nicolls and a hundred royal marines had joined Pensacola's garrison on August 14. Jackson demanded that the Spanish expel the British troops and Red Stick refugees.

The message did not intimidate González. The governor fired back with a letter he dictated to John Gordon, the courier who had carried Jackson's message to him, in which he condemned the American for his "impertinent . . . insult" and said that "the Spaniards would die before they would comply with such a demand."[21]

These words were a red flag to Jackson. As he readied his men to march, he escalated the rhetorical war, blistering the Spanish for violating their professed neutrality and letting the British arm a "murderous, barbarous, rebellious banditti." He passed a warning to González that either he embrace genuine neutrality or suffer a vengeance that reaped "an eye for an eye, tooth for tooth, scalp for scalp."[22] Finally, he bluntly wrote González that "you have thrown the gauntlet, and I will take it up."[23]

Meanwhile, a British expedition attacked Fort Bowyer, which guarded the entrance to Mobile Bay, on September 15, 1814. Although the Americans repulsed the attack, many feared that it was the opening act of a far larger expedition.

Word reached Jackson of the latest and most humiliating defeat suffered by the United States. A British expedition of forty-five hundred troops had burned Washington City on August 24. Although Baltimore's defenders repulsed the invaders on September 14, the damage to national prestige and morale was devastating. News of the catastrophe fired Jackson with an unquenchable desire for vengeance.

Jackson openly expressed his hope that his messages would provoke a war with Spain to justify his conquest of West Florida. This set off alarm bells in Washington. President Madison had War Secretary James Monroe directly order Jackson to "take no measures which would involve this Government in contest with Spain." Then, fearing this blunt message might offend hypersensitive Jackson, Monroe ended his letter with a more conciliatory note: "Very important interests are committed to you, and great confidence is entertained that you will meet the expectations of the Government in the discharge of your duties."[24]

The stand-down order reached Jackson too late. He had marched off with his army from Mobile on the road to Pensacola on October 25. He dispatched to Monroe a letter justifying his campaign:

> As I act without the orders of government, I deem it proper to state my reasons for it. I trust, sir, that the necessity of this act to the safety of this section of the Union; the hostility of the governor of Pensacola; resigning his forts to the British commander; his permitting them to remain there to fit out one expedition against the United States, return there and refit, now to be preparing for another; added to his having acknowledged that he has armed the Indians, sent them into our territory . . . will be a sufficient justification in the eyes of my government for having undertaken this expedition.[25]

Jackson and his men advanced within a few miles of Pensacola by the evening of November 6. As his troops set up camp, Jackson sent an ultimatum to Gonzáles: "I come not as the enemy of Spain, but I come with a force sufficient to prevent the repetition of those acts so injurious to the United States and so inconsistent with the neutral character of Spain." He then demanded that the governor promptly surrender his fortifications, arms, and men or else suffer the results: "But if they are not delivered peaceably, let the blood of your subjects be upon your own head. I will not hold myself responsible for the conduct of my enraged soldiers and the Indian warriors."[26]

González denied the accusations and rejected the surrender demand. Jackson promptly ordered his troops to attack. Two small forts protected the town's land side, while Fort Carlos de Barrancas guarded the entrance from Pensacola Bay. A diversion against Pensacola's west side drew off Spanish troops while most of Jackson's men assaulted the town's east side. After the Spanish troops in the town surrendered, Fort

Barrancas's commander, his troops, Nicolls and his marines, and hundreds of Indian allies rowed to British ships anchored nearby; behind them a long fuse burned toward the gunpowder magazine. The explosion destroyed the fort and thus inadvertently saved the Americans that labor. The British vessels sailed beyond the horizon. With his mission accomplished, Jackson withdrew his army to Mobile.

Jackson soon learned that Nicolls and his men had not gone far. The flotilla sailed to the mouth of the Apalachicola River, which divided West Florida from East Florida. There Nicolls set up a fort and equipped war parties against the American frontier. Jackson sent Maj. Uriah Blue with a thousand troops of the Thirty-Ninth Infantry and volunteer units to seal off the border. Jackson would have loved to have led his entire army against Nicolls, but word arrived of a much larger British expedition threatening a more crucial objective. On November 22, Jackson and two thousand troops marched westward from Mobile toward New Orleans.[27]

New Orleans was the key to the entire Mississippi River valley—whichever country controlled this city controlled the economic fate of the watershed between the Appalachian and Rocky Mountains. The United States took title to this vast region with President Jefferson's 1803 Louisiana Purchase. Now a British armada threatened to strangle the American West by capturing New Orleans.

The city and its twenty-five thousand inhabitants appeared to be low-hanging fruit. New Orleans was unfortified because at sea level diggers hit water just a few feet below ground, and there was no real local source for stone. However, two forts—St. Leon and St. Philip—guarded the Mississippi River's last sinewy hundred miles before it flowed into the Gulf of Mexico, twenty-five and sixty-five miles, respectively, below New Orleans. Two other approaches by water and land came much closer to the city. The Gulf reached just a dozen miles north of New Orleans by Lake Pontchartrain and thirty miles east by Lake Borgne; from either, troops could be conveyed by longboats through bayous to within a few miles of the city.

Shortly after leading his men into New Orleans on December 1, Jackson discussed with Governor William Claiborne and Commodore Daniel Patterson how best to defend the city. Patterson's naval forces were measly—just five gunboats guarded Lake Borgne's entrance and two sloops defended New Orleans. Jackson ordered detachments to defend the entrance to each bayou leading to the city and led most of his army down the river road a half dozen miles to set up camp.

Military necessity forced Jackson to set aside his harsh prejudices briefly and command the most culturally, linguistically, and racially mixed army in American history. He boosted their ranks by mustering local militia companies. Many spoke only French, while the languages of the other companies were as diverse as the city's polyglot population. This linguistic diversity would have astonished Jackson enough, but the sight of two of the companies, whose members proudly called themselves the Free Men of Color, would have ordinarily filled him with revulsion and fear; later, he praised them for their steadfast courage. Among the troops he brought with him were volunteer regiments from Tennessee, Kentucky, and Mississippi, two regular regiments manned mostly by Americans from many states but also by immigrants from foreign lands, and finally a contingent of Choctaws. And to this array he soon added some of the most exotic recruits of all.

Jean Lafitte headed a community of several hundred pirates and their followers on Barataria Bay, forty miles from New Orleans. Although he and his men largely confined their pillaging to British, Spanish, and other foreign vessels, they continually ran into trouble with American authorities. After Governor Claiborne put a public price on his head, Lafitte half-jokingly offered an even higher price for Claiborne's. An American expedition against Barataria in September destroyed the stronghold and captured eighty pirates, although Lafitte and most of his men escaped. At first Jackson was determined to destroy Lafitte and his pirate lair, but soon he had a change of heart. Lafitte paid an unexpected visit to Jackson and offered his services for the defense of New Orleans. Jackson reacted to Lafitte's bold appearance just as he had to Red Eagle's, with forgiveness rather than a hangman's noose. In exchange for amnesty, Lafitte and his best gunners manned most of the cannons along the American line.

For Jackson, warring against the British was about avenging personal as well as national honor. He wrote Rachel, "I owe Britain a debt of retaliatory vengeance; should our forces meet I trust I shall pay the debt."[28] In addition to his deep emotional wounds from losing his family during the Revolutionary War, he was constantly reminded of

British atrocities when he glanced down at the thick white scar across his hand or at a mirror, which revealed the scar across his cheek and forehead inflicted by a British officer's sword when he had refused to blacken the redcoat's jackboots.

During the weeks that Jackson prepared for and fought the British, he cast many a steely glance behind him. New Orleans unsettled Jackson. Although it was officially on U.S. territory, the city felt profoundly foreign to backwoods rustics like himself, with its French and Spanish communities; its Babel of languages spilling from the wharfs, streets, taverns, and brothels; its large free black community with its own militia companies; its countless mixed-race denizens, categorized exotically as mulattoes, quadroons, or octoroons, depending on skin color; not to mention the city's spicy food, exotic music, and pervasive sensuality. The annual Octoroon Ball epitomized this racial mingling as rich white men sought mistresses and wives among local mixed-race beauties. Americans were a minority who were largely shut out of high society, even though they made more money. Governor Claiborne reigned over rather than administered New Orleans and the rest of the territory.

Much more than multiculturalism provoked Jackson's unease. His nightmare scenario was a revolt by the city's Spaniards and French after a British army appeared before New Orleans. A decade of American rule could not eliminate traditional loyalties. From 1763 to 1800, Spain ruled New Orleans and the rest of Louisiana. Nearly all Spaniards were devoted to their king, Ferdinand VII, and by extension to Britain via Spain's alliance. The French community was only slightly less suspect since many had fled the French Revolution and Napoleon.

To deter rebellion, Jackson declared martial law on December 15, 1814, and warned that he would view anyone who violated that decree as a traitor, stating famously, "Those who are not with us are against us, and will be dealt with accordingly."[29]

Yet Jackson also knew that inspiration rather than intimidation could best mobilize the population behind him. He and his officers deliberately exuded an easy assurance that they would rout the redcoats. Jackson had spread the word among New Orleans's inhabitants that they should "not be alarmed" because "the enemy will never reach the city."[30] His certainty that a glorious victory was inevitable was genuine. Col. John Coffee wrote his wife that his men "have no pity for the redcoats, who, they declare, are to be responsible for all the devilment the Indians have done. Every one of my boys wants to get within fair buck range of a redcoat."[31]

As Jackson readied his men and the city for battle, a hundred British ships packed with eight thousand troops were fast approaching. Adm. Alexander Cochrane and Gen. Edward Pakenham commanded the fleet and army, respectively. Nearly all the redcoats were battle-hardened veterans of the Napoleonic wars. The armada dropped anchor at Lake Borgne's entrance on December 13. The next morning, Cochrane's warships wiped out the American gunboat flotilla. Pakenham loaded his troops, artillery, and supplies into boats, and local guides led them through the bayou maze toward New Orleans.

An advance force of eighteen hundred troops under Gen. John Keane appeared suddenly ten miles below the city on December 23. Jackson typically reacted decisively to word of the enemy's presence. When his officers gathered, he locked eyes fiercely in turn with each and then said, "Gentlemen, the British are below; we must fight them tonight."[32]

As Jackson and his army marched through the dark, the two sloops slipped downstream, anchored beside the British camp, and opened fire. After twenty minutes of sowing death, terror, and chaos among the redcoats, the sloops' guns ceased fire, thus signaling the infantry to surge forward. The battle was a wild frenzy of gunshots, the thud of musket butts against skulls, and the sickening squish of bayonets and swords thrust through flesh. Jackson finally recalled his men, leaving the enemy in possession of a field strewn with dead and maimed bodies. The onslaught stunned the British, who suffered 46 dead, 167 wounded, and 64 missing or captured, compared to 24 killed, 115 wounded, and 74 missing for the Americans.[33]

Jackson withdrew his army a mile, just behind the ten-feet-wide and four-feet-deep Rodriguez Canal, which ran between the river and a swamp three-quarters of a mile away. There he set his men to work digging an earthen wall at the canal's lip; nine cannons studded these earthworks. He established his headquarters in the McCarty mansion near the river, two hundred yards behind the line.

Pakenham arrived with the rest of his army and supplies at the devastated British camp. After a day's rest, he ordered his army to advance within two miles of the enemy and camp there, guarded by a half-dozen redoubts. Over the next two weeks, he sent his artillery and several regiments forward to within five hundred yards of the American line. There they erected batteries and opened fire. During the first barrage, the British gunners sank one of the sloops, but thereafter their balls and shells plopped harmlessly into the soft earth. Thanks largely to Lafitte's skilled gunners, the American fire was deadlier. The artillery duel on New Year's Day was the bloodiest; the British lost forty-four men killed and fifty-five wounded, and the Americans eleven dead and twenty-three wounded.[34]

Jackson hunkered down and awaited the massive British assault. During these weeks, he dispatched sharpshooters to pick off British gunners, officers, and other targets, but he did not try to capture the enemy's artillery. Time was a vital ally. Reinforcements swelled Jackson's army to five thousand men, of which thirty-five hundred were behind the earthworks on the city's side of the river, five hundred men and a battery fortified the opposite bank, and a thousand acted as a reserve and guarded other approaches to New Orleans. Food was plentiful.

In contrast, Pakenham could not expect any reinforcements, and his men rapidly devoured their provisions. His attempts to breach the enemy line had failed. He faced a grim choice—either attack or withdraw.

The British assault came shortly after dawn on January 8. Pakenham sent five thousand troops directly against Jackson's main army and a thousand against the enemy on the opposite shore. As the early morning fog dissipated, the redcoats resolutely marched into a hailstorm of cannon and musket balls. Only a few survived to wade across the foul canal and scramble up the slippery earthworks, where they were shot, bayoneted, or clubbed to death. The remnants of the main assault ran or limped beyond artillery range. The redcoats on the far shore succeeded in routing the defenders but withdrew after the main assault failed. The British losses were staggering. In less than a half hour of fighting, they suffered 291 killed, 1,262 wounded, and 484 captured, for 2,037 casualties altogether, or one of every three men in the army; Pakenham was among the dead. The Americans lost only thirteen dead, thirty-nine wounded, and nineteen missing.[35]

Jackson did not follow up his victory with an attack on the British camp. Had he done so he might well have captured or killed the entire army. Nor did he send his men to harass the redcoats after they broke camp and withdrew toward to their flotilla on Lake Borgne on January 18. For once the fierce warrior and high-stakes gambler played his cards cautiously. He may have hated the British, but he retained a healthy respect for their military prowess. It was just as well. Tragically, the war's bloodiest battle occurred after a peace treaty was signed on Christmas Eve, little more than two weeks earlier.

Jackson's authoritarian behavior after the battle smeared his victory's luster. He relished all the power that martial law gave him and refused to surrender it even though the British had sailed away and word had arrived that the Treaty of Ghent had ended the war. He rejected all appeals that he discharge the militia to their homes, rescind the strict curfew, or recognize civilian rule. Atop that he exiled all French citizens to at least 120 miles from the city and ordered the arrest of any found within that limit. On February 21 six captured deserters were executed in Mobile on his orders.

Influential people criticized his dictatorship. To crush this dissent, Jackson sought to apprehend someone in the act of "sedition" and make an example of him as he had Pvt. John Woods. That chance came when Louis Louaillier, a state legislator, penned a newspaper essay that condemned Jackson's "abuse of authority." Jackson had him arrested on charges of sedition and espionage. Although a court-martial found Louaillier innocent, Jackson kept him in prison. Federal judge Dominick Hall issued a writ of habeas corpus that required Jackson either to release Louaillier or file different charges. Jackson had the judge arrested, escorted to the city's outskirts, and ordered not to return until the Madison administration declared that the war was over.

Hall's exile was brief as a War Department dispatch officially announcing the war's end came the next day, March 13, 1815. Jackson rescinded martial law and his orders against Hall, Louaillier, and the exiled French. On March 21 Hall issued a summons to Jackson to answer contempt of court charges for refusing to obey a writ of habeas corpus. Jackson appeared on March 24.

In an essay that Jackson submitted to the court, he defended his behavior on what he claimed were constitutional grounds—a strategy that turned out to be legal quicksand. The framers were careful to permit martial law only in extraordinary and limited circumstances—during an insurrection or invasion in an area where civilian authority was incapacitated and where Congress specifically authorized the measure. None of these conditions was present after the British armada disappeared. Jackson refused to answer any of the prosecution's nineteen questions that challenged his argument. Hall then tried to get him to answer one essential question: "Whether the Law should bend to the General or the General to the Law."[36] Jackson remained defiantly silent. Hall found him guilty as charged and imposed a thousand dollar fine.

Jackson's rage against Hall and other civilian authorities and critics softened when Rachel joined him in New Orleans. Various members of the elite invited the Jacksons to dinners, balls, and teas. The motives for those who did so were mixed. Undoubtedly, the admiration expressed by some was as sincere as that expressed by others was feigned. One attendee rather meanly wrote,

> After supper we were treated to a most delicious pas de deux by the conqueror and his spouse, an emigrant of the lower classes . . . who explained by her corpulence that French saying, "She shows how far skin can be stretched." To see these two figures, the general a long haggard man, with limbs like a skeleton, and Madame la Generale, a short fat dumpling, bobbing opposite each other like half-drunken Indians, to the wild melody of Possum Up A Gum Tree, and endeavoring to make a spring into the air was . . . far more edifying a spectacle than any European ballet could possibly have furnished.[37]

After a final review of the troops, the Jacksons departed New Orleans on April 6, for the long, tedious keelboat voyage up the Mississippi and Cumberland Rivers to their home. Jackson's reemersion in domestic tranquility and the routine of plantation life would soon be cut short.

3

The Fate of Spanish Florida

I have long viewed treaties with the Indians as an absurdity
not to be reconciled to the principles of our Government.

ANDREW JACKSON

Our country! In her intercourse with foreign nations may she
always be in the right; but our country, right or wrong!

STEPHEN DECATUR

Beware how you give a fatal sanction, in this infant period of our Republic, scarcely yet two score years old, to military insubordination.

HENRY CLAY[1]

Jackson's mangling of a British army and the American Constitution
at New Orleans imposed a dilemma on the Madison administration.
Should they celebrate or censure the greatest hero and general to emerge
from the war? As Treasury Secretary Alexander Dallas explained, somehow they had to "manifest a just respect for the Constitution and laws
without wounding the pride or feelings of General Jackson."[1]

The stakes could have not been more profound for America's future.
The Constitution's framers constructed a system that completely sub-

ordinated the military to civilian rule and made the decision for and conduct of war the joint duty of Congress and the president. All this is clear enough in the Constitution's text. But letting a general get away with violating the Constitution can weaken that document by establishing a dangerous precedent that future generals can cite to justify their own violations. And thus might America's liberal democracy be subverted incrementally into a quasi-military dictatorship. This was among the framers' greatest fears. And now Andrew Jackson appeared to be doing just that.

Rendering a decision all the more perplexing for Madison and his cabinet was their fear of Jackson. Less than a decade earlier, Aaron Burr had tried to provoke a western rebellion against the United States. Although there was no hard evidence that Jackson contemplated, let alone conspired, doing the same, no one doubted his ability to do so. Tiptoeing around someone who was at once as powerful and as volatile as Jackson was incredibly stressful.

Dallas essentially advised Madison to let that sleeping dog lie with the excuse that a greater good trumped the wrongdoing: "Where no difference of opinion can occur as to the purity or the sincerity of the motive to action, where the exigency was great, and where the triumph has been complete, the judgment of a responsible and distinguished officer merits implicit confidence."[2]

Madison agreed and asked Dallas to express the sentiment in a letter to Jackson. Alas, try as he might, the treasury secretary tumbled from his high-wire balancing act. Jackson exploded in wrath at the following lines:

> The case of military necessity which creates its own law must not be confounded with the ordinary case of military service, prescribed and governed by the law of the land. In the United States there exists no authority to declare and approve martial law beyond the positive sanction of the acts of Congress. . . . If, therefore, [military commanders] undertake to suspend the writ of habeas corpus, to restrain the liberty of the press, to inflict military punishment upon citizens who are not military men, and generally to supersede the functions of the civil magistrate, he may be justified by the law of necessity, while he has the merit of saving the

country, but he cannot resort to the established law of the land for the means of vindication.[3]

Jackson fired off a short note acknowledging his receipt of the message and stating he would head to Washington to justify his behavior. His journey was a triumphal procession as crowds turned out in each town along the way to cheer the hero of New Orleans. He and his entourage reached the capital on November 16, 1815.

Madison and his secretaries greeted Jackson with sheepish praise. War Secretary William Crawford offered Jackson command of the Southern Military District. Jackson accepted. He would soon be in the field again, warring against familiar foes—hostile Indians, Spanish officials, and British agents.

The Jackson controversy was hardly the only unresolved conflict lingering after the War of 1812. Those who had so enthusiastically rushed the nation to war with Britain violated the most fundamental principles of the art of military power—know your enemy, know yourself, know your war, know your peace. The War Hawks deluded themselves into believing that the disputes between the United States and Britain were worth fighting for and that the United States would swiftly win the war. Compounding this core failure was how incompetently the civilian and military leaders had waged the war, with no one more inept than the commander in chief. James Madison lacked the gravitas, backbone, and know-how to run a war.[4] His cabinet secretaries were not much better. Jeffersonism proved to be as disastrous a formula for waging war as it was for developing the economy. Grounding the nation's defense on militia and gunboats was at once ideologically correct and militarily catastrophic.

The United States won nothing concrete from Britain in the war that remotely justified the tremendous sacrifice of blood and treasure. Instead, the Americans and British ended the war with a lose-lose deal. The Treaty of Ghent, named after the Belgian town where it was negotiated, made a mockery of the prewar War Hawk promises of spoils the nation would reap from a quick, easy victory. Canada's conquest was number one on the War Hawk's grandiose list of war aims. The United States did not win a square foot of Canada or any other British territory as the belligerents agreed to turn back the clock to the antebellum status quo. The Americans even failed to convince the British to renounce their practice of impressment, pay reparations for all the cargoes and ships they had confiscated, and pledge not to conspire with Indians in the United States, all of which were major excuses peddled by President Madison and the War Hawks to drive the nation to war. In all, the War of 1812 devastated American power, wealth, security, and honor.

Nonetheless, the United States did not emerge from the war completely empty-handed. Gens. William Henry Harrison and Andrew Jackson won the Battles of the Thames and Horseshoe Bend, respectively, which forever shattered the power of the Northwest and Southwest Indians. Jackson also asserted American control over Mobile in Spanish West Florida, the only land taken by the United States during the war. Yet critics questioned the cost of these gains. After all, the United States did not have to war against Britain to crush the Indians and grab land from the Spanish.[5]

Jackson's victory at New Orleans repolished America's tarnished honor in the minds of many Americans. People needed to believe, contrary to all evidence, that all the lives and money had not been squandered in vain. Such delusions are a deadweight on any nation's power. Throughout history, demagogues have wielded false conceptions of pride and honor to stampede weak-willed, ignorant, hateful, fearful, and hopeful followers into wars that ruin rather than bolster their national interests.

The Jacksonians took the nation to war and then to peace with myths. They brilliantly mass-marketed the belief that the war had been a glorious crusade that defended national honor. This notion would have been a tough sell without Jackson's decisive victory. In the minds of countless Americans then and thereafter, the Battle of New Orleans papered over the national disgrace of the two preceding years of mostly humiliating defeats and soaring deaths and debts. Few people could face the reality that their nation had callously wasted tens of thousands of lives and tens of millions of dollars in a war that was as unjustified as it was ineptly fought. Instead, the War of 1812 became a glorious second "War of Independence," a David-versus-Goliath struggle of common American citizens and their values against a tyrannical, rapacious British Empire.

The War of 1812 was a devastating failure of both the Jeffersonian and Jacksonian versions of the art of power. The war combined each philosophy's worst elements: the "government that governs least governs best" Jeffersonian delusion and the "our country, right or wrong" Jacksonian bluster. Hubris animated Jeffersonians and Jacksonians alike. The Jeffersonians cut off foreign trade and the Jacksonians declared war to uphold the nation's "honor," which had been sullied by the depredations of British, French, and other foreign navies against American ships, cargoes, and crews. In doing so, they ignored the pleas of the affected merchants that these policies would worsen their plight and devastate the United States.

And that is indeed what happened. From 1811 to 1814 American exports plunged from $61 million to $6 million, imports from $53 million to $13 million, the tonnage of ships involved in trade from 948,000 to 60,000, and government revenues from $13 million to $6 million. Inflation and insurance rates soared. Worst of all, the national debt skyrocketed from $45 million to $127 million.[6]

The war was not the Republican Party's only self-destructive act. As irony would have it, Republicans succeeded in destroying Hamilton's Bank of the United States in 1811 on the war's eve. The result was a speculative orgy. From 1811 to 1815 both the number of state banks and the amount of paper money circulating nearly doubled, respectively, from 117 to 212 and $66 million to $115 million. Hard specie plummeted as paper money soared. When it dissolved the bank, the federal government had to pay $7 million in gold and silver to European stockholders. Another $3 million in coin slipped from the United States during the war in payments to foreign smugglers.[7]

Some people did benefit from the war. As usual, the military contractors enriched themselves by selling the government high-priced and often shoddy goods or committing outright fraud. Farmers who sold their surpluses to the military at least kept their real income up with the inflation rate. Frontline states gained as generals requisitioned supplies and troops spent their money as they marched through or holed up in forts. Yet overall the war left most Americans much poorer as their incomes withered before soaring prices. Worst hit were those communities dependent on international trade. Thousands of ships rotted at anchor in port, and tens of thousands of men idled away their days jobless. The effects of this economic devastation surged far inland.

Then there were the countless Americans whose losses cannot be measured with a price tag. The official battle statistics record 2,260 men killed and 4,505 wounded. Disease most likely killed seven times this number, although an exact total will never be definitively known.[8]

This array of devastating blows to American power, wealth, security, and honor inflicted by Jeffersonians and Jacksonians through Republican Party policies would seem to provide an opportunity for a Hamiltonian comeback. But this did not happen. Jeffersonism and Jacksonism were populist movements whose leaders were brilliant at venting the rage of their followers against scapegoats rather than their own incompetence, prejudices, and delusions. In contrast, Hamiltonism was the outlook of worldly men guided by reason, history, and science. This was at once their greatest strength and weakness. They were incapable of distilling their practical skills and knowledge into the political slogans and grassroots organization that could impassion a mass movement. Their greatest ally was history. They could juxtaposition the 1790s, when Hamilton's policies promoted a decade of peace and ever greater prosperity, with the economic and military devastation of the Jeffersonian years. Exports, for instance, soared from $33 million in 1794 to $94 million in 1801. Then Jefferson and the Republican Party came to power. American exports went on a roller-coaster ride that ended with the crash eleven years later.[9] This stark contrast might have been enough to animate most Americans had the Hamiltonians not utterly lacked charismatic leaders to capitalize on it. No Federalist displayed more than a shadow of Hamilton's mind, passion, energy, and vision.

After voting against the war, the Federalists watched helplessly in worsening dismay as the Republicans utterly mismanaged it. They vented their frustration with the Hartford Convention of December 15, 1813, to January 5, 1814, during which they drafted several resolutions that they hoped might avert a similar catastrophe in the future. Among their proposals were two-thirds votes in both houses of Congress for wars, embargoes, or new states; a one-term presidency in which no incoming president could be from the same state as his predecessor; and the elimination of the tenet that counted slaves as three-fifths of a person, which bolstered southern representation in Congress. But convention delegates never translated these resolutions into constitutional amendments. Two powerful reasons held them back: one practical, the other philosophical. First, these amendments would have been dead on arrival in most state legislatures. Perhaps as important, they would have emasculated the powerful, problem-solving federal government that Hamilton envisioned.

Meanwhile, Madison and the Republicans redeemed themselves with a genuine military success. During the War of 1812, the dey, or ruler, of Algiers had allied with Britain as an excuse to raid American shipping in the Mediterranean Sea. American naval power could not then retaliate against Algiers given that it was fighting against the world's greatest naval power. But weeks after peace officially reigned with Britain, on February 23, 1815, Madison asked for and Congress granted a war declaration against Algiers. Commodores Stephen Decatur and William Bainbridge, both heroes of the War of 1812, each commanded a squadron bound for Algiers. Decatur's squadron captured two Algerian warships along the way, before sailing triumphantly into the Bay of Algiers. After threatening to destroy the city, Decatur convinced the dey to sign a treaty whereby Algiers would release ten American captives, compensate each of them with ten thousand dollars, and promise never again to demand tribute from the United States. In return Decatur would give back the two captured warships. Upon returning home to a hero's welcome, Decatur issued a toast at a banquet that captured Jacksonism's essence: "Our country! In her intercourse with foreign nations may she always be in the right; but our country, right or wrong!"[10]

As the Federalist Party faded into oblivion and the Madison administration chalked up a military and diplomatic victory, Andrew Jackson asserted his version of the art of American power. In 1815 he warred against the Seminoles.[11] The Spanish tolerated the Seminole presence as long as they confined their depredations to American territory. British agents supplied them with guns, ammunition, and other necessities.

Jackson's first target was Negro Fort, fifteen miles up the Apalachicola River from the Gulf of Mexico and sixty miles from the American frontier. About three hundred blacks and a mélange of Indians inhabited this fort and used it as a base for smuggling and raids. Jackson ordered Gen. Edmund Gaines, who commanded the Southern Military District in his absence, to mobilize an expedition and destroy the fort. He explained the rationale for the action: "This fort has been established by some villains for the purpose of murder, rapine, and plunder. . . . It ought to be blown up regardless of the ground it stands on."[12] This "ground" happened to be owned by Spain. Jackson fired off a stern letter to Governor Mauricio de Zuniga: "The conduct of this banditti . . . will not be tolerated by our government, and if it is not put down by Spanish authority will compel us in self-defense to destroy them."[13]

Gaines passed the mission to Col. Duncan Clinch and his Fourth Infantry at the newly established Fort Scott, where the Flint and Chattahoochee Rivers formed the Apalachicola River just north of the Florida border. Clinch decisively accomplished his mission. His expedition floated downriver, ground ashore within cannon range of the fort, and set up a battery. The guns opened fire on July 26. A cannonball hit a gunpowder magazine, which exploded with a force that obliterated the fort and nearly everyone in it. Clinch turned over the stunned survivors to his Indian allies, who tortured them to death.[14]

Gaines led the expedition against the Seminole village of Fowltown, the home of Chief Nemantha and his warriors, the most virulent raiders on the Georgia frontier. Fowltown was deserted when the soldiers warily marched in on November 12, 1817. Nemantha had gotten word of the enemy's advance and led his people to safety. Gaines ordered the village burned then withdrew to Fort Flint.

Rather than crush the Seminoles, the army kicked in a hornet's nest. Nine days later, Nemantha retaliated by wiping out a flotilla packed with supplies and fifty-one people on the Apalachicola River. Seminole attacks against the frontier worsened in number and violence. Gaines appeared ever less capable of winning the war. Eventually, Jackson would reenter the field and deal decisively with the Seminoles and their Spanish and British backers.

In the meantime, Jackson read an order from War Secretary Crawford that enraged him. He was to issue a proclamation that all squatters on Indian lands should either leave promptly or be driven off by the army. Jackson replied with a heated protest:

Candour . . . compels me to . . . state to you that the people of the West will never suffer any Indian to inhabit this country again that has been for thirty years the den of the murderers of their wives and helpless infants, and on the conquest of which, and for their security thereafter, they shed their blood and suffered every privation. I tell you frankly they never will unless coerced by the Government, and when this is attempted I fear it will lead to scenes that will make human nature shudder.[15]

Once again, Jackson got his way by defying his superiors, this time simply by refusing to obey his order. With the Constitution in hand, the commander in chief could have immediately cashiered Jackson. But neither the president nor the secretary of war seriously considered this. Instead, they sighed and ignored Jackson's latest blatant insubordination. Indeed, Madison fed Jackson's defiance by naming him one of three commissioners charged with settling the dispute between the tribes and the squatters.

Perhaps the president did so hoping to undercut Jackson's inevitable explosion when he learned of another administration policy. Madison had accepted Creek Indian complaints that the Treaty of Jackson was terribly unjust. On March 22, 1816, envoys signed a new treaty between the United States and the Creeks that returned 4 million of the 23 million acres confiscated by Jackson's treaty and awarded the tribe $25,500 in damages inflicted by Tennessee troops against friendly villages. Word of these concessions provoked Jackson's latest tantrum at what he viewed as a gross insult to his honor. That War Secretary Crawford had negotiated the deal made him a mortal enemy in Jackson's feverish mind.

Jackson sought to overturn Crawford's treaty in his subsequent negotiations with the tribes. He shunned any pretense of being an honest broker. Although the United States was officially at peace, Jackson treated the Southwest tribes—Cherokees, Chickasaws, Choctaws, and Creeks—as if they were still at war. From 1816 to 1818 he forced them to sign five separate treaties whereby they surrendered tens of millions of acres of land. At each council, when the tribal delegation pointed to the tenets of previous treaties that clearly granted them the disputed territory, he dismissed them as invalid and imposed upon them new treaties that deprived them of their land. When they continued to resist, he did not hesitate to weaken their resolve with bribes and bullying.

He first targeted the Cherokees. Under the Treaty of Turkey Town, signed on September 14, 1816, the Cherokees finally buckled to Jackson's demand to cede all their land south of a ridge dividing the Tennessee and Tombigbee Rivers and then east to the Coosa River. In return, the tribe would receive $5,000 within sixty days and $6,000 annually for ten years. Next came the Chickasaws. In a treaty signed on September 20, 1816, they yielded a huge triangle of land south to the Choctaw territory and east on both sides of the Tennessee River all the way to the Tombigbee River. The tribe would receive $4,500 within sixty days and $12,000 annually for ten years. The Choctaw cession came on October 24, 1816. They rendered all their land east of the Tombigbee River for $16,000 annually for twenty years atop a $10,000 payment in merchandise for signing.

In January 1817 Jackson received President Madison's authorization to cut another deal with the Cherokees that forced them to swap their ancestral lands for lands in the Arkansas Territory. On July 8, 1817, the Cherokee chiefs' resistance finally broke, and they agreed to cede 2 million acres of their Smoky Mountain homeland in return for the equivalent acreage far west of the Mississippi River. Jackson eventually became dissatisfied with his initial treaty with the Chickasaws. They occupied much of western Tennessee, land that he and a coterie of speculators longed to own for themselves. In a treaty signed on October 19, 1818, he browbeat and bribed the Chickasaws into surrendering the rest of their homeland for $300,000, to be paid in $20,000 annual installments for fifteen years. Finally, he revisited his first victims, the Creeks, for yet more cessions.

In all, Jackson forced the Southwest tribes to surrender territory that amounted to three-quarters of Alabama, one-third of Tennessee, one-fifth of Georgia and Mississippi, and one-tenth of Kentucky and North Carolina. Tens of thousands of settlers quickly spread across these lands, so many that Mississippi and Alabama became states in 1817 and 1819, respectively. But this astonishing transformation did not satiate Jackson's ambitions. A new president in 1817 gave him an opportunity to demand much more.[16]

James Monroe became the third consecutive Jeffersonian in the White House when he took the oath of office on March 4, 1817.[17] Like his predecessors, he was once a true believer who actually opposed the Constitution's ratification but who moderated his ideals as one after another crashed against the real world's harsh complexities. He was renowned for his congeniality and integrity, but by all accounts, his résumé was more impressive than his intellect. He graduated from the College of William and Mary; obtained a law license; rose to the rank of captain in the Continental Army and was wounded at Princeton; was elected to Virginia's assembly and then to Congress, first as a representative and then as a senator; was appointed the minister to France and then to Britain; was elected Virginia's governor; and acted as the secretaries of war and then state under Madison before he won the presidency. To his credit, Monroe picked first-rate minds for his cabinet: John Quincy Adams was his secretary of state, John Calhoun was his war secretary, William Crawford was his treasury secretary, and Richard Rush was his attorney general.

And then there was Andrew Jackson. Although he was physically hundreds of miles away, Old Hickory would be the stern ghost at the cabinet table. He fired off a series of letters to Monroe, giving him unsolicited advice on a range of issues.

For now, Jackson's number one ambition was trying to browbeat Monroe into a policy of dispossessing the Southwest Indians of all their lands by acts of Congress:

> I have long viewed treaties with the Indians as an absurdity not to be reconciled to the principles of our Government. The Indians are the subjects of the United States, inhabiting its territory and acknowledging its sovereignty. Then is it not absurd for the sovereign to negotiate by treaty with its subjects? I have always thought that Congress had as much right to regulate by acts of legislation all concerns as they had of Territories. . . . The United States . . . have the right to take it and dispose of it.[18]

Monroe gingerly shelved Jackson's idea and held his breath. Soon, the latest Jackson rant erupted, although for an unexpected reason. In 1817 the War Department bypassed him with a routine order to an officer in the vast Southern Military District. War Secretary Calhoun's subsequent apology was not good enough for Jackson. On April 22 he issued an order that henceforth no order should be obeyed unless it came through his own hands.[19]

Word of Jackson's act provoked another debate over what to do about the loose cannon. An anonymous pamphlet appeared castigating Jackson for his "mutinous" behavior; the author was rumored to be Gen. Winfield Scott, who commanded the First and Third Military Districts in the Northeast. Jackson fired off a letter to Scott demanding whether this was true. Scott disclaimed being the pamphlet's author, but he completely agreed that Jackson's behavior was indeed mutinous and urged him to rescind his policy. This sent Jackson into a violent paroxysm, which he vented with another letter to Scott, this one challenging him to a duel.[20] Fortunately, they were at opposite ends of the country, so meeting with pistols at dawn was problematic. And soon Jackson found another outlet for his rage.

He could not have received a better New Year's gift for 1818. Monroe authorized him to personally lead a campaign designed to crush the Seminoles. Jackson pledged to quickly "enter the territory of Spain and chastise the ruthless savages who have been depredating on the property and lives of our citizens."[21] He would be half-true to his word. The severest of chastisements lay ahead, although not for those who actually committed the depredations.

Jackson urged Monroe to authorize that "the whole of East Florida" be "seized and held as an indemnity for the outrages of Spain upon the property of our citizens. This done . . . saves us from a war with Great Britain or some of the continental powers combined with Spain." He vowed that "the possession of the Floridas . . . in sixty days . . . will be accomplished."[22] And his ambitions were not confined to conquering Florida for the United States. Later that year, he informed Monroe that with enough troops, transports, and supplies, "I will ensure you Cuba."[23]

Exactly what Monroe authorized remains hazy to this day. "Plausible deniability" lets the president or other officials get away with extralegal or outright illegal acts as long as no legal proof becomes public. The practice is as old as the first government supposedly restrained by law. In the United States, plausible deniability did not start with Jackson and the Monroe administration, although no previous administration exercised it quite so blatantly.

Monroe later denied that he understood Jackson's proposals or authorized him to invade East Florida. He rendered this "plausible," itself a highly pliable concept, by claiming "that when I received the letter . . . I was sick in bed and could not read it." He did admit to handing the letter to Calhoun and Crawford to read but claimed they did not discuss the startling message with him. His case is further bolstered with a letter to Calhoun, dated January 30, 1818, in which he instructs the secretary to warn Jackson "not to attack any post occupied by Spanish troops." But, whether from the president's secret spoken instructions or neglect, Calhoun never forwarded this order to the general.[24]

Jackson flatly rejected Monroe's version. He claimed that he received a written order but later was visited by John Rhea, one of Monroe's congressional allies, who asked him to burn it to prevent the chance it might "fall into the hands of those who would make improper use of it."[25] There is no question that Jackson complied with this request. The proof is in his letter book with the note that he burned the letter.[26]

Jackson acted believing that the Monroe administration fully backed his invasion of Florida and overthrow of the Spanish regime. On January 22, 1818, he led a thousand troops 450 miles from Nashville to Fort Scott, which they trudged wearily into on March 9. He gave them just a day's rest before pushing down the Apalachicola River. At Fort Gadsden, newly erected atop Negro Fort's ruins, the expedition received desperately needed supplies up from the gulf. He then marched his troops eastward to St. Marks, a Spanish fortress and supply center for the region's Seminoles and runaway slaves.

The Spanish commandant, Francisco Caso y Luengo, had only a handful of troops when the American army appeared on April 6. He opened a letter from Jackson that insisted he and his army were in Florida "not as the enemy, but as the friend of Spain."[27] The commandant can be forgiven if he begged to differ. Nonetheless, he swiftly obeyed Jackson's demand to surrender.

St. Marks served as Jackson's center for operations in the surrounding region. He immediately sought out two British agents and an Indian prophet, said to be the worst instigators of Seminole raids, for punishment. Alexander Arbuthnot was a trader who had spent years with the Southwest Indians. Robert Armbrister was a former royal marine who not only aided but also encouraged the Seminoles to war against the Americans. Francis, or Hillis Hadjo, was an Indian prophet who preached that salvation could come only by driving the Americans from their lands. Arbuthnot was arrested at St. Marks. Francis and Himomathle Mico, another chief, were lured aboard an American ship bearing the Union Jack. The general presided over a tribunal that swiftly found the chiefs guilty of torture, murder, and mutilation and watched triumphantly as they were hanged on April 8.

Jackson marched his men against the nearby Seminole village of

Billy Bowlegs, fought a couple of skirmishes along the way, and captured the town on April 16. Although the chief and most of his followers managed to escape, Armbrister was among the prisoners. Jackson
ordered the town burned and led his troops, captives, and loot back to
St. Marks. There Arbuthnot and Armbrister met the victor's version of
justice. Jackson convened a military tribunal. The trial lasted three days.
The court found both guilty but issued sentences based on the severity
of their crimes. Arbuthnot was to be hanged; Armbrister was to receive
fifty lashes and a year of hard labor in prison. Jackson asserted his power
to change one of the sentences. Armbrister would stand before a firing
squad. The executions were carried out on April 29.

The executions did not end the campaign. Jackson led his men east
on the trail to Miccoukee, the most populous Seminole town. There
his troops killed Chief Kinache and a score of other Indians and then
looted and burned the town. As usual, most Seminoles escaped to villages deep in northern Florida's forests and swamps. The general and
his army withdrew to St. Marks.

Word arrived of an atrocity committed by Georgia militia against
the friendly Creek village of Chehaw. There Capt. Obed Wright and
his men slaughtered the chief and seven other warriors, all of whom
had fought with Jackson on previous campaigns. This news incensed
Jackson. In a letter to Georgia governor William Rabun, Jackson not
only condemned Wright as "a cowardly monster in human shape" but
also assailed the governor himself for assuming "the right to make war
against an Indian tribe" at "peace with and under the protection of the
U[nited] States." He wrote that "Captain Wright must be prosecuted
and punished," and warned that the unjust act perpetrated by the governor and captain "will to the last ages fix a stain upon the character
of Georgia."[28]

Uncowed by Jackson's barrage, Rabun shot back a letter accusing the
general of perpetuating a "military despotism." Although a Georgia jury
acquitted Wright, the governor and legislature did allocate eight thousand dollars in compensation for Chehaw's survivors. Jackson offered
consoling words and gifts to the aggrieved.[29]

With that, Jackson declared the campaign's first phase over. The next
phase would complete his conquest of West Florida. He left a few hundred troops at St. Marks and marched west with twelve hundred men

to take over Pensacola. Hearing of his intention, Governor José Masot and the commandant, Luis Piernas, were determined to redeem the sullied honor of themselves and their nation by resisting. Masot bluntly warned Jackson, "If you proceed . . . I will repulse you by force." Jackson tried to dissuade him from doing so by explaining the severe consequences: "I am informed that you have orders to fire on my troops entering the city. . . . I wish you to understand distinctly that if such orders are carried into effect, I will put to death every man found in arms." He sent a gentler letter to the commandant: "Resistance would be a wanton sacrifice of blood. . . . You cannot expect to defend yourself successfully, and the first shot from your fort must draw down upon you the vengeance of an irritated soldiery."[30]

Jackson was bluffing. Although Spanish and American troops skirmished briefly on May 24, 1818, he did not unleash his troops for a vicious slaughter of the enemy or sack of the town. He respected the Spanish need to defend their honor even if lives were unnecessarily lost. Indeed, who better understood and lived up to this notion than Jackson himself?

But Masot continued to resist even after honor was satisfied. He withdrew to Fort Barrancas, which had been rebuilt since it was blown up during Jackson's last incursion, and refused the general's demand for surrender. This infuriated Jackson, who regretted that he "had not stormed the works, captured the Governor, put him on trial . . . , and hung him" for allegedly ordering atrocities against Americans.[31] Eventually, Masot agreed to Jackson's offer to capitulate with full honors of war, and afterward he and his men sailed to Havana, Cuba.

Jackson transformed West Florida from a Spanish into an American possession. He appointed Col. William King of the Fourth Infantry to serve as Pensacola's governor and Capt. James Gadsden to collect revenues for the U.S. Treasury. He proudly wrote the president that he had accomplished his mission: "I have established peace and safety, and hope the government will never yield it."[32] Then he headed north on the long road to the Hermitage.

The news that Jackson had conquered Florida and executed British agents provoked a political firestorm in Washington. Luis de Onís, Spain's minister to the United States, demanded that the American troops be withdrawn immediately and their commander severely punished.[33] Jackson's blatant violations of a neutral country and the laws of war appalled most members of Congress and nearly all of Monroe's cabinet. War Secretary Calhoun, Treasury Secretary Crawford, and Attorney General William Wirt urged Monroe to return Florida promptly to Spain and censure Jackson. House Speaker Henry Clay expressed the mingled outrage and fear that many Americans felt. He blistered Jackson's acts, warning that approving them would permit "a triumph of the military over the civil authority . . . a triumph over the constitution of this land."[34]

Only one prominent political leader backed Jackson. Secretary of State John Quincy Adams could not have been more pleased at the grand bargaining chip that Jackson had given him in his negotiations with Onís over the fate of Florida and related issues. He encouraged Monroe to retain Pensacola and St. Marks.

Monroe split the difference between these poles of advice. He did not censure Jackson but simply asked him to evacuate West Florida and return with his army to American territory. He had Adams issue Onís not an apology but an explanation that while Jackson had exceeded his authority, he did so out of military necessity.[35]

The controversy infuriated Jackson. He protested Monroe's denial that he had authorized the general to wage war as he saw fit.[36] For Jackson, Monroe's dishonesty was dishonorable enough, but atop that he could not fathom why the administration bothered with negotiations that dragged on with no resolution. He advocated declaring war on Spain. If the countries went to war, he guaranteed that "Florida shall be in possession of the United States in three months."[37]

Jackson eventually won some vindication for his behavior, but from the House of Representatives rather than from the president. On February 8, 1819, House Speaker Henry Clay introduced a resolution that criticized the invasion of Florida and execution of the British agents, and forbade any future invasions of foreign lands without congressional approval or any future executions of prisoners by the military without presidential approval. Although Clay was careful to include words of respect for Jackson, he also issued a dark warning to America: "We are fighting a great moral battle for the benefit, not only of our country, but of all mankind. . . . Beware how you give a fatal sanction, in this infant period of our Republic, scarcely yet two score years old, to military insubordination." Clay's resolution ensured that the general would hate him until his dying day. The House overwhelmingly rejected Clay's resolution by 63 votes for and 107 against.[38]

Unlike the House, the Senate did not let popular passions divert its duty to defend the Constitution. A Senate report castigated Jackson for invading Spanish territory and argued that the execution of Armbrister and Arbuthnot was "an unnecessary act of severity . . . and a departure from that mild and humane system . . . honorable to the national character."[39] But the Senate failed to take the next logical step and make that report the foundation for a vote to censure Jackson. Jackson once again received only the lightest official slap on the wrist.

How much Jackson's invasion of Florida affected the outcome of negotiations between Adams and Onís is impossible to determine. Onís angrily broke off talks until October 1818, when he received official word that the United States had withdrawn its forces from East Florida. Adams, however, warned Onís that should the Spanish resume aiding Indian raids against the American frontier, the United States would take and keep East Florida without compensation. On February 22, 1819, Adams and Onís signed the Transcontinental Treaty, which dramatically redrew the map of North America. Spain ceded Florida to the United States, and in return, the United States disavowed any claim to Texas and assumed $5 million in claims by American citizens against Spain. The boundary between the United States and the Spanish Empire now zigzagged from the Gulf of Mexico north up the Sabine River to the Red River and west up it to the 100th meridian, then north to the Arkansas River and west up it to its source, and finally north to the 42nd parallel and westward all the way to the Pacific Ocean. Adams won control of both banks of those rivers for the United States. The treaty was not legally consummated for another two years after it was signed. King Ferdinand VII finally approved it on October 24, 1820. The Senate ratified the treaty on February 19, 1821, five days after receiving the monarch's signed copy.

The treaty seemed like a good deal at the time, and even Jackson lauded it. But the official renunciation of America's claim to Texas later provoked bitter divisions and limited the nation's diplomatic options. And in the short run, Ferdinand pulled a fast one on the Americans. He delayed ratifying the treaty until he sold off as much land as possible to Spanish investors, at once reaping revenue and denying prime land to would-be American speculators and settlers and the subsequent revenue to America's treasury.[40]

Meanwhile, Monroe tried to compensate Jackson for unwillingly taking the hit to allow the White House plausible deniability for the Florida invasion. In the early autumn of 1820, the president asked the general to be the nation's hatchet man in cleaving away more territory from the Indians. Jackson relished this duty. He and his fellow commissioner, Gen. Thomas Hinds, met with the Choctaws at Doak's Stand on the Natchez Trace. The council opened on October 10 and concluded with the Treaty of Doak's Stand on October 18, 1820. In between, Jackson and Hinds made the usual mixture of threats, bribes, and pleas to the chiefs. The Choctaws finally agreed to surrender their ancestral lands east of the Mississippi for equivalent acreage far to the west and, unofficially, $4,674 in "donations" divided among twenty-six chiefs.[41]

Jackson's latest rage was provoked when Congress sought to reduce federal spending by cutting the peacetime army's budget in half. Among the cuts was a reduction in the number of major generals from two to one. Jacob Brown had seniority over Jackson, and so Old Hickory was forced into retirement. Monroe sought to appease Jackson's anger by tapping him to be the Florida Territory's first governor in January 1821. Jackson reluctantly accepted.[42] Jackson eventually warmed to the consolation prize, and Monroe later regretted naming him to the sensitive post.

Part of the face-saving deal was that Jackson would retire from the army before he became governor. He did so officially on June 1. But after assuming the governorship, he issued orders to troops in Florida, and those troops promptly obeyed. General Brown complained that Jackson was usurping his command over all American troops. The dispute was resolved only after Jackson resigned his post. This was hardly the only polemic that Jackson provoked during his brief tenure as governor.

Jackson stood with an honor guard alongside Governor José María Callava as the Spanish flag was lowered and the American flag was raised over Pensacola. He noted with pride that the ceremony on July 17, 1821, was "the third time I had planted the flag on that wall."[43]

Alas, after this dignified, poignant beginning, Jackson entangled himself in controversy. Callava barely concealed his hatred for him.

A court case required the transfer of Spanish documents to American control. Callava's subordinate, Domingo Sousa, had the documents and refused to render them. Jackson ordered Sousa arrested and the papers seized. Sousa managed to pass the documents to Callava before he was dragged off to jail. Under Jackson's interrogation, Sousa revealed who now held the documents. Jackson sent an order to Callava to surrender them. The summons interrupted a dinner party that Callava was attending at the home of Col. George Brooke. Federal judge Eligius Fromentin and other prominent American and Spanish officials were also in attendance. Callava said he would forward the documents later, and only after receiving a proper legal notice to do so. This was not good enough for Jackson; he had Callava arrested.

Callava exploded in wrath when he was ushered before Jackson, who replied with even more vitriol. Each shouted at each other in his own language; neither understood the exact meaning of the other but the essence of their rants was perfectly clear. Jackson "was turbulent and violent actions, with disjointed reasonings, blows on the table, his mouth foaming and possessed of the furies."[44]

The American was still furious the next morning when he received a writ of habeas corpus from Judge Fromentin, requiring him either to release Callava and Sousa or to charge them with crimes. Jackson angrily returned the writ to Fromentin, saying that it merited nothing but "indignation and contempt."[45]

The deadlock was broken when Callava rendered the papers. Jackson released him and Sousa. While Sousa sailed off to Cuba, Callava journeyed to Washington to protest his treatment to the Spanish minister. Fromentin was among many Americans and Spaniards who were appalled by Jackson's behavior. He complained that the governor acted like "a grand inquisitor" who had he discovered "in my library many books . . . prohibited . . . and among others the Constitution of the United States, he should send me to the stake."[46] But perhaps for this very reason, Fromentin never issued a contempt order against Jackson. Once again, Old Hickory succeeded in trampling the Constitution. It would be far from his last triumphant assertion of dictatorial powers.

Jackson resigned the governorship on November 13, 1821, just five months after taking power. He wrote President Monroe that his "duties have been laborious and my situation exposed me to heavy expenses . . .

that I should retire to resuscitate my declining fortune to enable it to support me in my declining years."[47] His health was in worse shape than his fortune. He was fifty-four, quite old by the era's life expectancy, and plagued by an array of chronic ailments and duel wounds. He would soon be called back to action, this time in the political arena. There he would fight as fiercely as ever, although without taking life, at least not directly. Meanwhile, he sat fuming on the sidelines as a political crisis threatened to tear America apart.

4

The Fire Bell in the Night

This momentous question, like a fire bell in the
night, awakened and filled me with terror.

THOMAS JEFFERSON

The states have no power, by taxation or otherwise, to
retard, impede, burden or in any manner control the
operations of the Federal government or its agencies.

JOHN MARSHALL

If you persist, the Union will be dissolved. . . . You have
kindled a fire which all the waters of the ocean cannot put out, which seas of blood can only extinguish.

THOMAS COBB

The War of 1812 pounded the last nails in the coffin of a viable national
Federalist Party. Much of the next decade became known as the "Era of
Good Feelings" as the Republican Party, an amalgam of Jeffersonians
and Jacksonians, dominated American politics, and the mostly New
England Federalists dwindled toward oblivion.[1] Despite the hypocrisy,
the Republicans stole shamelessly from the Hamiltonian playbook even

as they persisted in vilifying it. The reason was simple—fifteen years of disastrous Republican policies forced them to abandon their party's practices, if not the principles.

President James Madison led that flip-flop by calling on Congress to develop the national economy with new canals, better roads, and a protective tariff for infant industries battered by a postwar deluge of cheaper priced, better made British goods. To the astonishment and often dismay of his followers, Thomas Jefferson himself endorsed this idea: "We must now place the manufacturer by the side of the agriculturalist."[2] The 1816 Tariff Bill passed by large majorities in each house, and Madison signed it into law on April 27. He soon wielded his pen again for the National Road Bill, which appropriated a $100,000 downpayment on an ambitious scheme to construct a federal highway from Baltimore to Wheeling. The president, however, failed to muster enough votes to pass an internal improvements bill, as it proved impossible to spread the benefits to enough districts and states. A core of Jeffersonian purists known as Old Republicans and led by Virginia representative John Randolph shrilly denounced and voted against each of these heresies. The Federalists were at once vindicated and further diminished in ranks with each subsequent election.[3]

Among all the ideas that Alexander Hamilton conceived and brought to fruition, he was perhaps fondest of the Bank of the United States.[4] His finest creation launched and guided a decade of unprecedented American economic growth and prosperity. Hamilton was a student of history. Among history's most vital lessons is that markets left to themselves sooner or later self-destruct, either through frenzied speculative bubbles that burst or voracious businesses that eliminate their rivals and exploit consumers through monopoly or oligopoly rule. These disasters, however, are not inevitable. Sensible government policies and institutions can bring out the best market forces while restraining the worst.

Treasury Secretary Alexander Dallas understood all this. Although he was a devoted Jeffersonian in principle and politics, he embraced Hamiltonism for policies. In 1815 he issued a report with the dire conclusion that the nation faced a worsening and unbreakable vicious cycle of debt, joblessness, bankruptcy, and depression unless the Bank of the United States was reestablished. He proposed a structure nearly identical to that of Hamilton's institution. The bill that was hammered out in Congress provided for a second bank capitalized initially with $35 million, three and a half times more than the initial investment in the first bank. The government would own 20 percent of the institution and the public 80 percent. Investors had to pay coin for at least one-fifth of their shares. The second bank was headquartered in Philadelphia, and branches opened elsewhere. The government appointed the president and five of the twenty-five directors, and stockholders elected the others. The bank was empowered to serve as the sole deposit for federal funds. Finally, the bank would pay the federal government $1.5 million during its first four operating years.

Solid majorities of 80 to 71 in the House and 22 to 12 in the Senate approved the bill as hard practical realities edged out lofty ideals. Most western and southern congressmen voted in favor for two reasons—their own party proposed it, and they looked forward to the credit the bank might provide hard-pressed farmers and merchants in their regions. For this they were willing to deafen their ears to the Old Republicans' strict constructivist argument that because the Constitution did not specifically empower the creation of such an institution, it was unconstitutional. On May 10, 1816, Madison signed the bill establishing the Second Bank of the United States.

The president's flurry of Hamiltonian initiatives weighed heavily on his principles. On March 3, 1817, the day before he left office, Madison flip-flopped once again by vetoing the Bonus Bill, which would have allocated the $1.5 million fee that the bank paid the federal government to internal improvements, such as roads, canals, and ports. His veto sharply hit states with ambitious development plans. Without the start-up capital that the Bonus Bill would have provided, most states had to scrap their plans for better or new roads, ports, and canals.[5]

No plan was more ambitious than that of New York governor DeWitt Clinton. The Erie Canal was the core of his development program for New York, which was as farsighted as Hamilton's was for America.[6] By the time Clinton envisioned a canal linking the upper Hudson River and Lake Erie, he and his People's Party had already pushed a series of reforms through the New York State Assembly, including the promotion of factories, libraries, inventors, and retail banking; the abolition of slavery and imprisonment for debt; and voting rights for all adult white and black males alike. He overcame daunting political and then technical obstacles to realize this vision. Leading the opposition was Clinton's arch political rival, Martin Van Buren. He mustered his *Albany Register* and Tammany Hall political machines to deride "Clinton's Folly" as a chimera that would impoverish the state with higher taxes and labor costs. But for once the "Little Magician," a nickname bestowed on Van Buren for his brilliant political skills, did not prevail. Clinton rallied his own alliance of politicians and investors who would profit from the project. In the end, the state assembly approved the canal.

Work on the Erie Canal began at Rome, New York, on July 4, 1817, and was completed on October 26, 1825, after eight years of hard labor by nine thousand workers. The result was an astonishing engineering feat—the canal ran forty feet wide and four feet deep for 363 miles, with eighty-three locks, eighteen aqueducts, and a more than 675-foot watershed summit along the way. The longest American canal before the Erie was a mere twenty-six miles long.

The Erie Canal epitomized how Hamiltonism could create and distribute wealth and power that never would have existed had the private sector been left to its own motivations. Only a partnership of government and business could have amassed enough money and men to build the canal. The project stimulated the economy even before the first spade full of dirt was turned as the company began hiring workers and buying equipment and rights of way. Hard coin flowed into communities along the route as they provisioned and sheltered the workers. A mere nine years after the Erie Canal was completed, the fees paid off the $7,143,789 construction cost and thereafter generated steady revenues for the state government and private investors. From 1820 to 1850 New York City's population soared from 152,000 to 696,000, Syracuse's from 1,814 to 22,271, Rochester's from 1,502 to 36,403, and Buffalo's from 2,095 to 42,261. The "Empire State" had come of age.[7]

But this economic revolution lay ahead. Madison's Bonus Bill veto heartened the Old Republicans. Having won this struggle, they were dead set to eliminate the entire Hamiltonian program, and the second bank was number one in their crosshairs. Stymied in Congress, they hoped to kill the bank in the courts.

The Supreme Court ended up determining the fate of the bank's latest incarnation. James McCulloch, the Baltimore branch's director, refused to pay a tax demanded by Maryland. The state sued McCulloch for payment. A Maryland court issued the unsurprising verdict that the bank had to pay up. McCulloch appealed to the Supreme Court. The subsequent decision in *McCulloch v. Maryland* in 1819 not only saved the bank but decisively affected America's political and economic development. John Marshall and his four fellow justices unanimously upheld the bank's constitutionality and maintained that states could not tax the federal government or its institutions. Marshall's most memorable line in the decision was "the power to tax is the power to destroy." While this statement illustrates a cherished Jeffersonian and Jacksonian value, the context was thoroughly Hamiltonian as it asserted federal over state power and the Constitutional principle of "all necessary and proper" implied powers over a literal interpretation. In this, Marshall could not have been more clear: "The states have no power, by taxation or otherwise, to retard, impede, burden or in any manner control the operations of the Federal government or its agencies." The chief justice insisted that the national government's sovereignty lay in "we the people," the Constitution's opening words, rather than in the states.[8]

Although the bank survived the constitutional challenge, bad management nearly destroyed it. The first president, Capt. William Jones, had a solid résumé as a former navy secretary and Treasury Department official. Unfortunately, he was utterly corrupt and abused his power to speculate with the bank's funds. He resigned when Congress opened an investigation. The next president, Langdon Cleves, tried to clean up the mess by calling in questionable loans and tightening credit. From 1817 to 1819 he cut the bank's liabilities from $22 million to $10 million and increased its reserves from $2.5 million to $8 million.[9]

Jones's policies fed and Cleves's policies popped a swelling speculative bubble in cotton futures. Cotton prices rose steadily with the industrial revolutions in Britain and New England. As they did, British planters in India expanded their acreage. American cotton planters borrowed heavily against their rising prices. Although the soaring cotton prices eventually proved to be fool's gold, for now this was the only bright spot in an otherwise gloomy farm sector that had never recovered from its wartime heights. The average wholesale commodity price index fell from 182 when the War of 1812 ended in 1814 to 151 in 1817.

When the second bank sharply and suddenly restricted credit, other banks did the same. Anticipating a fall in prices, investors dumped their shares. The subsequent financial meltdown became known as the Panic of 1819. Cotton prices plummeted from a height of 33 cents a pound in October 1818 to 14 cents a year later. The wholesale commodity price fell below 100, with tobacco plummeting from 40 cents to 4 cents a pound, wheat from $2.41 to 88 cents a bushel, and average farm land prices from $2 to $1.25 an acre. Swelling numbers of farms, banks, and other businesses went belly up.[10]

A political crisis followed the economic crisis, with slavery the core issue. The words "slave" and "slavery" were nowhere mentioned in the Constitution hammered out by the framers in Philadelphia over the summer of 1787. Yet slavery was central to their debates over what kind of republic they were trying to construct. The Constitution empowered Congress to end the importation of slaves, but not before 1808; counted slaves as three-fifths of a person in the census; and required states into which slaves escaped to help their masters recapture them. Other than this, the Constitution left slavery largely in the hands of the states.

By 1820 the United States was split equally between slave and free states. The original northern states had either already ended or were in the process of ending slavery. The 1787 Ordinance banned slavery in the Northwest Territory between the Ohio and Mississippi Rivers, Great Lakes, and Pennsylvania; this vast swath of land eventually yielded five states. No restrictions existed on slavery in the original southern states or the new ones. Indeed, the 1790 Southwest Ordinance, which organized the territory south of the Ohio River, explicitly legalized it. Kentucky, Tennessee, Louisiana, Mississippi, and Alabama were admitted in 1792, 1796, 1812, 1817, and 1819, respectively, as slave states with no challenge from within or beyond Congress.[11]

Then, in February 1819, the territory of Missouri, having surpassed the population requirement of sixty thousand, applied to Congress for permission to hold a referendum for statehood. Until then Congress routinely granted such requests, but not this time. Representative James Tallmadge of New York declared that he would be happy to admit Missouri as a state, but only with one crucial stipulation. To the statehood bill, he submitted an amendment requiring Missouri gradually to abolish slavery by forbidding the importation of any new slaves and emancipating all young slaves when they reached age twenty-five. This provoked a firestorm of protests among southerners. Representative Thomas Cobb of Georgia fiercely denounced Tallmadge and his fellow abolitionists, warning that "if you persist, the Union will be dissolved. . . . You have kindled a fire which all the waters of the ocean cannot put out, which seas of blood can only extinguish." Tragically, Cobb's words were prescient. His attempt to bully Tallmadge, however, failed. Tallmadge angrily retorted, "Sir, if a dissolution of the Union must take place, let it be so! If civil war which gentlemen so much threaten must come, I can only say, let it come!"[12]

Thomas Jefferson vividly described his reaction to news of the crisis: "This momentous question, like a fire bell in the night, awakened and filled me with terror."[13] The crisis also deeply disturbed Andrew Jackson, who feared it "will be the entering wedge to separate the union. . . . Even more wicked, it will excite . . . insinuation and massacre." As a westerner, southerner, and slave owner, Jackson saw only one source of this evil: "the Eastern interest . . . who talk about humanity, but whose sole object is self aggrandizement regardless of the happiness of the nation."[14] Abolitionists, of course, wholeheartedly agreed with every word in that sentence except "Eastern," for which they would substitute "slave master."

The bullying by Cobb and other slavocrats did not intimidate Tallmadge and his allies. In fact, they upped the ante by adding a provision to the amendment that banned slavery not just from Missouri but from the entire Louisiana Territory. The measure narrowly passed by 82 to 78 in the House, where representatives from free states held a steadily expanding majority, but died in the Senate. The result was a deadlock that dragged on for a year.

To break it, House Speaker Henry Clay proposed a compromise bill, with slavery forbidden north and permitted south of 36 degrees 30 minutes in the Louisiana Territory, Missouri admitted as a slave state, and Maine as a free state. The bill preserved a tense power balance between senators across that political, ideological, economic, and moral chasm. The Missouri Compromise passed by 134 to 42 in the House and 24 to 20 in the Senate. President Monroe signed it into law on March 6, 1820. A second crisis erupted when Missouri's lawmakers inserted a tenet in their state constitution that forbade free blacks from residing in the state. Northerners condemned this tenet for violating the Constitution's equal protection clause and threatened to overturn the compromise. Clay eventually convinced the Missourians to drop the tenet in return for admission. Missouri officially entered the United States on August 10, 1821.[15]

As the Missouri Compromise's chief architect, Henry Clay achieved acclaim for being among the era's outstanding statesmen. For the next three decades, he would be Jacksonism's most powerful opponent. In many ways, he exemplified the "self-made man," a term that he coined. He was born in Virginia, attended William and Mary, and studied law under George Wythe in Richmond. In 1797 he headed west to Lexington, Kentucky, where he developed a thriving law practice and married into one of the state's most prominent families. He was soon celebrated as Kentucky's greatest trial lawyer; he nearly always won acquittals or reduced sentences for his defendants. His oratory and legislative skills were so renowned that he was elected Speaker of the House the day he entered as a freshman in 1811. He was tall and slender, with an impish face and a smile radiating confidence, energy, and wit. Ladies loved him for his courtly charms; men enjoyed his metamorphosis after hours into a boisterous madcap who gambled, drank, and whored.[16]

Philosophically, Clay began his political career as a devout Jeffersonian. He was appalled by the blatant unconstitutionality of the Adams administration's Alien and Sedition Acts of 1798. A dozen years later, he embodied all of Jacksonism's War Hawk zealotry. But the disastrous results of the 1807 embargo, the bank's destruction in 1811, and the War of 1812 discredited both Jeffersonism and Jacksonism for him. This left only Hamiltonism as a guiding political philosophy. Clay eventually called his version of this philosophy "the American System"; he focused on developing the nation through protective tariffs for infant industries, internal improvements, and the Bank of the United States. In 1816 he explained why he had opposed the first and championed the Second Bank of the United States: "It is I who have changed and not the Constitution. The bank was just as constitutional in 1810 as at the present moment."[17]

Missouri was vital to the union, not just as the source of a crisis over slavery. St. Louis became the gateway to the trans-Mississippi West shortly after the city was founded in 1764. Located on bluffs twenty miles south of where the Missouri River flows into the Mississippi River, St. Louis was the emporium for the upper Mississippi valley and jumping off point for fur-trading expeditions up the Missouri valley. Even before the Lewis and Clark expedition embarked in May 1804, fur traders had journeyed up the Missouri as far as the Mandan and Hidatsa villages near the Canadian border. The return of the Lewis and Clark expedition after a two-and-a-half-year journey that wintered where the Columbia River joins the Pacific Ocean electrified the nation and inspired entrepreneurs and adventurers to reach the Rocky Mountains and reap a fortune in beaver pelts from its streams and ponds.[18]

Manuel Lisa was an experienced businessman and frontiersmen who had traded with the Osage Indians and other tribes in the lower Missouri valley.[19] In 1807 he led forty-two men in the first trapping expedition to reach the Rockies. They built a fort in the Yellowstone River valley and dispersed in small trapping parties. In the spring, they paddled downstream to St. Louis in dugout canoes filled with hundred-pound packs of pelts. For the next five springs, Lisa's Missouri Fur Company launched grueling, months-long expeditions up the Missouri to resupply existing posts or establish new ones to replace those that were abandoned after trapping out the surrounding streams.

John Jacob Astor was an even greater entrepreneur and visionary than Lisa.[20] Unlike Lisa, he never ventured into the wilderness but instead directed his American Fur Company from his New York City headquarters. In 1810 he sent two expeditions of his subsidiary, the Pacific Fur Company, to the mouth of the Columbia River, one by sea and the other by land. Each reached the site in 1811 and, for the next two years, reaped furs from the region. Unfortunately, the timing could not have been worse as War Hawks were driving the nation into the War of 1812. Faced with being captured by a British navy flotilla or selling out to their rival, the British Northwest Company, the Pacific Fur Company's field leaders chose the latter in October 1813.

The fur trade collapsed with the war and remained depressed until 1821. That year several forces combined to revive the industry. Missouri achieved statehood, which brought an influx of new entrepreneurs and adventurers into the region. The national economy revived, after suffering a sharp downturn with Panic of 1819. Finally, Mexico won independence from Spain and its government announced that it would open its previously closed markets to trade.

William Becknell led a dozen men and scores of mules laden with trade goods from Franklin, Missouri, across the plains to Santa Fe, New Mexico, where he made a small fortune. Word of his successful venture inspired others to trod the Santa Fe Trail, with wagonloads of trade goods. Many men, after reaching Santa Fe, headed up into the southern Rockies to trap beaver and trade with the Indians. Meanwhile, the fur trade in the northern Rockies revived as four enterprises—the Missouri, French, Columbia, and Ashley and Henry Fur Companies—set forth up the Missouri River and leapfrogged each other to prime sites for trading posts or beaver-filled streams. [21]

The fur trade was further boosted in 1822, when the Monroe administration succumbed to heavy lobbying led by John Jacob Astor and abolished the nine government trading posts with the Indians known as the Factory System. The system was inaugurated in 1796 for a good reason. Among the many forces that provoked Indians to war against the American frontier was rage at being cheated by whites in trade and debauched with alcohol. The Factory System was designed to remove these causes by banning liquor from Indian country and requiring each factory or post to have fixed prices. Beginning in 1822, without fixed prices, traders reaped a bonanza from the trade, especially when they smuggled alcohol past the frontier army posts.[22]

After the Lewis and Clark expedition, the federal government played a secondary role in opening the Far West. The only significant federal government expedition was that of Maj. Stephen Long, which, in 1819, journeyed west up the Platte Valley to the Rockies, then south to the Arkansas River, and down it to Fort Smith. In the early 1820s the army had only four posts on the fringe of this vast region, Fort Jessup in northwestern Louisiana, Fort Smith on the Arkansas River, Fort Snelling at the forks of the Mississippi and Minnesota Rivers, and Fort Atkinson on the Missouri River. Fort Atkinson was founded in 1819, when Col. Henry Atkinson's Yellowstone expedition ground ashore there because its four steamboats were unable to further ascend the river.

A crisis erupted in 1823 on the middle Missouri River when Arikara Indians attacked a trapping expedition, led by William Ashley, that had stopped at their village to trade on June 1. Although the Arikaras killed a dozen of his men and wounded a dozen more, Ashley was not willing to give up. He holed up with the other survivors on an island downstream and sent an appeal to Col. Henry Leavenworth at Fort

Atkinson for help. The result was America's first Indian war west of the Mississippi River. Leavenworth eventually reached Ashley and his survivors with 230 troops of the Sixth Infantry and First Rifle Regiments. These troops were accompanied by 100 mountain men from the various fur companies and 750 Teton Sioux Indians. On August 9 the expedition neared two Arikara villages, which were surrounded by wooden palisades. The Sioux rode ahead and skirmished with the Arikaras, who withdrew into their villages. The next morning, Leavenworth had his artillerymen bombard the villages with the two cannons while the mountain men and riflemen crept close to pick off Arikaras who exposed themselves. That night the Arikaras slipped out of the villages and disappeared into the plains, leaving fifty dead behind. The Missouri River was once again open for the cutthroat rivalry among the fur companies. Ashley would soon inaugurate a new strategy that revolutionized the fur trade of the West.[23]

5

The Monroe Doctrine

We behold the glorious spectacle of eighteen millions of
people struggling to burst their chains and to be free.

HENRY CLAY

Wherever the standard of freedom and independence has
or shall be unfurled, there will her [American] heart, her benedictions, and her prayers be. But she [the United States]
goes not abroad in search of monsters to destroy.

JOHN QUINCY ADAMS

The American continents . . . are henceforth not to be considered
as subjects for future colonization by any European powers.

THE MONROE DOCTRINE

Somewhat astonishingly, the rage that led Congress to declare war against
Britain in June 1812 quickly dissipated after the Treaty of Ghent was
ratified in February 1815. Both nations, especially Britain, which had
waged nearly nonstop war since 1793, welcomed the peace. Relations
between the United States and Britain would remain largely constructive
if not warm for the next century. Here again the Republicans adopted a

sensible Hamiltonian policy, this one insisting that American interests were better served by negotiating with rather than confronting Britain.[1]

Secretary of State Richard Rush and Charles Bagot, Britain's minister to the United States, signed what became known as the Rush-Bagot Treaty on April 28, 1817. The treaty's intent was to reduce military forces and thus tensions along the American-Canadian border, especially on the Great Lakes. To this end, the United States and Britain pledged to maintain a minimal balance of naval power that consisted of one warship each on Lakes Ontario and Champlain and two warships each for the other four Great Lakes.

This sensible deal soon led to another. On October 20, 1818, they signed the Anglo-American Convention, which addressed three long-standing issues. The treaty more clearly defined the fishing rights of Americans off the coasts of Newfoundland and Labrador. It extended the international boundary westward along the 49th parallel from the Lake of the Woods to the Rocky Mountains. And, finally, it established a ten-year joint occupancy of the Oregon Territory in the Columbia River basin west of the Rocky Mountain divide.

The next issue that arose between Washington and London was their common interest in promoting trade and containing the European continent's great powers. Starting with a revolt in Mexico in 1810, Spain's Latin American colonies declared and fought for independence. Napoleon handicapped Spain's attempts to crush these revolutions. In 1808 he forced Charles IV and his son Ferdinand VII to renounce their rival claims for the throne and had his brother Joseph crowned as Spain's king. This sparked a five-year war for Spain. Although an alliance between British, Spanish, and Portuguese forces led by Gen. Arthur Wellesley, the Duke of Wellington, eventually drove the French from Spain and enthroned Ferdinand, the Spanish could spare few troops to battle the Latin American rebels. With Napoleon's final defeat in 1815, London abandoned its alliance with Spain and instead aided the Latin American struggle with arms and munitions in exchange for opening their markets to British trade.

Most Americans cheered the Latin American rebels on both commercial and ideological grounds. Merchants looked forward to selling in all the markets that the Spanish had kept to themselves for centuries. Liberals lauded the revolutionaries for espousing the same principles that fueled America's revolution and even modeling their constitutions on that of the United States. Henry Clay expressed the excitement that many Americans felt at the time: "We behold the glorious spectacle of eighteen millions of people struggling to burst their chains and be free." He called for Washington to recognize and encourage that struggle to give "hope, and confidence to the friends of liberty throughout the world."[2]

Secretary of State John Quincy Adams was not as sanguine. Although he welcomed the Spanish empire's collapse and opening of markets across the Western Hemisphere, he anticipated the future of these newly independent countries with dark pessimism. The rebels were trying to plant liberal institutions in authoritarian cultural soil. As a result, sooner or later the liberal institutions would wither and die. He accurately predicted that the Latin American states would suffer alternating periods of dictatorships, anarchy, and civil war and permanent corruption, poverty, and despair. To those who called on Washington to aid the rebels, he replied, "Wherever the standard of freedom and independence has or shall be unfurled, there will her [American] heart, her benedictions, and her prayers be. But she [the United States] goes not abroad in search of monsters to destroy."[3]

Adams thwarted efforts by Clay and others to pressure the Monroe administration into recognizing and aiding the rebels. He did so for a good reason. Ferdinand VII refused to ratify the 1819 Adams-Onís Treaty, which transferred Florida to the United States, unless the United States agreed not to do so. Only after Adams held the ratified treaty in his hands was he ready to develop diplomatic and trade relations with Latin America.

This policy was threatened by the chance that Spain, backed by other European powers, might reimpose its rule in the Western Hemisphere. Czar Alexander formed the Holy Alliance of Russia, Austria, and Prussia with a treaty signed in Paris on September 26, 1815, as a pact to crush any future liberal and nationalist revolts in Europe. The alliance's first order of business was deciding whether to help the Spanish scourge that New World plague of liberalism and nationalism before it infected the Old World. The seriousness of this potential threat was underlined when Czar Alexander I issued in 1821 a ukase, or decree, warning foreign vessels not to sail within a hundred miles of Russia's claims in the New

World, which then extended from Alaska down the coast to Fort Ross, just eighty miles north of San Francisco Bay. This claim cut across the joint American and British claim to the Oregon Territory.

Secretary of State Adams reacted to the czar's warning with one of his own. On July 17, 1823, he handed the Russian minister a letter warning the czar against any intrusion into the Oregon Territory. On November 27, 1823, he issued a second warning, this one not to wield the Holy Alliance with Spain against the Latin American rebels.

Meanwhile, on August 20, 1823, British foreign secretary George Canning suggested a joint statement by Britain and America not to tolerate any third power's intervention in the conflict between Spain and its colonies. On receiving this offer, Monroe asked Jefferson and Madison for their advice. Both recommended taking it. Adams, however, was firmly opposed. He explained that this was the time to step from the shadow of the British Empire, even if a joint statement implied equal status. The United States would assert its own sphere of influence over the Western Hemisphere.[4]

The president agreed and issued what became known as the Monroe Doctrine as part of his annual address to Congress on December 2, 1823. In words carefully crafted by Adams, Monroe asserted unequivocally that the Western Hemisphere would "henceforth not be considered as subjects for future colonization by any European power." The United States would view any European imperialism as "dangerous to our peace and safety." In return, the United States promised not to intervene in European affairs. Finally, the United States warned Spain not to transfer any of its New World territory to any other European state.[5]

Canning, meanwhile, received assurances from French ambassador Jules de Polignac that France did not intend to aid Spain's reconquest of its American empire. This prompted Canning to boast in a speech before the House of Commons, "I called the New World into existence to redress the balance of the Old."[6] In reality, the Latin Americans largely won independence on their own.

The Monroe Doctrine was at once a clear statement of American national interests and a bluff. It was certainly in American economic interests to trade with and invest in the dozen or so weak states that emerged from the Spanish Empire's ruins. But it was far beyond America's military power to thwart any attempt by a European state to aid the Spanish reconquest. Indeed, it would be decades before the United States massed the military power to enforce the Monroe Doctrine. Until then, only British naval power was capable of doing so. So, the Monroe Doctrine was actually asserted in the shadow of His Majesty's fleet without giving a hint of credit. The effect was somewhat like the scrawny kid in the playground warning one bully to back off while standing beside a rival bully. This same analogy holds for Adams's direct warnings to Czar Alexander not to intervene in the Oregon Territory or Latin America. Indeed, Russia or any other great power that took note of the Monroe White House's statements dismissed them as so much diplomatic hot air.

So, in an astonishing act of chutzpah, the Monroe administration asserted a sphere of influence over the entire Western Hemisphere and erected a "Keep Out" sign to European imperialism. To President Washington's admonition against entangling alliances, President Monroe added another powerful principle to guide American foreign policy for the indefinite future. What no one then anticipated was what the Monroe Doctrine would become. It was not until the late nineteenth century that Washington had amassed the power to begin acting on that principle, and since then this has dramatically changed relations among America, the Western Hemisphere, and the world beyond.[7]

6

The Corrupt Bargain

I feel much alarmed at the prospect of seeing General Jackson president. He is one of the most unfit men I know of for such a place. He has very little respect for law or constitutions. . . . He is a dangerous man.

THOMAS JEFFERSON

The people have a right to call for any man's services in a republican government, and when they do, it is the duty of the individual to yield his services to that call.

ANDREW JACKSON

The Judas of the West has closed the contract and will receive the thirty pieces of silver—his end will be the same.

ANDREW JACKSON

Andrew Jackson climbed back into the political ring in 1822 as much out of spite as anything else. He hated two leading politicians whose supporters were already mobilizing forces for the 1824 presidential race. Henry Clay and William Crawford had provoked his fury by criticizing his behavior during his second invasion of Spanish Florida. He especially loathed Crawford and often quipped that he would rather "support the Devil" as president.[1] He vowed to do all in his power to bar either man from the White House, and the best way to do that was to snatch the presidency for himself. As for his other likely rivals, Jackson respected both John Quincy Adams and John Calhoun, although these feelings would drastically change during the campaign. He admired Adams's "talents, virtue, and integrity" and thought "him a man of the first rate mind of any in America . . . and . . . never doubted of his attachment to our republican government." He "always believed Mr. Calhoun to be a high minded and honourable man, possessing independence and virtue. . . . The nation will be well governed by Mr. Calhoun or Mr. Adams."[2]

Jackson's political allies openly declared in June 1822 that they would nominate him for president. To this Jackson replied, "I have never been a candidate for office; I never will. The people have a right to call for any man's services in a republican government, and when they do, it is the duty of the individual to yield his services to that call."[3] This statement was as politically correct as it was false. Anyone openly ambitious for public office would automatically disqualify himself in the minds of most voters. Actually, Jackson had run not once but twice to be Tennessee's militia general; he had been appointed the state's representative and senator to Congress.

The "people's call" came on July 20, 1822, when Tennessee's assembly unanimously resolved to nominate Jackson. With the next presidential election more than two years off, this was a political gesture rather than an official nomination. The intent was to dramatically bring Old Hickory back in the national mind. Jackson responded appropriately, with gratitude and coy noncommitment.

The nomination shook everyone who either contemplated running or supported someone else. To avoid making a crowded, overheated race more so, Monroe tried to abort the Jackson run by offering him the post of minister to the newly independent nation of Mexico. Jackson turned it down.[4] Had Jackson taken that bait, his volatility, insensitivity, racism, and aggressiveness might well have provoked a war with Mexico a quarter century before it actually erupted.

The most powerful argument against electing Jackson president was his notion of power. His critics condemned him for being tyrannical by nature, a quality illustrated by his repeated violations of the Constitution and law whenever he held power. To dilute these charges, Jackson and his supporters marketed him as a virtuous and courageous defender of republican government against those who would usurp it. And the best way to prove this was to get him into a prominent public office. In August 1822 three of his of his political coterie, John Eaton, William Lewis, and Sam Houston, arranged for Tennessee's assembly to elect Jackson to the U.S. Senate. Old Hickory accepted the call.

Jackson and his entourage reached Washington on December 3, 1823, just before Congress reconvened. Two days later "the Hero of New Orleans" entered the Senate and took his seat amid the thunderous applause of his friends and even many of his foes. The changes in Jackson since his first brief appearance in this body more than a quarter century earlier were mostly physical. His leonine swept-back dark red hair had turned steel grey, deep wrinkles etched his gaunt face, his once lean muscular body was emaciated, and his former long-legged stride was now a deliberate stroll, aided by a cane. His character and convictions, however, differed little from those of his young manhood. If anything, they had hardened from a half-dozen years in the field commanding troops and warring against an array of enemies. He hated as fiercely as ever any men with ideas or interests that challenged his own. He warred politically as he did militarily—his enemies faced either complete annihilation or capitulation. Compromise was a reviled business that he would consider only as an inescapable last resort. Jackson's most notable change was that he was much more courtly and much less brusque than he had been during his younger Senate stint.

Andrew Jackson was not temperamentally suited to be a legislator. It was one thing to declare and defend his positions but quite another to roll up his sleeves with his fellow senators and engage in the time-devouring, painstaking political and legal work of lawmaking. He hated the latter and admitted as much: "Day after day talking and arguing about things that might be decided in a few hours requires a Job-like patience to bear; it does not suit me."[5] In all, he devoted little time to committee work or debate and none to compromise. He did most of his politicking after hours over meals, cigars, and whiskey, and this was mostly to line up potential supporters for his presidential ambitions rather than to assert any particular stand on an issue.

As irony would have it, his seat in the Senate was right beside some-

one with whom he had fought a vicious street brawl. Thomas Hart
Benton and his brother, Jesse, had squared off with Jackson and his
protégé, William Carroll, in September 1813. The exchange of gunshots and knife thrusts before bystanders pulled the belligerents apart
left Jackson near death. Shortly after the incident, the Benton brothers hightailed it from Tennessee to seek fortune and fame farther west.
Thomas Hart Benton was now Missouri's senior senator. Those who
looked forward to a renewal of hostilities were disappointed. Jackson
and Benton embraced affectionately on the new senator's first day in
office, and thereafter, Benton was a fervent Jackson supporter.

Henry Clay was among the Washington stars that Jackson and his
advisers hoped to pull into their constellation. Clay had earned Jackson's enmity for condemning his invasion of Florida and execution of
the British agents. As Jackson had with Benton, he was willing to let
bygones be bygones with Clay, if the latter made some sign of obei-
sance. Unfortunately, an arranged dinner between the two and their
respective coteries did not go well. Clay soon launched his own run
for the presidency.

Then there was John Quincy Adams. Of Monroe's cabinet, only he
had praised rather than condemned Jackson's takeover of Florida. To
show his continued esteem, he threw a dinner party for Jackson, Rachel,
and a host of other political luminaries to celebrate the anniversary of
the Battle of New Orleans. This potential alliance died with each man's
presidential ambitions. Adams tried to entice Jackson to become his
running mate. They would sweep the election, he argued, as they represented New England and the West. Jackson agreed but wanted to
reverse the front-runner order.

At this point, the most formidable potential rival for the White
House appeared to be William Crawford. Although Crawford is little
known today, he was highly regarded in the early nineteenth century.
Born in Virginia, he rose to political prominence in Georgia. Like Jackson and countless other politicians, he entered the elite by way of law.
He proved his mettle first as a lawyer and then as a lawmaker. Perhaps
his finest public service was to revise Georgia's law code. After several
stints in the state legislature, Georgia voters elected him to the Senate
in 1807. There he became a vehement War Hawk who helped push the
United States into the War of 1812. President Madison tapped Crawford

to be the treasury secretary in 1816, and he served in the post for the next eight years. He was renowned as much for his appearance as for his mind. He was a naturally huge, corpulent man who became more so with prodigious eating and drinking. This seems to have been his undoing. He was only fifty-one years old in the summer of 1823 when he suffered a stroke that briefly left him paralyzed, blind, and speechless. Although he recovered, his mental abilities were a shadow of what they had been before his stroke. Yet his followers so esteemed him that they hid his maladies and promoted him for the presidency.

The Republican Party was a coalition of coalitions. Factions formed around powerful figures rather than issues and ideas, and for presidential elections, they competed to call caucuses that backed their candidate. Although the "straw polls" were not binding, they helped forge a broader support for their man. Crawford's faction called a caucus among interested congressional representatives for February 14, 1824. It was hardly representative. Of the sixty-eight members who appeared, forty-eight were from only four states—New York, Virginia, North Carolina, and Georgia. Not surprisingly, Crawford received sixty-four votes compared to two for Adams and one each for Clay and Jackson. Crawford's backers then trumpeted the results through allied newspapers of which the most powerful was the *Richmond Enquirer*, edited by Thomas Ritchie. Crawford's most distinguished supporters were Thomas Jefferson and James Madison, who believed that he was the best candidate to advance the Jeffersonian agenda. With all this political firepower behind him, Crawford definitely appeared to be the man to beat.

Andrew Jackson relished the challenge. To win the White House, he had to weld northeastern support to his western base. To this end, he espoused vague centrist views that had the widest appeal and offended the fewest people. For instance, he and his staff contrived a stand on the tariff that appeared principled yet gave him plenty of political wiggle room: "I look at the tariff with an eye to the proper distribution of labor and revenue, and with a few to the discharge of the national debt."[6] Nor could voters find fault with this Jackson declaration: "I am Governed by Principle along—the articles of National Defense & National Independence. I will . . . foster & protect, without counting on dollars & cents, so that our own Manufactures will stand on a footing of fair competition with the laborers of Europe—in doing this, the articles all being of . . . our own country, tends to promote the agriculturalists, whilst it gives security to our nation & promotes domestic Labour."[7]

Jackson and his men realized that simply taking mainstream positions on the issues was not enough to win. Capturing hearts was far more important than capturing minds. For this, they ran a grassroots populist campaign that celebrated Old Hickory as an all-American hero. John Eaton wrote and mass-published an adulatory biography of Jackson. Under the pen name Wyoming, he also wrote eleven essays that expressed Jackson's political philosophy and idolized American union, liberty, and the common man.[8] Of all the groups a citizen could potentially join, none was more ubiquitous than the militia. Although peace and the receding frontier rendered that institution increasingly irrelevant as a military force, hundreds of thousands of American men were still nominal members. The Jackson campaign sought to bring out the militia vote by celebrating Jackson's military glories. The next president would take the oath of office nearly fifty years to the day after the Revolutionary War erupted at Lexington and Concord. As a young teenager, Jackson had fought in this war, a feat his campaign celebrated. His handlers arranged a meeting between Jackson and Gilbert du Motier, Marquis de Lafayette, who was in the middle of a nearly yearlong journey through the United States.

In the face of this swelling populist assault, Jackson's foes sharply questioned his fitness for the presidency. They reminded voters of his invasions of Florida, execution of the British agents, and other violations of the Constitution, laws, and commonly accepted morality. They worried that if he captured the White House, he might become a despot.

Ultimately, Andrew Jackson won 152,901 votes or a solid plurality compared to 114,023 for Adams, 47,217 for Clay, and 46,979 for Crawford. The trouble, of course, was that the American people do not elect the president, an electoral college does. When the electoral votes were tallied, Jackson still led with 99 to Adams's 84, Crawford's 41, and Clay's 37, but he was shy of the 131 needed to win. This threw the vote to the House of Representatives; each state delegation was allowed one vote.[9]

In the House vote, Jackson had a distinct disadvantage. He had spent only three months as Tennessee's first representative way back in 1796, and he had hated nearly every minute of the experience. In contrast,

Clay had served since 1811, understood every institutional and personal quirk, and thus knew where to horse-trade or arm-twist.

In the end, Clay and Adams struck a classic political deal. During a meeting on January 9, 1825, Clay yielded to Adams's political edge in return for being his secretary of state. On January 24 Kentucky's delegation announced that it support Adams, even though not a single Kentuckian had cast a vote for the candidate.

The House election took place on February 9. On the first ballot, Adams was elected with thirteen states, followed by Jackson with seven and Crawford with four. Although Jackson congratulated Adams, he later complained bitterly that the states did not follow their respective popular votes. He had won a plurality of popular votes in eleven states.

Jackson's bitterness turned to rage when he learned of the "corrupt bargain," as he and his cohorts dubbed it, between Adams and Clay. Of the two, he was less venomous against Adams, who had supported his behavior in Florida. Of Clay, he wrote, "The Judas of the West has closed the contract and will receive the thirty pieces of silver—his end will be the same. Was there ever witnessed such a bare faced corruption in any country before."[10] Jackson's comparison of Clay with Judas was outrageous enough; equating himself with Jesus was even more revealing of his egomania and megalomania. However, his other riposte was tougher to counter: "Mr. Clay never yet has risked himself for his country, sacrificed his repose, or made an effort to repel an invading foe."[11] Clay, like his fellow congressional War Hawks who stampeded the nation into the disastrous War of 1812, never resigned his seat to accept a field command.

In his rage, Jackson may have mulled provoking and leading a mass uprising like Coriolanus. Instead, he issued a vague appeal to "the people" to right the gross violation of their democratic rights: "The people are the safeguards of their own liberties, and I rely wholly on them to guard themselves. They will correct any outrage upon political purity by Congress; and if they do not, now and ever, then they will become the slaves of Congress and its political corruption."[12] However enraged many of his more zealous supporters were, there were no mass protests, let alone revolt against Congress and the Constitutional procedure it followed.

John Quincy Adams was anything but charismatic in personality or appearance. He was short, rotund, and balding, plagued by bouts of depression, and often irritable, impatient, and condescending. He tried to compensate for these flaws by being a model of stern probity, hard work, and piety. His finest attribute was his first-rate mind. He had not only absorbed the lessons of history but also played a role in shaping it in various European capitals and in Washington. Few Americans have served in a greater array of vital government positions. The presidency capped an astonishing résumé that included the posts of representative and then senator from Massachusetts to Congress; American minister to the Netherlands, Portugal, Prussia, Britain, and Russia; and finally secretary of state.[13]

The rancor of Jackson and his cohorts over the "corrupt bargain" failed to stymie the Senate's confirmation of the president's cabinet picks, including Richard Rush as treasury secretary, James Barbour as war secretary, William Wirt as attorney general, Samuel Southard as navy secretary, and Henry Clay, who received twenty-seven votes for, fourteen against, and seven abstentions, as secretary of state. The election for vice president was as one-sided as that for president was disputed. With 182 electoral votes, John Calhoun won an overwhelming victory over a half-dozen rivals.

Adams expressed his vision for America in his first message to Congress. One line epitomized the philosophy behind his agenda: "The great object of the institution of civil government is the improvement of the condition of those who are parties to the social compact." To this end, he proposed creating a national university, a naval academy, and an astronomical observatory; promoting innovation, manufacturing, and trade; linking the nation with a network of national canals and roads; and exploring the West. His call for government to guide the development of American wealth and power echoed Alexander Hamilton's vision more than three decades earlier. And for this the Jacksonians and Jeffersonians mercilessly pilloried Adams and fought him to a standstill on nearly every one of these issues.[14]

Among the president's goals was to better relations with other countries in the Western Hemisphere. Adams, after all, had authored the 1823 Monroe Doctrine, which asserted America's interest in preventing the Old World's great powers from recolonizing the recently independent New World countries. The best reason to do so was not to celebrate the liberal ideals the Latin Americans had used to justify their rebellions. America's Declaration of Independence and Constitution had inspired all these revolutionary movements to assert their own versions of republican government, but tragically, each nascent democracy was soon transformed into a dictatorship. The reason was simple: democratic institutions wither if planted in authoritarian cultures. America's liberal revolution succeeded because its democratic culture and institutions, along with a national identity, had developed slowly and steadily in the century and a half before independence. The Latin American rebellions were wars of national liberation innocent of genuine mass liberal values or institutions. Thus, the Latin American countries were valuable not for the ideals they espoused but for their markets, in which American merchants could peddle their products and bring profits back to the United States. This was common sense to any Hamiltonian.

This clear-cut American national interest was lost on Jeffersonians and Jacksonians alike. Jeffersonians were bent on minimizing foreign trade and promoting economic self-sufficiency. For Jacksonians, racism was a far more vital reason to keep the people of Latin America at arm's length. Sovereign states were equal in the eyes of international law, but Jacksonians could not condone establishing relationships with governments composed of mixed races or, in the case of Haiti, blacks. The latter possibility was especially troubling. The last thing slave owners wanted was for their chattel to learn that the United States had diplomatic and commercial relations with a country of former slaves who had achieved independence after a blood-soaked rebellion in which they slaughtered their masters. Not just Haiti but Mexico, Colombia, Argentina, Peru, and Chile had abolished slavery.

These fervently held Jeffersonian and Jacksonian dogmas explain the uproar when, on December 26, 1825, Adams announced his intention to send a delegation to a conference of Western Hemisphere states to be held in Panama City in the summer of 1826. The purpose of the meeting was to engage in friendly talks with America's neighbors about better ways to promote trade and other common interests.

But if this were the sole intent, those who were opposed to any meeting on ideological grounds would have had trouble justifying their opposition. So, the Jacksonians and Jeffersonians contrived and then vanquished a chimera: Adams intended to destroy American sovereignty and the Constitution. As Jackson put it, "To be represented at a congress of Independent confederated nations, is an event, which . . . the framers of our constitution never thought of, whilst deliberating upon those enumerated powers, which they conceived necessary & proper to be given to our confederated government." The conference in turn would lead to an alliance, and the "moment we engage in confederations or alliance with any nation we may from that time date the down fall of our republic."[15]

The battle over the Panama conference was long and hard fought. Senate opponents tried to filibuster the proposal to death. Proponents eventually mustered enough votes to cut off debate and approve sending two envoys. The final tally was 27 to 17 in the Senate and 134 to 60 in the House. But this victory proved to be hollow. One envoy died en route, and the other arrived after the conference had adjourned. Thus was an opportunity lost for the United States to promote its economic, political, and strategic interests in the Western Hemisphere.

Adams was able to push an internal improvement policy through the political backdoor. In 1823 his administration quietly put out word that federal lands would be given to the states if they used the sales to finance the building of infrastructure. From then through 1866, the United States granted 4.5 million acres to the states for canals, 3.5 million for roads, and 1.7 million for river navigation.[16]

Adams's most controversial act was to sign the 1828 Tariff Bill, which raised rates from 30 to 50 percent to protect mostly northeastern industries. Jeffersonians and Jacksonians condemned this bill as "the tariff of abominations." Vice President Calhoun attacked the bill on both constitutional and practical grounds. He argued that tariffs are forbidden because the Constitution does not explicitly allow them. He then pointed out that "the object in the tariff is to keep down foreign competition in order to obtain a monopoly of the domestic market. The effect on us is to compel us to purchase at a higher price, both what we purchase from them and from others, without receiving a correspondent increase of price for what we sell."[17] Yet the tariff passed with solid majorities in the House, by 105 to 94, and the Senate, by 26 to 21, on May 19.

In one of history's most astonishing coincidences, Thomas Jefferson and John Adams both breathed their last on July 4, 1826, fifty years after each signed the Declaration of Independence. This symbolic passing of two great revolutionary leaders reminded Americans how far their country had come in the half century since. The nation was in the midst of the revolution's second stage as one state after another abolished voting restrictions on adult white males and the northeastern states abolished slavery.

Yet Americans had not nor could they ever overcome the political malady of "factions" so dreaded by the Founders. Although superficially the United States was a one-party state as the Federalist Party faded into oblivion, the Republican Party had split between the "Democratic" wing led by Andrew Jackson and the "National" wing led by John Adams. As for political philosophies, Jacksonism, Jeffersonism, and Hamiltonism competed for hearts, minds, and power.[18]

Jackson had no sooner lost the 1824 election than he and his coterie began mustering forces for the 1828 election. His inner circle included such Tennessee cronies as John Overton, John Eaton, William Lewis, and Hugh White, with Felix Grundy and Sam Houston playing secondary roles. The Nashville Committee orchestrated one of American history's most populist election campaigns by mushrooming across the country Old Hickory clubs, parades, rallies, barbeques, dinners, balls, concerts, campaign slogans, songs, poems, cartoons, and even ceremonial plantings of hickory trees. Jackson's unofficial campaign song became the "Hunters of Kentucky" with its stirring tale of the Battle of New Orleans.

Faced with this political juggernaut, once-fierce rivals clambered aboard. Accepting the inevitable, John Calhoun and William Crawford prudently endorsed Jackson and urged their supporters to do the same. Jackson eventually agreed to accept Calhoun as his running mate, although he preferred DeWitt Clinton, New York's long-standing governor. Nonetheless, the Jackson-Calhoun alliance essentially sewed up the western and southern states. What Jackson needed was someone who could rally enough northeastern states to put him in the White House.

For this, his most important convert was Senator Martin Van Buren of New York, the Little Magician. He was short and plump, with a cherubic face and receding orange hairline. Sparkling eyes, a disarming smile, a soothing voice, refined manners, and natty attire alleviated his otherwise unprepossessing appearance. He first revealed his brilliance on the national stage by managing Crawford's 1824 campaign. Although

Crawford lost, he garnered respectable numbers of popular and electoral votes despite suffering a debilitating stroke.

Van Buren devoted his vast talents to helping carry Andrew Jackson to the White House in the 1828 election. He enlisted a network of newspaper editors for the campaign. The most powerful of these were Thomas Ritchie of the *Richmond Enquirer*, Dabney Carr of the *Baltimore Republican*, Edwin Crosswell of the *Albany Argus*, Gordon Bennett of the *New York Enquirer*, Nathaniel Greene of the *Boston Statesman*, Isaac Hill of the *New Hampshire Patriot*, and Mordechai Noah of the *National Advocate*. Two Washington newspapers served successively as Jackson mouthpieces during his presidency: first, Duff Green's *United States Telegraph* and then Francis Blair's *Globe*. Other newspaper editors sympathetic to Jackson carefully read and emulated the editorials of these newspapers.

Jackson's strategy was to avoid taking a clear stand on any controversial issue while running as a man and hero of "the people." His platform was carefully designed to bridge the chasm between Jeffersonians and Hamiltonians. He promised to "pay the national debt . . . & defense—then apportion the surplus revenue amongst the several states."[19]

The mudslinging in the 1828 campaign was among the most vicious in American history. Each side's supporters assailed the other side's candidates through speeches, newspapers, and pamphlets. Jackson contrasted his populism with Adams's gentility: "The present is a contest between the virtue of the people, and the influence of patronage." He charged Adams, an elitist who hobnobbed with the rich and disdained ordinary folks, with dispensing government patronage that corrupted "everything that comes within its influence and was capable of being corrupted."[20]

Although Adams refrained from sharply criticizing Jackson, his campaign leaders and editors were not so restrained. They described Jackson as a would-be tyrant who would destroy the Constitution. To back those claims, they cited Jackson's behavior during his military campaigns in Florida and New Orleans. Sadly, the critics did not confine their criticism to Jackson's public record. They brought up the old accusations that he had seduced and run off with another man's wife and committed bigamy by marrying Rachel before her divorce was finalized. Rachel was described as having been a woman of easy virtue before she eloped with Jackson.

Rachel innocently picked up a campaign pamphlet in a store and was mortified by these calumnies. She became terrified that should her husband win, she would suffer a hellish existence as the First Lady amid the mean people in Washington City. As if the vicious attacks on Rachel were not painful enough, the Jacksons suffered a terrible blow when their beloved adopted child Lyncoya died at age sixteen on June 1, 1828.

The real Rachel was an adoring wife and unassuming hostess. One guest recalled her as "stern—but always courteous and affable. . . . Side by side with [Jackson] stands a coarse-looking, stout, little old woman, whom you might mistake his washerwoman were it not for the marked attention he pays her, and the love and admiration she manifests for him. . . . Mrs. Jackson, as was her favorite custom, lighted her pipe, and having taken a whiff or two, handed it to my father, saying: 'Honey, won't you take a smoke?'"[21]

The 1828 presidential election was far more democratic than previous elections. The recorded votes tallied 1,155,340, three times more than the number cast in the 1824 election, and voter turnout was also higher, at 57.5 percent. Over the previous four years, New York, Vermont, Georgia, and Louisiana had changed their systems to allow citizens to vote for the state's delegates to the Electoral College. As important as these institutional changes in bringing more people to the polls was Andrew Jackson, who inspired his supporters and enemies alike to turn out.

When the votes were counted, Jackson won an overwhelming majority of the popular vote, with 647,276, or 56 percent, to 508,064 for Adams, and an even more overwhelming number of electoral votes, 178, or 68 percent, to 83, or 32 percent. Yet the race was closer than the numbers indicated. Had a mere nine thousand voters in New York, Ohio, and Kentucky supported Adams instead of Jackson, the electoral vote then would have been 149 for Adams and 111 for Jackson. One can only imagine the uproar had Jackson been defeated by that quirk.[22]

Tragedy overshadowed Jackson's victory. Rachel died of an apparent heart attack on December 22, 1828. They had spent thirty-eight mostly happy years together, and now she was gone forever from his life. Her loss devastated him. "My heart is nearly broke," he wrote.[23] He blamed his political foes for her untimely death. Andrew Jackson would come to Washington City ready to avenge himself on his enemies.

2

The Presidency, 1829–1837

7

The Scandals

I did not come here to make a cabinet for the
ladies of this place, but for the nation.

ANDREW JACKSON

By the eternal! I'll smash them!

ANDREW JACKSON

Andrew Jackson took his first oath as president of the United States
on March 4, 1829. His inaugural speech was short and gave few details
of what he intended to do with his power. His calls to stamp out corruption, pay off the national debt, and enact a just tariff were crowd-
pleasing clichés rather than plans. He certainly gave no hint of the
political convulsions he would provoke over issues such as the Bank of
the United States or Indian removal. But these omissions came more
from uncertainty than from guile. At this point, he and his advisers had
only the haziest notion of how to translate election campaign platitudes
into public policies and laws.

If Jackson's inaugural address was noteworthy because he said nothing
of note, the inaugural "party" that followed became the most notorious
in presidential history. A boisterous mob of "the people" descended on

the White House and barged through the doors or climbed through the windows. The revelers stuffed into their gullets as many glasses of liquor and fistfuls of food as they could snatch from the long tables. Thousands of dollars' worth of crystal, china, furniture, and windows were smashed; shrubbery was trampled; curtains were ripped; and silverware and heirlooms were pocketed. Jackson's critics later pointed to this orgy as a harbinger of how his political and business cronies would trash and loot the country.

Meanwhile, the People's Hero mounted a white stallion outside the Capitol and slowly walked it down Pennsylvania Avenue; he was surrounded each step of the way by a huge adoring crowd. At his new home, he dismounted and tried to push his way through the throng, but it was too thick and excited to give way. He remounted and rode to Gadsby's Boarding House, where he had stayed in the days leading to the inauguration.

Jackson chose nearly all his cabinet secretaries for their political worth rather than any personal ties. Winning the Senate's swift confirmation were John Branch, a former governor and current North Carolina senator, as navy secretary; John Berrien, a prominent Georgian politician, as the attorney general; and William Barry, who was defeated in his run for Kentucky's governorship, as the postmaster general. The Senate thwarted Isaac Hill, Jackson's initial choice for treasury secretary, for two reasons. As an abrasive senator, Hill had alienated many of his colleagues who now retaliated. Plus, the more financially sophisticated senators deemed Hill too openly critical of the Second Bank of the United States to provide unbiased oversight of it. For treasury secretary, the Senate did approve with little debate Samuel Ingham, a Pennsylvania politician with solid ties to the financial world.

Of Jackson's political picks, the most prominent was Martin Van Buren, who had just realized a long-standing ambition by being elected New York's governor. Yet when Jackson offered him the senior cabinet post of secretary of state, he eagerly accepted. So far the post had been the stepping stone for four presidents. Van Buren hoped to be the fifth. But he could not just abruptly pack up and hurry down to Washington to assume his duties. It would take several months for him to settle his public and private affairs and for a new governor to be named.

Meanwhile, James Hamilton covered the position. Hamilton was a prominent New York lawyer who became a trusted Jackson adviser. What made this relationship extraordinary was that he was Alexander Hamilton's son and had broken decisively with his father's political philosophy to adopt Jacksonism.

The exception to these politically expedient choices was Jackson's selection of his protégé and friend John Eaton as secretary of war. He wanted to have one person in the cabinet that he trusted completely. He described Eaton as "more like a son to me than anything else; I shall as long as I live estimate his worth and friendship with a grateful heart."[1] This bond soon came under an enormous strain and nearly derailed Jackson's presidency.

Aside from running mate John Calhoun and Secretary of State Van Buren, Jackson packed his cabinet with either sycophants or mediocrities. He did so deliberately, to control them all the easier. He held weekly cabinet meetings on Tuesday and Saturday to discuss issues. During the meetings, he asked the secretaries' advice not for what to do—on virtually all issues his mind was already firmly set—but for how best to get it done. Once this was decided, he expected them promptly and unquestionably to fulfill their duties. When they failed to do so, he did not hesitate to replace them. During his eight years in office, Jackson had five treasury secretaries, four secretaries of state, three attorney generals, three navy secretaries, two war secretaries, and two postmaster generals.

Cabinet secretaries were the Jackson administration's front men who implemented policies through their respective bureaucratic and legal channels. Unfortunately, politics often clogged those channels. To avert the clogs, the president relied on a coterie of skilled and devoted political operatives. Pundits eventually distinguished his "Kitchen Cabinet," the group that debated issues and decided policies, from his "Parlor Cabinet," which generally rubber-stamped and implemented decisions.[2] Three of these pundits were confidants from Tennessee. John Eaton served in the Kitchen and Parlor Cabinets. William Lewis was Jackson's unofficial chief of staff. Andrew Donelson acted as his personal secretary. Of the members of the Kitchen Cabinet, Eaton already had a day job. Jackson put the others on the government payroll with minor posts at various departments, but they spent little time at their desks. The president revealed how media savvy he was by rounding out his inner circle with five allied newspaper editors—Amos Kendall of Kentucky's *Argus of Western America*, Duff Green of Washington's *United States Telegraph*, Isaac Hill of the *New Hampshire Patriot*, Thomas Ritchie of the *Richmond Enquirer*, and Francis Blair of the *Washington Globe*; their loyalty was rewarded with lucrative government printing contracts.

An administration is more than a policymaking team. Among a president's many duties is to be the "entertainer in chief." With Rachel dead, Jackson needed a White House hostess. Andrew Donelson's wife, Emily, admirably performed that role. Like any president, Jackson was concerned with spinning his administration's history in the most favorable light. His nationwide network of editors and newspapers churned out fawning articles, pamphlets, and books, but these, he decided, were inadequate. He invited the painter Ralph Earl to reside in the White House and record the likenesses of himself and his entourage for posterity.

Although Jackson did not invent the spoils system, no president before him and few since have exploited the opportunity to reward their followers as systematically and shamelessly. His first important presidential decision was to issue orders to purge all federal officeholders beholden to other administrations and political factions. When required to confess their political loyalty, many made a quick conversion and claimed to be enthusiastic Jackson supporters. Those who were honest tended to suffer the consequences. During the first eighteen months of the Jackson administration, 919 of 10,093 federal employees lost their jobs. Over the next six and a half years, thousands more followed. Their places were filled with Jackson loyalists, regardless of merit or experience. John Quincy Adams observed that "the persons appointed are . . . some good, the greater part very indifferent, some notoriously bad—on the average much less respectable than those dismissed."[3]

To his credit, Jackson insisted that bookkeepers carefully go over the accounts of each federal bureaucracy. He had the attorney general investigate and, if need be, prosecute any evidence of wrongdoing. What was exposed was shocking. Embezzlement and inside deals were widespread; millions of dollars were squandered or outright stolen annually. While Jackson's purge did briefly cleanse the government's Augean stables of much corruption, his own team soon surpassed their predecessors in the scale and venality of their plunder. When his critics pointed this out, Jackson angrily denied it and refused to open an investigation.

The exposure of the Jackson administration's financial corruption lay in the future. Jackson no sooner settled into the White House than his administration became entangled in a much more prosaic scandal that dismayed his allies, delighted his enemies, and stalled action on an array of pressing issues for months. The scandal revealed a hitherto unrealized and surprising source of national power—Washington's political wives. This world had its own political culture, pecking order, and conflicts, but after the inauguration, it united around one issue—the wife of Secretary of War John Eaton.[4]

Margaret "Peggy" Eaton née O'Neil was the ultimate nightmare for any wife with a virile and frisky husband. Peggy was renowned for her beauty, vivacity, and sensuality. Her father owned a boarding house that many out-of-town members of Washington's elite called their home away from home. She was an enthusiastic hostess, beguiling many a lonesome congressman, senator, and military officer with her natural coquetry. She had hoped to snare a rich, powerful, famous, and handsome husband, and she found one in John Eaton, who fell head over heels in love with her. Having married on New Year's Day 1829, they were newlyweds when Jackson was inaugurated.

There were two catches to their living happily ever after. Both were recent widowers, and Peggy's spouse had died tragically. Lt. John Timberlake was smitten, talked her into marrying him, and then was forced to leave his bride for an extended naval voyage. The separation was pure torture for Timberlake, who not only terribly missed Peggy but imagined her in the arms of one or more of her many suitors. The agony finally overwhelmed him, and he killed himself. Eaton's wife, in contrast, died of disease rather than a broken heart. The deaths freed Eaton and Peggy to legalize a long-standing passion between them. Throwing decorum to the winds, they married within the one-year period of mourning for a departed spouse.

Washington's political wives used the hasty marriage as an excuse to vent their scorn for a woman whose beauty and behavior they secretly envied. Led by Vice President Calhoun's wife, Floride, they snubbed the Eatons at weekly formal dinners for leading politicians, diplomats, and other luminaries at the White House and left the couple off the guests lists for their own parties.

Jackson exploded in wrath when he learned of the mean-spirited united front of disrespect. He too was enchanted by Peggy and, probably with manly enthusiasm, had encouraged his protégé to marry her when Eaton asked his advice. The scandal reminded him of all the vicious slander that his enemies had heaped upon his beloved Rachel during the presidential campaign. In Peggy's defense, he argued that she was "as chaste as those who slander her," bitterly dismissed the wives as a "group of gossips," and asserted that "I did not come here to make a cabinet for the ladies of this place, but for the nation."[5]

The Eaton affair was not the only sex scandal that engulfed someone close to Jackson. Sam Houston had first stirred Jackson's deepest respect for his unsurpassed bravery at the battle of Horseshoe Bend. Thereafter, Jackson did what he could to assist Houston's rise, first in the army and then in Tennessee politics.

As he had with Eaton, Jackson played cupid with Houston. This protégé was a lady's man still blissfully unmarried at age thirty-five. Jackson explained to Houston that his lack of nuptials disadvantaged him politically. He then introduced Houston to what he thought was an appropriate potential bride. Eliza Allen was from a wealthy family of Jackson supporters in central Tennessee. Houston fell in love. Eliza succumbed to her parent's ambition that she hitch her life to a rising political star. The wedding was that year's social event in Tennessee and the perfect accompaniment to Houston's inauguration as governor.

Alas, their marriage suffered its first devastating blow on the wedding night. Houston discovered that his wife was no virgin. Eliza knew that her husband was a heavy drinker, but she was likely also repelled by his body's gruesome battle scars, some of which still seeped with infection. She fled to her parent's home a few weeks later. The rumor mill went into overdrive as Houston's enemies attributed the breakup to the vilest array of accusations about his sexual tastes and diseases.

Houston resigned the governorship on April 16, 1829, and fled to his old friends the Cherokees. This time his sobriquet was not the Raven but Big Drunk, as Houston drowned his sorrow. In a poem to Jackson, he described his life, not inaccurately, as Byronic: "What am I! An exile from my home and my country, a houseless, unsheltered wanderer among the Indians. . . . I am myself . . . a proud and honest man! You, General, will ever possess my warmest love and most profound veneration."[6] Jackson would continue to reciprocate his prodigal surrogate son's love and veneration. However, his first reaction to news of the scandal and resignation was, "My God, is he mad?"[7] The exile eventually roosted in Texas, where he helped lead the war of independence from Mexico and govern the new republic. And in doing so, Houston became the second greatest Jacksonian of all that man's many emulators.

The "petticoat war" dragged on for more than two years, and Jackson became increasingly exasperated. He finally resolved the conundrum much as Alexander the Great had when confronted with the Gordian knot. He simply cut it to pieces. He asked for his entire cabinet to resign in April 1831. The first to go were John Eaton and Martin Van Buren; they were followed by Samuel Ingham and John Berrien.

Having cleaned house, Jackson then reinhabited it. Lewis Cass of Michigan, the secretary of war, and Roger Taney of Maryland, the attorney general, were Jacksonian zealots. Louis McLane, the treasury secretary, and Edward Livingston, the secretary of state, were moderates. Jackson compensated Eaton by naming him governor of the Florida Territory and later minister to Spain. After the mass resignation, Jackson eliminated regular cabinet meetings and relied solely on his Kitchen Cabinet for critical decisions.

The petticoat war represented another challenge to Jackson's conception of honor, and he soon targeted a key villain for retaliation: his vice president, whose wife had led the parade of smears and snubs against Peggy. Jackson was stuck with John Calhoun until the 1832 election, but in the meantime, he would try to politically emasculate him. The question was how? Jackson eventually found a potentially powerful weapon in a letter from William Crawford to John Calhoun. In the correspondence, Crawford had referenced a letter in which Calhoun had excoriated Jackson for his Florida campaign.

Jackson demanded that Calhoun explain and defend his criticism. Calhoun did so in a fifty-two-page reply that he submitted to the president on May 25, 1830. His opening line was a red flag to Jackson: "I cannot recognize the right on your part to call in question my conduct."[8] Jackson refuted each of Calhoun's points in a much briefer reply.[9] Knowing his letter would likely be made public, he held his rage in check, while unleashing his attack dogs against Calhoun. On February 21, 1830, the *Globe* condemned Calhoun's pamphlet as "a firebrand wantonly thrown into the [Democratic] party. Mr. Calhoun will be held responsible for the mischief which may follow." Variations on that attack were echoed by the chorus of pro-Jackson newspapers across the country.[10] However, one hitherto allied newspaper defected. Duff Green, the editor of the *United States Telegraph*, had been a Calhoun man before he threw his support to Jackson. Now he reverted to Calhoun. This provoked Jackson's newspaper chorus to attack Green as viciously as it did Calhoun.

The imbroglios steadily ate away at Calhoun's once seemingly inevitable future as Jackson's heir in the White House. Almost like a seesaw, John Calhoun's political fall permitted Martin Van Buren's rise. The Little Magician had the perfect credentials. He was a brilliant politician from a powerful state and was devoted to Jackson.

Calhoun unwittingly granted his rival a huge political boost. Jackson nominated Van Buren to be minister to Britain in January 1832. The Senate split evenly at 23 votes for and against the nomination. The vice president's vote breaks all ties. The best choice for both the nation and Calhoun was to send his rival to the court of St. James. But vindictiveness trumped pragmatism in Calhoun's mind. He voted against the nomination. This at once kept his rival in Washington and sharply raised the temperature of Jackson's hatred for Calhoun. Jackson learned of the vote while he was presiding over a formal White House dinner party. He leapt to his feet and shouted, "By the eternal! I'll smash them!"[11]

The latest scandal of Jackson's administration erupted on June 9, 1834, when the Senate released a report on the Post Office Department. The conclusions were disturbing—the department was $803,625 in debt. Postmaster General William Barry was accused of making unauthorized loans and packing the department with people better known for their loyalty to Jackson than their competence. Jackson's foes rejected with derision a Democratic proposal that Congress let the president handle the accusations but failed to appoint a committee charged with its own investigation.[12]

The scandal deeply embarrassed and enraged Jackson. It revealed that he had failed to fulfill his promise to make honesty, efficiency, and economy his administration's guiding values. In Jackson's fevered mind, to fire Barry would admit that failure. Instead, he appointed Barry the minister to Spain and replaced him with his close adviser Amos Kendall. He ordered Kendall to thoroughly clean up the mess. Kendall got to work, alleviated many of the problems, and sent a set of reform proposals to Congress. The subsequent Post Office Act of July 2, 1836, provided the administrative, fiscal, and legal reforms necessary to completely overhaul the department.

The worst scandal of all was not revealed until after Jackson left the White House. Samuel Swartwout, the tariff collector at the Port of New York, absconded to Europe with $1,222,705. Jackson had appointed Swartwout despite an explicit warning from Martin Van Buren of these likely consequences. Although Swartwout's justification for his grand larceny is not on the record, if asked he might have quoted another loyal Jacksonian, War Secretary William Marcy, who defended the administration's rapacious policies against congressional critics with this venerable maxim: "To the victor belongs the spoils."[13]

8

The Monster Bank

The Bank . . . is trying to kill me. But I will kill it.

ANDREW JACKSON

This worthy President thinks that because he has
scalped Indians and imprisoned judges, he is to have
his way with this Bank. He is mistaken.

NICHOLAS BIDDLE

It will come to this, whoever is in favor of that
Bank will be against Old Hickory.

AMOS KENDALL

Andrew Jackson rarely obscured his stand on the issues. He shared his
views with his correspondents, on the campaign trail, in interviews with
journalists, and in official speeches. But saying was not doing. The scan-
dals scuttled any good chance of tackling his agenda during his first year
in power. He was determined to change all that in his second year. For
this, he wanted his congressional allies to know his intensions so that
they could busy themselves with implementing them. He articulated

his agenda in his first State of the Union address, which he submitted to Congress on December 8, 1829.

Number one on his agenda was a tariff that promoted national and sectional interests: "Local feelings and prejudices should be merged in the patriotic determination to promote the great interest as a whole. . . . Discarding all calculations of political ascendancy, the North, the South, the East, and the West should unite in diminishing any burthen of which either may justly complain."[1] Writing an acceptable tariff bill would be up to congressional leaders. The tariff's most vital purpose was not to promote manufacturing through protection but to eliminate the national debt, which now stood at $49 million. Jackson vowed to eliminate this burden by the time he left office.

But resolving this problem would lead to another—what should be done with Washington's growing surpluses? Politicians would naturally demand that the money be distributed among the states for "internal improvements." Jackson opposed this for two reasons. First, dispensing this cash would lead special interests to try to corrupt Congress in order to get a share of the funds and would make the states dependent on federal handouts. Second, as if this were not reason enough, because the Constitution did not specifically permit "internal improvements," they were impermissible.

Jackson then abruptly shifted to another priority. All Indians east of the Mississippi River, he said, should be expelled from their lands and transferred far west of that boundary. The move would save the Indians from destruction through assimilation with the American population or decimation from disease. He argued, "Humanity and national honor demand that every effort should be made to avert so great a calamity."

Finally, Jackson pointed out that the charter for the Second Bank of the United States would expire in 1836. He noted that the bank was controversial on both economic and constitutional grounds. Yet he did not then openly call for the bank's destruction; he only hinted at what lay ahead.

House Speaker Henry Clay had his own agenda and, with a majority behind him, could trump Jackson's. His immediate priority was to revive work on the National Road.[2] In doing so, he deliberately reignited a controversy that had begun in 1811, when Congress passed and a skeptical President Madison signed the National Road Act, which authorized a federal road westward from Cumberland, Maryland, that would link the East with the Ohio River valley states.

Like all other issues, the National Road had three dimensions—ideological, practical, and political. Did the Constitution empower the federal government to launch such a project? Hamiltonians argued most certainly yes by citing the Constitution's "implied powers" and "necessary and proper" doctrines. The Jeffersonians and, more recently, the Jacksonians vehemently argued no, noting that the Constitution's text did not explicitly grant road-building powers. Would the National Road boost America's economic development by stimulating the creation and distribution of more wealth? Here again Hamiltonians replied of course and cited statistics of the economic boom along the stretch so far completed. The Jeffersonians and Jacksonians dismissed these facts and insisted that only free markets and private investors could create wealth. As for the political dimension, it just so happened that the spur of the National Road that Clay wanted built ran through his home state of Kentucky, from Maysville on the Ohio River to Lexington, and was the first segment of a road that would eventually extend to the Natchez Trace's terminus in Nashville, in Jackson's home state, just a dozen miles from his plantation. The Maysville Bill appropriated $150,000 for this road. In April 1830 it passed the House with a solid 105 to 86 vote majority and the Senate by 21 to 19.

Jackson and most of his followers opposed the Maysville Bill on ideological, political, and fiscal grounds—it was unconstitutional, it was the hated Clay's special project for his state, and it would delay eliminating the national debt. However, some Jacksonian congressional allies agreed with these arguments but backed the bill hoping they could win similar projects for their own states.

Jackson vetoed the Maysville Bill on May 27, 1830. Congress failed to override his veto, but did pass the Washington Turnpike Bill. Jackson killed this bill as well, this time with the first exercise of what became known as a "pocket veto." Rather than formally vetoing the bill, the president simply refused to sign it before Congress went into recess. Then, he finished off the National Road by eliminating the board of engineers that was in charge of it and transferring control of the project to each state through which it passed. Having successfully destroyed two Hamiltonian measures, Jackson then launched an offensive against an institution and its president that increasingly became scapegoats for all that he hated.

The financial power of the Second Bank of the United States peaked in 1833, when it had $79 million in assets and $37 million in liabilities. The bank could not have been in better hands.[3] Nicholas Biddle, the bank's president, succeeded brilliantly at everything he attempted. After he graduated from Princeton University at age fifteen, his gift for languages got him appointed James Monroe's secretary in Paris. After returning to his native Philadelphia, he plunged into the study of law, passed the bar exam, and opened a practice. His love of fine books and minds prompted him to found a literary magazine; for his writing skills, he was chosen to edit the Lewis and Clark journals for publication. He won elections to first the lower and then the upper houses of Pennsylvania's legislature. In 1823 he was appointed to be the president of the Second Bank of the United States. There he proved to be a financial and managerial wizard akin to Alexander Hamilton and Robert Morris. In all, Nicholas Biddle was a Renaissance American man, renowned not just for his wit, learning, and erudition but even more for mastering the practical skills of diplomacy, law, business, and finance. He epitomized the worldly, sophisticated easterner that Andrew Jackson and other westerners loved to hate.

Within a few years, Biddle transformed a corrupt, ineptly run institution that hemorrhaged money and handed out insider loans into a model of professionalism and profitability. He did so by purging corrupt and clueless officials; tightening lending, reserve, and investment standards; and constantly assessing the business and political world so that he could make the best-informed decisions. All this was challenging enough. But Biddle never let himself get lost in the myriad of daily operating details and become blind to his foremost duty. The bank operated like a modern central bank by loosening credit during economic downturns and tightening credit when the economy overheated. With his hand firmly on the bank's tiller, Biddle guided the nation's development between the extremes of recession and runaway inflation.

Yet a dilemma haunted his brilliant record. The bank's future could be threatened more by good than bad management. A powerful mix of creed and greed had destroyed the first bank and might well doom the second. Jeffersonians and their ideologically similar Jacksonian cousins denounced any federally sponsored banks or other enterprises as unconstitutional because the Constitution's text did not explicitly permit them. This stance was bolstered by special interests, like speculators and debt-ridden enterprises, that demanded easy credit and no regulations. The bank's success at once vindicated the Hamiltonian assertion that a muscular, problem-solving government best promoted American wealth, power, security, and liberty, and repudiated the Jeffersonian and Jacksonian claims that unfettered markets and weak government were superior. And therein lay the danger, especially during Jackson's presidency. No one hated to have his beliefs or behavior revealed as inadequate more than Andrew Jackson.

So, Biddle tried to tiptoe the bank around those dozing ideological dogs that were so vicious when aroused. He explained to Daniel Webster, "I have been so anxious to keep the Bank out of view in the political world and bring it down to its true business character as a counting house that I have been reluctant to apply to Congress for anything."[4] He was scrupulous to keep a firewall between finance and politics, at least those in which he was not involved. He insisted that "no officer of the Government, from the President downward, has the least right, the least authority, the least pretense, for interference in the concerns of the Bank."[5]

Despite these precautions, Biddle had flaws that led to his undoing. He was not above dispensing bank loans to current or potential political allies. He did not suffer fools easily, and he reckoned Andrew Jackson the king of that pack. When Jackson vowed to "destroy the monster Bank," Biddle miscalculated the popularity and power of the president relative to the institution. Rather than try to deftly outmaneuver Jackson, Biddle politically head butted him and came away a sore loser.

Jackson's hatred for the bank was as driven by psychology as by ideology. His seething inner demons demanded that he always have an enemy against whom he could unleash his poisonous bile. To this end, he was hypersensitive to any insult to his "honor." In 1821 he asked the bank's New Orleans branch for a ten thousand dollar advance to cover his administrative costs as he assumed Florida's governorship. The branch refused. Jackson appealed to Biddle. Biddle refused. Jackson could only fume and vow to one day avenge this gross insult. His time had come.[6]

The bank's fate involved more than a duel between Jackson and Biddle. An array of egos and interests took sides in that struggle. The war's opening shots erupted in December 1830. Jackson's Senate attack dog against the bank was Thomas Hart Benton of Missouri. In a typically long-winded speech, Benton vented all the anti-bank arguments. The following day, Daniel Webster rose to rebut Benton point by point in one of his most memorable speeches. A long cease-fire followed as more pressing issues took precedence.

Meanwhile, Treasury Secretary Louis McLane did what he could to prevent Jackson from wrecking the bank and thus the economy. He understood that Jackson's twisted psyche constantly drove him to search for hated monsters to slay. So he tried to divert Jackson's aggression from eliminating the national bank to eliminating the national debt. In the autumn of 1831 McLane presented a plan to pay off the national debt by the end of Jackson's first term. The debt then stood at $24 million. This could be liquidated by anticipated revenues of $16 million and the sale of the federal government's $8 million share in the bank. This feat would be a brilliant coup for Jackson's presidency and legacy in American history. After Jackson eagerly pounced on the idea, McLane explained that for the plan to work, the president had to avoid attacking the bank in word let alone deed. This admonition transformed Jackson's elation to anger. McLane eventually quelled the president's tantrum by patiently explaining why. Vilifying the bank scared off investors and lowered its stock values. The lower the share prices, the less money the federal government would make when it sold its shares and thus the less debt that could be paid off. The president grudgingly agreed to hold fire for now. In his December 1831 speech to Congress, he simply placed the bank's fate in Congress's hands.

The "bank war" might have ended there had the Jackson movement's radical wing not interpreted his innocuous statement as a sellout of his principles. "Let Jackson be Jackson" a chorus of congressmen and editors demanded. Destroying the monster bank would be the issue that spearheaded Old Hickory's reelection campaign. Within the administration, Attorney General Roger Taney led the assault. The criticism that Jackson had betrayed his values sharply stung him. Yet for now McLane's arguments appeared stronger than Taney's.

Henry Clay was eager to confront Jackson over the bank issue. He was confident that most Americans would realize that Jackson's obsession with destroying the institution that provided the United States economic stability and growth was utterly crazy. He did not think Jackson was reckless enough to veto a bank renewal bill that enjoyed such broad congressional and popular support in an election year, but if he did, he would lose the White House. Even if the current Congress did not override his veto, the next president, who Clay jauntily assumed would be himself, would happily sign the next bill into law.

Wielding that logic, Clay talked a skeptical Biddle into asking Congress to recharter the bank as soon as possible. Biddle submitted the request on January 6, 1832. Clay and his Senate ally Daniel Webster started drafting bills in their respective chambers.

Although for now Jackson remained publicly mute on the issue, his congressional followers wielded every possible measure to destroy this bill. Benton revealed their smear and obstruct strategy: "Attack incessantly, assail at all points, display the evil of the institution, rouse the people—and prepare them to sustain the veto."[7]

The trouble was that the legislators' anti-bank arguments were as intellectually feeble as they were ideologically powerful. Their charge that the bank was corrupt was refuted by an investigation by the House Ways and Means Committee, chaired by George McDuffie of South Carolina, a John Calhoun ally. The committee report found absolutely no evidence of wrongdoing and instead lauded the bank's efficiency and fairness. When the Jacksonians attacked the bank on constitutional grounds, proponents cited the Supreme Court's 1819 decision in *McCulloch v. Maryland* and other rulings that proved the bank was indeed constitutional. Rather than accept this reality, the enemies of the bank turned their ideological guns on the federal court system itself.

What the anti-bank forces lacked in rational arguments, they made up for with pure emotionalism. They stoked populist fires by marketing themselves as the champions of "the people" against "the big moneyed interests." Passions flared as the bill appeared more likely to pass. Amos Kendall captured Jackson's Manichean approach to the issue: "It will come to this, whoever is in favor of the Bank will be against Old Hickory."[8] No one worked himself into a worse frenzy over the issue than Jackson himself. He repeatedly declared that the bank was "a monster" that was "trying to kill me. But I will kill it."[9] Passion was not confined to Jackson and his followers. Jackson's vow provoked a sharp retort from Henry Clay: "Should Jackson veto it, I will veto him!"[10]

The bill passed the Senate by 28 to 20 on June 11, and the House by 107 to 85 on July 3. The majorities were solid but not veto proof. To maximize the political impact, Clay and his colleagues ensured that the bill was delivered to the White House on July 4, 1832.

It took Jackson and his advisers six days to write a reply. They sent the bill and the president's veto message back to Congress on July 10. Jackson's arguments for killing the bill boiled down to the literal interpretation of the Constitution held so zealously by himself and his followers—the Constitution does not mention creating a bank, and therefore a bank is unconstitutional.[11]

The Senate fell far short of a two-thirds override, with a vote of 22 to 19, on July 16. Jackson's web of newspaper editors trumpeted the veto as a victory for the downtrodden in their class war against the rich. The *Washington Globe's* pontification was typical: "The Jackson cause is the cause of democracy and the people against a corrupt . . . aristocracy."[12]

As if the vituperation between the Democrats and National Republicans was not nasty enough, a new political party arose with a special target against which to vent its hatreds. The Masons were a secret, elite society that promoted reason, knowledge, and good works among its members. Many prominent Americans had been Masons, including Benjamin Franklin, George Washington, Alexander Hamilton, John Quincy Adams, Henry Clay, and Andrew Jackson. A scandal arose in September 1826, when a Mason named George Morgan in Batavia, New York, threatened to publish the group's secret rituals. He was arrested on apparently trumped-up shoplifting charges, kidnapped as he left the jail, and later found drowned in the Niagara River. The assumption that the Masons had instigated these events triggered an outpouring of rage.

Starting in 1828, anti-Masonic parties sprung up across the country, opposing not just Masons but all elitists everywhere. But they were for as well as against things, including Henry Clay's "American System." And they made an important contribution to the development of democracy in America when they held the first national political party convention. On September 26, 1831, at Baltimore, they nominated William Wirt, a brilliant lawyer who had prosecuted Aaron Burr for treason, defended the Cherokees against Georgia, and served as attorney general for a dozen consecutive years in the Monroe and Adams administrations. Other leading Anti-Masons were Thurlow Weed, the editor of the *Rochester Evening Telegraph*, and Senators William Seward of New York and Thaddeus Stevens of Pennsylvania.[13]

Historically, third parties unwittingly tend to siphon votes from a centrist candidate and thus aid the more radical candidate. This is certainly what happened in the 1832 election. Had Henry Clay not been a Mason, he would have garnered the lion's share of votes that went to William Wirt. National Republicans and Anti-Masons were in essential agreement on such critical economic issues as the internal improvements, the tariff, and the second bank. They were also united in their fear and loathing of Andrew Jackson's character and policies. Yet they never formed a coalition.

Instead, the National Republicans, increasingly known informally as the Whigs, not only emulated the Anti-Masons by calling a convention but also held theirs at Baltimore. The city was the perfect place to gather, given that it was only thirty-four miles from Washington City and even closer to the Mason-Dixon line, with railroads radiating in all directions. Shortly after meeting on May 7, 1832, the delegates chose Henry Clay as their presidential candidate.

Not to be outdone, the Democrats opened their own convention at Baltimore on May 21, 1832, and unanimously chose Jackson for renomination. Jackson tapped Martin Van Buren as his running mate. As for a platform, Jackson and the Democratic Party targeted for elimination the monster bank and the "1828 Tariff of Abominations."

Although the National Republican and Democrat Parties each had its own distinct platform, the 1832 presidential campaign had one core issue—Andrew Jackson. For most Americans, this was no issue at all. They voted enthusiastically for him and all that he symbolized. Jackson crushed Clay and Wirt in the general election with 688,242 votes to 473,462 and 101,051 and in the Electoral College with 219 votes to 49 and 7. In the end, Wirt's third-party candidacy did not keep Clay from the White House; it merely deepened his defeat.[14]

The decision rendered Jackson and his supporters exhilarated and vindicated. They pointed to the overwhelming popular support as a mandate to do whatever the president wanted. Yet the Democrats emerged from the election weaker than they entered it. Congress was split with

26 National Republicans, 20 Democrats, and 2 independents in the Senate, and 143 Democrats, 63 National Republicans, and 34 independents in the House. Nonplused by the congressional results, Jackson would bury the weapon of his own popularity to the hilt in all who opposed him.

9
The Nullification Crisis

As the nation weathered the bank war and national elections of 1832, a long-simmering dispute erupted into a crisis that threatened to break up the United States into civil war. Ironically, the crisis was sparked when moderates tried to placate rather than confront southern radicals. Henry Clay crafted the 1832 Tariff Bill, which slashed average rates to 25 percent from 45 percent under the 1828 Tariff Bill, hated by southerners as the "Tariff of Abominations." However, he wrote the bill so that all tariffs on goods, like wine, that were not produced in the United States were eliminated, while those that protected American industries that fueled the nation's prosperity were upheld. He explained that the tariff cuts would cost the Treasury $5 million a year in revenues and delay the national debts' elimination. The 1832 Tariff Bill passed in July with overwhelming majorities of 132 to 65 in the House and 32 to 16 in the Senate. Jackson signed it into law on July 14.

Despite, or more likely because of, the bill's popularity, South Carolina radicals seized it as an excuse to assert their "nullification" doctrine, the creed that each state held sovereign power and thus could nullify or violate any federal law. The doctrine's father was none other than Thomas Jefferson, who developed the notion with James Madison in their respective 1798 Kentucky and Virginia Resolves, whereby these states refused to abide by the Alien and Sedition Acts. The trouble was that nothing in the Constitution remotely hints at "nullification." This would seem to make its assertion an intellectual abyss for anyone, but especially for the Jeffersonians, who otherwise insist on a strict literal interpretation of the Constitution.[1]

Oblivious to these glaring realities, Senator Robert Hayne of South Carolina launched a blistering attack against Daniel Webster for arguing that helping to unify the nation was among the tariff's benefits. For Hayne, "a money interest in the Government is essentially a base interest, and . . . is . . . opposed to all free government, and at war with virtue and patriotism."[2] Webster replied in a three-hour speech that spilled into the next day's session and ended with the stirring words "Liberty and Union, now and forever, one and inseparable."[3]

This long-standing dispute led to a memorable duel in 1830 between Andrew Jackson and John Calhoun. Mercifully, they fought with toasts rather than pistols. The occasion was a banquet for the Democratic Party's elite to celebrate Jefferson's birthday on April 13. As president, Jackson proposed the first toast. Raising his glass and staring hard into Calhoun's eyes, he proclaimed, "Our Union, it must be preserved." Calhoun notably grimaced at these words. As vice president, protocol allowed him the second toast. He retorted, "The Union. Next to our liberty, the most dear."[4]

Fortunately, the tension between the nation's leading Unionist and Nullifier did not snap into outright rancor. Jackson was not quite as restrained a few days later. When asked by a South Carolina congressman whether the president had a message for the people of his state, Jackson retorted, "Yes I have. . . . Please give my compliments to my friends in your State, and say to them that if a single drop of blood shall be shed there in opposition to the laws of the United States, I will hang the first man I can lay my hands on engaged in such treasonable conduct upon the first tree I shall reach."[5]

Jackson had reason for concern. No state was more dominated by radical states' righters than South Carolina. Slavery and radicalism were inseparable—the larger the portion of slaves in a population, the greater the paranoia and thus virulence of the radicals. South Carolina was the only state in which most people were slaves.

Yet support for nullification in South Carolina was hardly universal. The state was split economically and politically between the Tidewater and Piedmont. Nullifiers dominated the Tidewater, whereas Unionists had a slight edge in the Piedmont. Two reasons explain this division. The Piedmont held fewer slaves and large plantations and was less dependent on foreign markets for its wealth. Although Nullifiers outnumbered Unionists across the state, they magnified their advantage by blatantly gerrymandering the districts to favor their candidates. Nonetheless, Jackson had a valuable ally inside South Carolina's legislature. Joel Poinsett was a leading Unionist and Jacksonian who had left a distinguished diplomatic career to return to his home state and fight the nullification movement. During the crisis, he kept the president informed of the latest developments.

Governor James Hamilton reacted to the 1832 Tariff Bill by leading the formation of a States' Rights and Free Trade Association to lobby Congress. But the Nullifiers recognized that protest was not enough, they had to act. Hamilton called a special session of the state's legislature on October 22. The legislature in turn called for a convention to be held at Columbia on November 19. After a week of fierce debate, on November 26, the convention voted 136 to 26 to declare the 1828 and 1832 tariff laws "null, void, and no law, nor binding" upon South Carolina as of February 1, 1833. On that date, federal officials would be forbidden from collecting tariffs within South Carolina.

During the 1832 election, the Nullifiers trounced the Unionists by capturing 61 percent of the vote. Two electoral outcomes were crucial. John Hayes had been one of the state's federal senators. He resigned his seat and was elected the governor. John Calhoun resigned his post as vice president and was elected to fill Hayes's vacated Senate seat in Washington.

Calhoun could not have been happier than he was returning to the Senate floor. For someone as bright, impassioned, and opinionated as he was, it must have been utterly frustrating to preside mute over the Senate for four years. The 1832 election unmuzzled him. Back at his old desk, he could unleash his oratorical gifts and ideological obsessions with no regard for time or moderation.

Jackson was incredulous that Calhoun and his fellow Nullifiers would dare cross swords with him: "Can any one of common sense believe the absurdity that a fraction of any state, or a state, has a right to secede and destroy this Union, and the liberty of our country with it?"[6] He and Secretary of State Edward Livingston composed the ultimatum that the president issued to South Carolina on December 12, 1832. Typically, Jackson did not mince words. He denounced the nullification doctrine as unconstitutional and its adherents as guilty of treason: "I consider, then, the power to annul a law of the United States, assumed by one State, incompatible with the existence of the Union, contradicted expressly by the letter of the Constitution, unauthorized by its spirit, inconsistent with every principle upon which it was founded, and destructive of the great object for which it was formed." To confirm that, one need look no further than the Constitution's preamble, in which the United States and its government were established by "we the people" rather than by the states. The United States was a nation and government, not a league. Upon ratifying the Constitution, the states transferred their sovereignty to the United States. Indeed, the United States preceded the individual states. The Constitution permits neither nullification nor secession. Thus, nullification and secession are acts of treason to be treated accordingly.[7]

Jackson fired up Secretary of War Lewis Cass and the rest of his cabinet and advisers with declarations such as "We must be prepared to act with promptness and crush the monster in its cradle."[8] He vowed that "in forty days I can have within the limits of South Carolina fifty thousand men, and in forty days more another fifty thousand. . . . The wickedness, madness, and folly of the leaders and the delusion of their followers in the attempt to destroy themselves and our Union has not its parallel in the history of the world. The Union will be preserved."[9]

For all his smoldering rhetoric, Jackson hoped to resolve the crisis as much with a carrot as a stick. He asked Congress to pass two bills.

The Tariff Bill was designed to placate the Nullifiers by further slashing rates. The Force Bill would empower him to mobilize what military force was necessary to resolve the crisis if all else failed. To those ends, he had Treasury Secretary Louis McLane outline a tariff bill and submit it to Gulian Verplanck, who chaired the House Ways and Means Committee, on January 8, 1833, the anniversary of the president's victory at New Orleans. The bill would cut tariffs roughly to their 1816 level. McLane also wrote much of the Force Bill and passed it to Congress on January 16. Meanwhile, Jackson had Cass order the commanders of federal Forts Moultrie and Pinckney at Charleston "to defend them to the last extremity."[10] He sent two warships to anchor in Charleston Bay and then withdrew the federal revenue collectors from Charleston and placed them on those warships. All ships parting or arriving at Charleston would be stopped and their cargoes assessed for revenues.

Jackson's finest political hour may have been the special message he sent to Congress on January 16, 1833. For once, he actually reflected the framers' original intent when he wielded the Constitution to assert his position. Referring to the Preamble, he argued that this

more perfect union made by the whole of the people of the United States granted the federal government certain powers and retained others. But nowhere can it be found where the right to nullify a law or to secede from the Union, has been retained by the states. . . . Therefore when a faction in a state attempts to nullify a constitutional law of Congress, or to destroy the Union, the balance of the people in this Union have a perfect right to coerce them to obedience. . . . The Union must be preserved. I will die with the Union.[11]

Privately, he was even fiercer: "The Union will be preserved and treason and rebellion promptly put down when and where it may shew its monster head."[12]

Andrew Jackson insisted that the Tariff and Force Bills proceed in tandem. On February 20 the Senate voted 32 to 1 for the Force Bill. John Tyler of Virginia was the sole holdout. Calhoun and his fellow Nullifiers boycotted the vote in protest. Two notable senators did not vote, although they backed Jackson. With presidential ambitions in mind, Henry Clay and Thomas Hart Benton sought to avoid alienating southern voters.

Clay immersed himself in drafting a compromise tariff bill that would drop the rate to 20 percent for a decade, after which Congress could revisit the issue. He defended this level as essential for federal revenues and was wise enough not to mention that it was also high enough to enable most industries to compete with British and other foreign rivals. The 1833 Tariff Bill passed the House by 119 to 85 on February 26 and the Senate by 26 to 16 on March 1. Also on March 1 the Force Bill passed the House by 149 to 48 and the Senate by 29 to 16. The following day, Jackson pointedly signed first the Force Bill and then the Tariff Bill into law.[13]

Andrew Jackson took his second oath as president of the United States on March 4, 1833. In his inaugural speech, he summed up his view with these immortal words: "Without union, our independence and liberty would have never been achieved; without union they never can be maintained."[14]

The crisis effectively ended on March 11, when South Carolina's legislature rescinded its nullification bill by a vote of 155 to 4. Although Jackson and his followers celebrated their victory, he later expressed regret that he was not tough enough during the crisis. He lamented his failure to execute John Calhoun for treason: "My country would have sustained me in the act, and his fate would have been a warning to traitors in all time to come."[15] Nonetheless, the nullification crisis was Andrew Jackson's finest display of presidential leadership, as it enhanced rather than diminished American power.

Yet Jackson's misgivings were prescient. He and his supporters had simply kicked the poisonous political can of worms down the road another eighteen years to President Abraham Lincoln. South Carolina Unionist James Pettigrew understood that a far worse crisis was inevitable: "Nullification has done its work. It has prepared the minds of men for a separation of the states, and when the question is moved again it will be distinctly union or disunion."[16]

IO

The Spoils

The Jackson cause is the cause of democracy and
the people against a corrupt . . . aristocracy.

GLOBE

I tell you gentlemen, it's all politics.

ANDREW JACKSON

Money is power.

ANDREW JACKSON

Among the worst mistakes a foe of Andrew Jackson could make was
not to take him at his word. Jackson never hid his intention eventually to break the Bank of the United States by yanking out its federal
deposits. Yet reasonable people had trouble believing that even Jackson
would commit such a devastating economic and political act. When
Senator Daniel Webster expressed his fear that the president would carry
through his threat, second bank president Nicholas Biddle dismissed
the notion. He "will not dare to remove them" because to do so "will be
a declaration of war which cannot be recalled."[1] After years of struggle
between them, Biddle still misunderstood his nemesis.

Jackson always spoiled for a fight whereby he could portray himself as championing all that was good and his enemies all that was evil. Of course, in doing so, he simply projected his own deep unresolved pathologies onto hated others. Previously, this reality had been lost on his followers, who always zealously backed him to the hilt no matter what. This time was different. His announcement that he would withdraw the bank's federal deposits and spread them among "pet banks" at first provoked mostly embarrassed silence and throat clearing. Nearly all of his closest advisers were afraid of such a blatantly vindictive measure, which would most likely wreck the economy even as it reimbursed the president's financial allies. James Hamilton gingerly suggested that the withdrawal might lead to a "great disturbance in commercial affairs."[2] Vice President Martin Van Buren, Treasury Secretary Louis McLane, and Secretary of War Lewis Cass urged Jackson to postpone the removal at least until January 1834 so that Congress might be convinced to back the policy. Jackson curtly dismissed the notion. He knew that he could never muster majorities in both houses of Congress to support his scheme to destroy the bank. He derided the naysayers as "overawed by the power of the bank. It cannot overawe me. I trust in my God and the virtue of the People."[3]

Jackson's angry denunciations of any compromise cowed nearly all of his inner circle. Then there were Amos Kendall and Roger Taney, who egged him on. Jackson embarked Kendall on a trip around the country to identify allied banks to reward with financial chunks of the institution's carcass. Kendall promised Jackson that he would "raise up powerful friends."[4]

Jackson's strongest congressional allies were Representative James Polk and Senator Thomas Hart Benton. In their respective chambers, they vilified the bank in one long impassioned speech after another and spearheaded official investigations into allegations of bank corruption. The investigations backfired when the reports not only cleared the institution and Biddle of any wrongdoing but lauded the bank's efficiency, fairness, and profitability. This simply spurred Polk, Benton, and others to inject more venom and lies into their speeches. They insisted that Jackson alone could determine the fate of the monster bank's deposits and simply denied the reality that its charter clearly charged Congress with this power.

Jackson had hoped that Treasury Secretary McLane would be his hatchet man in destroying the bank. When McLane balked, Jackson transferred him to the unfilled secretary of state position on May 29; he then tapped William Duane to be the treasury secretary on June 1, 1833. The shake-up, however, did not resolve the impasse. Duane also refused on both legal and practical grounds Jackson's request to loot the bank. Doing so would clearly violate the bank's charter, and depositing the funds in the pet banks would wreck the economy. Jackson tried to break Duane to his will during several meetings and exchanges of letters from June through September. Finally, Jackson's ever-brittle patience snapped. On September 20, 1833, he ordered Duane to transfer the deposits. When Duane stood fast, Jackson fired him three days later.[5]

Once again, Jackson racked up a first in American political history—no president had ever before fired a secretary for refusing to obey an order. That same day, the president named Roger Taney his new treasury secretary and replaced him as attorney general with Benjamin Butler, a New York lawyer and member of Van Buren's political machine. Since Congress was in recess, Jackson's new appointments could immediately get to work and face the approval process only after the Senate reconvened.

Taney wasted no time. On September 25 he declared that as of October 1, 1833, all federal deposits would be moved to select state banks. He then set in motion the initial distribution of $2.3 million to the seven pet banks that Kendall had identified. Other banks naturally complained that their rivals were enjoying an unfair advantage. The political returns of spreading the public funds as widely as possible proved to be irresistible. By the year's end, the Jackson administration had expanded its number of pets to twenty-two, and within three years the tally jumped to eighty-seven with $26 million split among them.[6]

And thus was the dirty work done. The result was to shove the bank war into a more destructive stage. Jackson crowed triumphantly that his act would "have Mr. Biddle as quiet and harmless as a lamb in six weeks."[7] But Jackson no more understood his adversary than Biddle understood him.

Biddle explained that because Jackson "has scalped Indians and imprisoned judges," he believed he could "have his way with this Bank. He is mistaken."[8] On October 7, 1833, Biddle began calling in outstanding loans and sharply curtailing the issuance of new ones. Within a few months, he cut the bank's liabilities by $9 million. His motives for doing so were both financial and political. He sought to protect the bank from destruction while squeezing the economy. He hoped that the subsequent outcry from the business world would force Jackson to reverse course.

A delegation of prominent New York businessmen did indeed visit the president and implore him to spare the country the worsening economic damage. To this, Jackson gleefully retorted, "We have no money here, gentlemen. Biddle has all the money. He has millions of specie in his vaults, at this moment, lying idle, and yet you come to me to save you from breaking. I tell you gentlemen, it's all politics."[9]

Much like Jefferson with his embargo, Jackson rejected any suggestions that his policy was akin to economic suicide. "There is no real general distress," he declared confidently. "It is only with those who live by borrowing, trade on loans, and the gamblers in stocks." And he was as eager to ruin them as he was Biddle and his monster bank, insisting that it would "be a god send to society if all such were put down."[10]

No prominent politician blistered Jackson's destruction of the bank more than Henry Clay. He ominously warned that Jackson's behavior toward the bank and an array of other issues had brought the nation "in the midst of a revolution, hitherto bloodless, but rapidly tending toward a total change of the pure republican character of the Government."[11] Jackson exploded in wrath at word of Clay's speech: "Oh if I live to get these robes of office off me I will bring the rascal to a dear account."[12]

Clay increased the pressure on Jackson. By a vote of 23 to 18 on December 4, 1833, the Senate passed a motion that Jackson deliver all his administration's documents concerning the bank policy. The president refused, citing executive privilege. Clay played yet another powerful political card. He introduced a censure motion that condemned Treasury Secretary Taney's removal of the deposits; it passed by a vote 28 to 18 on February 5, 1834. Finally, he aimed a resolution straight at Jackson, condemning him for having "assumed upon himself authority and power not conferred by the Constitution and laws, but in derogation of both." The Senate censured him by a vote of 26 to 20 on March 28, 1834.

Thus did Jackson rack up yet another "first" in American political history—the Senate had never before censured a president. Naturally, this rendered Jackson apoplectic. In his rant, he swore that no matter what "the monster must perish."[13] He then issued on April 15 a "Protest" to the Senate in which he defended his firing of Duane and transfer of the bank deposits. "The President is the direct representative of the American people," he declared, and "the entire executive power is vested in the President of the United States." He went on to argue that secretaries are merely there to carry out the will of the president and thus the people.[14] His argument did not sway the Senate majority that with a vote of 27 to 16 upheld its censure of Jackson.

If Jackson could not bend the Senate to his will, he prevailed in the House of Representatives. His point man there was James Polk, the Speaker. On April 4, 1834, Polk pushed through a series of resolutions that vindicated Jackson's war against the bank. First, the House voted 134 to 82 not to recharter the bank, thus reversing its vote the previous year in favor of rechartering. Then, the House voted by 117 to 105 that the deposits should be transferred to state banks. Finally, the House voted by 175 to 42 to appoint a committee to investigate the bank's operations. Word of these measures exhilarated Jackson: "I have obtained a glorious triumph."[15]

These resolutions drove the final nails into the bank's coffin. Yet the bank still had some life in it. And this mattered because the economy was tottering. In the game of brinksmanship between Jackson and Biddle, the bank president eventually stepped back from the abyss. To prevent a financial and economic meltdown, Biddle issued $15 million of loans during the first six months of 1835. This combined with looser credit from the pets and a hundred other banks helped boost the nation's money supply from $172 million in 1834 to $276 million in 1836.[16] But this transformed a looming depression into a speculative bubble that would sooner or later burst.

Jackson meanwhile tried to alleviate mounting concern over the viability and trustworthiness of his pet banks by proposing a reform on April 21, 1834. He called for letting the treasury secretary deposit funds in any bank after giving his reasons to Congress; requiring each deposit bank to submit monthly reports on its financial activities; empowering the federal government to examine any deposit bank's books; preventing deposit banks from issuing notes worth less than five dollars;

and revaluing gold to parity with silver. Congress started work on these and other issues.

Congress first passed the Coinage Act, which the president signed on June 28, 1834. This bill addressed a serious flaw in the U.S. currency. The 1792 Coinage Act set a 15 to 1 ratio between gold and silver for the gold eagle, which was askew from the commercial rate of 15.5 to 1. As a result, a $10 coin was actually worth $10.66. This encouraged people to hoard rather than spend the coins to avoid buying something for less than it was worth. The new ratio of 16 to 1 had the opposite effect. Although now silver was undervalued, people tended to spend their gold eagles rather than hoard them, which boosted the economy.

The speculative boom fueled a surge in exports and imports that brought in more revenues. Indeed, so much money poured into government coffers that Jackson was able to fulfill yet another of his promises, this one actually beneficial for the nation. The national debt stood at $58.4 million when he took power in 1829. Six years later, on New Year's Day 1835, the debt disappeared. For the first and, sadly, last time in American history, the United States owed no money to anyone. The *Washington Globe*, the leading Jacksonian mouthpiece, trumpeted this achievement and linked it with the thirtieth anniversary of another shattering victory: "New Orleans and the National Debt—the first of which paid off our scores to our enemies, whilst the latter paid off the last cent to our friends."[17]

Although Jackson took credit, the debt was paid despite rather than because of his policies. He did not cut total government spending. When he took his second oath of office in 1833, the federal budget was $22,713,755, double the $11,490,460 budget of 1825. In 1835 the federal government directly employed 60,294 people, and when pensioners were counted, the number receiving a government stipend rose to 100,079.[18]

Hamiltonian-style tariffs that promoted industry and reaped revenues were vital for eliminating the national debt, with public land sales a distant second cause. And for this, Henry Clay deserves the most credit. Protective tariffs, internal improvements, and the second bank were the key elements of his American System, which was designed to spur related industrial, commercial, financial, technological, and agrarian revolutions for the United States.

A seemingly odd problem emerged after the debt was eliminated.

What should be done with the federal budget surplus, which reached $17 million in 1835 and $42 million in 1836? Before the question could be answered, the "problem" disappeared with the Panic of 1837 and subsequent depression—the nation's debt reappeared and soared once again.

Although the budget surplus "problem" was all too fleeting, the issue of what to do with surplus federal lands had been hotly debated since the birth of the United States. For the first century, the key question was how to sell them as quickly and profitably as possible. Land sales at once brought desperately needed revenue to the government and developed the economy. Everyone agreed on this but differed over whether it was better to auction off huge swaths to speculators or sell segments at a fixed price to settlers. The 1820 Land Act was a compromise between these positions. Sales began with auctions. When the speculators were satiated, the leftovers were sold off in eighty-acre tracts for $1.25 an acre (down from 160-acre tracts and $2 an acre under the previous act), with a 25 percent down-payment and four years to pay off the balance.

This policy satisfied both speculators and farmers but was not good enough for the president. Jackson favored selling public lands at a pittance to all who would till it. To accelerate this process, he called for transferring all public lands from the federal government to the states, much as he had spread the federal deposits from the bank to his pet state banks. Indeed, this was a good analogy. Had Jackson gotten away with his public land giveaway, the result would have been even more catastrophic for America's development than was his federal money giveaway.

A related issue was what to do with the revenues derived from these sales. Although he had lost the election, Henry Clay was determined to enact as much of his American System as possible. Internal improvements were a key element of his vision. In 1832 he proposed a bill that diverted 10 percent of the revenue from land sales to the states for internal improvements. A Senate majority approved the idea and a House majority killed it. With some backroom deals, his 1833 version passed both houses.

Jackson vetoed this bill on December 4, 1833, arguing that public lands belong to all Americans and thus could accrue only to the common treasury. Besides, the divvying of federal money to the states was a form of welfare that made them greedy, lazy, and dependent. Thus did he protect states' rights from the federal government. This, of course, was the same president who looted the second bank's federal deposits to distribute them among the state banks.[19]

Jackson's veto spurred Clay to try again. Reasoning that a veto-proof bill could be purchased at the right price, his 1834 version gave 15 percent of the revenue to the states in which land sales occurred, while the rest was spread among the other states. He then packaged that bill with the Deposit Bill, which authorized Jackson's policy of diverting federal money from the second bank to his pet banks, whose number had increased to eighty-one. The 1834 bill overwhelmingly passed the Senate by 155 to 38 and the House by 40 to 6.

Jackson faced a dilemma. He loved the bill's deposit element and hated the land sale distribution element. Holding his nose, he signed the bill into law on June 23, 1836.

Then, in vengeance against Clay and his allies, he committed a typically destructive act. After Congress adjourned, he issued on July 11, 1836, a decree that became known as the Specie Circular. The decree asserted that beginning August 15, 1836, public lands would be sold only for hard silver or gold coins. His legal justification for the decree was an 1816 bill empowering the Treasury Department to determine what type of currency it would accept for deposits or payments. His practical justification was the dangerous buildup of paper money or certificates of dubious value. Jackson hated paper money as much as he loved hard money. The trouble was that, once again, Jackson's passions dealt a devastating blow to American power.

The policy cut speculation and inflation by rendering worthless millions of dollars in paper certificates that bought land. But it also caused financial harm to more than the get-rich-quick speculators—it threatened foreclosure and destitution for countless families. Hardscrabble farmers could purchase land only by borrowing not hard coin, which was scarce virtually everywhere across the country, especially on the frontier, but a paper certificate for the amount. They then handed the certificate to the land office. Of course, the land title was held by whoever had lent the money to the settler. In effect, the champion of the common man had become his worst enemy. With the Specie Circular, public and private land sales and federal revenues plummeted, and that helped pop the speculative bubble created when Jackson distributed the federal deposits to his pet banks.

The resulting uproar was politically deafening. A bill to rescind the Specie Circular passed by overwhelming numbers of 41 to 5 in the Senate and 143 to 59 in the House. The bill landed on Jackson's desk on March 2, 1837, two days before he had to vacate the White House. As the second-to-last important act of his presidency, Jackson gleefully vetoed the bill the next day.

The final shots in the bank war were fired on January 16, 1837, when the Senate voted 24 to 19 for Thomas Hart Benton's resolution to expunge that body's previous censor of Andrew Jackson from the record. But this whitewash of Jackson's destruction of the bank could not erase its disastrous effect on America's economic development and power. The short-term consequences—the economic meltdown known as the Panic of 1837—lasted for years. The long-term results for American wealth and power are incalculable. Henry Clay's lament for the vetoed land bill could have been levied against the Jacksonian legacy: "What immense benefits might not have been diffused through the land! . . . What new channels of commerce and communities might not have been opened! What industry stimulated and labor rewarded!"[20]

II

The Master's Nightmare

We have the wolf by the ears and we can neither hold him nor safely let him go.

THOMAS JEFFERSON

We owe an obligation to the laws, but a higher one to the communities in which we live.

AMOS KENDALL

I yield slowly and reluctantly to the conviction that our constitution cannot last.

JOHN MARSHALL

Am I gagged or not?

JOHN QUINCY ADAMS

It is not surprising to learn that Andrew Jackson was the first president
to be physically assaulted and the first to be targeted for assassination.
Although each of his predecessors had his share of political foes, all of
them put together could not rouse a sliver of the hatred that Jackson
provoked in his enemies. Several caught up to him during his presidency.

One was former navy lieutenant Robert Randolph, whom Jackson had cashiered for theft. On May 6, 1833, he stepped before the president. "You've injured me," he stated, and then he slapped Jackson's face. Several members of Jackson's entourage pounced on Randolph and pinned him to ground. One of his defenders offered to murder the assailant if Jackson would promptly pardon his crime. Jackson tersely shook his head no, but his disapproval was rooted in upholding his honor rather than the law: "I cannot do that. I want no man to stand between me and my assailants, and none to take revenge on my account." Should anyone wonder whether a man of sixty-four years was still capable of defending himself, he intended to disabuse them with these words: "Had I been prepared for this cowardly villain's approach, I can assure you all that he would never have the temerity to undertake such a thing again."[1]

Yet another Jackson hater confronted him on the frigid afternoon of January 30, 1835, as he emerged from a memorial service at the Capitol. A man stepped before Jackson, pulled a pistol from his coat pocket, pointed it at his heart, and pulled the trigger. The pistol clicked with a misfire. The act was so unexpected and surreal that it briefly froze Jackson and his companions in their tracks. The man pulled a second pistol from his other pocket and aimed it at Jackson. Once again the pistol misfired. This murder attempt incensed rather than frightened Jackson. He lunged forward, slashing the assassin with his cane. His followers tackled the man.

The assailant was marched off to the nearest jail for questioning and booking. He revealed himself to be Richard Lawrence, a jobless housepainter who blamed the "tyrant" Jackson's policies for rendering himself and countless others unemployed and destitute; the president had thus made a mockery of their "freedom." By killing Jackson, he hoped to liberate all those suffering from his tyranny. He got off lightly. He was not executed for the attempted murder, but rather judged insane and locked away in an asylum.[2]

The would-be assassin was the first to try to murder a president. Tragically, he would not be the last. His failure, however, further fortified Jackson's belief that Providence had selected him as Its special instrument for bettering the lot of the common man and strengthening the nation. With God on his side, he could do no wrong.

If a president's worst nightmare is assassination, a similar terror haunted the nights and days of countless other Americans. Slave masters were stalked by the specter of being murdered in their beds by their vengeful chattel. Yet virtually all slave owners would do anything to protect and expand their "peculiar institution," including fighting for it.[3] Only a few recognized the moral and political dilemmas that slavery posed to themselves and the nation, and no one better expressed these than Thomas Jefferson: "We have the wolf by the ears and we can neither hold him nor safely let him go."[4]

The fear of a slave revolt was nowhere greater than in South Carolina. This was not an irrational fear. The state's blacks outnumbered its whites, and nearly all those African Americans were enslaved and hated their condition. This fear was nearly realized.

Denmark Vesey had purchased his liberty after winning a lottery and thereafter devoted himself to freeing all others from slavery. In 1822 he organized a revolt in Charleston to take place on July 14, Bastille Day, but several of the conspirators got cold feet and tipped off authorities. The subsequent investigation led to the arrest of 135 people. Thirty-five, including Vesey, were executed; forty-three were sold out of the state; fifteen were acquitted; thirty-eight were questioned and released; and four white men were imprisoned for aiding the conspiracy.[5]

Luck nipped this conspiracy in the bud. Although the near catastrophe provoked greater alertness among most southerners, it failed to prevent mass death and destruction less than a decade later. In August 1831 Nat Turner led a slave revolt in Hampton County, Virginia, that murdered fifty-seven whites, of whom forty-six were women and children. Militia eventually captured Turner and most of his followers. Trials resulted in the execution of Turner and twenty-two others, the transport and sale of ten, and the acquittal of fifteen suspects; perhaps another score of blacks were killed during the roundup.[6]

Educated, articulate black Americans struck nearly as much existential fear in slave owners as murderous ones. The case for slavery weakened as the number of blacks who proved themselves equal to whites in all human endeavors increased. The next round of slavery-related violence erupted in the heart of the nation's capital and nearly engulfed the president himself. But this time a white mob was hunting down blacks who had committed the "crime" of calling for abolition.

Reuben Crandell was a free black who sought to liberate his fellow

African Americans. To this end, in August 1835, he wrote and distributed an abolitionist tract in Washington City. He was arrested, but several other free blacks proclaimed his ideas in the streets. This provoked a white mob to rampage through the black neighborhood where the tracts and speakers had appeared. The whites torched three homes and forced terrified blacks to seek shelter in other neighborhoods. The mob then advanced on the White House, armed with a rumor that one of Jackson's servants was part of the conspiracy. This infuriated Jackson. He met the mob on the White House steps, insisted that his people were innocent of any crime, and ordered the rioters to disperse. Later, he castigated the Washington authorities for their failure immediately to suppress that mob.

David Walker, another black activist, may have died for the cause. Walker was the Boston correspondent for the abolitionist newspaper *Freedom's Journal*. He summarized his views in his 1829 pamphlet, *An Appeal to the Colored Citizens of the World*, which called on African Americans to liberate themselves but stressed the importance of education and nonviolence. Most southerners reacted with outrage when they learned that Walker's newspaper and pamphlet were circulating through the slave underground. Authorities did what they could to suppress the smuggling, and many slavocrats openly called for the author's murder. In conformity with countless hopes, Walker died abruptly on August 6, 1830; many suspected poison was the cause.

Frederick Douglass became this age's most celebrated black leader. He escaped from a Maryland plantation in 1838, changed his name from Bailey to Douglass, and eventually joined the abolitionist movement. His *Narrative of the Life of Frederick Douglass, Written by Himself* caused a sensation when it was published in 1845. Supporters eventually raised enough money to purchase his freedom from his former owner. Without fear of being kidnapped and dragged back into slavery, Douglass went on the lecture circuit and attended numerous meetings of abolitionist and other progressive groups. He worked tirelessly for the realization of America's ideals for blacks until his death in 1895.[7]

The ability of Douglass, Walker, and countless other free blacks to become productive, educated members of a society parallel to that of white America actually undermined the arguments for a different fate advocated by many abolitionists. On December 21, 1816, Henry Clay,

John Randolph, Richard Bland Lee, and a score of other interested citizens met at the Davis Hotel in Washington City. By the meeting's end, they agreed to found the American Colonization Society, dedicated to assisting free blacks and liberated slaves settle in Africa. Over the next three years, the group raised money by selling memberships and lobbying Congress and the White House for federal financial support. Such other prominent Americans as Andrew Jackson, Daniel Webster, Francis Scott Key, Bushrod Washington, and James Monroe became members. In 1819, after becoming president, Monroe had Congress appropriate $100,000 to finance a ship and supplies for the colonists. In 1820 eighty-eight blacks and three members of the American Colonization Society boarded a ship that eventually dropped anchor on a stretch of West African coast that they called Liberia and where they founded their capital, Monrovia, in honor of the president. For the next twenty-seven years, the colony gradually expanded in numbers. In 1847 the Liberians felt secure enough to ask for and receive full independence. Although in this sense the policy succeeded, it was anything but a solution to race relations in America. By 1843 only 4,291 blacks had voluntarily settled in Liberia, whereas the 1840 census counted 2,487,355 slaves in the United States.[8]

Most abolitionists were dedicated to liberating and integrating blacks into American society. This certainly was true of William Lloyd Garrison, the age's most influential and fiery abolitionist leader.[9] At age twenty-five, Garrison joined the American Colonization Society. His intelligence and eloquence so impressed Benjamin Lundy, who published the Baltimore newspaper *The Genius of Universal Emancipation*, that he hired Garrison as a coeditor. Among the features that Garrison introduced to the newspaper was "The Black List" of the latest horror stories of the abuse of slaves by their masters. One of the masters targeted by Garrison won a lawsuit against him. Unable to pay the fine, Garrison was sentenced to six months in prison. He was released after serving seven weeks when the abolitionist and philanthropist Arthur Tappan settled his debt. Garrison moved to Boston, where he vented his views through weekly editions of his newspaper, the *Liberator*, which ran for thirty-five years, from January 1, 1831, to January 1, 1866. Garrison and his followers founded the New England Anti-Slavery Society in Boston's African American Meeting House on January 6, 1832. The following year in Philadelphia, Garrison joined with Lewis and Arthur Tappan to found the American Anti-Slavery Society.

The abolitionist movement split in 1840, when the Tappans led a group to defect from the American Anti-Slavery Society and form the American and Foreign Anti-Slavery Society. The new group emphasized evangelism and gradualism in contrast to Garrison's impassioned calls for the immediate liberation, integration, and full rights of citizenship for slaves. Most other leading abolitionists, like Theodore Weld, Angelina and Sarah Grimké, and Charles Finney, leaned toward the Tappans. While those groups publicly advocated abolition, hundreds of Americans secretly served as "conductors" in the "Underground Railroad," a system of safe houses that helped slaves escape to freedom in northern states and Canada. Many of the women who participated in the abolitionist movement began advocating liberation for their own gender; Lucretia Mott and Elizabeth Cady Stanton began the feminist movement in a convention at Seneca Falls, New York, in 1848.[10]

It took tremendous courage to be an abolitionist. The notion of liberating slaves and granting them and other free blacks all the rights of American citizenship appalled nearly all whites, even those who hated slavery. Those who expressed abolitionist sentiments openly risked suffering assault and outright murder. Antiabolitionist violence peaked in 1835, with records of seventy-nine southern and sixty-eight northern mobs lynching sixty-eight and eight people, respectively. The most sustained violence erupted in New York City in 1834, after the abolitionist movement and black community celebrated, on July 4, the seventh anniversary of the state's outlawing of slavery. After five days of preparation and mobilization, a horde of white racists began a three-day assault on hundreds of blacks and white sympathizers; the mob also looted and burned scores of shops, homes, and churches.[11]

Elijah Lovejoy was a New Englander, minister, journalist, editor, and eventually the abolitionist movement's most famous martyr. As a young man, he moved to St. Louis and started the *St. Louis Observer*, a newspaper with an abolitionist and anti-Jacksonian message. Founding such a paper in a citadel of slavery and Jacksonism was either courageous or foolhardy, depending on one's point of view. After a mob destroyed his printing press and threatened to kill him, Lovejoy courageously purchased a new press and resumed publishing. Another mob destroyed that press, and so he moved to Alton, Illinois, just upriver from St. Louis; bought a new press; and resumed publishing his abolitionist views. A third mob forever silenced him on November 7, 1837.

The most nationally important conflict between slavocrats and abolitionists during Jackson's presidency erupted in Charleston on July 29, 1835, when Postmaster Alfred Huger opened a stuffed mailbag from up north and to his horror discovered hundreds of abolitionist tracts sent by the American Anti-Slavery Society. Huger set aside the tracts and fired off a letter to Postmaster General Amos Kendall asking what he should do with them. That problem was soon taken out of his hands.

Word of the incendiary tracts spread like wildfire. The next day, a mob stormed the post office, seized the bag, and burned it along with effigies of the Tappans, Garrison, and Weld in the public square. South Carolina's government appointed a five-man committee led by former Governor Robert Hayne to inspect all incoming federal mail.

Meanwhile, Kendall sent an ambiguous response to Huger. He acknowledged the importance of the Constitution's First Amendment and federal law: "I am satisfied that the postmaster general has no legal authority to exclude newspapers from the mail, nor prohibit their carriage or delivery on account of their character or tendency." Yet he questioned whether the law should protect the voices of those who sought its destruction. The tracts appeared to be "most inflammatory and incendiary—and insurrectionary in the highest degree." While "we owe an obligation to the laws," he wrote, there is "a higher one to the communities in which we live."[12] So what should Huger do? It was his unenviable call.

Jackson was of two minds on the issue. He was angry that a mob had looted a federal post office but was outraged that the abolitionists had dared send antislavery tracts to a slave state. He called for having the author's names "exposed thro the publik journals as subscribers to the wicked plan of exciting the negroes to insurrection and massacre."[13] Yet, surprisingly, he agreed with Kendall that the federal government could not censor the mail. He was willing to go along with whatever side congressional majorities took on the issue. But Congress was in recess until December.

In his annual address to Congress, Jackson raised the issue of what limits, if any, should be imposed on free speech. His argued that Congress should enact a law prohibiting the dissemination of incendiary tracts through the mail. Ironically, the most powerful voice against such a law came from South Carolina senator John Calhoun, who naturally rooted his objection in states' rights. He insisted on a bill that forced the federal government to respect any state and local restrictions on freedom of the press. A majority in Congress rejected both censorship proposals. The Post Office Act that passed on July 2, 1836, forbade postmasters from censoring the mail. Although Jackson reluctantly signed the bill, he sent word to the postmasters that he would not enforce it.

The same Congress that upheld freedom of speech through the mail imposed a gag rule on itself. Petitioning those in power is among the rights protected by the First Amendment. Each year thousands of petitions arrived in Congress and were distributed among the various committees for discussion and action. No group submitted more petitions to Congress than abolitionists.

Slavocrats condemned these abolitionist petitions as incendiary and seditious. In the Senate and House, John Calhoun and James Hammond, respectively, introduced measures whereby abolitionist petitions would be automatically discarded without being submitted to a committee, let alone the floor and debate. Majorities voted down these rules as unconstitutional.

Vice President Martin Van Buren hoped to finesse this objection by proposing that Congress receive the petitions but automatically and permanently table them. This way, Congress could maintain the appearance of the First Amendment while avoiding its contentious substance. He talked South Carolina congressman Henry Pinckney into writing up his proposal but failed to find a Senate sponsor.

Pinckney did so and submitted it on May 26, 1836. To the dismay of the rule's supporters, slavocrats and abolitionists alike condemned it but for opposite reasons. Defenders of slavery wailed that it did not go far enough to stifle any mention of the issue. Those who championed freedom denounced it as a "gag rule" that grossly violated the Constitution's First Amendment. Nonetheless the motion carried by 117 to 68.

John Quincy Adams, the former president and now the representative from his home district in Massachusetts, led the effort to resist this assault on the Constitution. He bypassed the censors by receiving petitions and presenting them in speeches on the House floor. Meanwhile, the House restriction spurred abolitionists to redouble their petition efforts. By early 1839, 1,496 antislavery petitions with 163,845 signatures from 101,850 people had piled up in the office of the clerk who kept them from being formally introduced.[14]

Conservatives retaliated against Adams and other congressmen sympathetic to abolitionism by getting the House to approve even stricter censorship rules by in a close vote of 114 to 108 in 1840. Adams redoubled his efforts to bring antislavery petitions to the House floor. In 1842 he presented one from a town in his district whose inhabitants requested the dissolution of the United States so that they would not be associated with the evil of slavery. Slavocrats angrily motioned that Adams be censured for violating the House rules.

This was a strategic mistake. Adams, then seventy-four years old, seized his chance to eloquently attack slavery and triumphantly present two hundred other abolitionist petitions during the week of hearings. Thus did the slavocrats invoke the very debate they had tried to stifle with their censorship rule. During the course of the hearings, Adams famously asked, "Am I gagged or not?" In the end, he escaped censure. Two years later, in December 1844, the House voted to lift the censorship rule by a vote of 108 to 80.

Adams's most famous attack on slavery was before the Supreme Court. In 1839 fifty-three slaves led by Jose Cinqué took over the Spanish ship, the *Amistad*, on which they were being transported along Cuba's coast. They killed all the crew members except the pilot and forced him to sail them back to Africa. He sailed them instead toward the United States. An American coast guard vessel intercepted the *Amistad* and escorted it to New Haven, Connecticut, where officials debated whether to release or incarcerate the Africans. Meanwhile, President Van Buren accepted a Spanish diplomatic request to transfer the Africans back to Cuba. Lewis Tappan sued for their release in a federal court on the grounds that they had been wrongfully enslaved under international law, which had abolished the slave trade, and thus had the right to free themselves by any appropriate means. The district federal judge ruled in the Africans' favor and ordered them sent back to Africa. The Van Buren White House appealed. The case—*United States v. the Amistad*—went before the Supreme Court, and Adams mounted a brilliant case for the defendants. The Supreme Court rendered its verdict on March 9, 1841. By a vote of six to one, the Africans were free to go. Adams's case was so legally airtight that even Supreme Court Justice Roger Taney, a zealous slavocrat, voted with the majority.[15]

This was the last progressive Supreme Court ruling for several decades. John Marshall had died on July 6, 1835, after serving as the chief justice for thirty-five years. He went to his grave deeply pessimistic about America's future. He wrote fellow justice Joseph Story, "I yield slowly and reluctantly to the conviction that our constitution cannot last."[16]

Jackson's choice to replace Marshall as chief justice was Roger Taney. A fervent Jacksonian and the president's hatchet man for looting the bank, Taney faced fierce resistance from Senate progressives. As Jackson mulled strategies for pressuring the Senate to approve Taney, another vacancy opened on the court when Justice Gabriel Duval resigned. The president proposed a package deal of Taney and Philip Barbour on December 28, 1835. The Senate Judiciary Committee tabled the nominations.

The deadlock eventually broke in Jackson's favor. Four new senators took the seats of men who had resigned for varying reasons; each replacement was a Jacksonian. On March 15, 1836, Thomas Hart Benton, Jackson's key Senate ally, determined that he had rounded up enough votes for confirmation. Taney was approved by 29 to 15 and Barbour by 30 to 11.

With the addition of Taney and Barbour, the Supreme Court was now solidly Jacksonian. Old Hickory had already seated three of his followers—John McLean, Henry Baldwin, and James Wayne—on the seven-man court, yet Marshall had continued to hold sway with usually unanimous positions because his powerful reason trumped emotional ideological convictions. Jackson would seat two more justices on the eve of his departure from the White House, when his congressional allies passed a bill expanding the Supreme Court from seven to nine. Taney's appointment decisively shifted the Supreme Court's ideological orientation from Hamiltonism to Jacksonism. On the question of race, this revolution would culminate with the 1857 Dred Scott decision, whereby Taney denied not just citizenship but humanity to black Americans.[17]

Of course, Jackson's packing of the Supreme Court with slavocrats did not prevent but helped provoke the ultimate nightmare for "masters" and all other Americans—a horrendous Civil War in which 750,000 Americans died, hundreds of thousands more were maimed, and billions of dollars' worth of property was destroyed. From the ruins, a race emerged with the shackles of slavery forever broken.

12

The Trail of Tears

Toward the aborigines of the country, no one can indulge a more friendly feeling than myself.

ANDREW JACKSON

It would be as cruel as unjust to compel the aborigines to abandon the graves of their fathers and seek a home in a distant land.

ANDREW JACKSON

How under these circumstances can you live in the country you now
occupy? Your condition must become worse and worse, and you
will ultimately disappear, as so many tribes have done before you.

ANDREW JACKSON

I concluded it was best to obey our Great Father and say nothing contrary to his wishes.

BLACK HAWK

Andrew Jackson's attitudes toward Indians were a complex mixture of
condescension, loathing, admiration, paternalism for them as a people, and greed for their land. Yet hatred rarely animated his racism. He

bullied recalcitrant Indians like he bullied anyone who opposed him. It was rarely personal.

To those who accused Jackson of being a vicious Indian hater who wielded all his powers to destroy the native peoples, he had this reply, "Toward the aborigines of the country, no one can indulge a more friendly feeling than myself." He insisted that his policies actually served their best interests. The Indians were savages bound for extinction. By taking their ancestral land and sending them westward, he saved them from being immediately overrun and either wiped out or assimilated by white settlers: "It puts an end to all possible danger of collision between the authorities of the general and state governments on account of the Indians. . . . It will separate the Indians from immediate contract with settlements of whites, free them from the power of the states, enable them to pursue happiness in their own way and under their own rude institutions; will retard the progress of decay." Yet he also acknowledged that the westward push would only delay the inevitable extinction of the Indian way of life. It will "cause them gradually, under the protection of government and through the influence of good counsels, to cast off their savage habits and become an interesting, civilizing and Christian community."[1]

In justifying his Indian policies, Jackson was being more sincere than cynical. He shared a view held by countless Americans over the centuries. He was an unyielding and decisive perpetrator of the practice of stealing Indian lands and destroying their cultures, which originated with the first settlement at Jamestown in 1607. Thereafter, for nearly three centuries, one tribe after another was driven from their homes because they were decimated by war or disease and the settlers took their land with or without a treaty. However rapacious and violent this process of land theft was, there was never a crown or federal policy of genocide or the mass murder of a defiant tribe, let alone the entire Indian race; King Philip's War of 1675–76 was the closest a colonial government came to genocide. Ethnic cleansing or the deliberate destruction of a tribe's culture was not an official policy until the 1887 Dawes Act. Before then ethnic cleansing certainly occurred, but mostly as the sporadic by-product of trade, intermarriage, and Christian proselytizing.[2]

Congressional majorities mirrored Jackson's views of the Indians. Each house produced a version of what became known as the Indian

Removal Act. The Senate passed its bill by 28 to 19 on April 26, 1830. The House vote was nearly a dead heat, 102 to 97. A conference committee reconciled the differences between the bills. Both houses voted for the final version, and Jackson signed it into law on May 28, 1830.

Jackson now had uncontested power to realize his vision. During his eight years as president, the United States signed more than seventy treaties and acquired more than 100 million acres of land east of the Mississippi River in exchange for $68 million and 32 million acres of land west of the Mississippi. As a result, more than forty-five thousand Indians were removed or resettled; perhaps as many as one in ten died on the way to their "promised land." It was a stunningly lopsided victory of America's military, economy, and population over the Indians, but the cost in the violation of America's constitutional and moral values was incalculable.[3]

Jackson later admitted that "it would be as cruel as unjust to compel the aborigines to abandon the graves of their fathers and seek a home in a distant land."[4] Having said so, he lacked the intellectual honesty and emotional maturity to admit that in reality his policies had blatantly done just that. Despite all contradictory evidence, he clung to his assertion that the tribes had voluntarily rendered their lands and migrated toward the setting sun. In his mind, succumbing to bribes and bayonets had nothing to do with what liberal "do gooders" dubbed the "Trail of Tears."

The president himself presided over treaty negotiations with the Chickasaws in August 1830. To them, he expressed his "earnest desire . . . that you may be . . . preserved as a nation; and this . . . can only be done . . . by your consent to remove to a country beyond the Mississippi . . . where . . . you can live contented." He then darkly warned them that should they "reject this opportunity," they would become subject to the state and "by becoming amalgamated with the whites, your national character will be lost" and "you must disappear and be forgotten."[5] The Chickasaws protested but in the end had no choice but surrender. They finally signed the treaty thrust before them on August 31, 1830. Accusations of malfeasance in Congress forced the Jackson administration to renegotiate the treaty, the final version of which was not signed until October 30, 1832.

Meanwhile, the Choctaws and Creeks also bowed before the Jackson administration's demands and bribes. In signing the Treaty of Dancing Rabbit Creek on September 15, 1830, the Choctaw chiefs promised to migrate in three divisions over the next years until not a single Choctaw remained behind. The Senate ratified that treaty on February 25, 1831. The Creeks surrendered their lands with a treaty signed on March 24, 1832.

The Cherokees were one of three eastern tribes that dug in their heels. Like every tribe, they faced the cruel choice of assimilate, adapt, flee, or die before the crushing advance of American civilization. They chose to adapt to American economic practices and political institutions. In 1827 they devised a democratic constitution inspired by America's. Most lived on farms that they owned and tilled themselves; a few amassed enough wealth to emulate southern aristocrats and establish plantations worked by slaves. Many lived in towns and enriched themselves through a variety of trades. Cherokee silversmith Sequoyah developed an alphabet, and Cherokees became literate in their own language and the white man's. The Cherokee *Phoenix* newspaper had parallel columns in both languages. But despite these stunning accomplishments, most whites clung to the conceit that the Cherokees were savages with land for the taking.[6]

Georgia spearheaded the campaign to dispossess the Cherokees. On December 20, 1828, the legislature passed and Governor John Forsyth signed a bill that asserted Georgia's legal jurisdiction over all Indian lands by June 1830. The drive to steal Cherokee land grew into a frenzy when gold was discovered in their territory in July 1829. A horde of whites rushed into the region, staked claims, and drove off the Cherokee owners. Georgia's legislature passed and the governor signed laws forbidding Cherokees from mining gold on any land, from suing or testifying in court against whites, and from meeting politically unless it were to cede land to Georgia.[7]

The federal government had a legal and moral duty to protect the Cherokees from trespassers, thieves, and murderers. President Jackson soon revealed which side of the law he stood on. He had all federal troops withdrawn and replaced by Georgia's militia, which blatantly aided the invaders.

The Cherokee National Council and Principal Chief John Ross debated three responses to the American injustices—they could fight, yield, or sue. They chose to sue for the protection of their rights in federal court. Their champion was William Wirt, a former attorney general who was appalled by Georgia's blatant violations of the Constitution and morality. Wirt grounded the Cherokee suit against Georgia in the argument that the tribe was a long-established and legally recognized sovereign nation and thus was immune from Georgia's law.

The Supreme Court decided *Cherokee Nation v. Georgia* on July 18, 1831. Chief Justice John Marshall found that the "Acts of Georgia are repugnant to the Constitution, laws, and treaties of the United States." But he also rejected Wirt's contention that the Cherokees or any other Indian tribe were sovereign nations. Instead, the Indians were "domestic dependent nations" that were "subject to the United States as a ward to a guardian." All Indian lands were ultimately owned not by the tribes that inhabited them but by the federal government.[8]

Jackson had always hated John Marshall for his assertion of judicial review and the subsequent court decisions rooted in this principle. His hatred exploded into rage when he heard the *Cherokee Nation v. Georgia* decision. The president is alleged to have exclaimed, "John Marshall has made his decision, now let him enforce it."[9] Whether or not he did, the retort certainly vented his prejudices and bullying spirit.

Jackson had upped the ante in February 1831, by informing Congress that he would no longer uphold the 1802 Indian Intercourse Act, which extended to Indians federal protection from rapacious whites. The announcement had rendered official his existing policy. When Thomas McKenney, who had led the Bureau of Indian Affairs since its creation in 1824, protested, Jackson fired him.

Meanwhile, Georgians predictably erupted in rage at Marshall's ruling. The legislature was dead set to defy the Supreme Court and savage anyone else who backed that ruling and the Cherokees. In December 1831 it passed a law forbidding whites from entering Indian lands without a state permit after March 1, 1832. The measure was designed to thwart sympathetic lawyers and Christians from aiding the Cherokees. Georgia officials arrested the missionaries Samuel Worcester and Elizur Butler for violating this law and gleefully sentenced them to four years of hard labor in the state penitentiary.

The missionaries sued. Not surprisingly, they lost at each level of Georgia's court system. They appealed to the U.S. Supreme Court. On March 3, 1832, John Marshall ruled in *Worcester v. Georgia* that all

Georgia laws affecting the Cherokees were unconstitutional and thus must be rescinded and the missionaries released.[10]

In throwing his administration's weight behind Georgia and against the Cherokees, Jackson unwittingly contradicted the arguments he had made against South Carolina's nullification doctrine. He dismissed any notion of being hypocritical in doing so. What mattered was not intellectual or legal consistency but the assertion of his will. Georgia's courts, legislature, and governor waved the nullification banner by rejecting being bound by law to the United States and its governmental institutions. Jackson initially backed the defiant Georgians to the hilt, declaring that the Supreme Court "cannot coerce Georgia to yield to its mandate."[11] But then South Carolina's leaders hurled his words against him to assert their own nullification arguments. Jackson finally admitted angrily that championing Georgia's assertion of nullification was hampering his attempts to deter South Carolina's assertion of the same principle. He quietly encouraged the Georgians to release the missionaries, who were becoming increasingly powerful symbols of martyrdom to humanitarians. Governor Wilson Lumpkin ordered them freed on January 14, 1833, after they had endured seventeen grueling months in prison.

To deprive the Cherokees of their land, Jackson again wielded the strategy of talking only with the minority of chiefs willing to sell, usually because they had pocketed huge bribes to do so. He refused to recognize the Cherokee people's own National Council and principal chief.

Nonetheless, Jackson accepted Ross's request for a meeting. They shook hands at the White House on February 5, 1834. The chief began by asking the president to take the Cherokee side in their dispute with Georgia. Jackson bluntly refused and informed Ross that the tribe would have to resettle far west of the Mississippi River. Ross then asked for $20 million for their territory along with millions of dollars more in compensation for all the times the United States had violated its treaties with the tribe. For this, Jackson sent Ross to War Secretary Lewis Cass, who informed him that the Senate would pay not a penny more than $5 million for title to all Cherokee land and to cover any previous claims.

Ross and the National Council boycotted any treaty negotiations. Jackson had several score "chiefs" led by John Ridge rounded up to meet with the American commissioners. They signed a draft treaty on March

14, 1835. In return for surrendering their ancestral lands, the Cherokees would receive $4.5 million to distribute equally for each man, woman, and child, and an equal swath of territory in the Far West to live on. As usual, Jackson tried to soften a tribe's rage and sorrow at what they were being forced to give up by insisting that they were being saved from oblivion: "How under these circumstances can you live in the country you now occupy? Your condition must become worse and worse, and you will ultimately disappear, as so many tribes have done before you."[12]

The National Council rejected the treaty, and the White House summoned the unofficial chiefs back to council. Once again, a generous distribution of bribes convinced nearly all of them to rubber-stamp the document thrust before them. By a vote of 79 to 7, the chiefs signed the Treaty of New Echota on December 29, 1835; the new treaty essentially repeated the draft treaty's tenets.

Ross campaigned to urge first his people and then the U.S. Senate to repudiate the treaty. He and his followers secured the signature of twelve thousand Cherokees in Georgia and 3,250 in South Carolina to protest the treaty. He gathered scores of documents revealing all the corruption, deceit, and bullying that had led to the series of treaties that the United States had forced upon the Cherokees. Ross spent months in Washington in the spring of 1836 lobbying senators to reject the treaty and let the Cherokees stay in their ancestral homes.

Ross's efforts nearly succeeded. The Senate ratified the Treaty of New Echota by a vote of 31 to 15, just above the two-thirds requirement. Jackson signed the treaty into law on May 23, 1836. The Cherokees had to vacate their land within two years of ratification.

Of 18,000 Cherokees who embarked on that long road, the government officially recorded 424 as dying along the way. Some native sources estimate that at least four thousand graves marked the Trail of Tears. North Carolina allowed several hundred Cherokees living in the state's western mountains to remain; many of their descendants live there today.[13]

Jackson's Indian troubles were not confined to the defiant Cherokees. As the chief of a band of Sauk and Fox, Black Hawk faced a terrible dilemma in early 1832. For years, the U.S. government had failed to uphold an 1804 treaty that guaranteed the tribe land straddling the upper Mississippi River between Illinois and Iowa and an annual annuity. The discovery of lead around Galena, Illinois, had led to an invasion of miners and settlers that drove the Sauk and Fox west of the Mississippi. Now Black Hawk's people were starving, and he had no way to feed them. Drought and storms had destroyed much of the autumn 1831 harvest in their farmland along the Iowa side of the Mississippi. In April 1832 Black Hawk led his people east of the river in a desperate search for food.[14]

Upon hearing terrified accounts of the "invasion," Illinois governor John Reynolds called out the militia and sent an urgent message to the White House for military aid. Jackson ordered Gens. Winfield Scott and Henry Atkinson to muster their commands and hurry to the region.

Fighting erupted on May 14, when militia fired on a delegation dispatched by Black Hawk to assure the whites of his peaceful intent and to request food. The Indians retaliated by routing a militia force at the Battle of Silliman's Run. Black Hawk then led his people north as different army and militia columns pursued. Col. Henry Dodge's troops caught and defeated Black Hawk's band at Wisconsin Heights on July 21. Black Hawk abandoned his hope of eventually leading his people to Canada and instead veered west toward safety beyond the Mississippi. They almost made it. On August 1 they were building rafts on a Mississippi riverbank a few miles south of the mouth of the Bad Axe River when two American forces converged on them: General Atkinson and thirteen hundred regulars and militia on land and Capt. Joseph Throckmorton with troops packed aboard a steamboat on the river. Atkinson's troops attacked and slaughtered or captured most of the five hundred men, women, and children along the shore. Black Hawk and a hundred or so others managed to escape across the river. The survivors found no shelter there. America's Sioux allies tracked them down and brought sixty-eight scalps and twenty-two captives to Atkinson's camp. Black Hawk and a few followers surrendered on August 27.

Jackson used the Black Hawk War as yet another excuse for his Indian removal policy. To those who criticized the mass deaths inflicted by American troops on the Indians, he retorted that the Fox and Sauk deserved it because of "their unprovoked aggression." Furthermore, he lauded the death toll's deterrent value: "It is to be hoped that its impression will be permanent and salutary."[15]

Two ancient warriors met on April 26, 1833, when Black Hawk was ushered before Jackson at the White House. The president was anything but cordial as he sternly informed Black Hawk that he and his chiefs would be incarcerated in Fortress Monroe to ensure that his people lived up to the peace treaty. Black Hawk accepted the harsh news stoically, later explaining, "I concluded it was best to obey our Great Father and say nothing contrary to his wishes."[16]

No eastern tribe resisted Jackson's campaign to steal their land and drive them like cattle far beyond the Mississippi more fiercely than the Seminoles.[17] Jackson's administration bribed and bullied seven Seminole chiefs into signing away their land with the Treaty of Payne's Landing on May 9, 1832. Like other tribes, most Seminoles exploded in wrath when the chiefs explained what they had done. A young chief named Osceola articulated the most persuasive arguments. The tribal council refused to ratify the treaty.

Upon learning this decision, Jackson sent the Seminoles a stern message warning that if they did not yield, "I have directed the commanding officer to remove you by force."[18] This alarmed Florida governor John Eaton, Jackson's friend, former secretary of war, and Peggy's husband, who conveyed his fear to the president that any strong-armed measures would provoke rather than cow the Seminoles. Jackson, as usual, dismissed this view so contrary to his own. But Eaton's fear was tragically realized.

Certainly no eastern tribe was more capable of resisting. The lands of other tribes were diminishing islands amid seas of ever larger white populations; army forces could easily surround and destroy any resistance. In contrast, the Seminoles had the entire Florida peninsula of nearly impenetrable swamplands and forests behind them. Should the army drive them from their villages in northern Florida, the Seminoles could simply withdraw southward deeper into that marshy wilderness.

The war erupted in August 1835, shortly after troops seized Osceola, forced him to sign the treaty, and then released him. Osceola led his followers not westward but to war. For the first five months, the fighting was a sporadic series of hit-and-run attacks by Seminole war parties on frontier farms and army patrols with relatively few casualties on either side. Then, on December 23, a Seminole war party wiped out Maj. Francis Dade and his two companies of 110 troops, while losing only three killed.

News of the humiliating massacre infuriated Jackson, but he was hamstrung to destroy the Seminoles. He was already immersed in the French and Texas crises. The two top-ranking American generals, Edmund Gaines and Winfield Scott, despised each other and refused to cooperate. Although the army numbered around seventy-five hundred men, they were scattered among fifty-three posts across the country.

Jackson ordered Scott to take command. Although Scott proved his brilliance against regular troops in the War of 1812 and the Mexican War, he was ill-suited to fighting Indians, especially the Seminoles, who were so familiar with Florida's terrain and climate. He devised and launched a plan for three columns to converge in the heart of the Seminole territory. The columns got lost, ate up their supplies, and found themselves bogged down in the swamps and forests. Warriors ambushed patrols and picked off stragglers. When a column approached a village, the Seminoles simply abandoned it for another site deeper in the wilderness. Scott finally called off the campaign.

Jackson shook up Florida's political and military leadership. He replaced Eaton with Richard Call as the governor; Call had served with Jackson in his Creek campaign. He ordered Scott to yield his command to Gen. Duncan Clinch. When Clinch declined the post, Jackson handed it to Call. Despite his experience fighting Indians, Call was no more capable than Scott of running down the Seminoles.

This second failure enraged Jackson. He ranted against the "mismanagement of all the military operations in Florida, all of which are so humiliating to our military character, that it fills me with pain & mortification."[19] The failures hurt Jackson's pride and empowered his enemies in Congress and the press to attack him.[20]

With all this assailing his mind, in November 1836 Jackson replaced Call with Gen. Thomas Jessup and ordered him to destroy the Seminoles "before Congress meets." This was a tough job given that Congress would reconvene in December. Although Jessup missed the deadline by nearly eighteen months, his troops eventually captured three thousand Seminoles, including Osceola, who was treacherously taken under a truce flag on October 22, 1837. Osceola was chained in Fort Marion, at St. Augustine, where he died on January 31, 1838. The other captives were herded to their new homes west of the Mississippi. But more than a thousand Seminoles evaded the troops and fought fiercely for their freedom.

By then, Martin Van Buren was in the White House. The new president relieved Jessup and placed Gen. Zachary Taylor in charge of mopping up the resistance. The war sputtered on through 1842, when the government finally called it off. Although troops captured most of the refugees and dispatched them westward, hundreds more evaded capture and fought a third war against the United States from 1856 to 1858.

The American "victory" in the Second Seminole War came at the terrible cost of more than $40 million and 1,446 dead soldiers, who mostly succumbed to disease. How many Seminoles died in the fighting will never be known.[21] During these seven years, Jackson frequently vented his disgust at how the war was being fought. He lamented that the "Florida war from the first to the present time has been a succession of blunders and misfortune." He explained a simple but effective means to vanquish the Indians: "The commanding general ought to find where their women are, and with his combined forces by forced marches reach and capture them. This done, they will at once surrender."[22]

Theoretically, winning an Indian war was indeed as simple as Jackson asserted. But every war poses unique challenges. In nearly three centuries of fighting Indians across the continent, no terrain was more advantageous for the defenders and more baffling for the invaders than that of Florida.

The two Seminole wars revealed the limits of American power during the Age of Jackson. More important, ever since then they have provided vital lessons in the nature of fighting an insurgency in hostile terrain. Alas, given the track record of America's counterinsurgency wars, it appears that few commanders have bothered to study these lessons. The "trail of tears" in American history has not been confined to the paths of vanquished Indians.

13

The World Beyond

This cannot protect our national character and must
at last lead to war—the only way to preserve our honor
is to carry into effect my maxim "Ask nothing
but what is right and permit nothing that is wrong."

ANDREW JACKSON

We occupy a high standing in all Europe, and will now take
our stand on a level with the greatest powers of Europe.

ANDREW JACKSON

During Jackson's eight years in the White House, four secretaries of state—Martin Van Buren, Edward Livingston, Louis McLane, and John Forsyth—served him. The turnover had little effect on the administration's diplomacy. Each man was able enough and quickly took charge. More important, each acted as the president's secretary. Jackson was his own man when it came to both foreign and domestic policy. He decided what to do and had each secretary realize his decisions as best as he could.[1]

Although Britain remained America's largest trading partner, the volume could have been even bigger. Six decades after the United States won independence, the British persisted in restricting American merchants from its West Indian colonies. Jackson sent a message to Congress on May 26, 1830, asking for the authority to resolve the deadlock on the basis of reciprocity. Three days later, Congress granted this authority with a bill that let the president open American ports to British vessels filled with West Indies products if the British let American ships drop anchor in West Indian ports.

Prime Minister Arthur Wellesley, Duke of Wellington, thought this proposal was reasonable enough. He sent word that his cabinet was willing to accept it if the Americans moved first. Upon learning of this concession, Jackson proclaimed on October 5, 1830, the opening of American ports to British vessels bearing West Indian goods. Wellington's government announced the opening of West Indian ports to American traders on November 7, 1830.

Meanwhile, another dispute festered much closer to home. America's northeastern border with Canada was vaguely defined in the 1783 Treaty of Paris, whereby Britain accepted an independent United States. The American and British claims overlapped. Jackson did not believe that America's case for the full extent of its claim was strong. Maine's political leadership, however, refused any compromise. Jackson offered Maine the proceeds from the sale of a million federal acres in Michigan if it cut back its claim. Maine refused.

The King of the Netherlands offered to mediate. Jackson agreed. Unfortunately, the envoy Jackson sent to the Hague, William Preble, was no diplomat. When the king split the difference between the two countries, Preble rejected the compromise, and the British in turn severed negotiations.

Upon learning what had happened, Jackson convened his cabinet to mull the deal spurned by Preble. The consensus was to oppose it, mostly to avoid offending Maine and the other northern states that backed its claim. Jackson asked Secretary of State Edward Livingston to find a solution. Try as he might, Livingston could not bridge the chasm between the parties. The Maine dispute was the only significant conflict with Britain that the Jackson White House was unable to resolve.

Another dispute flared between the United States and Britain in 1831. When a storm wrecked an American ship transporting 164 slaves on a Bahamas reef, British authorities freed the survivors. The owners complained to the Jackson administration. The president had Secretary of State Livingston demand compensation from the British government. For years, the British rejected the demand but ultimately paid it in 1836.

The Jackson administration won trade deals with the Ottoman Empire and Russia by manipulating the perennial animosities between them. This strategy first worked with the Turks, who agreed to a treaty that granted most-favored-nation status and opened the Black Sea to American trade. The American mission in St. Petersburg pointed to this deal with Russia's ancient enemy and asked for the same. When the Russians expressed an interest, Jackson appointed John Randolph, the mercurial Virginia senator, as the minister. Randolph had no sooner arrived at his post when he abruptly left for home. Jackson then sent over James Buchanan, a prominent Pennsylvania politician. Buchanan succeeded in signing a trade treaty based on the most-favored-nation principle on December 18, 1832, a half year after he arrived in Russia. This was quite a coup. The United States was the first country with which Russia agreed to extend most-favored-nation status.

Although a generation had passed since the end of the Revolutionary and Napoleonic Wars, some European states still refused to pay for seizures of American vessels and their cargoes during that era. Americans had claims against a number of countries, including Russia, the Netherlands, Portugal, Spain, Denmark, and the Kingdom of Naples, but France owned more than the others combined. The universal excuse for not paying up was that prize courts had already rendered unappealable judgments.

Had Jackson upheld the long-standing "freedom of the seas" principle, the deadlock would have persisted. Instead, he indicated his willingness to settle financially for less. The first breakthrough came with Denmark. In a convention signed on March 27, 1830, the Danes agreed to pay $650,000 of $2,662,280 of outstanding claims.[2]

American claims against France amounted to $6,256,647. For decades, Paris had stonewalled any American diplomats who raised the issue of the seized vessels. Finally a political upheaval appeared to offer a diplomatic opening. In July 1830 a revolution toppled the absolute monarchy of Charles X and established a constitutional monarchy led by Louis Philippe.

Jackson launched a diplomatic offensive. He lauded France's new king and his liberal revolution in his December 1830 address to Congress. He had William Rives, his minister in Paris, indicate his willingness to settle for less if French markets widened for American merchants. Louis Philippe agreed to talks. After several tough rounds of haggling, a treaty was signed on July 4, 1831, that required France to pay about $5 million in installments over six years and cut its import tariffs on cotton in exchange for lower American tariffs on French wines. The Senate unanimously approved the treaty after Jackson submitted it on December 6, 1831.

Jackson followed up the successes with Denmark and France by signaling his ministers posted elsewhere to press their claims. The next deal came swiftly: a treaty with Portugal was signed on January 19, 1832. After that, the diplomacy was tougher. The Kingdom of Naples rejected any talks. John Nelson, the minister, advised Jackson to pressure Naples with military force. Jackson agreed. He penned a letter to the king and sent it via the frigate USS *United States*, which anchored with its cannons pointed to the crowded city. A treaty was signed on October 14, 1832, whereby the kingdom would pay the United States $1,755,450, a significant settlement. In contrast, in a treaty signed with Spain on February 17, 1834, America received only $600,000, or about half of its claim. Yet Cornelius Van Ness, the diplomat, reckoned that was the best possible deal given the chaos engulfing Spain after King Ferdinand VII died in 1833. He met blunt refusals every time he requested that Spain open Cuba to American trade and recognize the independence of its former colonies elsewhere in the Western Hemisphere.

Getting a legal promise from France to pay up was the easy part. Actually securing payment took years as France's Chamber of Deputies refused to appropriate the money. In his latest cabinet shakeup, Jackson named Edward Livingston his minister to France and had Louis McLane take his place as secretary of state. Livingston got a sympathetic hearing from the French foreign minister, but he could only express his regret that nothing could move a majority in the Chamber of Deputies to honor the treaty. Livingston sent back word of the deadlock along with the advice to retaliate by cutting off trade with France.

This message infuriated Jackson. Simply severing trade would not satisfy American honor. He convened his cabinet and told them he would ask Congress for the authority to issue letters of marque to privateers to prey on French shipping. Louis McLane and Lewis Cass, the respective secretaries of state and war, promptly agreed. Treasury Secretary Roger Taney was bold enough to urge caution. Jackson was already in the midst of one war—against the monster bank—and he was poised to eliminate the national debt. Entering a war with France might jeopardize these priorities.

Jackson reluctantly agreed to one final diplomatic effort. McLane summoned France's minister and warned him that his country had better pay or prepare for war. A frigate was dispatched to France with the same message for Livingston to convey to the king. Jackson explained to Livingston why he had rejected severing trade relations for sterner measures: "This cannot protect our national character and must at last lead to war—the only way to preserve our honor is to carry into effect my maxim 'Ask nothing but what is right and permit nothing that is wrong.'"[3]

Livingston redoubled his efforts to no avail. Jackson had a report written on the French failure to honor their promise and sent it to Congress, along with a request to authorize retaliation with military force. The House Foreign Relations Committee, headed by Jackson's nemesis Henry Clay, issued its own report on January 6, 1835. Although the committee largely concurred with Jackson's view, it called for giving the Chamber of Deputies one last chance.

Louis Philippe and his government knew of the ultimatum before Livingston delivered it. The king announced that he was recalling Louis Serurier, his minister to the United States. This was a serious step toward war. The Chamber of Deputies convened in March and began a debate on the issue that ground on for weeks. The deputies again voted on whether to pay on April 18, 1835. This time the measure passed by a vote of 289 to 137.

This vote appeared to stymie the possibility of war between the United States and France. But there was a final snag. Even after passing a law to do so, the French still refused to pay. They had been insulted by Jackson's belligerent saber rattling. They demanded that he explain his behavior before they handed over a penny.

Nothing could have been better calculated to enrage Jackson. He instructed Livingston to do anything compatible with American honor to convince the French to fulfill their legal duty. But the entire French government, including Louis Philippe, had rallied around the excuse not to pay. When Livingston resigned in disgust, Jackson replaced him with Thomas Barton, the deputy minister in Paris. Barton did what he could to pressure the French government to fulfill its pledge but came away empty-handed. Barton's last diplomatic card was to leave. He set sail for America in November 1835 and arrived in Washington on January 14, 1836.

After debriefing Barton, the president once again played the dangerous game of brinksmanship with France. He sent to Congress all the correspondence and reports on relations between the two countries, noting the seriousness of France's "refusal to execute the treaty except on terms incompatible with the honor and independence of the United States." He called for Congress to empower him to defend "that which we owe our constituents, our national character, and to the world." He specifically asked for Congress to build up the navy and costal fortifications.[4]

Fortunately, Britain interceded with an offer to mediate the conflict. Jackson accepted on February 3, 1836, with the condition that he would never explain his behavior to any foreign government. The British talked the king and his government into reconsidering their stance. When they received word of Jackson's latest message to Congress, they accepted it as an adequate explanation even though it was even more belligerent than his previous message. Sheltered by the diplomatic fig leaf, Paris promised to promptly pay what was owed. Jackson informed Congress on February 22, 1836, that the crisis was over. This time, the French were good to their word and settled their bill on May 10, 1836.

Jackson exulted in his diplomatic victory: "We occupy a high standing in all Europe, and will now take our stand on a level with the greatest powers of Europe."[5] The great powers might have begged to differ with the president on the exact status of the United States in their eyes. A chasm always splits how Americans and Europeans view the United States, and it is usually unbridgeable.

Nonetheless, Jackson had proved his worth as America's diplomat in chief. Indeed, on the compensation issue alone, he far outshone his predecessor. In all, the Jackson White House recovered $12.5 million in claims, whereas Adams, who was renowned for his diplomatic experience, was unable to recover a dime.[6]

Jackson did not resolve all of America's international disputes with reason and handshakes. On February 7, 1831, Sumatran pirates swarmed aboard and plundered an American ship. Jackson did not learn of the attack for half a year. He authorized Capt. John Downes of the frigate *Potomac* to set sail for those waters and negotiate compensation from the local ruler. In the spirit of Jackson himself, Downes violated his instructions. On February 6, 1832, he ordered his men to bombard and burn the town of Quallah Battoo. Having demonstrated his might, Downes forced the local rulers to pay compensation and promise not to engage in further acts of piracy. When Jackson issued a report on Downes's "gunboat diplomacy" to Congress, the Whigs condemned him for waging war without a formal congressional declaration.

Although Jackson bristled at the criticism, he dispatched Edmund Roberts, a sea captain with years of experience in those waters, on a peace and trade mission. Roberts signed a treaty with Siam's king on March 30, 1833, and Muscat's sultan on October 3, 1833. The Muscat treaty was especially far reaching as it opened the markets of Oman and Zanzibar in East Africa, which Muscat ruled. The Senate ratified both treaties, thus inaugurating America's formal diplomatic relations with parts of the Indian Ocean basin.

Jackson then sent Roberts on his most challenging mission. In April 1835 Roberts sailed for Japan to open that hermit realm to American trade. For more than two centuries, the Tokugawa dynasty that ruled Japan had sealed it off from the world except for the Port of Nagasaki, through which a limited trade with China and the Netherlands was allowed. Merchants dreamed of being the first to sell shiploads of goods in a long-closed market of 30 million Japanese. It would be another generation before this dream was realized. Roberts never made it to Japan. He died at Macao in June 1836. By the time word of his demise reached Washington, a new president with new priorities was in power.

Jackson's diplomacy also bore fruit much closer to home. In the Western Hemisphere, with one exception, his trade missions to Mexico, Colombia, Peru-Bolivia, Venezuela, and Chile all brought back treaties that opened markets to American merchants. Argentina was the sole hold out, and this nearly led to war.

The dispute was over islands several hundred miles southeast of Buenos Aires known by the Argentineans as the Malvinas and by the British as the Falklands. Both countries claimed these islands, but they remained uninhabited until 1821, when the Argentineans planted a small colony. In 1831 the governor seized three American ships on charges that their captains had violated the law. The USS *Lexington* was anchored off Buenos Aires when its captain, Silas Duncan, learned of the incident. He ordered his crew to sail for the Malvinas, where, on New Year's Day 1832, the Americans destroyed the settlements and transported the population to Montevideo.

Upon learning of the seizures and retaliation, Jackson sent Francis Baylies to Buenos Aires to seek compensation for the ships and secure a most-favored-nation treaty. Baylies was an excellent choice—he spoke Spanish and was a skilled lawyer and politician from Massachusetts. But try as he might, the Argentinean government rejected his requests. Baylies left for home on September 3, 1832. Upon meeting Jackson, Baylies pressed for seizing the islands and holding them as a bargaining chip to pressure the Argentineans for reparations and trade.

Jackson was considering this when word arrived that Britain had seized the islands. This posed a dilemma for Jackson. The 1832 Monroe Doctrine, which he upheld, opposed any recolonization of the Western Hemisphere by any European power. But in this case practical American interests undercut the principle. For now, Jackson chose not to act.

With one glaring exception, America's foreign relations during Jackson's presidency did not involve crucial elements of national security. Nonetheless, Jackson deserves high marks for his foreign policies. He resolved several challenges with low-key but effective policies that protected or advanced American interests. In all, he displayed a sensitive, patient, and compromising spirit in his relations with the European powers that was totally void in his approach to his domestic foes. Jackson's diplomacy failed with only one country—Mexico.

14

The Texas Revolution

I have traveled near five hundred miles across
Texas . . . and I have no hesitancy in pronouncing
it the finest country to its extent upon the globe.

SAM HOUSTON

If they touch the hair of the head of one of our citizens,
tell him to batter down & destroy their town &
exterminate the inhabitants from the face of the earth!

ANDREW JACKSON

Like the mentor he all but worshiped, Sam Houston could not stay out
of trouble. A quick temper, obsession with honor, and alcoholism was a
volatile brew that often led him to explosive behavior. His most recent
public roil had been the most self-destructive. After three months of
marriage in early 1829, his wife fled him and filed for divorce. Utterly
humiliated, Houston resigned as Tennessee's governor and spent a couple of years in drunken exile with the Cherokees.

At some point, his self-loathing pushed him to a crucial crossroads—
step either into the abyss or back into the political arena. He roused
himself and headed back to Tennessee. There he found a forgiving pub-

lic, or at least enough voters willing to back him rather than his rival for a seat in the House of Representatives.

His devotion to Jackson swiftly made him enemies in this bitterly divided chamber. After William Stanberry of Ohio expressed on the floor an especially pointed criticism of the policies of the president and his supporters, Houston challenged him to a duel. Stanberry refused. On April 17, 1832, Houston ambushed him on Pennsylvania Avenue and severely beat him with his hickory cane. Stanberry filed a complaint with the House Speaker, who had Houston arrested, brought before Congress, charged with assault, and then released to prepare his defense.

After inviting the miscreant to the White House, Jackson explained, "It's not you they are after, Sam. . . . They are after your old commander."[1] He gave his protégé money to buy a new suit for his trial and the advice to present himself as the people's champion. The new suit and old excuse failed. His colleagues found him guilty by 106 to 89 and expelled him from their ranks. This provoked Jackson to rant against the expulsion as "the greatest act of tyranny and usurpation ever attempted under our government."[2] Of course, Jackson was projecting; his enemies were saying similar things about his policies.

Houston was once again jobless and humiliated. Jackson soon came up with a task to occupy his time. He handed Houston five hundred dollars and pointed him to Texas. His mission was to rally the American settlers there behind an attempt to shake off Mexican rule, ideally by peaceful means. His cover was to serve as Jackson's envoy to the Texas Indians, especially the Comanches.[3]

What Houston reported was electrifying. Nineteen of twenty Texans despised the corrupt, inept, brutal Mexican rule and wanted to join the United States or, failing that, Britain. It was essential that the United States act quickly or else the British might win Texas for themselves. And this would be a grand prize indeed: "I have traveled near five hundred miles across Texas . . . and I have no hesitancy in pronouncing it the finest country to its extent upon the globe."[4]

Jackson had hungrily eyed Texas for many years. He was not alone in his desire. Thomas Jefferson had insisted that the 1803 Louisiana Purchase included not just the Mississippi River's western watershed but the Floridas and Texas as well. Madrid angrily dismissed such claims. It was another sixteen years before the United States and Spain resolved this conflict. The 1819 Transcontinental Treaty swapped Florida to the United States for Washington's disavowal of any claims to Texas and acceptance of the Sabine River as the border with Spanish Texas. Although Jackson had initially backed this treaty, he denied doing so after the 1824 election and the corrupt bargain that put Adams in the White House. Thereafter, one of a quiver of political arrows that Jackson fired at Adams was labeled the "giveaway of Texas."

Jackson shrewdly foresaw the ultimate result of Mexico's generous immigration and land grant policies: When those American transplants "get possession and become permanently fixed, they will soon avail themselves of some pretext to throw off the Mexican authority and form an independent government of their own. This would beget great disquietude, and might eventually endanger the peace and tranquility of the United States and Mexico."[5]

This understanding brought a degree of trepidation to the usually aggressive Jackson after he entered the White House. He wanted Texas as long as annexation did not spark a war with Mexico or a political crisis between the slave and free states. He first tested these treacherous political waters by contradictorily denouncing the Sabine River boundary and insisting that its western branch, the Neches River, was the proper frontier. Houston was instrumental in asserting this claim for a slice of Texas. He and six other Texans set up a "committee of vigilance and safety" for Nacogdoches and the surrounding region east of the Neches River.

Mexico's failure to act decisively against this provocation emboldened Jackson. On August 13, 1829, he dispatched Anthony Butler to Mexico City to instruct American minister Joel Poinsett to buy Texas for $5 million. To facilitate the deal, Poinsett was authorized to bribe the most powerful people in the country, particularly Antonio Lopez de Santa Anna, then the army commander. Butler reported that bribery was no problem as Mexican officials were "selfish, corrupt, utterly unprincipled. Any of them may be successfully appealed to through their cupidity." The going price for Santa Anna and his key underlings might run up to $700,000. Yet trying to buy off Santa Anna was a gamble. The general would not come cheap and might well take the money and then denounce his would-be paymaster.[6]

All this may have been true, but Poinsett and Butler missed a key element of Mexican political culture. Corruption was packaged with deco-rum. Crass, demanding Americans waving fistfuls of dollars in the faces of officials grossly offended the etiquette of Mexican kickbacks. Thus, Poinsett's machinations backfired. Rather than sell out their country, the Mexican government sought to kick out Poinsett by demanding his recall. Jackson replaced him with Butler but did not change the mission

Rumors of Jackson's questionable means of trying to acquire Texas reached the newspapers. The president denied the bribery. To cover his tracks, he sent Butler an unciphered letter that admonished him "to give these shrewd fellows no room to charge you with hampering with their officers to obtain the cession through corruption." Yet he gave his envoy considerable wiggle room when he said he would not pay a penny more than $5 million for Texas. What the officials did with all that money was solely their concern.[7]

The loyal but rather dim-witted Butler failed to see the nod and wink so obviously embedded in the president's letter. He replied that Jackson's advice to be cautious "proves how little you know of the of Mexican character. I can assure you, sir, that bribery is not only common and familiar in all ranks and classes, but is familiarly and freely spoken of. Resort must be had to bribery—or by presents, if the term was appropriate."[8]

Jackson, of course, understood how essential corruption was to Mexican political culture and thus that bribing key officials was necessary to get anything done, with the price related to the undertaking's ambition and the official's rank. Indeed, he informed Butler that he had "scarcely ever knew a Spaniard who was not the slave of avarice, and it is not improbable that this weakness may be worth a great deal to us."[9] Buying Texas would demand huge bribes, and this was not an issue. Keeping the sordid business hushed up, however, was crucial to pulling it off. Two of three senators had to approve any treaty that transferred Texas to the United States. Those concerned with having another slave state in the Union would pounce on any allegations of nefarious acts by the president or his envoys to that end.

The president's man in Mexico City achieved nothing during his half-dozen years there. Yet, rather than give up his goal of buying Texas, Jackson widened the mission. He had Secretary of State John Forsyth authorize Butler to offer a half-million dollars for San Francisco Bay atop what was already on and under the table for Texas. But, once again, Butler overplayed his hand. The Mexican government complained. Forsyth recalled the hapless envoy on November 9, 1835. This would have been no great diplomatic loss in any event, but Butler's presence was rendered especially frivolous given the electrifying news—the Texans had rebelled against Mexico. If the rebellion succeeded, the United States could annex Texas without paying Mexico a penny.

Sooner or later Mexico was going to lose Texas. By 1835 the American population in the territory included thirty thousand American whites along with their five thousand black slaves, nearly five times the seventy-eight hundred Hispanics. Most Americans were eager for any excuse to haul down the Mexican flag and run up the American one.[10] How had it come to this?

What appears to work for a nation's interests in one era can work against them in the next. This certainly proved true for Mexico's Texas policy.[11] Shortly after declaring independence in 1821, Mexico's leaders opened the country to trade and immigration. They were especially eager to attract well-armed, hardworking Americans to Texas, the region most vulnerable to Indian attacks and least economically viable. Comanche raids devastated the frontier. The vast majority of Tejanos were peasants who scratched a bare existence from the land; the rest were a tiny elite of landowners and merchants who garnered what little wealth was produced. Texas's settled portions extended no more than a hundred or so miles from the Gulf of Mexico, mostly along the valleys of the Neches, San Antonio, Colorado, Brazos, and Trinity Rivers. The Camino Real, or Royal Road, ran through Texas, tenuously linking it with the rest of Mexico to the south and terminating at Natchitoches on the Red River in Louisiana.

Moses Austin was an entrepreneur and visionary who made a fortune developing lead mines in Missouri only to lose everything in the Panic of 1819. Mexico's immigration policy offered him a chance to renew his quest for wealth and power. In 1821 he journeyed to Texas and obtained an "empressario" land grant for promising to settle three hundred families across it. When Moses died, his son, Stephen, realized his vision. By 1825 he had settled three hundred families in the Brazos Valley, and by 1829 he had enticed another nine hundred families to farms and businesses elsewhere across the region.[12]

Mexico's 1824 constitution was modeled on that of the United States with two deviations—slavery was outlawed and Catholicism was mandatory. Most American immigrants to Texas were southern slaveholders and Protestants who brought their chattel and creed with them. Mexican officials generally turned a blind eye and an extended palm to these infractions. The constitution had also eliminated Texas as a separate province and established the state of Coahuila y Tejas with its capital at Saltillo.

Alarmed by the swelling American population in Texas, New Mexico, and California, the Mexican government suspended its free immigration and trade policies in April 1830 and began to enforce the constitution's tenets on slavery and faith. Austin worked tirelessly to convince those in power to reverse these policies as well as let Texas separate from Coahuila and become a state within the Mexican federation. To give weight to their interests, he and fifty-five delegates gathered in a convention at San Felipe de Austin in October 1832. The delegates wrote up a list of grievances to send to both Saltillo and Mexico City. The refusal of either government to respond provoked Texan delegates in April 1833 to reconvene at San Felipe de Austin. They voted to have Austin carry their petition directly to the federal government in Mexico City. There he would confront one of the most reviled characters in Texas or Mexican history.

One man above all provoked the loss of Texas—Antonio Lopez de Santa Anna.[13] Santa Anna dominated Mexico from the 1820s through the 1850s, much as Andrew Jackson did in the United States from 1815 to 1848. His impact on Mexican history was as colorful as it was disastrous. In many ways, he was the political vampire of Mexican history. In each of the six times that he took power, he drained the nation of blood and treasure and then fled into exile as rivals rallied against the devastating effects of his megalomania, greed, and blunders. He first became a Mexican hero when he led the repulse of a Spanish invasion in 1829. He was elected the president on April 1, 1833, the same day that the Texas convention reconvened. In 1834 he dismissed Congress, assumed emergency powers, and sent reinforcements to Texas to ensure that the laws were obeyed.

A Texas revolt was primed and just needed a spark to set it off.[14] The spark came on October 2, 1835, when a Texas militia company at

Gonzáles refused to surrender a cannon to Mexican forces. Hearing of the standoff, other militia companies swelled the Texas ranks around a flag with the outline of a cannon and the words "Come and Take It." Fighting broke out and the Texans routed the Mexicans. This easy success inspired attacks on all Mexican garrisons across the region. Texans captured the presidio or citadel at Goliad on October 11 and besieged Gen. Martin de Cos in the walled mission of the Alamo outside of San Antonio de Bexar. On December 11 Cos surrendered with the promise that he and his men would never again fight against the Texans and that the Mexican government would restore the 1824 constitution.

The Texans organized a state government with Henry Smith as the governor and Sam Houston as the commanding general. From his headquarters at San Felipe, Houston tried to scrape up men and supplies. Two forts guarded the approaches from Mexico to Texas—Cols. William Barret Travis and Jim Bowie jointly commanded the Alamo at San Antonio and Col. James Fannin the Presidio La Bahia at Goliad.

Even before he learned of Cos's humiliating surrender, Santa Anna issued on December 15, 1835, his Seven Laws, which attempted to legitimize his dictatorship and concentrate power in his hands by transforming the states into departments ruled from Mexico City. Those laws enraged most Texans whether they were of American or Hispanic origin. Then, to crush the Texas revolt, Santa Anna ordered a two-pronged offensive, with Gen. José de Urrea advancing with fifteen hundred troops along the coast road to Goliad, while he himself led twenty-five hundred troops along the Camino Real to San Antonio.[15]

Santa Anna's army reached San Antonio on February 23, 1836, and began what would become a thirteen-day siege of the Alamo. Within the Alamo, Travis took sole command after Bowie was bedridden with illness. Lining the parapets were perhaps as many as 250 men. Among them were a dozen brought in by David Crockett, who had headed west after losing in his third reelection bid as a Tennessee congressman the previous November. Santa Anna ordered his army to assault the Alamo in the early morning of March 6. The fighting did not last long. By dawn, the Mexican troops had slaughtered the defenders, while suffering perhaps 650 dead and wounded of their own.[16]

Upon learning of the Alamo's fate, Fannin ordered Goliad evacuated and led his men east. After defeating several small forces along the way, Fannin and his 350 men encountered Urrea and his army at Coleto Creek on March 19. Fannin surrendered the next day, and he and his men were disarmed and marched back to Bahia. On March 27 Urrea obeyed Santa Anna's orders to execute his prisoners.[17]

Meanwhile, a convention at Washington on the Brazos declared Texas an independent nation on March 2, 1836, and elected David Burnet the president. The delegates did not have time to enjoy their assertion of freedom. News of first the Alamo's fall and then the Goliad massacre caused thousands of people to flee east in what became known as the Runaway Scrape. Among the refugees were Houston and the Texan army. Mexican forces chased them, looting and often burning the abandoned houses in their path.

Houston finally halted his retreat at the San Jacinto River. With the river at their back, he and his seven hundred men awaited the enemy. On April 21 Santa Anna and fifteen hundred footsore troops encamped a quarter mile from the Texas position. After the Mexicans settled down for a siesta, Houston led his men in an attack. Shouting "Remember the Alamo!" they surged through the Mexicans, shooting, stabbing, and clubbing. The Texans won a bloody vengeance for the Alamo and Goliad by slaughtering around 650 Mexicans and capturing another 700, including Santa Anna.

Although President Jackson officially maintained a strict neutrality during the rebellion, he did nothing to impede Texas agents from gathering money or men in the United States or lobbying Congress for aid and recognition. He also dismissed the protests of Mexico's minister to the United States. Two powerful voices urged him to do much more. Secretary of War Lewis Cass and Gen. Edmund Gaines, who commanded the Southwest Region with his headquarters at Fort Jessup near the Texas frontier, called for occupying Nacogdoches to boost Texan and deflate Mexican spirits.[18]

Jackson approved but wanted the orders to Gaines to be written vaguely enough to claim "plausible deniability" if need arose. He knew that occupying Nacogdoches would more likely provoke than intimidate the Mexicans. The result could be a war that Jackson felt the country was then too politically fractured to fight effectively. Cass's instructions to Gaines gave Jackson the leeway to declare a misunderstanding and withdraw if necessary. Gaines was to occupy "such position, on either side of the imaginary boundary line, as may be best for your defensive operations." This "imaginary boundary," however, included Nacogdoches "within the limits of the United States."[19]

The Mexicans committed their own provocative acts against the United States. At Tampico, officials harassed the American consul and other residents and refused to allow American warships in the harbor to take on water and food.[20] This news enraged Jackson, who had War Secretary Cass fire off orders to Commodore Dallas "to blockade the harbour of Tampico, & to suffer nothing to enter till they allow him to land and obtain his supplies and water & communicate with the Consul, & if they touch the hair of the head of one of our citizens, tell him to batter down & destroy their town & exterminate the inhabitants from the face of the earth!"[21]

Jackson wanted to rivet his attention on the epic events unfolding in Texas. To his chagrin, he had to keep glancing down Pennsylvania Avenue, where powerful voices warned against any meddling in Mexican affairs, let alone consider adding Texas to the United States. No one was more vociferous or eloquent in expressing these admonitions than John Quincy Adams, who condemned Jackson and his followers for instigating "a war between slavery and emancipation" between the Texans and Mexican government and for "rushing" the nation "into a war of conquest, commenced by aggression on your part, and for the reestablishment of slavery where it has been abolished. . . . In that war, sir, the banners of freedom will be the banners of Mexico and your banners . . . will be the banners of slavery."[22]

The news of the massacres at the Alamo and Goliad and Houston's retreat with the Texas army's remnants forced Jackson to weigh a heavy question. What if Santa Anna's army chased Houston and his men all the way to Nacogdoches? Should Jackson launch Gaines and his troops against Santa Anna or withdraw them into uncontested American territory? To Jackson's relief this question was rendered moot with news of the crushing Texan victory at San Jacinto where a captured Santa Anna fearfully agreed to relinquish Texas.

The fever for summarily executing Santa Anna was understandable— he was reviled for ordering the massacres at the Alamo and Goliad. Houston acknowledged that a lynch mob among his officers and men had gathered after the dictator was apprehended, but he talked them out of it. Vengeance, however just and immediately gratifying, might actually destroy their cause given that a couple of thousand Mexican troops remained in Texas. Only Santa Anna could order them to march back to Mexico, and he would do so only if the Texans promised to spare his life. As a bargaining chip, the dictator's value was priceless, at least for several crucial weeks after San Jacinto. On May 14, 1836, Santa Anna signed the Treaty of Velasco, whereby he, as Mexico's president, recognized Texas independence and promised to withdraw all Mexican troops immediately and permanently from Texas, restore or make restitution for all looted or destroyed property, and release all prisoners. Houston encouraged Santa Anna to write Jackson and request "relations to the end that your nation and the Mexican, may strengthen their friendly ties."[23]

Jackson replied on September 4 with letters to Houston and Santa Anna. After lauding Houston for his brilliant victory, he added a cautionary note: "I have seen a report that General Santa Anna was to be brought before a military court, to be tried and shot. Nothing now could tarnish the character of Texas more than such an act at this late period." It was good policy as well as humanity that spared him.[24] This advice could not have been at once so sound and ironic. The author was the same man who as a general had been condemned for drumhead trials that ended with the execution of two British agents in Florida and a wayward sentry in the Creek territory. Of course, the execution of a head of state, albeit a deposed one clearly guilty of horrendous war crimes, would far exceed Jackson's deeds in notoriety and diplomatic damage. Jackson informed Santa Anna that "your powers ended with your capture." Thus, "until the existing government of Mexico ask our friendly offices between the contending parties, Mexico and Texas, we cannot interfere, but should Mexico ask it, our friendly offices will . . . be afforded to restore peace and put an end to this inhuman warfare."[25]

The president retained the fiction that the United States was a neutral, uninvolved bystander willing to provide assistance purely from humanitarian motives. He was genuinely concerned that the United States annex Texas only through strict adherence to international law and morality that "secured to us respect and influence abroad and inspired confidence at home."[26] He deemed this crucial to convincing the northern free states to accept the latest slave state in the Union. To this end, he ordered General Gaines to withdraw from Nacogdoches, explaining that "ours is a state of strict neutrality in . . . the struggle of Texas for independence and you as commander of our forces on that frontier must religiously observe and maintain it."[27] Of course, Andrew Jackson not only was deeply involved in helping foment the Texas rebellion, he was vital to its outcome. Although the Texans would have revolted regardless of whether Jackson sent Houston to provoke such a rebellion, they would not have won independence when and how they did had another man led the Texas army after the debacles at the Alamo and Goliad.

Houston sent Santa Anna with an escort all the way to the White House, along with a letter expressing the hope that the two leaders would resolve all the outstanding issues among Mexico, Texas, and the United States.[28] However, a crucial turn of events would negate any subsequent deal. Santa Anna was no longer Mexico's dictator. Carlos Maria de Bustamante had taken power and was mobilizing an army and supplies to retake Texas. So, Jackson received Santa Anna, not as a head of state but as an influential private Mexican citizen. On January 17, 1837, the president hosted him at the White House with an official reception, and the following day they met informally. He sent Santa Anna back to his homeland aboard an American frigate with an offer to pay $3.5 million for Mexican recognition of the transfer of Texas, New Mexico, and California to the United States. The new government in power in Mexico City responded to Jackson's offer with silent, seething contempt.[29]

Jackson had many a meeting with William Wharton, the Texas minister. They spoke frankly of how best to orchestrate America's annexation of Texas. The slave question was crucial. To finesse the issue, the president urged Texas to declare that its borders extended westward all the way to the Pacific, thus embracing New Mexico and California. This would allow for a deal with northern politicians whereby Texas entered the Union as a slave state and New Mexico and California as free states.[30]

Jackson's tenure in the White House was rapidly drawing to a close. He would have loved to have had Texas annexed as his last act as president and his career's capstone. Although he fell short of this prize, he was able to coax the United States to take a decisive step in that direction. A bill recognizing Texas independence passed the House on February 28 and the Senate on March 1. President Andrew Jackson signed the bill into law on March 3, 1837. The same day, the Senate approved his choice of Alcée La Branche as America's first minister to Texas. That evening, he welcomed to the White House William Wharton as the minister of Texas to the United States. The next day, he stood proudly by as his protégé was sworn in to follow him as president of the United States. He expected Martin Van Buren to carry on his agenda, with the annexation of Texas the top priority. In this, he would be cruelly disappointed.

3

The Protégés,
1837–1848

15
The Little Magician

> If the Union is once severed, the line of separation will grow
> wider and wider, and the controversies which are now de-
> bated and settled in the halls of legislation will then be tried
> in the fields of battle and determined by the sword.
>
> ANDREW JACKSON

The Democratic Party convention that opened at Baltimore on May 20, 1835, was the largest such gathering yet, with six hundred delegates attending from all states but South Carolina, Alabama, Tennessee, and Illinois. It also may have been among the most stage-managed in history. There was little doubt whom the convention would nominate for its presidential candidate. Martin Van Buren was Andrew Jackson's protégé and headed a political machine that maneuvered the delegates into first letting him chair the proceedings and then unanimously endorsing him for the White House. Finally, by a vote of 178 to 87, the delegates nominated Richard Johnson, a windbag Kentucky politician best known for his disputed claim to have killed Tecumseh, as the vice presidential candidate.

In contrast, the Whig Party, which had morphed from the National

Republicans in 1832, was still a loose coalition of factions. The Whigs could not decide on one presidential candidate, so four ended up running—William Henry Harrison, Daniel Webster, Hugh White, and William Mangum, the respective favorite sons of Indiana, Massachusetts, Tennessee, and South Carolina. Fratricide was the natural result.[1]

The Whig Party got its name in derision and wore it with pride. Critics accused people like John Quincy Adams, Henry Clay, and Daniel Webster of being secret aristocrats who should wear wigs to identify themselves. Regardless of how its members adorned their heads, Britain's Whig Party was more liberal than its rival Tory Party. Thus, the American Whig Party was so dubbed in a mixture of humor and history.

The candidates contended for the votes of citizens in two new states that year. Jackson signed bills admitting Arkansas on June 15, 1836 and Michigan on January 26, 1837. The ideological and political balance was maintained in the Senate as slavery was permitted in Arkansas and forbidden in Michigan.

Van Buren nosed ahead of his rivals with 764,198 popular and 170 electoral votes against the combined Whig totals of 736,147 popular and 124 electoral votes; Harrison received the lion's share of the Whig's popular and electoral votes with 548,966 and 73, respectively. The winner could claim no popular mandate from such a narrow victory. The new president would have to govern from the center and forge plenty of compromises along the way.

This did not bother Van Buren, who was as naturally conciliatory as his predecessor was confrontational. In 1833 he had displayed the epitome of his political skills in a celebrated confrontation with Henry Clay. As the newly elected vice president in Jackson's second term, he took his desk to preside over the Senate. Clay rose to deliver a long speech that blistered Van Buren along with the president and the rest of his administration. At the conclusion of his polemic, Clay sat down triumphantly at his desk. Looking serious, Van Buren descended and approached Clay. Silence abruptly descended on the usually noisy chamber as each senator wondered what fireworks might ensue. "Mr. Senator," he intoned, "allow me to be indebted to you for another pinch of your aromatic Maccoboy." This unexpected act rendered Clay for once speechless. He gestured toward the gold snuffbox on his desk. Van Buren took a pinch, sniffed, thanked Clay with a broad smile, and returned to his desk.[2]

Van Buren's refreshingly amiable style did not obscure in his own mind the role he was expected to play. He promised "to tread generally in the footsteps of President Jackson, happy if I shall be able to perfect the work he has so gloriously begun."[3] He had little choice in doing so. Jackson may have been about six hundred miles away, as a crow flies, at the Heritage, but he cast a long dark shadow over Van Buren and his administration. To nearly the day he died, Old Hickory meddled in and fumed at Washington City politics and fired off streams of letters to his cohorts telling them what to do.

As Jackson prepared to pass the torch to Van Buren, he submitted a farewell address that touted his accomplishments over the preceding eight years. Some of his claims likely provoked irritated snorts from his political foes. The loudest most likely greeted his insistence that he had fulfilled rather than violated the Constitution: "Our Constitution is no longer a doubtful experiment. . . . We find that it has preserved unimpaired the liberties of the people" and "secured the rights of property." Yet, after that upbeat assertion, he ended with a dire warning:

> We behold systematic efforts publicly made to sow the seeds of discord between different parts of the United States, and to place party divisions directly upon geographical distinctions, to excite the South against the North and the North against the South. . . . If the Union is once severed, the line of separation will grow wider and wider, and the controversies which are now debated and settled in the halls of legislation will then be tried in the fields of battle and determined by the sword.[4]

In that, of course, he was prescient.

Jackson's most immediate legacy was a devastating economic depression. He promised that regular folks would enjoy easier credit after he slew the monster bank and distributed the money to his pet banks. They did for a while. Hard currency drained from the country as foreign investors, who owned 84,055 of the 350,000 Bank of the United States shares, spirited away their money to safe havens in Europe or elsewhere in anticipation of the inevitable crash that would wallop the United States. As coins disappeared, the pet banks and others printed ever more paper money. The result was a fast-swelling speculative bubble. If Jackson's pet-bank policy fueled this bubble, his Species Circular that required hard cash for public land helped pop it as millions of dollars' worth of paper certificates that formerly paid for these sales were rendered all but worthless.[5]

The Panic of 1837 was triggered on March 17, when the financial firm of I. and L. Joseph declared bankruptcy after cotton prices on the New Orleans Exchange collapsed. This unleashed a domino effect as one overleveraged financial house after another shut its doors. The banks accepted only hard coin for payment. The reserves of New York City banks alone plummeted from $7.2 million to $1.5 million from September 1, 1836, to May 1, 1837, and banks across the country experienced similar losses.[6]

To deal with the crisis, Van Buren called Congress back into a special session. Once everyone had assembled, the question was, of course, what to do. The trouble was that those responsible for destroying the second bank had eliminated the one institution that, in Nicholas Biddle's capable hands, could have either prevented the economic collapse in the first place or subsequently alleviated it. As a Jackson loyalist, Van Buren would have committed heresy had he called for establishing a third Bank of the United States. Instead, he did the next best thing. On September 8, 1837, he asked Congress to pass a bill setting up a Treasury account for federal deposits. The Senate approved the bill, but the House killed it. Van Buren then issued an executive order to this effect. The policy actually worsened the depression as more money was drawn from the economy. However, over the long term it made speculative bubbles less frequent and virulent. The economic depression dragged on until 1843.

Although Henry Clay was the Whig Party leader, his potential presidential campaign for 1840 was burdened with some heavy political baggage—he had lost his two previous White House bids. When the convention opened at Harrisburg, Pennsylvania, in December 1839, he was soon eclipsed. The Whigs were in desperate search for their own party's version of Jackson. They found him in William Henry Harrison, who had fought at Fallen Timbers in 1795 and led the armies that defeated the Shawnees at Tippecanoe in 1811 and the British and Indians at the Thames in 1813. His political résumé was as impressive. After competently governing Indiana Territory for a dozen years, he had moved to Ohio, where he was elected successively as a state assemblyman, congressional representative, and senator. Given Harrison's good showing in the 1836 election, he won on the third ballot at the 1839 convention with 148 votes to 90 for Clay and 16 for Gen. Winfield Scott.

Harrison offered the vice presidential slot to the runner-up. Clay's polite refusal drastically affected the course of American history. The party leaders mulled which candidate best upped the odds of a Harrison victory. As a westerner, Harrison would undoubtedly carry most of that region's vote. Whig power was rooted in the Northeast and that region could be expected to vote for him too. Then there was the South.

To contend there, the Whigs tapped John Tyler as Harrison's running mate. Like most ideas that go bad, it seemed like a good one at the time it was made. Tyler had graduated from William and Mary at age seventeen, had passed the law bar within two years, and in 1817, at age twenty-seven, was elected to the House of Representatives. After four terms, he ran for and won Virginia's governorship in 1825. Two years later, the legislature sent him to the U.S. Senate, where he had served ever since. As a bonus, he was bright, personable, and ambitious. Finally, as a Democrat, Tyler and Harrison posed a bipartisan political juggernaut.

Alas for the Whigs, Tyler's dazzling credentials obscured his ideological orientation. And in this the Whigs could not have picked a worse vice presidential candidate. Tyler broke with Jackson and the Democratic Party over nullification. He fervently believed that the United States was merely a confederation of sovereign states. He was also a plantation slave master who hated and feared abolitionism. Indeed, all his beliefs warred against those of the party that foolishly embraced him.[7]

Harrison himself was hardly the perfect candidate. At age sixty-eight, he was the oldest so far to run for the presidency and was not in the best of health. Then there was the misleading way his candidacy was promoted. Taking another page out of the Jackson playbook, the Whigs mass-marketed their hero with a populism that celebrated images over issues and ideals. The campaign slogan was the catchy if silly "Tippecanoe and Tyler Too." Although Harrison was born into a plantation manor in Virginia's tidewater aristocracy, he was depicted as a frontiersman who lived in a log cabin, drank hard cider, and wore a coonskin cap.

Meanwhile, the Democrats took much longer to pick their candidate. Their convention opened at Baltimore on May 5, 1840, and was immediately mired in rancorous debate. A reform faction attacked political and business corruption, championed free trade, and at once hated but tolerated slavery. The conservative wing condemned the reformers as radicals and derided them as "Locofocos," after the matches they used to light candles during a New York conference when conservatives turned off the gas lamps in a mean-spirited attempt to shut them up. Like the Whigs, the Locofocos converted a political epithet into a distinct label. They fared poorly in this and subsequent elections; many ended up joining the Whigs and later the Republicans.

Fuming with rage at the dissenters, Jackson rallied his political cohorts behind Martin Van Buren, who ultimately received the required two-thirds vote to get the nomination. Amos Kendall resigned as postmaster general to manage the campaign and edit the *Extra Globe*. Heavyweights such as Thomas Hart Benton, James Polk, Felix Grundy, and Silas Wright stumped widely for the ticket. But this time all the joint firepower of the Jackson and Van Buren machines was not enough to prevail; most Americans were ready for a change.

That year, a third party emerged to run a candidate for the presidency. The Liberty Party called for the gradual emancipation of slaves and the immediate abolition of slavery in Washington City and the interstate slave trade. James Birney was a Kentuckian, lawyer, politician, planter, newspaper editor, and convert from slave master to fervent abolitionist. The Liberty Party tapped him as their standard-bearer.

Harrison won by a landslide with 1,275,612 popular and 234 electoral votes to Van Buren's 1,130,033 popular and 60 electoral votes and Birney's 7,053 popular votes. The turnout was the largest in American history to that point, with 80.2 percent of eligible voters going to the polls, up from 57.8 percent in 1836. In all, mass democracy triumphed in the 1840 election along with Harrison.[8]

William Henry Harrison holds the dubious distinction of giving the longest inaugural address and spending the shortest time in office. He was also the first president to die in office, when he succumbed to pneumonia on April 3, 1841, less than a month after taking the oath.[9]

Jackson was ecstatic at news of Harrison's death, partly because he had convinced himself that Harrison was Clay's puppet and once in power would destroy the country by imposing the American System upon it.

But a poisonous dose of petty jealousy also animated Jackson's hatred. With his victories at Tippecanoe and the Thames, Harrison was the only living general whose fame came close to matching Jackson's own. In reporting the news to Jackson, Francis Blair insisted that Harrison's demise resulted from his "pampered vanity added to the tension of the other passions which strained all his faculties beyond their capabilities, and at last every thing gave way at once."[10]

John Tyler was sworn in as president on April 4, 1841, and soon imposed his ideological stamp on his administration and the nation. Clay painstakingly led an effort to craft a bill establishing yet another Bank of the United States and rounded up the votes to pass it on August 6. Tyler vetoed the bill on August 16. This "betrayal" incensed the Whigs. Clay and his team then drafted a compromise bill that passed both houses. Tyler vetoed it on September 9.

Tyler's vetoes had powerful economic and political impacts as they robbed the nation of the growth and stability that a Bank of the United States would have nurtured. The Whigs drummed Tyler out of the party. He was happy to abandon a ship that he did so much to sink. The Whigs split into conciliatory and confrontational wings. All the Whig department heads quit Tyler's administration except Secretary of State Daniel Webster. Tyler filled the slots with conservative Democrats.

Tyler was not completely intransigent. With mixed feelings, he signed three bills in 1841. The Internal Improvements Act of 1841 allocated 500,000 acres of public lands to each state that held them. The Land Act sold off federal lands in 160-acre allotments for $1.25 an acre to settlers. Finally, the Bankruptcy Act let individuals who held bank notes rendered worthless through no fault of their own escape foreclosure by declaring bankruptcy. Encouraged by these economy-boosting measures, the Whigs designed a tariff bill that extended the rates of the 1833 bill rather than let them drop to 20 percent as scheduled. This new bill would have at once protected American manufacturers and retained revenues needed to service a rapidly rising national debt. Tyler vetoed it on June 29, 1843.

Although most Whigs condemned Daniel Webster for not resigning, the criticism subsided as he adroitly managed the nation's foreign relations. The most pressing problem he encountered was reversing the deteriorating relations with Britain provoked by a series of incidents.

Sympathetic Americans blatantly aided a Canadian independence movement that fortified itself on an island in the Niagara River and in 1838 launched two raids into Canada. Canadians retaliated by crossing over and burning the rebel vessel *Carolina*. In 1839 the militias of Maine and New Brunswick mustered against each other over where to draw the international line between them. Fortunately, the Aroostook War was bloodless because the American and Canadian governments convinced their respective local officials to stand down. In 1841 slaves took over an American vessel named the *Creole*, which was transporting them to the States, and sailed to asylum in Nassau, in the Bahamas. British officials freed 129 of the slaves but handed over the *Creole* and five slaves who wished to return to American custody.[11]

Webster's greatest achievement as secretary of state was to resolve the boundary dispute with Britain that had festered since American independence. On August 9, 1842, he signed with Minister Alexander Baring, Lord Ashburton, the Webster-Ashburton Treaty, which drew the definitive line between Maine and New Brunswick. With the international boundary's eastern end finally settled, the next administration would focus on the disputed far western frontier.

And then there was Andrew Jackson. Although he was far away at his beloved Hermitage plantation near Nashville, he remained close to the hearts and minds of countless Americans. In the presidential election year of 1844, his devotees in Congress mustered overwhelming votes to reward their hero with a controversial gesture. A bill compensated Jackson with interest for the thousand-dollar fine he had paid to the court of Judge Dominick Hall in February 1815. Hall had imposed the fine for Jackson's violations of various constitutional principles when he imposed martial law on New Orleans long after the British invaders had sailed away. The bill passed the House by 158 to 28 on January 8, the anniversary of the Battle of New Orleans, and the Senate by 30 to 16 on February 10; Tyler signed the measure into law as soon as he got it. Jackson received a check for $2,732.90 on February 27, 1844.

In passing the bill, a congressional majority and the president essentially rewarded Jackson for blatantly violating the Constitution. Although the gesture was politically and financially symbolic, as a precedent it could have enormously harsh consequences for the nature of American power.

16

The Industrial and
Cultural Revolutions

❧✦❧

America is the country of the future. It is a country of beginnings, of projects, of vast designs and expectations.

RALPH WALDO EMERSON

I do not know a country where the love of money holds a
larger place in the heart of man and where they profess a
more profound scorn for the theory of equality of goods.

ALEXIS DE TOCQUEVILLE

America's industrial revolution began during the age of Jackson despite
Jacksonian policies that rewarded speculation, corruption, and insider
trading and fought protective tariffs, internal improvements, and the
Second Bank of the United States, which nurtured industrialization.[1]
These were only the latest challenges that industrialists had to overcome.
The worst constraint was America's colonial legacy. Britain's navigation
acts kept the colonists from producing a lengthening list of manufactured goods. Even after winning political independence, the United
States remained economically dependent on Britain for more than half
of its trade. For decades, America exported raw and semirefined goods
to Britain in return for sophisticated goods and credit; the value of

imports was twice that of the exports so that much more hard coin left than entered the United States.

Paradoxically, as if all this were not hobbling enough, America's industrial revolution was further inhibited by the nation's seemingly endless cornucopia of natural resources. For centuries, labor and money were relatively scarce, whereas water, soil, timber, game, and eventually coal, iron ore, and precious minerals were either free or cheap for the taking. When producers exhausted a farm's soil or mine's vein, they simply abandoned it for a lode as rich or richer elsewhere. This was not just extremely wasteful; it also retarded the nation's economic development as people lived off producing crude commodities rather than refined goods.

During the 1790s Treasury Secretary Alexander Hamilton freed America from some of its economic fetters with policies that promoted finance, infrastructure, innovation, industry, and education. The resulting economic renaissance was short lived. The Jeffersonian Revolution of 1800 sacrificed these initiatives on the altar of minimal government, market purity, and trade embargoes. Enterprising individuals were left to sink or swim with their innovations; mostly they sank.

Yet some inventers and entrepreneurs succeeded despite the odds against them. The best known exception in the early republic was Eli Whitney, who invented the cotton gin in 1793. This simple yet profound devise ignited not just an economic but also a political revolution. Before the gin, cotton seeds were laboriously picked by hand, a time-devouring process that limited cotton's supply and thus kept its price high. Now a slave with a gin could clean fifty times more cotton. Prices fell, demand rose, and plantations spread across the cotton belt, a swath of rich soil in central Georgia, Alabama, and Mississippi, and across stretches of northern Louisiana and east Texas. The white and slave populations soared in these states along with the planter elite's wealth and power. Between 1800 and 1820 American cotton production surged ten times and surpassed that of India. The halls of Congress reverberated with the swelling chorus of shrill Senate and House voices defending slavery and demanding its expansion.[2]

The South's cotton revolution combined with Jefferson's embargo of 1807 to stimulate a New England textile boom. With English textiles scarce and expensive, demand grew for the American-made version. The number of spindles soared from 8,000 in 1807 to 80,000 by 1811, 191,000 by 1820, and 1.25 million by 1831. This expansion preceded, stimulated, and was in turn stimulated by the Cotton Kingdom's growth across the Deep South. New England cotton cloth production soared from 4 million pieces in 1817 to 323 million in 1840. This industrial revolution also fed and was fed by expanding wool production, which rose from 400,000 pounds in 1810 to 15 million in 1830. Carpets skyrocketed from 9,948 square yards in 1810 to 1,147,500 in 1831.[3]

An earlier innovation lacked the cotton gin's political punch but eventually stirred economic tsunamis. Oliver Evans is not a household name but should be. In 1782 he quietly introduced both standardized interchangeable parts and assembly line production to his flour mill. These techniques remained a local wonder for decades until one by one other entrepreneurs emulated them, thus forcing their rivals to do the same or go out of business.

The nation's chronic shortage of skilled labor forced entrepreneurs to improve or invent machines that required fewer workers. One profitable innovation in an industry inevitably led to others. The number of patents rose steadily from 535 during the 1820s to 646 during the 1840s and then skyrocketed to 2,525 during the 1850s.[4] Inventions—such as Cyrus McCormick's grain reaper and Ichabod Washburn's wire maker of 1831, Samuel Colt's revolver of 1835, John Deere's steel plow of 1837, Charles Goodyear's process for vulcanizing rubber in 1839, Samuel Morse's telegraph in 1844, and William Morton's anesthesia in 1846—revolutionized entire industries. The shift from charcoal to coke in fueling blast furnaces generated far greater heat and thus stronger iron and steel.

Farm production benefited from the industrial revolution. Iron-edged plows, shovels, and hoes lasted much longer than the all-wooden tools they replaced and let laborers dig deeper and more efficiently. Cheaper fertilizer and more refined seeds boosted crop yields. Rising food production fed growing numbers of factory workers and city dwellers.[5]

Not all the inventions that fueled America's industrial revolution originated in the United States. It is easier to catch up than stay ahead in the economic race. The latecomer can sidestep all the innovator's promising paths that proved to be economic dead ends, and he can copy at a fraction of the money and time the inventions that cost the innovator so much.

America's industrial revolution got a major boost with just such a catch-up strategy. In one of history's most far-reaching acts of industrial espionage, Francis Lowell stole the design for elaborate water-powered loom machinery used to produce textiles. He did so during a two-year sojourn in Manchester, England, by visiting a factory day after day, memorizing all the details of the machinery that he could, and then writing them down at night. He brought the blueprint home, had mechanics build the stolen designs into machinery, and formed the Boston Manufacturing Company to mass-produce textiles in 1813. Although Lowell died in 1817, his partners carried on his work. In 1821 they set up a model factory town in Massachusetts where the Merrimac River falls thirty feet and named the site Lowell. The complex included factories, repair shops, stores, churches, and dormitories where young women resided after putting in twelve-hour days running the machinery. Eventually, business rivals copied both the machines and the organization that Lowell and his successors at the company had mastered.[6]

Water fueled the early industrial revolution. Entrepreneurs built factories in the low piedmont, where falling water spun their machinery. The next step was to convert that water to steam, but this took a while. In 1850 steam-generated horsepower accounted for only 181,000 units compared to 2.5 million units from inanimate sources and 8.5 million units from all sources, including humans.[7]

A transportation revolution at once stimulated and was stimulated by the industrial revolution.[8] Although Robert Fulton gets the credit, John Fitch actually designed, built, and tested the first steamboat in 1787. Witnesses viewed the trial run on the Delaware River as a novelty rather than the economic future. The idea languished in the United States until 1807, when Fulton launched on the Hudson River a steamboat that he had developed in France. The maiden voyage chugged the three-hundred-mile trip from New York City to Albany and then back in thirty-two hours. This inaugurated America's steamboat revolution. Within a few years, steamboats plied all navigable waters across the East, and beginning in 1811, they could also be found on western rivers. Increasingly powerful and reliable engines led to faster trips and larger cargoes. By the mid-1820s steamboats journeyed upstream from New Orleans to St. Louis in eight days. Shipping costs plummeted as more goods arrived more quickly to more distant markets.

The steam railroad was invented in Britain in 1814 as a device to haul coal from mines. The first steam-driven railroad capable of carrying passengers and freight quickly over a long distance was inaugurated between Manchester and Liverpool in 1830. In 1828 the Baltimore and Ohio Railroad Company was the first to lay track in the United States, but the trains were drawn by oxen along the twenty-three miles. The first steam-engine train, so diminutive that it was named the Tom Thumb, opened on a test track in 1830. The Tom Thumb's power to outrace a horse inspired a slew of entrepreneurs to build engines on a larger scale. This in turn launched a railroad revolution that at once shaped and was shaped by the industrial revolution. A decade later, in 1840, 450 locomotives hauled passengers and freight along thirty-two hundred miles of track, mostly across the northern states. The federal government eventually spurred the railroad revolution with massive giveaways of public lands.[9]

Canals were a more tranquil form of water transportation that emerged as the steamboat revolution churned ahead. Prosperity spread with the chains of canals. The digging alone distributed money along a canal's path as workers spent their hard-earned coin in taverns, stores, boardinghouses, and less reputable establishments. Ever more goods were exchanged at lower prices. Once-isolated farm hamlets were enriched from ties with national and international markets. The canals would never have been built—and all the new wealth created and distributed—without massive government aid, including $98.5 million of the $130.8 million total costs of the network before the Civil War, a nearly 4 to 1 ratio between the public and private sectors.[10]

The comfort and efficiency of travel along roads lagged far behind that of railroads and waterways. Stagecoaches and wagons still hauled passengers and goods at the old high rates and low speeds. The more money invested in cutting-edge transportation often meant that even less was devoted to improving the wretched roads. Shipping fees on the Erie Canal fell to 2 cents per ton-mile compared to anywhere from 30 to 70 cents for wagon transport.[11]

A communication revolution was yet another essential component of the industrial revolution. No invention of this age was more electrifying than the telegraph. On May 24, 1844, Samuel Morse sat before a small black machine in the Supreme Court building, surrounded by hundreds of distinguished onlookers. A wire led from the machine to an identical one in Baltimore, thirty-four miles away. In the code he had devised, Morse tapped out the message "What hath God wrought." The crowd murmured anxiously, wondering whether his associate in Baltimore had received the message and could reply. Soon the machine began clattering. Morse rapidly jotted down the message, rose, and triumphantly declared that he had received the same message that he had sent. The crowd burst into applause at witnessing the birth of an invention that would change the world. By 1850 ten thousand miles of telegraph wires stretched across the United States.[12]

An insidious but no less profound transformation of national communications took place in the decades before the telegraph's invention. From 1815 to 1830 the number of post offices rose from three thousand to eight thousand. Each office was a distribution point not just for letters but newspapers, journals, and other information. The post office was also a great patronage source for whichever party held the White House.[13]

The industrial and transportation revolutions caused the prices for most goods to plummet and the variety of goods to proliferate. Wages for most people either stayed roughly the same or rose. The result was a virtuous economic cycle, whereby people bought cheaper and more plentiful goods, that enriched the factory owners and raised salaries for more workers, shopkeepers, haulers, and others, who in turn demanded more goods. Supply kept up with demand as more factories mass-produced less expensive and more diverse products, such as textiles, guns, glass, paper, hats, blankets, carpets, leather, brooms, barrels, shoes, stoves, plows, pots, pans, clocks, chairs, beds, tables, cutlery, and books, to name the more prominent. The largest industrial complexes turned out the steam engines that ran the factories, trains, and boats.

Culture was the final and perhaps most important force fueling America's industrial revolution. Alexis de Tocqueville observed, "I do not know a country where the love of money holds a larger place in the heart of man and where they profess a more profound scorn for the theory of equality of goods."[14] Americans' obsessive materialism, worship of the marketplace, notion that everything and everyone has a price, belief that greed is good, and freedom to act on these values were all vital for the entrepreneurship that led to industrialization.

Yet industrialization as much shaped as was shaped by American culture. American society gentrified as more people enjoyed more wealth and education.[15] Ironically, gentrification spread from the upper to the middle class during the age of Jackson, which was notorious for its vulgarity, violence, and corruption. With their fundamental needs of food, shelter, and clothing satisfied, people looked for ways to enrich themselves emotionally and materially. Class differences blurred as "the middling sort" adopted the manners of and deferred less to their "betters." For upper-class males, especially those with political ambitions, appearing as a Jacksonian man of the people was no longer a display of vulgarity. Comfort in dress became increasingly important for men if not women. For men, pantaloons, stovepipe hats, short hair, and beards replaced knee breeches, cocked hats, wigs, long hair, and shaven faces. Alas, for women, respectability was measured by the number of petticoats worn at once and how tight corsets pinched waists. Starting first with the wealthy and then trickling down to the middle class were such practices as honeymoons, travel for pleasure, and journeying to resorts such as Saratoga Springs, Niagara Falls, the Greenbrier Hotel, or Cape May.

The parlor became a key symbol of respectability. There family and friends were entertained. Bare walls disappeared behind cheap framed engravings and wallpaper. Carpets hid bare floors. Rocking and upholstered chairs made sitting a less rigid and more soothing experience. An Argand lamp burning sperm oil generated ten times more light than a candle. A popular form of evening entertainment was singing to tunes led by someone playing the pianoforte. Privacy was increasingly valued and guarded by venetian blinds, curtains, locks, and separate bedrooms. The kitchen also experienced an industrial revolution. Cast-iron stoves made cooking easier and safer as women wearing long dresses no longer needed to bend over the open flames of the fireplace. The connection between filth and disease was less opaque. Cleanliness drew closer to godliness with cheap mass-produced brooms and soaps. Women washed clothes and sheets more frequently. Folks ensured that barnyard animals stayed outdoors rather than entering the home through open doors and windows.

Schools and literacy expanded across the United States during the age of Jackson, despite the prevailing anti-intellectualism. Not surprisingly, the New England states took the lead, with each making elementary public school mandatory for boys and girls. One by one other states—first those in the Midwest and eventually those in the South—enacted their own versions of this law. Many Protestant and Catholic churches opened their own schools. Girls caught up to boys in literacy, and children spent more years behind a desk. The *McGuffy Reader*, devised by William Holmes McGuffy, promoted civil duties along with reading skills. Stories emphasized hard work, charity, churchgoing, and deferred gratification. Private academies and boarding schools flourished for those who could afford them. The number of colleges soared from 33 in 1815 to 113 in 1848.[16]

As a result, despite the haphazard schooling of most of its youth and the slavery of most blacks, America became a surprisingly literate country. Among the questions of the 1840 census was whether one could read and write. The tally, which included African Americans, found that 78 percent of Americans could.[17]

The demand for things to read, especially books, expanded with the ability to read. In ever more homes, books were displayed, read, and talked about. Book prices fell as the volume and types of books rose. Writers enjoyed a swelling potential audience for their work, although then as now most had to keep their day jobs. The 1790 copyright law offered scant protection to writers from pirated editions of their work. The book publishing industry expanded from $2.5 million in 1820 to over $12.5 million in 1850. Newspapers were even more popular with the number of weekly and daily editions soaring from 375 in 1810 to 2,526 in 1850.[18]

Of all the intellectual contributions individuals made to America, perhaps none has delighted more people than that of James Smithson, a rich English scientist who bequeathed $550,000 to the United States to found "an establishment for the increase and diffusion of knowledge." President Andrew Jackson was flabbergasted when this inheritance arrived on his desk in 1835. On one hand, he was disinclined to look a gift horse in the mouth. On the other, the notion of a public institution devoted to learning insulted his entire notion of government. After consulting with his congressional cohorts, Jackson diverted the money to his pet banks, which soon gambled nearly all of it away in get-rich schemes. An outraged John Quincy Adams resurrected Smithson's legacy by shaming congressional majorities into appropriating the same amount of money to a trust that in 1846 become the Smithsonian Institute.[19]

Women led the way in many social refinements. Advice books, including *The Lady's Guide to Perfect Gentility*, *A Guide to Politeness*, and the bestselling *The American Frugal Housewife* by Lydia Maria Child and *Godey's Lady's Book* by Sarah Hale, inspired women to be more refined wives, mothers, friends, and neighbors. Being a lady involved learning the arts of conversation, letter writing, penmanship, needlework, dancing, and charity. The challenges of parenting were rendered less so through such books as Child's *The Mother's Book*, John Abbott's *The Mother at Home*, and William Abbott's *The Young Mother's Guide*. Both mothers and fathers learned to nurture their children's natural development with affection rather than the rod.

America's cultural revolution at once reflected and shaped an increasingly literate, curious, refined, and knowledgeable society. Yet the revolution's scope was limited. John Quincy Adams echoed George Washington's and Alexander Hamilton's calls for a national university, and like them, he suffered mostly indifference broken by derision. The Northeast was the cultural revolution's epicenter, and its power diminished as one journeyed farther south and west. At some point, the "parlor culture" dissolved into a "bowie-knife culture."

The industrial revolution benefited most people, but there were also plenty of losers. The growing wealth spawned by industrialization was hardly shared equally across the country. While most whites in the northern free states were solidly middle class, more whites were poor than middle class in the southern slave states. Plantation owners enjoyed the lion's share of the wealth created in the South.[20]

America's factories may not have produced the horrors of Dickensian England, but they were bad enough. All that whirling, pounding machinery steadily destroyed one's hearing and often caught and mangled or ripped off workers' hands and fingers. Mass production threw legions of craftsmen out of their shops. Middle-class families lost income and members as daughters abandoned their looms for the drudgery, dangers, and clamor of a factory a dozen hours a day, six days a week. Industrialization and urbanization caused average longevity to drop from fifty-two to forty-seven years and average height from 1/3 to 171 centimeters between 1815 and 1845. People ate less nutritiously and were assailed by more diseases in the city than in the countryside.[21]

Laborers began to organize themselves. The first Working Man's Party was founded in New York in 1829, and others soon mushroomed in other industrial cities. These groups demanded more pay, better conditions, and ten-hour days. Until the mid-1840s the relative scarcity of labor gave workers bargaining power that their English counterparts lacked. But thereafter, the mass immigration of Irish, Germans, and others rapidly diluted their initial edge.[22]

A powerful part of Jackson's populist appeal was his claim to represent the common working man. Indeed, he went so far as to argue, "Let labor have security, prosperity will follow—all other interests rest upon it, and must flourish if it flourishes."[23] Yet, understandably, he drew the line when labor demands became violent. When workers on the Chesapeake and Ohio Canal rioted in 1834, he became the first president to restore order with federal troops, even though the labor dispute "had not arisen out of a violation of federal law or a defiance of the federal government."[24] For this, Jackson was once again criticized for violating the Constitution. And once again Jackson replied by ranting against his critics.

Henry Clay coined the term "self-made man" in an 1832 speech. In doing so, he stuck a label on an increasingly common phenomenon. Individualism, or the right of each person to freely develop and express oneself, is a crucial component of American culture. During the age of Jackson, individualism in America came to be viewed as solely positive and something that all should strive for. Before then, during the colonial and well into early republic era, communitarianism prevailed and condemned individualism as leading to selfishness and alienation. A church was every community's heart and soul, and that church demanded the strict conformity of its members to its strictures.

Yet, even from the earliest colony, extraordinary individuals, including John Smith, Thomas Morton, Anne Hutchinson, Roger Williams, William Byrd, and above all, Benjamin Franklin, defied convention and asserted themselves. With time, communalism's bonds weakened, and people were freer to express themselves. By the late eighteenth century, Franklin's individualism as an inventor, editor, philosopher, bon vivant, deist, and libertine provoked more admiration than scorn.

Franklin is, in so many ways, the quintessential American because he was the first to popularize liberalism as both a lifestyle and a political philosophy. More than anyone else, he led the way to the revolution of American creativity.[25]

Yet some Americans sought refuge from the merciless Darwinian marketplace in communalism. Robert Owen, a British industrialist, pioneered a humanitarian labor system for his factory at New Lanark, Scotland, that included high wages and safety standards, comfortable living quarters, hearty food, ten-hour workdays, child care, and after-work activities that promoted learning and community. He made these values the foundation for a community he founded at New Harmony, Indiana, in 1825, but the experiment only lasted four years before it broke up from worsening quarrels among its members.

Some visionaries went even further in their quest for communalism and egalitarianism. In 1774 Ann Lee founded the United Society of Believers in Christ's Second Appearing, better known as the Shakers, on the values of equality between men and women, the equal sharing of work and wealth, craftsmanship, joyful prayers, hymns, dance, and chastity. By 1840 the Shakers reached their height with six thousand members in a score of communities in New York, Massachusetts, New Hampshire, and Kentucky. But eventually, the chastity requirement caused the sect's demise. John Noyes founded his Oneida Community on the diametrically opposed value of free love in upstate New York in 1848, but his experiment lasted only until 1879, when its last members drifted away. Brook Farm was a utopian community founded on transcendental and unitarian principles by George and Sophia Ripley in 1841, but it closed in 1847; Nathaniel Hawthorne later satirized the community's pretentions and squabbles in his novel *The Blithedale Romance*.

Communalism was a rare, fleeting, and heartily mocked sideshow in Jacksonian America. Materialism consumed virtually all Americans then and has ever since. The industrial revolution gave more people the power to buy more things; the greater their buying power, the more they wanted, and their insatiable demand proliferated the factories and rewarded the inventers, entrepreneurs, financiers, managers, and workers who produced all those things and the merchants who sold them. Tall chimneys belched smoke from more factories; cities spread, devouring farmlands; houses grew bigger and more crowded with stuff;

clocks, rather than seasons, governed the working lives of more people; and steamboats, trains, and barges propelled people and products via a web of narrow lines across the nation. Most folks marveled at these extraordinary changes. Ralph Waldo Emerson conveyed that wonder with these words: "America is the country of the future. It is a country of beginnings, of projects, of vast designs and expectations."[26]

17

The Transcendentalists

I went to the woods because I wished to live deliberately, to front
only the essential facts of life, and see if I could not learn what it had
to teach, and not, when I came to die, discover that I had not lived.

HENRY DAVID THOREAU

Standing on the bare ground—my head bathed by the blithe
air and uplifted into the infinite space—all mean egotism
vanishes. . . . I am nothing; I see all; the currents of Universal
Being circulate through me. I am part and parcel of God.

RALPH WALDO EMERSON

We can make our lives sublime, and departing leave
behind us footprints in the sands of time.

HENRY WADSWORTH LONGFELLOW

Creativity can at once profoundly reflect and shape national power. Inventors, engineers, and scientists clearly do so with the wealth they help make and distribute from their respective enterprises. But painters, writers, composers, sculptors, architects, and choreographers can also empower a nation by creating sources of unifying pride, inspiration, and criticism.

American arts and letters achieved unprecedented heights during the age of Jackson. Charles Peale's painting *The Artist in His Museum* (1822) wonderfully depicted this American renaissance. Peale painted himself drawing a curtain aside and revealing his Museum of Curiosities, the nation's first. His collection brought together elements of the artistic, scientific, and natural worlds. Peale was not just a fine painter and promoter of art and science; he also passed on his vocation and skills to four of his sixteen children—Raphaelle, Rembrandt, Rubens, and Titian—whose work spanned the early republic and Jacksonian eras.

It was during an age of mass and crass materialism that art and literature caught up to commerce in the power of its expression. The Hudson River and Luminist schools of painters and the Concord school of writers produced brilliant, insidiously subversive works that provided an alternative vision to the prevailing national obsession with making money, exploiting others, and often devastating the natural world in the process. And in doing so, they have ever since inspired those who are profoundly restless, curious, questioning, and searching.[1]

Thomas Cole and Ralph Waldo Emerson were the founders and leading theorists for the respective schools of painters and writers that drew inspiration from and developed the philosophy of transcendentalism. Asher Durand's painting *Kindred Spirits* captured the dynamism between the genres by depicting the poet and publisher William Cullen Bryant and the painter Thomas Cole talking amiably atop a crag deep in wilderness.

Transcendentalism is the belief that God and nature are one and thus that people are the closest to God when they immerse themselves in nature. Emerson described a transcendent experience as follows: "Standing on the bare ground—my head bathed by the blithe air and uplifted into the infinite space—all mean egotism vanishes. . . . I am nothing; I see all; the currents of Universal Being circulate through me. I am part and parcel of God."[2]

This outlook reflects a revolution in American thought. For their first couple of centuries in the New World, Americans viewed nature through a Bible-thumping Puritan prism that condemned wilderness as the abode of evil. Any American who ventured there must be constantly vigilant against the temptations of savage life, much as Jesus resisted the devil's entreaties during his sojourn of forty days and nights.

During the seventeenth century, anyone who expressed the belief that God and nature were inseparable would likely have been condemned for heresy and witchcraft.

Transcendentalism was inspired by Europe's Romantic movement, which celebrated the sublime in nature. It was also a conscious attempt by writers and painters to assert a unique dimension of American civilization. Nature across most of the continent was still largely wild, whereas Europe's environment had been manipulated by thousands of years of history.[3]

The transcendentalists celebrated a pristine nature rapidly being destroyed by a civilization obsessed with getting rich and amassing more things. The awareness that all life is transient provokes at once wonder and melancholy. In his journey around the country, Alexis de Tocqueville was strongly moved by his "consciousness of the destruction, of quick and inevitable change that gives such a touching beauty to the solitudes of America. . . . One is in some sort of a hurry to admire them."[4]

Henry David Thoreau was a close friend of Emerson and for a while lived with his family and tutored his children. He began his famous two-year sojourn at Walden Pond in 1845, deliberately on the symbolic date of July 4. He later explained, "I went to the woods because I wished to live deliberately, to front only the essential facts of life, and see if I could not learn what it had to teach, and not, when I came to die, discover that I had not lived."[5] Thoreau was no Daniel Boone. Walden Pond was just a two-mile stroll through the woods from Concord, and he frequently stayed in town at his mother's house or with friends. Likewise, his much-celebrated civil disobedience during the Mexican War hardly made a martyr of him; he was jailed overnight for refusing to pay a $1.50 poll tax in protest against the war. Yet the beauty and profundity of his writings on these experiences have ever since inspired countless people around the world to explore and realize the meaning behind them.

Transcendentalism is a theme in James Fenimore Cooper's Leatherstocking Tales, of which *The Last of the Mohicans* is the most famous. Cooper modeled Nathaniel Bumppo, the series hero, on Daniel Boone. Bumppo is at home in the wilderness, solitary by nature but social when necessary, a reluctant killer who is compassionate toward the needy, and a man who revels in the sublimity of nature.[6]

Cooper imagined, often inaccurately, a world that he never visited let alone inhabited. Two contemporary writers—Washington Irving and Francis Parkman—did trek for months through wilderness, although neither embraced transcendentalism. Irving's histories *Astoria* (1836) and *The Adventures of Captain Bonneville* (1837) are enlivened by his journey onto the Great Plains in 1832 as a member of a surveying expedition, while Parkman's *Oregon Trail* (1847) recounts his previous year's hunting expedition on the plains. Irving's other writings are diverse and include short stories, biographies, histories, novels, and travel accounts. Parkman, in contrast, wrote a series of histories of colonial America characterized by meticulous research and a vivid style.

The relationship between man and nature was the central theme of this age's greatest American writer, Herman Melville, who experienced wilderness at sea rather than on land. He drew deep from his experiences to write a series of thought-provoking novels and short stories, including *Typee* (1846), *Omoo* (1847), *White Jacket* (1850), and most powerful of all, *Moby Dick, or the Whale* (1851), that explored with mingled skepticism and wonder the most profound existential questions. Nathaniel Hawthorne was a much better known and critically acclaimed writer at that time and Melville's friend. His greatest work, *The Scarlet Letter* (1850), explores not man and nature but human nature through the spectrum of passion, conformity, courage, cowardice, hypocrisy, and fulfillment in a Puritan village in colonial Massachusetts, as a young woman is seduced and abandoned with child by the church minister, a seeming paragon of virtue. In his macabre short stories and poems, Edgar Allan Poe journeys even deeper into the wilderness of one's mind, exploring the darker passions and terrors that lurk within. The frontiers of style and psyche that these writers explored opened the way for Walt Whitman to celebrate passion, sensuality, and forbidden sexuality in his poetry collection *The Leaves of Grass* (1855).[7]

If America's literary renaissance had a Florence, it was Concord, Massachusetts, where such luminaries as Emerson, Thoreau, Hawthorne, Louisa May Alcott, Margaret Fuller, and Elizabeth Peabody for varying lengths of time lived, wrote, and inspired each other. Yet Concord had a rival in New York City, where John O'Sullivan edited his *Democratic Review*. O'Sullivan promoted a cultural as well as territorial manifest destiny for the United States by publishing essays, short stories, and poetry by Hawthorne, Melville, Whitman, and other writers. For him, American literature was "another ligament to the ties which bind a people together."[8]

Painters expressed transcendentalism through the Hudson River and Luminist schools. Hudson River painters—including Thomas Cole, Asher Durand, Jasper Cropsey, Gifford Sanford, George Inness, Thomas Doughty, and Frederick Church—depicted sublime scenes of pure wilderness or lonely settlements surrounded by thick forest and soaring mountains. Luminism turned to another great wilderness against which humans are insignificant yet from which they can derive great meaning—the sea. Martin Heade, Robert Salmon, John Kensett, and Fitz Hugh Lane painted magnificent and often haunting seascapes. Many paintings of Salmon and Lane depicted majestic sailing ships at anchor in tranquil port waters illuminated by sunsets. Civilization was often absent in the seascapes and beachscapes of Heade and Kensett. Heade's most famous canvas, *Approaching Thunder Storm*, depicts a sailor sitting on driftwood on a lonely shore gazing across an inlet leading out to sea, where a distant vessel sails beneath leaden clouds that appear about to release a deluge.

No painting more beautifully conveys transcendentalism's essential values than Cole's *The Oxbow* (1836). The foreground is a forested mountain overlooking an oxbow twist of the Connecticut River in the valley below. The oxbow is a symbol of man's attempt to yoke nature, whose hubris and futility is revealed by the tranquil sunny summer day on the painting's right half that will soon be devastated by a storm surging in from the left. In the foreground, amid a tangle of undergrowth and trees, is a painter who, with brush in hand and canvas before him, looks curiously back at us.

Transcendentalism contrasts the transience of individual human lives with nature, which at once constantly changes and perpetually endures. Civilizations are often compared to people, who pass through stages of infancy, youth, adulthood, and finally, death. Cole expressed this idea through his most famous series of paintings, the Course of Empire (1836) and the Voyage of Life (1839–40). These series, especially the Course of Empire, can be profoundly unsettling for most Americans, who celebrate the notion of unending linear progress and emotionally bury death. Although most people may accept, if not dwell upon, the reality that one day they will die, the thought that America may decline or outright collapse is radically at odds with the people's belief that their nation will live on, not just indefinitely, but ever better.

While transcendentalism inspired some of this age's greatest paintings and writings, many artists and writers created profound works unrelated to that philosophy. Indeed, no one better depicted ideal versions of the age of Jackson than George Caleb Bingham, although his best paintings appeared shortly after the nation entered a new era. In his *The County Election* (1851–52), *Canvassing for a Vote* (1852), *Stump Speaking* (1854), and *Verdict of the People* (1854–55), "the People" are almost invariably prosperous, well dressed, well fed, male, and white. Whether they are at work, politics, or play, they express a remarkable mix of skill, fun, humor, progress, freedom, and equality, in other words the noblest and most joyful expressions of being an American. Among them, there is no discernible inequity, poverty, racism, violence, corruption, incompetence, or injustice. On the fringe of the crowd or activity is the occasional reveler who has overindulged, but he is depicted with knowing winks of amusement rather than disdain, let alone condemnation.

In his only truly haunting painting, Bingham hints at another world distant, alien, parallel, and at times, overlapping with American civilization. The *Fur Traders Descending the Missouri* (1845) depicts a grizzled older man, a half-Indian youth who is likely his son, and a chained bear cub in a dugout canoe on a luminous river that merges into a hazy sky. Whether Bingham consciously intended it or not, his painting can be seen as a metaphor for the American experience. The trappers—the older white and the younger of mixed blood—are returning to civilization in a canoe riding low in the water beneath the weight of furs that they have trapped or hunted in the wilderness. These furs will materially enrich both civilization and themselves. Yet trouble may lurk downstream from that tranquil, timeless scene. The chained bear cub will grow up; whether it stays tamed or reverts to its wild instincts remains to be seen. The man has left the boy's mother behind. Had he brought her with him, he would have suffered jeers, snubs, and possible violence for being a "squaw man" with a "savage" wife and "half-breed" son. The youth will face a hard time in a racist society.

Bingham was not the only painter of the common man, nor was he the best at the genre. William Sidney Mount, Eastman Johnson, and Henry Inman painted individual Americans with far more refined techniques and profound expressions. In contrast to Bingham's crowded, clamorous scenes, theirs are intimate with a few people horse-trading, whittling, fiddling, courting, cornhusking, or lazing. And, unlike Bingham, they often depicted black people serving, observing, and occasionally working alongside whites. In Mount's most famous painting, *Eel Spearing at Setauket*, a large black woman stands ready with a trident in the prow of a boat paddled by a white boy; together they will bring back and probably share that evening's meal of eel.

Although most painters of the era rarely depicted blacks, let alone deeply explored their world, Indians were a primary subject of Charles Bird King, George Catlin, Alfred Jacob Miller, William Ranney, and Charles Deas. All five journeyed through parts of the American West. Catlin and Miller made it all the way across the plains to the Rockies during the golden age of the mountain men and returned with portfolios of buffalo hunts, war dances, rendezvous, trap setting, and even romance. Miller's *The Trapper's Bride* (1845) depicted a young trapper taking the hand of a comely Indian girl being given away in marriage by her family, which likely received horses and other gifts in return. The painting shows harmonious relations between Americans and Indians that were often observed in the Far West but were unthinkable back in the "civilized" East. Deas symbolically expressed a much more common reality in his stunning and disturbing painting *The Death Struggle* (1845), in which a frontiersman and a warrior on horses are plunging together off a cliff; the warrior hugs tight the frontiersman, who grips the reins with one hand and a frail tree branch with the other.

These painters tried to capture images of a race that they believed was doomed. Although Indian peoples would never completely vanish, they were devastated by war, disease, forced removal, deliberate ethnic cleansing, and the inability of most either to assimilate or segregate themselves completely. This sense of impending doom was evocatively captured in *The Last of the Race* (1847) by Thompkins Matteson, who painted from a sentimental imagination rather than firsthand experience of his subjects; the painting depicts an Indian family on a lonely shore or perhaps an island staring morosely out to a sun setting into the sea.

Surprisingly, only one painter of this era tried to inspire a patriotism that transcended political parties and philosophies. Through four marvelous paintings now hanging in the Capitol's rotunda, John Trumbull captured the American Revolution's highlights. Of them his *The Signing of the Declaration of Independence* (1820) is the most famous. The roomful of luminaries, with Jefferson and Adams in the center, at once contrasts with and eventually leads to the anonymous but prosperous, happy, hardworking, and free spirits of Benton's Jacksonian America.

During the age of Jackson, one art form explicitly expressed the theme of democracy. Architects of the Greek Revival style evoked Athenian democracy in their buildings and, in doing so, launched a revolutionary departure from established styles like the Salt Box, Georgian, and Federal. Greek Revival's massive pillars, supporting a triangular capital and grounded on a wide poach, epitomized at once the nation's democratic ideals and the ability of ever more Americans to afford beautiful homes. More than anyone, Thomas Jefferson founded and developed this style by realizing his vision for his own home, Monticello (1767–1807); Virginia's State House (1785–99); and the complex of buildings for the University of Virginia (1822–26). Jefferson took his ideas for Greek Revival from four key sources. Two were from the past: the ancient Roman Maison Carée in Nîmes, France, and the seventeenth-century masterpieces of Italian architect Andrea Palladio. Two were contemporary: Charles Bulfinch, whose greatest work was the Massachusetts State House, and Benjamin Henry Latrobe, renowned for his Bank of Pennsylvania (1800) and the Capitol (1816–17). These public buildings inspired scaled-down designs for countless houses across the nation. Architecture was democratized with 188 books on the subject appearing from 1799 to 1860.[9] Owners and builders worked together to design unique features into houses.

How much did the arts during the age of Jackson at once reflect and shape the national image and thus enhance American power? Lovers of painting, literature, and philosophy can patriotically revel in the dazzling expressions of genius created during these decades. Yet these thrills are shared by only a tiny sliver of the population. America's renaissance did not create any enduring national icons that stirred mass emotions. The only paintings that come close are Miller's *The Trapper's Bride* (1845), Charles Deas's *Long Jakes, or the Rocky Mountain Man* (1844) or, better still, *The Death Struggle* (1845), and Bingham's *Daniel Boone Escort-*

ing Settlers through the Cumberland Gap (1852). Alas, few people other than art aficionados are familiar with these paintings. Although the names of Irving, Parker, Emerson, Thoreau, Hawthorne, Melville, and Poe may resonate with more Americans, few have actually read any of their works, even when they were assigned in class.

A set of ideas rather than books or paintings has been far more enduring, although few are aware of the genesis. Transcendentalism was the nation's most powerful intellectual movement during the age of Jackson. Indeed, that philosophy was inspired partly in reaction to Jacksonism's pervasive greed, corruption, aggression, and violence. But this philosophy remained confined to the hearts, minds, and souls of a handful of devotees for more than a century until the late 1960s, when it finally blossomed into the related environmental and New Age movements. Since then, New Age ideas have enriched the lives of countless people and environmentalists have scored vital victories that have curbed some pollution and saved some natural habitats, but these movements are clearly outgunned by their nemeses.

In the end, Jacksonism was and remains either indifferent or scornful of painting and literature. And thus, Jacksonians neglect an essential element of the art of American power. The sublimity of their work aside, artists and writers tend to be devil's advocates, and their skepticism is crucial for American democracy to survive, let alone thrive, with a powerful quasi-authoritarian ideology and movement like Jacksonism in its midst. But, of course, Jacksonians must always disdain this tool of power. If Jacksonians embraced self-awareness, unbridled creativity, and irony, they would no longer be Jacksonians.

Although Jacksonians and transcendentalists are bitter and implacable foes, each might find inspiration in these lines by Henry Wadsworth Longfellow:

Life is real! Life is earnest!
And the grave is not its goal . . .
Lives of great men all remind us
We can make our lives sublime,
And departing leave behind us
Footprints in the sands of time . . .

18

The Annexation

We must regain Texas, peaceably if we can, forcibly if we must.

ANDREW JACKSON

Annexation and war with Mexico are identical.

HENRY CLAY

We want a war with Mexico and . . . we may be blessed
with an opportunity to give the Mexicans a drubbing, (which
they have long deserved) and acquire Northern Mexico
and Upper California, which has of late become indispensable to . . . complete our defense and wants on the Pacific.

ARCHIBALD YELL

The annexation of Texas topped the to-do list of American expansion-
ists for one practical reason—if the United States did not take Texas,
Britain or another European power would.[1] Nearly all southerners carried fear of a European takeover a huge step further. A European over-
lord might well abolish slavery in Texas, thus depriving the owners of
their God-given right and converting that land into a refuge for escaped
slaves, much like Florida once was.

Andrew Jackson naturally championed this view: "We must regain Texas, peaceably if we can, forcibly if we must."[2] In a letter to the Nashville Union, he warned, "If Texas be not speedily admitted into our confederacy, she must and will be inevitably driven into alliances and commercial regulations with the European powers, of a character highly injurious and probably hostile to this country. . . . She is the key to our safety in the South and the West. She offers this key to us on fair and honorable terms. Let us take it and lock the door against future danger."[3]

This was not an irrational fear. Britain's minister to Mexico, Charles Elliot, had proposed that Britain would pay off Texas's national debt if Texas eliminated slavery and trade barriers. News of this proposal provoked an uproar among American southerners. Secretary of State Daniel Webster requested a formal explanation from his counterpart. Although Foreign Secretary George Hamilton-Gordon, Lord Aberdeen, replied that Elliot had expressed his personal rather than his government's view, this did not mend the political damage.[4]

Within John Tyler's administration, only Webster opposed annexation, but his voice and mind were so powerful that he stymied the president and other secretaries. This restraint disappeared when he resigned in May 1843. Tyler replaced him with Abel Upshur, the navy secretary and an unabashed slavocrat. Even then, Tyler was careful to line up most senators and representatives informally before he acted. By September 1843 he felt secure enough to give the nod to his secretary of state.

Upshur informed Isaac Van Zandt, the minister from Texas, that the White House now favored annexation. To the shock of many, President Sam Houston rebuffed the notion. Britain and France had offered to convince Mexico to recognize Texas independence if it remained an independent country. When Jackson learned of this, he shot off a letter to Houston, asking his old friend and protégé to reconsider. But Houston held firm until he learned the Mexican response. The Mexicans would agree only to an indefinite truce; they refused to recognize Texas independence under any circumstances. Houston then put the matter before Texas's congress, which in December 1843, voted overwhelmingly for annexation and, to this end, authorized negotiations with the United States.

A tragedy disrupted the process. President Tyler; most of the cabinet;

leading senators, representatives, and businessmen; and many of their wives—some four hundred people—packed aboard the newly launched state-of-the-art warship, the steam-driven, ironclad USS *Princeton*, on the frigid morning of February 28, 1844. This pride of American naval power was celebrated by the test firing of its two most powerful cannons followed by a banquet. After each of the guns, dubbed the "Peacemaker" and "Oregon," with their fifteen-foot barrels shot a 212-pound shell three miles, the dignitaries retired below decks for the feast. For several hours, they devoured one delicious dish of food after another and washed them down with numerous glasses of champagne. Finally, most of the stuffed and tipsy revelers stumbled back on deck for the second round of test firing. Tyler lingered below, but Secretary of State Upshur, Navy Secretary Thomas Gilmer, and Senator Thomas Hart Benton crowded with others around the huge guns. When the gunner yanked the lanyard, the barrel exploded with a deafening roar. The fiery hot iron chunks instantly killed eight observers, including Upshur and Gilmer; knocked Benton flat; and wounded dozens more.

Tyler replaced Upshur with John Calhoun, who began talks with Houston's two envoys. Under the annexation treaty that they signed on April 12, 1844, Texas would enter the Union as a territory, not a state. In the short-term, this appeased northerners who opposed Texas as a slave state. Texas would transfer its vast public lands to the United States and Washington would assume its $10 million public debt. No specific boundaries were cited. Tyler submitted the treaty to the Senate on April 22.

Henry Clay and Martin Van Buren were leading antiannexation voices. They stirred political tempests when newspapers published their letters on the topic. On April 17 Clay bluntly wrote, "Annexation and war with Mexico are identical." As troubling was that annexation would "proclaim to the world" America's "insatiable and unquenchable thirst for foreign conquest or acquisition of territory." It would be "far more wise and important to compose and harmonize the present confederacy . . . than to introduce a new element of discord and distraction into it." In another letter, Clay declared that he had "no objection to the annexation of Texas, but certainly would be unwilling to see the existing Union dissolved or seriously jeopardized for the sake of acquiring Texas." He later explained that he favored taking Texas only if it were done "without the loss of national character, without the hazard of foreign war, with the general concurrence of the nation, without any danger to the integrity of the Union, and without giving a reasonable price for Texas." And as if these conditions were not daunting enough, he warned that annexation would also reignite the shrill, divisive slavery debate and explode the national debt. On April 20 Van Buren also strongly opposed annexation with mostly the same reasons, adding that it would violate America's highest ideals: "It has hitherto been our pride and our boast that, whilst the lust of power . . . has led other . . . governments to aggression and conquest," the United States had "always been regulated by reason and justice."[5]

Clay and Van Buren articulated a version of national security diametrically opposed to that advocated by the Jacksonians. American power ultimately lay in adherence to the principles upon which it was founded. Imperialism, or the conquest and exploitation of other people, was an anti-American value and practice and thus should be shunned.

These were courageous stands given each man's presidential aspirations. Upon reading Clay's words, Jackson chortled that his rival was "a dead political duck." But Van Buren's stand against annexation provoked "tears of regret" in Jackson, who was heartbroken and angry at his disciple's betrayal. Old Hickory abruptly threw his support from Van Buren to James Polk as the Democratic Party candidate for the presidency. Jackson had many reasons to embrace the protégé dubbed Young Hickory, but the most important was his public declaration on April 23 that "I am in favor of the immediate re-annexation of Texas to the territory and government of the United States." Jackson summoned Polk to the Hermitage on May 13 and promised to do what he could to secure his nomination.[6]

At this point, probably two of three senators favored the treaty, just enough for ratification. But Secretary of State Calhoun killed the chance of approval by writing British minister Richard Pakenham that the core reason for annexing Texas was to prevent Britain from taking over the realm and abolishing slavery. Calhoun insisted that abolishing slavery in the region would be evil because slaves were better off and happier than northern laborers. The secretary's letter appeared in the *New York Evening Post* on April 27.[7]

Calhoun's message provoked outraged protests from those senators who had no intention of defending slavery. Not just the Whig Party but moderate Democrats like Thomas Hart Benton announced that henceforth they opposed ratification. The Senate crushed annexation with a 35 to 16 vote against the bill on June 8, 1844. News of the rejection caused an uproar in Texas. Now twice spurned in their suit for union with the United States, Texans faced two unsavory choices. They could go it alone, continue to pile up their national debt, and exist under the shadow of another Mexican invasion. Or they could seek shelter as Britain's protectorate at the cost of their pride, sovereignty, and slaves.

Despite their defeat, President Tyler and other annexation advocates did not give up. The president sent Andrew Jackson Donelson, Old Hickory's nephew, to Austin with the promise that his administration remained committed to annexation. Donelson was a good choice for this job. He graduated second in his class at West Point and had served as Jackson's aide during his Florida campaign and his secretary during his White House years. After arriving in Texas on November 11, 1844, he conducted a series of talks with President Sam Houston and Secretary of State Anson Jones. He grimly reported to Secretary of State Calhoun, "Every day's delay is adding strength to the hands of those who are playing the game for the ascendancy of British influence in this Republic."[8]

Meanwhile, the political parties chose their standard-bearers for the 1844 election. Baltimore again hosted two conventions. The Whig Party met there on May 1 and unanimously acclaimed Henry Clay as their nominee. It was Clay's third run for the White House. He was confident of victory after learning his Democratic opponent's identity.[9]

The Democrats took far longer to choose a candidate as they were split between two bitterly opposed factions, each derogatively nicknamed by the other. Van Buren's followers were known as the Barnburners for reputedly being so radical that they would burn down their own barn to drive out the rats. The Barnburners rather contradictorily called for eliminating both the national debt and the national tariff, even though the former would be impossible without the latter. The Jacksonian loyalists were called the Hunkers because they hunkered after the political spoils they would reap with their candidate in the White House. The Hunkers were willing to cut deals on issues like the tariff, land sales, and internal improvements.

When the Democrats met on May 27, five men contended openly—Martin Van Buren of New York, Lewis Cass of Michigan, Richard Johnson of Kentucky, John Calhoun of South Carolina, and James Buchanan of Pennsylvania. A winner would be declared only after receiving the votes of two of three delegates. On the first vote, Van Buren garnered an impressive 146, compared to 83 for Cass, 24 for Johnson, 6 for Calhoun, 4 for Buchanan, and 1 each for Levi Woodbury and Charles Stewart, but short of the 177 needed for victory. Backroom horse trading caused the numbers to fluctuate widely in subsequent votes during the next week but put no aspirant over the top.

Although he was far away at the Hermitage, Jackson pulled what political levers he could to convince the convention to embrace James Polk. His protégé was considered the long-shot, or "dark-horse," candidate, the first-known political use of that term. Tennessee's legislature originally nominated him for the vice presidency, but as a stalemate emerged between Van Buren and Cass, Polk increasingly seemed like a sensible compromise with his excellent political résumé and Jackson's backing. He got his first votes on the eighth ballot, after his supporters mustered the backers of lesser candidates. Polk won decisively with 233 votes on the ninth ballot on May 29. For vice president, the first choice was Silas Wright. When he refused, the delegates picked George Dallas, who had served in Pennsylvania's assembly, the U.S. Senate, and in St. Petersburg as America's minister to Russia. It took a while for word of the convention's decision to reach Polk at his home in Nashville, Tennessee. On June 12 he sent them his acceptance and cleverly rallied the disappointed losers behind his campaign by pledging that he would be a one-term president.[10]

The election was a contrast in personalities, with the charismatic, crowd-pleasing Clay versus the pedantic, somber Polk. But Clay's seeming advantage obscured critical weaknesses. Over the years, he had alienated countless potential supporters with his acerbic wit. More important, he had enraged slave owners and abolitionists alike by opposing both slavery and abolition. He compounded the hatred of many westerners and southerners against him by rejecting Texas annexation. In contrast, Polk ran a low-key but effective campaign. His unabashed championing of slavery and annexation won him the South and the West. Although these stands alienated most northeastern voters, he gleaned some votes there with his record of backing various tariff bills for revenue if not for protection of manufacturing.

Polk nosed ahead of Clay in the popular vote with 1,337,243 to 1,299,062, a 38,181 vote margin, or 49.5 percent to 48.1 percent. But he won decisively in the Electoral College, with 170 to 105 votes. The Liberty Party fared much better in this election than the last; James Birney's 62,300 votes undoubtedly played a spoiler role in Clay's defeat by siphoning support in New York, which Polk carried by 5,106 votes. Winning New York would have put Clay over the top with 141 to 134 electoral votes. Had this happened, the course of America's development and power, and thus the fate of the world, would have deviated sharply from what actually occurred.[11]

Lame-duck John Tyler had not garnered much of a legacy for his presidency. So far the word "no" best characterized his four years. He was either renowned or reviled for vetoing several Whig bills, while the Senate had rebuffed his Texas treaty. Yet he still had several months in office and was determined to do what he could to leave behind an enduring gift to the nation.

An appeal for annexation was the core message of his last State of the Union address, which he delivered on December 2, 1844. He rooted his arguments in democratic principles: "A controlling majority of the people and a large majority of the states have declared in favor of immediate annexation. It is the will of both the people and the states that Texas shall be annexed to the Union promptly and immediately." He then called on Congress to invite Texas into the United States with a joint resolution.[12]

The subsequent debate in both houses was fierce. Most Whigs opposed annexation for any reason, but the idea of offering annexation by resolution rather than by treaty alarmed them on constitutional grounds. Those in favor split between admitting Texas immediately as a state or as a territory that would earn statehood.

The House first reached a consensus. Texas would be admitted as a state with the duty to service its own public debt and the right to retain all its public lands and laws, including slavery. Washington would determine the state's boundaries. In the future, with Austin's agreement, territory could be split off to make up to four additional states. The House passed this resolution by 120 to 98 on January 25.

The idea that Texas could potentially be split into five slave states, each with two senators, horrified northerners. This would destroy the delicate sectional balance and let the slave states rule America. When a similar resolution was introduced in the Senate Foreign Relations Committee, a majority voted it down. Thomas Hart Benton of Missouri then proposed that Texas be admitted as a state and that Congress work out the details later. Critics condemned this on the grounds that Texas would likely reject the plan for its uncertainties. Robert Walker of Mississippi offered the compromise of giving the president the choice of offering Texas either the House or Benton resolutions. Walker's resolution passed the Senate by 27 to 25 on February 27, 1845, and the House by 132 to 75 the following day. Tyler signed the resolution into law on March 1, 1845, and sent the House version to Donelson in Austin to present to the Texas republic.

It took weeks before Washington learned how Texans replied to the resolution. News of Mexico's reaction, however, was almost immediate. Ambassador Juan Almonte acted on standing instructions to leave the United States promptly if it officially resolved to annex Texas. He did so, condemning America's takeover as "an act of aggression the most unjust which can be found recorded in the annals of modern history."[13] Almonte did not confine such gross exaggerations to an American audience. His disparagement of American military power to the Mexican government was a major reason why Mexico City stonewalled the Polk administration's attempts to resolve the U.S.-Mexican conflict over Texas peacefully.[14]

Those who hoped that Almonte's departure was just a gesture soon learned otherwise. On March 28, 1845, Foreign Minister Luis Cuevas wrote American minister Wilson Shannon, "Diplomatic relations between the two countries cannot be continued." Shannon appealed for the conflict's amicable resolution. Cuevas replied that his government rejected relations with a country that "usurped a portion of territory which belongs to Mexico by a right which she will maintain at whatever cost." And with this, Cuevas ended all official communication with Shannon.[15]

The incoming president faced what appeared to be an intractable conflict with a neighboring country that perhaps only war could resolve. As if this were not challenging enough, Polk soon provoked a crisis with another neighbor that also seemed destined to end in war.

James Polk took the oath of office from Chief Justice Roger Taney on March 4, 1845. This was a triumphant moment in Jacksonism's history as two of Old Hickory's disciples looked into each other's eyes across a Bible before the Capitol, where Democratic majorities dominated each chamber. Jacksonism dominated all three branches of the federal government.

In his inaugural address, Polk articulated Jacksonism's essence. He condemned the Whig platform that promoted a U.S. bank, internal improvements, and protective tariffs. While upholding states' rights, he took a swipe at radical Democrats by rejecting nullification. He applauded the resolution for Texas annexation and promised to take the Oregon Territory. He defended slavery with the peculiar American talent of not directly naming it. Above all, he insisted, "Our Federal union—it must be preserved."[16]

So who was James Polk?[17] He has been described as "a smaller-than life figure" with "larger-than-life ambitions."[18] He was born on a farm in Mecklenburg County, North Carolina, about twenty miles and more than a generation apart from Andrew Jackson. Like his future mentor, he migrated to Tennessee, became a lawyer, and rose steadily in the state's political and plantation ranks. Yet he differed from Jackson in crucial ways. He was no warrior and never even served in the military. He had been a frail child who suffered from kidney stones until a gruesome operation removed them, and most likely his virility, when he was seventeen. He graduated with honors from the University of North Carolina in 1818. Then, he journeyed to Nashville and studied law under Felix Grundy. He entered the political world the following year, when Grundy secured him the post of senate clerk in Tennessee's assembly.

Polk was that rarity in politics, an introvert in an extrovert's profession. He stood out for approaching life with somber-minded, humorless rigor. He was often two-faced; hating confrontation, he preferred to thrust a political stiletto when his foe's back was turned. His speeches were constructed and delivered much like legal briefs, void of the soaring imagery and oratory of a Clay or Webster. Sam Houston mocked Polk as being "a victim of the use of water as a beverage."[19] Others found worse faults. Gideon Welles, then a Navy Department official, damned Polk's "trait of sly cunning which he thought shrewdness, but which was really disingenuousness and duplicity."[20] Through his diary,

Polk revealed that he was a control freak, workaholic, and Jacksonian dogmatist who was fiercely partisan and could be vindictive but truly believed that right was on his side. He was a stickler for detail and procedure and persisted doggedly until his work was done. He wearily confided to his diary that "no president who performs his duty faithfully . . . . can have any leisure time. . . . I prefer to supervise the whole operations of the Government myself rather than entrust the public business to subordinates, and this makes my duties very great."[21]

Yet Polk had a gentle and nurturing if not romantic side. Nothing else can explain his ability to woo, wed, and keep content Sarah Childress, the vivacious, bright, well-educated daughter of a wealthy merchant and plantation owner. Nonetheless, to his dying day he ended his letters to her as "James K. Polk," as if he were signing an official document. Andrew Jackson played cupid in that courtship, which led to nuptials in 1824. By then, Polk was a Jackson protégé. It was a natural alliance if not friendship. Polk was an earnest, skilled, untiring, and loyal disciple. Jackson was a national hero whose coattails could carry his loyalists to the heights of power, wealth, and prestige.

The following year, Jackson encouraged Polk to enter the political arena as a candidate for the House of Representatives. With Jackson's political machine behind him, Polk won that election and five reelections. In 1833 his colleagues rewarded his diligence by naming him chair of the Ways and Means Committee. Yet, later that year, he suffered his first election defeat when John Bell won his seat. After a two-year hiatus, he not only retook this seat but was elected House Speaker. In 1839 Jackson and his other backers talked him into running for the Tennessee governorship. He won but then lost his 1841 reelection bid. Suddenly he was out of politics. He ran for governor and failed again in 1843. His public career appeared dead until Jackson raised him from the political grave and helped carry him to the White House.

At age forty-nine, James Polk was the youngest of the first eleven presidents. His cabinet picks displayed geographic diversity and either personal or party loyalty. He tapped James Buchanan of Pennsylvania as secretary of state; Robert Walker of Mississippi as treasury secretary; William Marcy of New York as secretary of war; George Bancroft of Massachusetts as navy secretary; James Mason of Virginia as attorney general; and Cave Johnson of Tennessee as postmaster general. Mason and Johnson were Polk's friends, and Walker, Marcy, and Bancroft loyally followed the president's lead.

Bancroft was the cabinet's most intellectually distinguished member. He attended Phillips Exeter Academy, Harvard, and Gottingen University, where he earned a doctorate, and then embarked on a grand tour of Europe to seek the age's finest minds. Back in Massachusetts, he founded a school, edited a journal, and began writing what would be a five-volume *History of the United States*. In 1837 Van Buren appointed him Boston's tariff collector. In this post, he became renowned for his honesty, efficiency, and loyalty as a Democrat in a largely Whig region. He was defeated in his 1844 governorship run. Polk saw him as a perfect choice to give his administration regional balance and intellectual heft.

Buchanan became the cabinet's wild card. Jackson dismissed him as an "inept busybody" and "Aunt Nancy," referring to his not-so-closeted homosexuality. Defying convention, the Pennsylvania senator lived openly with another "confirmed bachelor," Senator William King of Alabama.[22] Like loose cannons, Buchanan's stands on the issues would career erratically across the Polk administration's deck.

In his first cabinet meeting, Polk articulated his goals. He would obtain all foreign or disputed lands stretching westward to the Pacific coasts of Oregon and California. He would replace the 1842 protective tariff with one solely designed to raise revenue. He would establish an independent treasury to hold federal deposits. Finally, his work done, he would retire after his term was up. He fulfilled each promise.[23]

He then asked his secretaries to sign a pledge to uphold his agenda and do nothing to aid aspirants for the 1848 Democratic Party nomination or promptly resign should he desire to be a candidate. Whatever his private misgivings, each secretary promptly obeyed the president's request. This in itself was an extraordinary achievement and provides insights into Polk. No president before or since ever imposed such a political straitjacket on his cabinet.

Throughout his four years as president, James Polk coordinated his diplomatic and military moves as if he were playing chess. The only problem was that his board was a continent wide and most of the spaces obscured the actual terrain, resources, and opposing forces. And at one point, he nearly got the United States into simultaneous wars with Britain and Mexico over Oregon and California, respectively.

Polk ultimately succeeded in this deadly game largely because his party controlled Congress. There were 143 Democrats to 77 Whigs and 6 others in the House, and 31 Democrats to 25 Whigs in the Senate. In national politics, the powers to manipulate votes and information are inseparable. Polk tried to control Democratic Party newspapers as tightly as his cabinet. In Washington, a newspaper war raged between the Democrat's *Union*, edited by Thomas Ritchie, and the Whig's *National Intelligencer*, edited by Joseph Gales and William Seaton. Although the *Washington Globe* was the nation's leading Jacksonian newspaper, its editor, Francis Blair, had not spared Polk criticism on various issues over the years. As the Democratic Party's leader, Polk could now avenge himself. He gave Blair a choice: either resign as the *Globe*'s editor or Polk would start a new Democratic Party newspaper. Blair sold the *Globe* for $35,000 to Thomas Ritchie and John Heiss of the *Nashville Union* on April 12, 1845. The new owners renamed their newspaper the *Washington Union* and published the first issue on May 1 with a pledge to be nonpartisan. The pledge was a blatant lie. In return for lucrative government printing contracts, the *Union* served as the Polk administration's zealous mouthpiece.

The first order of business was Texas. Polk and the rest of the nation eagerly awaited news of how Austin had received the annexation resolution. Anson Jones was now the Texas president. His journey to the peak of the republic's power was extraordinary. He was born into poverty in Massachusetts and, as a young man, sought to break free by studying medicine. Apparently, he lacked the confidence and enterprise needed to make a good living from this usually lucrative and prestigious profession. After a dozen years of struggle, he finally gave up in 1832 and moved to New Orleans, where he failed at various businesses. He escaped his debts in Texas, where he resumed practicing medicine. When the Texas rebellion erupted, he enlisted as a private but was soon named a surgeon. Finally, he had a flourishing practice. This naturally shy man found his voice as others lauded his skills. He was elected to Texas's congress, was named the minister to the United States, and finally, was elected president.

Unlike Houston, Jones feared rather than welcomed annexation. He would rather be the president of an independent republic than the governor of one state in a union of many. He had his secretary of state Ashbel Smith ask British consul general Charles Elliot to help broker a deal whereby Mexico recognized the republic's independence if Texas never joined another country. Elliot wrote London for instructions and tried to interest Alphonse de Saligny, France's minister to Texas, in joining this effort. Elliot and Saligny received permission from their governments to proceed with the deal. After informing Jones, they journeyed to Mexico City to press their case. Elliot carried an astonishing letter from one president to another whereby Jones asked for recognition if Texas would not "annex herself or become subject to any country whatsoever."[24]

The Texan reaction to Congress's annexation resolution was unknown when Polk dispatched his friend Archibald Yell to Austin. His mission was to reassure the Texas government that the United States was fully committed to defending the state with borders at the Rio Grande. To back this pledge, he dispatched Cdre. Robert Stockton with official orders to sail with his four ship flotilla to Galveston and there go ashore and determine the people's disposition toward annexation and related issues. These public assignments cloaked a covert operation.[25]

Exactly what Polk had in mind will never be known. No documents have been uncovered and probably never existed. The instructions were most likely delivered verbally with the warning that if all went wrong, what is now called "plausible deniability" would shield the president and his cabinet, and the "rogue" agents would figuratively have to fall on their swords. Perhaps Polk sought only to muster auxiliary forces to defend Texas. Or perhaps even then he sought to provoke Mexico to war against the United States.[26]

Stockton was a good choice to carry out either plan. He was a Jacksonian in conviction and temperament. He dropped out of the College of New Jersey for adventure at sea as a midshipman. When posted in the Mediterranean, he fought duels with British officers when they insulted his country. Ironically, during the War of 1812, he never had a chance to exchange broadsides with a British warship. He eventually was promoted to captain. In 1823 he retired from the navy, went into business, and over the next fifteen years became rich developing New Jersey canals and railroads. But he never lost his love of the sea, and so he rejoined the navy in 1838.

Polk also dispatched another agent to Texas. Charles Wickliffe was a Kentucky politician, previous postmaster general, and fervent Jacksonian. His mission was to secretly explain Polk's intentions to Maj. Gen. Sidney Sherman, who commanded the Texas army, and thus prepare for Stockton's visit. Sherman was a good soldier, having commanded a regiment at the Battle of San Jacinto. His marketing skills surpassed his martial skills. After independence was won, he talked Texas's congress into creating the rank of militia major general and appointing him to the post. Most important for Polk, Sherman was a maverick who defied authority unless he could be convinced of the need to conform.

Wickliffe began conspiring with Sherman shortly after reaching Texas on May 2. Stockton joined these talks after he arrived on May 12. Stockton and Sherman began not-so-secretly mustering an army. That army's purpose remains unclear to this day. The circumstantial evidence points to Sherman and Stockton planning to provoke war with Mexico by assaulting Matamoros, at mouth of the Rio Grande, with their respective land and sea forces.

Stockton sent his flotilla's surgeon, Dr. John Wright, to explain the plan to President Jones and seek his support. The last thing Jones wanted was to war against the country whose recognition he sought. He told Wright that any decision depended on Texas's congress, which would not reconvene until June 16. By then, Jones hoped, Elliot and Saligny would have talked Mexico into acknowledging Texas independence.

Word of Mexico's acknowledgment arrived in a letter from President José Joaquín de Herrera on May 30. Jones promptly announced that because Mexico had agreed to recognize Texas independence, his government would cease all hostilities against that country. When Texas's congress reconvened, he presented it two documents, the American annexation resolution and the Mexican recognition treaty. To the president's dismay, the Texas Senate unanimously rejected the proposed treaty with Mexico, and both houses unanimously accepted annexation by the United States. The lawmakers then began rewriting their constitution as a state rather than a sovereign document. Every man in each chamber approved the revised constitution on July 4, 1845. Finally, in October, a vast majority of Texas citizens approved both annexation and the constitution in a referendum. America's Congress then approved both measures, and Polk signed them into law on December 28, 1845. Texas officially joined the United States on February 19, 1846. It would be the only one of the fifty states whose admission led to a war.

A powerful group of politicians and newspaper editors did everything possible to provoke this war. Archibald Yell, Polk's friend and envoy to Texas, offered a vivid and explicit rationale for armed conflict: "We want a war with Mexico and . . . be blessed with an opportunity to give the Mexicans a drubbing, (which they have long deserved) and acquire Northern Mexico and Upper California, which has of late become indispensable to . . . complete our defense and wants on the Pacific."[27] Senator Stephen Douglas of Illinois was among the most outspoken of those demanding that America's frontier be thrust westward to the Pacific coast. He encouraged Polk to embrace his vision: "the northern provinces of Mexico including California . . . belong to this Republic, and the day is not far distant when such a result will be accomplished."[28] The only questions were how to start a war with Mexico and what to take after winning it.

Andrew Jackson did not live long enough to see Texas's official admission into the Union. His health was fast declining as he passed his seventy-eighth birthday on March 15, 1845. His life finally yielded to an array of diseases on June 8, 1845.

Learning that his mentor's end was near, the disciple who most resembled Jackson hurried to be at his side when he passed. Sam Houston and his family reached the Hermitage just hours after his death. Although he missed a final word with and embrace of his mentor, Houston was there as Jackson was lowered into the ground a couple of days later.

As might be expected, Jackson's death stirred a profusion of eulogies, with his partisans extolling him as a great American and his enemies condemning him as a villain whose policies devastated the United States. The *National Intelligencer* was open to either possibility: "He has occupied a large space in the history of his country during the greater part of the last thirty years, and, for good or evil, has exercised an irresistible influence on public affairs."[29]

Jackson had a worthy successor in the White House. James Polk may have appeared dull, diminutive, and pedantic beside his hero, but he lacked none of his audacity. Like Jackson, Polk rolled for high stakes. If his diplomacy had failed, he might have plunged the United States into simultaneous wars against two countries, another dubious first for the age of Jackson.

19

The Manifest Destiny

It is now time for . . . the fulfillment of our manifest destiny
to overspread the continent allowed by Providence for the
free development of our yearly multiplying millions.

JOHN O'SULLIVAN

The United States ought to provide its less fortunate sister republics with support [and] assume the role of a sublime
moral empire, with a mission to diffuse freedom by manifesting its fruits, not to plunder, crush, and destroy.

WILLIAM ELLERY CHANNING

For we must consider that we shall be as a city on
a hill. The eyes of all people are upon us.

JOHN WINTHROP

A war would probably be the best mode
of settling our affairs with Mexico.

JOHN SLIDELL

If we do have war it will not be our fault.

JAMES POLK

In justifying Texas's annexation, John O'Sullivan, who edited the *Democratic Review*, extolled it as merely the latest large step in "the fulfillment of our manifest destiny to overspread the continent allowed by Providence for the free development of our yearly multiplying millions."[1]

O'Sullivan coined the term "manifest destiny" to describe a belief that Americans had had about themselves from virtually the beginning of their history. As early as 1630, Massachusetts governor John Winthrop explained to his fellow colonists that they had embarked on a divine mission in the New World that all the world would admire and emulate one day: "For we must consider that we shall be as a city on a hill. The eyes of all people are upon us." Thomas Jefferson described America's destiny as peacefully spreading an "empire of liberty" across the continent. "Westward the star of empire takes its way" appears like a national motto on the 1837 cover of George Bancroft's *History of the United States*. In a public letter to Henry Clay, the liberal minister William Ellery Channing insisted, "The United States ought to provide its less fortunate sister republics with support [and] assume the role of a sublime moral empire, with a mission to diffuse freedom by manifesting its fruits, not to plunder, crush, and destroy." Clay captured manifest destiny's essence by explaining that Americans desired continual expansion because "it fills a space in our imagination, and we wish it to complete . . . our territory. It must certainly come to us."[2]

Although most Americans believed in their nation's manifest destiny, they split bitterly over how far to go and how to get there. As politicians, newspaper editors, and the common man debated the issue back east, American frontiersmen on land and sea were leading the way to the ends of the earth.

No one developed the American West during the 1820s more than William Ashley.[3] He was among those many restless Virginians who headed West at a young age in search of adventure, fortune, and fame. In 1808 he reached St. Louis and was soon enriching himself as a merchant, land speculator, and fur trader. His success was grounded in his skill in sizing up and manipulating the strengths and weaknesses of others and an almost reckless courage in the wilderness and marketplace.

Ashley faced his life's toughest choice in June 1823. Arikaras had killed or wounded nearly half of his expedition after he ordered his keelboats and land party to stop to trade at their two villages on the

Missouri River. Rather than withdraw in defeat to St. Louis, he holed up his expedition's remnants on an island and requested help in chastising the Arikaras from Lt. Col. Henry Leavenworth at Fort Atkinson. On August 9 Ashley stood beside Leavenworth as 230 infantry, 100 frontiersmen, and 750 Sioux allies bloodied the Arikaras with cannon shots, rifle shots, arrows, lances, and war clubs. After the Arikaras fled that night onto the plains, the gateway to the upper Missouri River and Rockies beyond was once again free for American enterprise.

Ashley split his men in two groups. He and a score of men ascended the river in a keelboat while Jedediah Smith headed west overland with a dozen men on horseback. Over the next two years, these parties trapped a fortune in beaver pelts, which not only paid off Ashley's debts but made him rich. More important for the nation's development, they discovered South Pass, where the Rocky Mountains disappear into a broad plain across the divide between waters that eventually flow into the Pacific and Atlantic Oceans. Now explorers, trappers, settlers, and other footloose, enterprising folks could journey by wagon across the continent all the way to Oregon or California. Finally, Ashley revolutionized the fur trade by abandoning the expense of building, manning, and supplying trading posts. Instead, he met his trappers annually with a mule supply caravan at a site close to that year's trapping grounds.

At the 1826 rendezvous, Ashley sold his enterprise to Jedediah Smith, William Sublette, and David Jackson. The partners split the men among them and then headed in different directions. Sublette and Jackson trekked north into the Rockies to trap in the beaver-rich streams in Blackfoot country; Smith led his men west into unchartered territory.

Jedediah Smith was already a mountain legend for his astonishing exploits of courage and leadership since he first entered the fur trade in 1822.[4] His party discovered South Pass and eventually the Great Salt Lake far beyond. He had been mauled by a grizzly bear, raised his rifle against the Arikaras, and all along uplifted his men's spirits through nearly incessant drudgery, which was broken only by eruptions of perilous dangers from predatory Indians, beasts, and weather. Unlike most of his devil-may-care, hell-raising comrades, he did not drink, cuss, smoke, or dally with Indian women. Instead, he often sat alone reflecting on passages from the Bible that he carried in his saddlebag. He was about six feet tall with lean muscle, but it was his keen intelligence and quiet but powerful charisma that calmed the most aggressive of his hardened men or the Indians whom they traded and tarried with and at times fought. He was driven primarily, not by a desire for wealth or fame, but by an insatiable curiosity to discover what lay behind the next horizon.

What Smith did after leaving the 1826 rendezvous made him an American Odysseus. He led his men west into the then-unexplored Great Basin and reached California by November. There, Mexican officials in San Diego retained Smith and his men for a month for trespassing before they released them with the promise that they would return the way they came. Instead, Smith and his men headed into California's Central Valley and trapped their way north. Although over the winter they took nearly fifteen hundred pounds of beaver pelts, they found no pass by which their heavily laden pack animals could cross the Sierras. So, Smith and two other men trekked on foot over the mountains and Great Basin and had a joyful reunion with their partners. Smith led eighteen trappers on the same immense loop around the Great Basin and California back to his men. Mohave Indians attacked as they crossed the Colorado River and killed a dozen of them. Smith and six survivors finally reached the party he had left behind in the Central Valley. They headed north into Oregon Territory toward Fort Vancouver, where Smith hoped to sell his furs and then head east with his men and profit. Umpqua Indians attacked and killed all but Smith and two others. Smith was able to convince Governor John McLoughlin, the Hudson's Bay Company leader at Fort Vancouver, to force the Umpquas to return most of the furs and equipment they had stolen. McLoughlin then bought from Smith the furs the Umpqua had rendered. Smith arrived at the 1829 rendezvous for yet another astonishing reunion; Sublette and Jackson had given him up for dead.

From 1826 to 1830, despite the disasters that Smith and his expeditions suffered, the partners made a fortune. At the 1830 rendezvous, they sold out to Jim Bridger, Tom Fitzpatrick, Milton Sublette, Henry Fraeb, and John Baptiste Gervais, who dubbed their partnership the Rocky Mountain Fur Company. Smith, Sublette, and Jackson exited the business just in time. Another revolution soon convulsed the fur trade.

John Jacob Astor was to the American West in the 1830s what Ashley had been in the 1820s. Astor was no mountain man.[5] He was born in Baden, Germany, immigrated to New York City as young man, and stayed there, steadily amassing more wealth as a merchant and financer until he became America's first multimillionaire. His business empire thrived on an array of enterprises of which the most lucrative were real estate, opium, and furs. He bought and sold land in the city and beyond. His agents peddled opium mostly among China's swelling market of addicts through the Port of Canton.

As for furs, Astor launched the operations of his American Fur Company in upper New York state in the 1790s and then spread the business westward across the Great Lakes. His boldest venture, the Pacific Fur Company, was designed to scour the Columbia River valley of beavers and the Pacific coast of sea otters, whose furs would be sold at Canton. This enterprise initially succeeded, but the field leaders were forced to sell out to their rival, the Northwest Company, during the War of 1812. For the next two decades, Astor focused on dominating and exploiting the Great Lakes but the decimation of beavers and other fur-bearing animals across this region forced him to look west, far beyond the Mississippi River.

During the late 1820s the American Fur Company bought out the operations of the Missouri, Columbia, and French Fur Companies and combined them into the Upper Missouri Outfit, skillfully managed by Kenneth McKenzie at his headquarters at Fort Union, across from the mouth of the Yellowstone River. This Missouri River monopoly brought down yearly fortunes in buffalo robes and beaver pelts. In 1832 Astor had McKenzie dispatch trapping expeditions into the northern Rockies. The result was a bitter rivalry among three enterprises: the American, Rocky Mountain, and Hudson's Bay Fur Companies. The fur trade peaked at the 1834 rendezvous, when more than a thousand trappers and Indians gathered in Pierre's Hole. In the following years, the trade declined rapidly as the three giants and a half-dozen smaller ventures undersold each other, beavers were trapped to near extinction, and silk replaced beaver felt as the fashionable material for hats. The last rendezvous was held in 1840 and was a melancholy affair as the several score free trappers and Indians had little to trade other than vivid memories of an exciting, colorful era about to disappear forever.

The mountain men explored and mapped the West, opening the way for countless others to follow. Emigration characterized a new era as wagon trains plodded from Missouri across the continent on a trail that split in the Great Basin with spurs to Oregon and California. The first wagons rolled into Oregon in 1836 and California in 1841.[6] Whereas most of the tens of thousands of emigrants eventually reached either destination, one remarkable group decided to settle in the heart of the Great Basin itself.

Mormonism was manifest destiny's most unlikely spearhead.[7] Joseph Smith founded the religion based on the sacred Book of Mormon, which he claimed was given him by an angel. He had also received teachings during visitations by God and Jesus. By 1830 he had a community of followers in Palmyra, New York, who believed that their sacred book revealed Christianity's purest version. Mainstream Christian sects condemned Mormonism as heretical. Discrimination and threats forced Smith and his swelling community into a series of migrations that led to Kirkland, Ohio; New Jerusalem, Missouri; and Nauvoo, Illinois. In December 1843 Smith and his followers petitioned Congress to make Nauvoo and its surrounding land a federal territory so that they might receive military protection from the worsening violence against them. In February 1844 Smith announced that he would run for president in that year's election. On June 27 he and his brother were arrested in Carthage, Illinois, on charges of treason. A mob broke into the jail and murdered both men. This provoked the latest migration.

Under Brigham Young's leadership, most Mormons sold their holdings in Nauvoo and elsewhere and headed west. In February 1846 they arrived at Winter Quarters on the Missouri River, twenty-five miles north of the mouth of the Platte River, and there most stayed for the next two years. In April 1847 Young led a hundred men westward. Upon reaching Salt Lake Valley on July 24, he announced, "This is the place." He sent back word for all Mormons to hasten and join him.[8]

Although the age of Jackson's sea captains are much less appreciated than the mountain men in America's collective consciousness, they were no less vital to the nation's development. Vessels packed with provisions and manufactured goods sailed from northeastern ports on voyages that usually lasted three years and stopped to trade on the coasts of Latin America, Mexico, California, Oregon, Hawaii, Canton, Southeast Asia, South Asia, and Africa, before finally heading for the home port.

Along the way, the captains did what they could to prevent their sailors from jumping ship for the allures of women or better jobs or just relief from the vessel's tedium, danger, and at times, brutality. American communities in California, Oregon, and Hawaii amassed ever more economic, and thus political, power and would lead in the nation's eventual conquest of these realms. By 1842 America's commercial and strategic interests in Hawaii had grown so great that President John Tyler asserted an American protectorate over these islands, a policy that became known as the Tyler Doctrine.

Of all the markets in that steadily expanding global trade network, China's was the most desired. Chinese silk, tea, and porcelain were the world's finest and least expensive. American trade with China began in 1784, when the appropriately named *Empress of China* set sail for Canton, then the only port open to commerce with western countries. Several years later, the vessel returned with a hull full of goods worth many times what it had departed with, and this encouraged other entrepreneurs to launch similar voyages. At first, the problem for American merchants was finding goods that the Chinese wanted. With time, they discovered that the Chinese prized cow hides and tallow from California, sea otter and beaver pelts from the Oregon coast, sandalwood from the Hawaiian (then known as the Sandwich) Islands, and raw opium from India and Turkey.

Faced with a worsening addiction problem, the Chinese emperor declared that opium was illegal. The new law did not stop British, American, and other western traders from smuggling opium into the kingdom, however. In 1839 Chinese officials arrested a number of smugglers and confiscated and publicly burned tons of opium in Canton. This prompted Britain to launch the Opium War against China. Over the next three years, the British military repeatedly slaughtered hordes of Chinese armed with antiquated weapons and tactics or blasted to splinters the vessels defending ports. Under the 1842 Treaty of Nanjing, China was forced to cede to Britain Hong Kong Island and open five ports for free trade in perpetuity.

Upon learning of this treaty, President Tyler dispatched envoys to China to secure a similar deal for the United States. The result was the 1844 Treaty of Wangxia, which allowed Americans to trade at the five open ports and enjoy most-favored-nation status, whereby they automatically received any benefits that China granted other foreign governments.

Although the American flag mostly followed trade, at times it led. The Wilkes expedition was to the world's oceans what the Lewis and Clark expedition was to the West. Representative John Quincy Adams mustered support for the South Sea Exploring Expedition, led by Lt. Charles Wilkes. During its four-year circumnavigation of the globe from 1838 to 1842, the six vessels sailed eighty-five thousand miles, and its half-dozen scientists charted 280 islands and eight hundred miles of the Oregon coast and compiled nineteen volumes of scientific reports on biology, climatology, geology, oceanography, ethnography, philology, and botany. Wilkes's narrative of his journey became a bestseller.[9]

Beyond the Rockies, the Americans and British asserted conflicting claims over the Columbia River valley. In May 1792 merchant sea captain Robert Grey ordered his crew to sail fifteen miles up a previously uncharted river that he would name after his vessel, the *Columbia*. As *terra nullius*, it was free for the taking, so he claimed the discovery for his country, the United States. Several months later, Grey revealed his discovery to Capt. George Vancouver, who commanded a British naval expedition of exploration. Vancouver promptly sailed to the Columbia River and then up it nearly a hundred miles to the first set of rapids, and in doing so, he claimed this vast territory for Britain. These were the only known foreign incursions of the territory for more than a dozen years. Lewis, Clark, and their men were the first whites to linger where the Columbia River flowed into the Pacific Ocean. They spent the dreary, drenched winter of 1805–6 at Fort Clatsop on the south shore. The field leaders of John Jacob Astor's Pacific Fur Company planned to stay much longer. Expeditions over land and sea reached the mouth of the Columbia River and established Astoria in 1811. But, learning of the outbreak of war with Britain, the leaders sold Astoria to their Canadian rival, the Northwest Company, to avoid being conquered by a British military expedition. The Northwest Company abandoned the site and established Fort Vancouver seventy miles upstream, across from where the Willamette River flows into the Columbia.

America and Britain each had strong legal and political cases for their overlapping claims to the Columbia River valley. In the Anglo-American Treaty of 1818, they amicably agreed to resolve this and most other disputes along the border between the United States and Canada. The treaty extended the border along the 49th parallel from Lake of the Woods to the Rocky Mountain divide and let them jointly own the Oregon Territory for ten years. The Oregon Territory's southern boundary was defined by the 1819 Adams-Onís Treaty, which said the border ran up the Sabine River to the Red River, then up the Red River to the 100th meridian to the Arkansas River and up it to its headwaters, then north to the 42nd parallel, and finally westward to the Pacific Ocean. In 1826 the Adams administration signed a treaty with Russia defining Alaska's southern boundary at 54 degrees, 40 minutes. Oregon now had a potential northern border. In an 1827 treaty, the Americans and British extended their Oregon arrangement for an indefinite period with each party able to withdraw from the treaty after a year's notice.

For most of this time, only the British enjoyed the ability to exploit the Oregon Territory. From its Fort Vancouver headquarters on the Columbia River, the Hudson's Bay Company, which acquired the Northwest Company in 1821, dispatched trapping brigades in all directions to scour the streams for beavers and other fur-bearing animals. Few American trapping brigades ventured deep into Oregon Territory. Indeed the British did everything possible to keep them out. Their most notorious policy was to create a "fur desert" around the territory's southern and eastern approaches by trapping out every beaver stream they found.

Britain's containment policy did not so much deter as anger Americans who wanted their fair share of Oregon's resources. An Oregon lobby emerged among groups with trapping, whaling, mercantile, and missionary interests in the region. As more of America's prosperity was reaped from and dependent upon foreign trade, Oregon was viewed as an increasingly vital link in the expanding global network.

The point man in Congress for taking Oregon was Representative John Floyd of Virginia. In December 1828 Floyd introduced a bill that would construct a chain of forts across the West all the way to the Columbia River mouth. Ironically, Representative James Polk of Tennessee led the opposition to this bill on the grounds that it violated the joint-occupancy treaty with Britain.

The first missionaries reached Oregon in 1834. The previous year, the Methodist Church had advertised for volunteers to proselytize among the Oregon Indians. Jason Lee and his nephew, Daniel Lee, accepted that calling and joined a trading venture led by Nathaniel Wythe that trekked across the continent all the way to Fort Vancouver. There, John

McLoughlin, the Hudson's Bay Company's chief factor or leader, graciously helped them establish a mission forty miles up the Willamette River valley. The mission gradually developed into a settlement as trappers, seamen, and emigrants were attracted to farming the rich bottomlands.

Two missionary couples, Marcus and Narcissa Whitman and Henry and Elizabeth Spaulding came west in 1836. The couples reckoned that they would save more souls by splitting up so they set up their missions at Wallilaptu and Lapwai in eastern Oregon. Narcissa and Elizabeth were the first white women to journey along the Oregon Trail, and they created quite a stir when they camped for a few days at that year's rendezvous.

During the 1840s more Americans seeking a better life journeyed the Oregon Trail to an expanding cluster of settlements. Gradually, the balance of population, and thus power, shifted in Oregon from the British to the Americans. In 1845 the British presence largely disappeared when the Hudson's Bay Company shut down Fort Vancouver and moved operations to Fort Victoria on Vancouver Island's southern tip. Time was definitely siding with the United States. A census in 1849 revealed that of 5,414 males and 3,673 females in Oregon Territory, all but 298 were Americans.[10]

These developments emboldened the Tyler administration to assert sole American control over the region. In London, American minister Edward Everett proposed to Foreign Secretary George Hamilton-Gordon, Lord Aberdeen, that they simply extend the border along the 49th parallel to the Pacific Ocean and then bend it south below Vancouver Island. Aberdeen promised to share Everett's proposal with Prime Minister Robert Peel. Everett sent word back to the White House that a resolution might well be pending. But before any official deal was reached, a new president came to power and upset the diplomatic table.

President Polk articulated his view in his inaugural address: "Our title to the whole of the territory of Oregon is clear and unquestionable."[11] This stirred a fierce debate among politicians, newspapers, and interest groups over how, when, and even whether to take sole title to Oregon. Many, such as Senator Henry Clay of Kentucky, preferred a gradual progress: "I think our true policy is to settle and populate our immense territory on the east of those [Rocky] mountains and within the United States before we proceed to colonize the shores of the Pacific; or at all events postpone the occupation of Oregon some thirty or forty years."[12] Others, such as Senator E. A. Hannegan of Indiana, not only demanded that the United States take Oregon as soon as possible but also insisted that its border run north all the way to 54 degrees, 40 minutes, to Russian Alaska. This inspired the belligerent Fifty-Four Forty or Fight movement.

America's newspapers were nothing if not hyperbolic. The Whig newspaper, the *Intelligencer*, condemned Polk's determination to take Oregon at all costs as "extreme and violent," whereas Horace Greeley, the *New York Tribune*'s editor, blasted it as "palpable knavery and babbling folly." An editorial by the *Washington Union*'s Thomas Ritchie, in contrast, attacked the "insolent tone of the British public" for assuming "that we are weak and cowardly; devoid of public spirit and patriotism." He later insisted that the nation faced a stark choice: "The Whole of Oregon or None."[13]

The Polk administration's first diplomatic initiative on Oregon came with a long letter on July 29, 1845, from Secretary of State Buchanan to Richard Pakenham, Britain's minister to the United States. After reciting American claims, Buchanan presented Everett's plan to extend the boundary along the 49th parallel from the Rocky Mountain divide to the Pacific Ocean. Pakenham replied by refuting these claims and rejecting any deviation from the existing treaty.[14]

Polk laid the Oregon conflict before the cabinet on August 26. He expressed his disappointment at Pakenham's blunt dismissal of what he believed was a reasonable proposal. In response, he would pressure the British by withdrawing his offer and awaiting a counteroffer. Buchanan worried this might turn a dispute into a crisis, which, if mishandled, might lead to war. This would be terrible enough but could be catastrophic if war also broke out with Mexico over America's annexation of Texas and ambitions to take the entire southwest. Buchanan advised shelving Oregon until they resolved the crisis with Mexico.

Confronting and possibly fighting both foreign powers did not faze Polk. He replied, "If we do have war it will not be our fault." He was just as optimistic in private, confiding to his diary, "We should do our duty towards both Mexico and Great Britain, and firmly maintain our rights, and leave the rest to God and the country." He criticized Buchanan for

being "too timid and too fearful of war on the Oregon question, and
. . . most anxious to settle the question by yielding and making greater
concessions that I am willing to make."[15]

Polk forged a consensus to inform Pakenham that the United States
had rescinded the 49th parallel offer. Buchanan did so on August 30.
Pakenham made no immediate response. Word of British intransigence
angered the Fifty-Four Forty or Fight movement, and its ranks swelled
with adherents. Pakenham informed London of what had transpired and
asked for instructions. In turn, he received a reprimand from Aberdeen
for transforming an issue into a crisis by stonewalling the original offer.

Polk first learned of Aberdeen's reprimand on October 21, when
Buchanan brought him a dispatch from Louis McLane, America's minister in London. Aberdeen had shared his regret and a desire for compromise with McLane, who promptly sent word to Washington. Pakenham
was contrite when he met Buchanan on October 22. He apologized for
his dismissal of the 49th parallel offer and asked that the Polk White
House resubmit it.

The following day, Polk summoned his Senate point man on Oregon, Thomas Hart Benton. The senator advised pressuring Britain by
giving the one year's notice of withdrawal from the treaty. The next step
would be to announce that the United States was extending its laws to
the territory. Forts would be established in a chain across the Oregon
Trail to the Pacific. Finally, all Oregon tribes would be subject to the
nation's Indian policy. After agreeing to consider these steps, Polk told
Benton he intended to invoke the Monroe Doctrine in his next address
to Congress and to secure at least San Francisco Bay and all lands eastward to the United States. If America did not take these lands, Britain
or some other great power would most likely do so. Although Polk did
not embrace the Fifty-Four Forty or Fight position, he promised decisively to assert the 49th parallel boundary.

American interests in California swelled steadily after Mexican independence in 1821, when the government opened the entire country to
trade and immigration. Adventurous Americans searching for distant
wealth traveled to California; marveled at the natural beauty, pretty
senoritas, and easy acquisition of land and money; and stayed. At first,
most came by sea. Whaling ships briefly dropped anchor to replenish
their supplies, and merchant vessels lingered in the bays of San Diego,

Monterey, San Francisco, and elsewhere, buying hides, tallow, and salt beef and selling textiles and other goods mass-produced in factories at the continent's other end.[16] Despite this growing influx, California's ports were rarely an end in themselves for American sea captains; instead, they were considered vital links in a global trade network that started and ended in northeastern and mid-Atlantic ports. Starting in the early 1830s, more Americans came overland. The first were trapping parties exploring for beaver-filled streams. Many a mountain man bid farewell to his comrades and happily exchanged his wild, dangerous life for a California ranch or business and wife. The next to arrive were pioneer families, with the first wagon train reaching California in 1841.

By the mid-1840s California was inhabited by about forty-five hundred Mexican citizens and twelve hundred foreigners, mostly Americans. About forty-five hundred Indians resided among the twenty-one missions, and perhaps 100,000 others lived free in small bands far beyond the settlements. Nearly all of Mexico's population lived within twenty or so miles of the sea. With thirteen hundred inhabitants, San Diego was the largest town, followed by a thousand at Monterey, and eight hundred each at Santa Barbara and San Francisco.[17]

The United States faced the same opportunities and perils in California that it had in Texas. National interests in California rose with the value of the business Americans conducted and the number of Americans who settled there. At first Mexicans welcomed the wealth that the newcomers created. But the Americans did not confine their activities to making money. They increasingly used California's political factions to advance their own interests. American economic and political power steadily expanded and made local officials increasingly nervous.

Americans and Mexicans both worried about another foreign presence. British merchant and war ships crowded California ports. Mexico's government and people did not just owe money to Americans. British financiers also lost money when their Mexican clients refused to pay what they owed. In Washington, rumors that the British government was willing to write off these debts in return for California were rife. Or the British might just seize California in the chaos following an outbreak of war between the United States and Mexico over Texas's annexation.

Until recently, another foreign power had had a foot in California. There was a Russian fur trading post at Fort Ross, eighty miles north of

San Francisco Bay, from 1811 to 1839. The governments of first Spain and then Mexico grudgingly tolerated this intrusion on land Russia claimed as its own. The fur trade eventually played out and the post became a drain rather than source of wealth. Nicholas I ordered it abandoned.

Determined not to let the British seize California, the Tyler administration issued a standing order to Cdre. Thomas Jones, who commanded the Pacific flotilla, to conquer the province if war erupted with Mexico. On October 18, 1842, on hearing from John Parrott, America's consul in Mazatlan, that war was imminent, Jones landed marines at Monterey, raised the Stars and Stripes, and declared America's annexation of California. Unfortunately, he had not consulted the local American merchants before acting. They produced months-old American newspapers that revealed the rumor was myth. Jones rather sheepishly ordered the flag lowered, and the marines rowed back to their ships.

The diplomatic damage far surpassed the commodore's personal embarrassment. Mexicans had long suspected a hair-triggered American plan to seize California at the first chance. Now they had proof. American settlers faced greater scrutiny and at times harassment by officials. As in Texas, this provoked rather than cowed the Americans. They too began looking for an excuse to take over and assert their "rights."

The diplomatic gaff prompted President Tyler to appoint a consul at Monterey. After consulting sea captains who had dropped anchor in West Coast ports, he chose Thomas Larkin. Shortly after first settling in California in 1833, Larkin had started a flour mill and a family. By the early 1840s he was among the American community's most prosperous and prominent members. He spoke fluent Spanish and was liked and trusted by Mexican officials and most of the other elite. He received his appointment on April 2, 1844.

Larkin sent back reports in the summer of 1845 that alarmed the Polk administration. The British and French had established their own consulates in California. It was rumored that Britain was urging the Mexican government to clamp down on the growing American presence in both California and New Mexico to prevent those provinces from suffering Texas's fate. Meanwhile, the Hudson's Bay Company, whose trade links with California were challenged by the growing American presence, supplied the Mexican government with money and guns to suppress that province's slow pull into America's sphere of influence.

Should push come to shove, the British readied themselves for action by bolstering their navy flotilla in California's waters.[18]

For decades, American businessmen and politicians had resented Mexico's government and people. Americans trying to do business in Mexico suffered shakedowns for bribes, refusals to repay loans, outright robbery, and incarceration on trumped-up charges. The first American complaints arose shortly after Mexico's opening but worsened with time. By Jackson's last year as president, the accumulated claims of Americans against Mexicans surpassed $3.5 million.

Jackson offered to wipe this debt clean for the transfer of California and New Mexico to the United States. The Mexican government's refusal even to respond to this offer infuriated him. In February 1837 he issued a fiery report to Congress that condemned those "wanton . . . outrages" that "would justify, in the eyes of all nations, immediate war." Yet, for now he advocated a policy tempered by "wisdom and moderation . . . to give Mexico one more opportunity to atone for the past, before we take redress into our own hands." The Foreign Relations Committees of both houses of Congress agreed. The Senate's reported that it could indeed "with justice, recommend an immediate resort to war or reprisals." The House's concurred that "ample cause exists for taking redress into our own hands."[19]

But neither subsequent presidents nor Congresses did anything for another eight years as other issues took precedence. A legal catch also diminished any rush to war. A tenet of the 1831 friendship treaty between the United States and Mexico appeared to subject the citizens of each to the laws of the other when they were in that country. Mexican officials claimed that what Americans alleged were confiscations or refusals to pay back loans were actually justified under Mexican law. Most important, Mexico's government reduced some of this tension in 1839, when it agreed to form a joint committee with the United States to review any claims. In August 1840 the committee convened in Washington for eighteen months. Eventually, Mexico agreed to pay $2 million of $6.5 million worth of submitted claims in twenty installments of $100,000 each. It made three payments before suspending them for lack of money. The timing could not have been worse for Mexico. James Polk was about to enter the White House.

Although it would negotiate the debt issue, Mexico rejected any discussion of Texas's boundaries. Washington upheld the Texas claim that the Rio Grande was the proper southern and western boundary. The Mexicans rejected this claim as lacking historical or legal foundations. The boundary had always been the Nueces River whose mouth on the Gulf of Mexico was about 150 miles north of the Rio Grande's mouth. A Rio Grande boundary was absurd not just because virtually no legal documents supported it, but also because, if accepted, Texas would consume half of New Mexico, including its capital Santa Fe and most other towns, whose founding predated Texas by nearly two and a half centuries. Americans replied by pointing to the Treaty of Velasco that Santa Anna signed in 1836, after his defeat and capture at San Jacinto; the dictator conceded an independent Texas with a Rio Grande boundary. Mexicans denied any legal standing to the treaty since Santa Anna made it under duress and the Mexican government subsequently repudiated it and him.

President Polk first sought to gain Mexico's acceptance of America's annexation of Texas through diplomacy. Among his first presidential acts was to send Dr. William Parrot to Mexico City to interest the government in talks. Parrot certainly had the credentials for this mission. He had lived for years in Mexico City as a dentist and entrepreneur and spoke fluent Spanish. More than patriotism motivated his mission. His $690,000 claim against the Mexican government for confiscating his shipment of port wine was the largest of any American. He sought any settlement that forced Mexico to compensate him for what it took. He reached Mexico City on April 23, 1845, and, after spending frustrating weeks trying to meet with officials, reported that Mexico's elite was united on preferring war over talk with the United States.[20]

This report prompted Polk and his cabinet to take a tougher stand. In their minds, the Mexicans clearly only respected strength. With annexation all but a certainty, Texas had to be secured. The closest American troops were at Fort Jessup in northwestern Louisiana, just twenty miles from the border. In mid-June, Gen. Zachary Taylor, Fort Jessup's commander, received orders from War Secretary Marcy to encamp his men at the frontier and there await official word that Texas had accepted annexation. He was then to march into Texas and prepare to defend it "from foreign invasion or Indian incursions." As Taylor readied his troops, he received a follow-up letter in which Marcy directed him to send the bulk of his force to Corpus Christi at the mouth of the Nueces River.[21]

Taylor sent a contingent of soldiers to San Antonio to guard the Comanche frontier and pointed the rest of his troops to Corpus Christi, the dragoons by land and the infantry by boat down the Red and Mississippi Rivers to New Orleans, where they crowded aboard steamships. By late August, his dragoons and infantry reunited at Corpus Christi. There Taylor received his latest order from Marcy. He was to send patrols into the disputed region between the Nueces River and Rio Grande to assert America's claim but should fire at any Mexican forces only in self-defense. Meanwhile, Navy Secretary Bancroft sent orders to Cdre. David Conner, whose flotilla was scattered off ports along the Texas and east Mexican coasts. Conner was "to preserve peace, if possible; and, if war comes, to recover peace by adopting the most prompt and energetic measures."[22]

In ordering Taylor to occupy Corpus Christi on the Nueces River's south bank in the disputed zone and send patrols toward the Rio Grande, the Polk administration initiated aggressive acts that could have sparked a war. Yet it was not for another month, in late August 1845, that the president convened his cabinet to discuss what do should war erupt with Mexico. During the meeting the president urged an offensive strategy, whereas Secretary of State Buchanan advised a defensive strategy. The president's views prevailed. Taylor and Conner received standing orders to advance on Matamoros and take this city at the Rio Grande's mouth if war erupted. After Matamoros fell, Conner would split his flotilla to blockade key Mexican ports.[23]

Disturbing news from Mexico prompted this discussion and subsequent policy. On August 21 President José Joaquín de Herrera issued a fiery anti-American statement and appointed Anastasio Bustamante to command the Mexican army. Gen. Mariano Paredes y Arrillaga threatened to march back to Mexico City and depose both Herrera and Bustamante. The threat apparently convinced Herrera that cutting a deal with the Americans might actually strengthen his grip on power. Parrot reported that Herrera now welcomed an envoy with whom to "settle over a breakfast, the most important national question."[24] Polk sought from both American consuls, John Black in Mexico City and Francis Dimond in Veracruz, corroboration of Parrot's optimistic report.

With urgent news for the president, Secretary of State Buchanan strode into the White House on November 7. Foreign Minister Manuel Peña y Peña was willing to talk, but he had two conditions. He would have nothing to do with Parrot, and the United States had to withdraw its fleet from Mexican waters near Veracruz as a sign of good faith.

Polk issued two orders. Navy Secretary Mason would have Commodore Conner withdraw his ships in Mexican waters beyond the horizon. Buchanan would invest John Slidell with full diplomatic powers and a draft treaty to negotiate with the Mexican government. William Parrot would serve as Slidell's secretary.

Linguistically, Slidell and Parrot were an impressive team as both spoke Spanish fluently. This, however, was their only diplomatic strength. The two abrasive Americans had alienated many influential Mexicans during their sojourns in the country. Thus did Polk's choices appear more like an insult than a genuine attempt to resolve differences.

The ends and means of Slidell's instructions were straightforward. He was to convince Mexico to recognize the annexation of Texas with a Rio Grande border and sell New Mexico and California. In return, the United States would assume the roughly $3.5 million of Mexico's public and private debt to American investors and pay $5 million for New Mexico west of the Rio Grande, $20 million for western New Mexico and California from San Francisco north, and $25 million for New Mexico and California from Monterey north. If need be, Slidell could go as high as $40 million.[25]

Polk's diplomacy with Mexico and Britain dominated his annual message to Congress on December 2, 1845. He assured Congress that negotiations to assert American interests were ongoing with both countries. Congress could help with Oregon by giving Britain notice of the abrogation of the 1827 Oregon treaty, extending American law and jurisdiction to American settlers in that territory, and appropriating money for a chain of forts across the Oregon Trail to the Pacific. After the year's notice expired, "we shall have reached a period when the national rights in Oregon must either be abandoned or firmly maintained. That they cannot be abandoned without a sacrifice of both national honor and interest is too clear to admit of doubt." He then quoted the 1823 Monroe Doctrine's assertion that "the American continents . . . are henceforth not to be considered as subjects for future colonization by any European powers." Americans "must ever maintain the principle that the people of this continent alone have the right to decide their own destiny."[26] Polk was more circumspect in discussing Mexico. He regretted that relations "have not been of the amicable character which it is our desire to cultivate with all foreign nations." But for this, Mexico was to blame for stonewalling on the reparations and annexation issues. He reassured Congress that an American envoy was currently addressing these problems in Mexico City. He was hopeful to resolve the conflicts with both countries diplomatically, but he hinted that Congress and the nation should prepare for the worst.

To this largely "good cop" presentation, Polk could rely on "bad cops" in Congress to rattle sabers for him in the face of either country. For now, saber rattling would be counterproductive with Mexico because Slidell was assumed to be negotiating with its government. But the British remained intransigent over Oregon's future. So Polk gave the nod to his allies in Congress to heat up the rhetoric.

A few days after Polk's speech, Senator Lewis Cass of Michigan noted that a "crisis is fast approaching" between the United States and Britain and issued a resolution to ready American forces in case war erupted. That war would be solely Britain's fault because "England has placed herself in the path that is before us; and if she retain her position, we must meet her. If the last proposition she has submitted is her ultimatum, it is effectively a declaration of war."[27] The resolution passed unanimously.

The House of Representative acted first on abrogating the Oregon treaty with a vote of 163 to 54 on February 9. The resolution gave Britain the required one year's notice but suggested that the president continue negotiating. The Senate Foreign Relations Committee, chaired by William Allen, produced its own resolution that simply issued the notice. In releasing the committee's resolution to the full Senate for debate, Allen urged his colleagues to pass it with one voice. The rancorous debate raged on for sixty-five days. The April 16 vote was far from unanimous—40 to 14. A conference committee took up the two resolutions. The Senate version eventually prevailed and passed by 42 to 10 there and 142 to 46 in the House on April 23. The final resolution extended an olive branch to Britain by calling for the "amicable settlement of all their differences."[28]

Meanwhile, the Polk administration suffered a harsh setback on the other diplomatic front. Slidell reached Mexico City on December 6. The Mexicans soon dashed any hopes for a swift diplomatic resolution. When Consul Black informed Foreign Minister Peña of Slidell's arrival, he "manifested great surprise" and said he would have preferred a more tardy appearance.[29] Neither President Herrera nor any other high-ranking Mexican official would see Slidell. On December 20 Slidell was formally told that his credentials as an "envoy extraordinary and minister plenipotentiary" implied that standard diplomatic relations prevailed between the United States and Mexico. In fact, Mexico had severed diplomatic relations with the United States after it annexed Texas. Thus, Mexico would only accept an envoy armed solely with powers to address the Texas issue. Slidell withdrew from Mexico City to Jalapa, on the road to Veracruz, and there awaited further instructions. On December 29 he sent a letter to Polk reporting his failure and noting that "a war would probably be the best mode of settling our affairs with Mexico."[30]

What explains the Mexican government's intransigence? Herrera and his ministers were afraid that even talking with an American diplomat about selling the nation's northern half would cost them their jobs and even their lives. This fear proved rational. Paredes deposed Herrera and seized power on January 2, 1846.

This coup was only the latest. Mexico was essentially a failed state. Since winning independence in 1821, Mexico had suffered political instability, violence, and repression as one dictator after another deposed his predecessor and took over the presidential palace. Since 1836 the Texas issue had exacerbated Mexico's political turmoil. Mexicans were enraged at President Santa Anna's defeat and capture at San Jacinto and his signing of the Treaty of Velasco. Carlos Maria de Bustamante took power, repudiated the treaty, and issued the 1836 constitution to legitimize his rule. In 1841 Gen. Mariano Paredes y Arrillaga tried to overthrow Bustamante. A desperate Bustamante invited Santa Anna back from exile to help him ward off Paredes. Santa Anna returned, overthrew Bustamante, and suspended the 1836 constitution. In 1843 he proclaimed a new constitution that justified his takeover; henceforth he would serve officially as Mexico's president rather than as dictator. Then, in September 1844, Santa Anna fled again to exile after he was trounced by Paredes in battle. Paredes turned over the formal government to Herrera but maintained power behind the presidential throne. He then retook the throne to forestall any deal with the Americans.

Texas was not the only explosive issue. Mexico had its own version of a two-party system. Much like Hamiltonians and Jeffersonians in the United States, Centralistas favored a strong national government and Federalistas advocated a decentralized political system in which the provinces held most power. The party system was divisive enough, but Mexico's political elite was also split between Moderados (Moderates) and Puros (Purists). The moderates sought to avoid an unwinnable war by selling some of Mexico's thinly populated northern territory for hard, desperately needed cash to pay off part of a swelling mountain of national debt. The purists insisted that to uphold national honor, it was far better to fight and lose than never fight at all.

After learning the fate of Slidell's mission, Polk convened a cabinet meeting on January 13. The secretaries agreed that only military pressure could bring the Mexicans to the negotiating table. War Secretary Marcy ordered General Taylor to march his army across the disputed boundary zone from the Nueces River mouth at Corpus Christi to the north bank of the Rio Grande mouth, 150 miles south.[31] Secretary of State Buchanan wrote Slidell praising him for his efforts and asking him to do what he could "to throw the odium of the failure of the negotiation on the Mexican government."[32] This way the Polk administration could justify a subsequent war not only to Congress and to the American people but also to the international community. The stronger America's case, the less likely other countries would be to offer financial or military aid, let alone an alliance, to Mexico.

Meanwhile, a shady soldier of fortune appeared at the White House for three days of meetings in February 1846. Col. Alexander Atocha was born in Spain, insisted that he was a naturalized American citizen, and was among those foreign investors who had gotten burned in Mexico and subsequently filed claims for reparations. The reason for his visit was to offer a deal from Santa Anna, who was then living in exile in Havana, Cuba.

Santa Anna is among history's greatest survivors and most inept leaders. Americans recalled him as the dictator who ordered the massacres at the Alamo and Goliad, then suffered his army's devastating defeat at San Jacinto, and finally promised Texas independence for his release. Yet after San Jacinto, rather than face a prison cell or firing squad back in Mexico, he simply retired for a while before staging another comeback. Indeed, the presidential palace had a revolving door during Mexico's age of Santa Anna. In all, he took and lost power a half-dozen times from 1832 to 1855. The pattern never varied. He negotiated, bribed, and fought his way to the presidential palace, ruthlessly pursued ambitious plans far beyond his abilities, got the bum's rush by his rivals when those plans exploded in the face of himself and the nation, then bided his time as his political foes proved to be even more incompetent. An astonishing mix of luck, chutzpah, and charisma explains how he not just survived but repeatedly reaped vast wealth and power during these violent, catastrophic decades.

For a generous fee, Santa Anna would return to Mexico and retake power, whereupon he would settle all outstanding issues with the United States. He suggested that America could gain title to the swath of the continent from Texas to San Francisco Bay for $30 million. But this offer alone would not cinch the deal. It had to be backed with force. No Mexican government could yield this territory and survive in power unless it looked like it had been coerced. So Atocha urged the president to reanchor America's Gulf of Mexico fleet before Veracruz and Tampico. Finally, the president had to show his good faith by giving Santa Anna and his associates a half-million dollars up front.[33]

Atocha's scheme certainly tempted the president. A half-million dollars seemed a small price to pay compared to war's costs and uncertainties. Then again, what if Atocha were a charlatan or he and Santa Anna simply took the money to enhance their Havana lifestyles? Not surprisingly, the cabinet split over whether to gamble on this covert action, so for now, Polk shelved the option.

Meanwhile, President Paredes vowed never to surrender a foot of Mexican territory to the Americans. However, he did not let Slidell know this until March 12. Slidell packed his bags and headed back to Washington City. He sent ahead word to Buchanan "that nothing is to be done with these people until they shall have been chastised."[34] Polk took those words to heart when he read them on April 7, 1846.

Gen. Zachary Taylor certainly lived up to the nickname bestowed by his troops: "Old Rough and Ready."[35] He was a plainspoken soldier's soldier who shared his men's discomforts and dangers. Then sixty-one years old, he had spent most of his life in the army. He received his lieutenant's commission in 1808 and served with distinction in the War of 1812 and the Seminole and Black Hawk Wars. In battle, he was an unimaginative tactician who preferred headlong bayonet charges to elaborate maneuvers. His indifference to the bullets and arrows whizzing past inspired both affection and emulation among his men.

Taylor's 3,550 troops included five infantry regiments, an artillery regiment deployed as infantry, seven companies of the Second Dragoons, and four light artillery companies, split among three brigades. Most of these troops, trailed by 307 oxcarts packed with provisions and munitions, began their march on March 8; the siege guns, heavy supplies, and about five hundred troops went by water to Port Isabel, where a fortified supply base was established.[36]

Taylor and his men first encountered Mexican cavalry at the Arroyo Colorado on March 20. As the general deployed his troops for an attack, the Mexicans cantered off without a shot fired from either side. Taylor and his weary army reached the Rio Grande's north bank across from Matamoros on March 28. The general immediately put his men to work constructing Fort Texas. His supply base was at Port Isabel, twenty-five miles away on the gulf coast. Across the river were three thousand Mexican troops commanded by Gen. Francisco Mejia.

Taylor dispatched Gen. William Worth to Mejia with a message assuring him of his peaceful intent. The Mexican officer at the ferry demanded that Worth wait while he sent word of the general's mission to his commander. Mejia refused to accept the letter from Worth personally, insisting that he would address only Taylor, who was of equal rank. He sent his artillery commander, Gen. Rómulo Díaz de la Vega, to meet Worth. The American general first asked Vega whether Mexico had declared war on the United States. To his relief, Vega explained that their countries remained at peace. Worth then insisted that General Taylor and his army hoped to uphold that peace.[37]

So far the exchanges had been polite if tense. The American and Mexican troops warily eyed each other across the river, wondering if they would eventually receive orders to kill. This possibility became much likelier on April 12, after Gen. Pedro de Ampudia arrived with three thousand troops and took command from Mejia. Ampudia demanded that Taylor withdraw his army north of the Nueces River "while our governments are regulating the pending questions in relation to Texas." If Taylor refused, then "arms and arms alone must decide the question."[38]

Although outnumbered, Taylor was not intimidated. He politely but firmly replied, "I regret the alternative which you offer; but at the same time wish it understood that I shall by no means avoid such an alternative."[39] He then upped the ante by sending, on April 12, a request to Commodore Conner to blockade the Rio Grande's mouth and thus sever the most vital supply source to Ampudia and his six thousand troops.

A blockade is an act of war. Taylor justified this decisive step by dubiously assuming that war began with Ampudia's ultimatum. Ampudia, of course, held that the war began as soon as Taylor and his army marched south of the Nueces River. Regardless of who technically started hostilities, blood had already flowed. On separate days, Mexicans had waylaid and murdered two American officers riding in the countryside. The victims' comrades called for vengeance.

Gen. Mariano Arista took command of the Mexican army on April 24. The next day, he committed two critical acts. He passed word to Taylor that the war had begun, and the American general expressed his regret. He also sent Gen. Anastasio Torrejón and sixteen hundred cavalry and light infantry about fourteen miles up the Rio Grande to a ford. Their mission was to cross the river and arc around to sever Taylor's army from its supply base at Port Isabel.

Learning of this incursion, Taylor dispatched Capt. Seth Thornton and sixty-eight dragoons to determine the Mexicans' whereabouts and intentions. On April 25 they were about twenty-five miles from Fort Texas when they rode into an ambush of several hundred Mexican lancers. The Mexicans killed eleven Americans and captured the rest. Taylor received word of the attack on the morning of April 26, when a released dragoon rode into Fort Texas. In his report to the White House, he laconically stated, "Hostilities may now be considered as commenced."[40]

Polk received this message on the evening of May 9, after he and his cabinet had spent the afternoon debating whether to ask Congress to declare war against Mexico. All saw ample justification for war except Navy Secretary Bancroft, who insisted that the Mexicans must attack first. With the message that the Mexicans had indeed drawn first blood in his hand, Polk immediately recalled his cabinet, and they unanimously agreed on war.[41]

Late into the night and for much of the following day Polk, Buchanan, and Bancroft carefully crafted a message for Congress not to declare but to recognize an existing state of war: "Mexico has . . . invaded our territory and shed American blood upon . . . American soil. She has proclaimed that hostilities have commenced, and that the two nations are at war."[42] The Polk administration then asked for authority to call fifty thousand volunteers and spend $10 million to fight this war.

Congress received this message on May 11. The result in the House of Representatives was a fierce but short debate. Months earlier, a handful of peace advocates had condemned Polk's order to Taylor to invade the disputed zone. They now argued that the action had started the war and thus the blood was on the president's hands. They called for withdrawing American forces beyond the Nueces River and opening talks with Mexico. Most congressmen decried Mexico's refusal to negotiate and blatant aggression. The debate ended a mere thirty minutes after it began. The House then voted 173 to 14 for war, with 35 abstentions.

The Senate debate took longer. To the surprise of many, John Calhoun opposed the war. He argued that constitutionally, the president as commander in chief can repel an invasion but cannot start a war; only Congress has the power to declare war. With this reasoning, he condemned the line in the president's message that read, "A state of war exists." "I will not agree to make war upon Mexico by making war upon the Constitution," Calhoun said.[43] In the end, he abstained. Others objected on practical grounds. Thomas Hart Benton worried about warring with Mexico before the Oregon dispute was settled with Britain, although in the end he voted for war. Others questioned whether they had enough information to make an informed decision. In contrast to those who urged caution, Lewis Cass of Michigan spoke for the War Hawks when he called for a total war that crushed Mexico. The Senate voted 40 to 2, with 3 abstentions on May 12.

President Polk signed this message into law on May 13, 1846. The United States was now officially at war with Mexico.[44]

20

The Mexican War

A more effectual means could not have been devised to encourage
the enemy and protract the war than to advocate and
adhere to their cause, and thus give them "aid and comfort."

JAMES K. POLK

If an earnest desire to save my country from ruin
and disgrace be treason, then I am a traitor.

DANIEL KING

Experience proves that the man who obstructs a war
in which his nation is engaged, no matter right or wrong,
occupies no enviable place in life or history.

ULYSSES S. GRANT

I believe if we were to plant our batteries in Hell the
damned Yankees would take them from us.

ANTONIO LOPEZ DE SANTA ANNA

In warring against Mexico, the United States certainly appeared to enjoy
overwhelming superiority by most measures of hard and soft power.

In just raw numbers, America's 17 million people dwarfed Mexico's 7 million. More vitally, an industrial revolution was rapidly transforming America's economy and enriching an already middle-class society; virtually all Mexicans were peasants mired in mass poverty and feudalism. Most Americans could read and write; only Mexico's elite enjoyed those skills. The American republic so far had resolved a series of political crises with compromises and expanded its electorate to include all white males; coups, authoritarianism, and violence beset Mexico's political system. Most citizens of the United States considered themselves Americans despite their nation's grave regional and racial divisions, although the importance of this identity varied greatly; only Mexico's elite was clearly nationalistic, and the country was plagued by regional, racial, cultural, and linguistic chasms.

When these political, economic, and social advantages were transformed into military power, the contrasts were just as striking. America's industrial revolution mass-produced weapons, munitions, and provisions and, with rail and steam power, rapidly transported all this to distant army and navy forces; Mexico imported rather than made most of its weapons and equipment. American naval power dwarfed that of Mexico. American troops were all enthusiastic volunteers and were far better trained, led, fed, equipped, disciplined, and motivated than were Mexican troops, who were nearly all sullen conscripts. In particular, the quality of American cannons and crews far exceeded those of Mexico. Whether or not they were West Point graduates, most American officers were proficient in the science and art of military leadership; Mexico's officers were ill trained. Finally, America's commanders repeatedly outgeneraled their Mexican opponents.[1]

In retrospect, an American victory seems inevitable. Yet this was not what European military observers anticipated. They reckoned that Mexico had the edge. Certainly when the war began, Mexico's army outnumbered America's. Its officers and troops had far more military experience from trying to crush a series of rebellions. The Mexicans had a natural advantage fighting on the defensive in their own land. They could scour the countryside of food, forage, and livestock ahead of the invaders and could choose and fortify battle sites. When they withdrew, they were closer to most sources of supplies and reinforcements. In contrast, America's government, as usual, entered the war unprepared to fight and spent months raising, equipping, training, supplying, and transporting volunteer regiments to the distant fronts.

Handicaps plagued both armies. Most soldiers shouldered muskets with poor range and accuracy. Disease killed many times more troops than battle. Water was often scarce and foul, and food was not much better. Draft animals and riding horses were increasingly hard to obtain and keep alive. Finally, the fierce patriotism and rivalries of Mexico's elite prolonged the war long after its outcome was certain, thus causing the fruitless waste of treasure and lives.

A potential wild card lurked in a war between the United States and Mexico. The president and congressional War Hawks had also rushed America to war's brink with Britain over Oregon. If they plunged into the abyss, America would end up fighting two wars at once and could well lose both of them. Even if a war did not erupt with Britain, the Polk White House would have to battle Mexico with one military arm tied behind its back as long as the Oregon conflict festered.

Fortunately, cooler heads in London prevailed. Prime Minister Robert Peel was forced to dissolve his government when Parliament split bitterly over the Corn Laws and free trade. John Russell tried to form a government but failed. Had the belligerent, anti-American Russell replaced the conciliatory Peel, hot heads would have ruled in both London and Washington, and war quite likely would have ensued. Instead, Queen Victoria convinced Peel to reshuffle his cabinet and stay on as prime minister. Peel did as instructed but wisely retained the conciliatory George Hamilton-Gordon, Lord Aberdeen, as foreign secretary. By promising to repeal the protectionist Corn Laws, Peel convinced a majority in Parliament to vote his government to power.

Aberdeen's persistent attempts to seek compromise had been thwarted by British hard-liners, especially Richard Pakenham, the minister in Washington City. In a letter to Pakenham, Aberdeen explained the need for compromise to avoid war, sagely noting the likelihood that "the President and his Government are more afraid of the Senate than they are of us."[2]

Louis McLane, America's minister in London, explained these nuances of British politics and the consequences for American interests. Insisting on "Fifty-Four Forty or Fight" might not win that boundary, he noted, but would definitely lead to a fight. He strongly advised the president to split the difference at the 49th parallel.[3]

After five months of debate, majorities in both houses of Congress voted on April 23, 1846, to send Britain an abrogation notice for the 1827 Oregon treaty. The notice reached London on May 15, 1846. Peel convened his cabinet for four days of intense talks. They forged a consensus to extend the boundary along the 49th parallel to the Pacific Ocean and then bend it south through the Strait of Juan de Fuca and thus around Vancouver Island, which would remain part of Canada. Absent from the offer was the former insistence on British navigation rights to the Columbia River; only the Hudson's Bay Company would be allowed free access and only until its operating charter expired in 1859. Aberdeen drew up the consensus and sent it to Pakenham.

Meanwhile, the possibility of simultaneously fighting Mexico and Britain dampened some of the war zeal in Washington City. As the crisis and political rhetoric with Mexico worsened, foreign observers noted with alarm the likelihood that America was preparing for a war of conquest. Secretary of State Buchanan sought to alleviate these fears with a bold gesture. On May 13 he presented to the cabinet the draft of a message he intended America's diplomats to issue to their hosts— the United States promised not to acquire any territory from its war with Mexico. When Polk scornfully rejected this suggestion, Buchanan warned, "Then you will have war with England as well as Mexico and probably with France also, for neither of those powers will ever stand by" as "California is annexed" to the United States. The other secretaries heatedly attacked Buchanan's proposal. Buchanan stood his ground until Polk said the decision was final and then stalked wordlessly from the room.[4]

As soon as Polk received Pakenham's official British proposal via Buchanan, he gathered his cabinet to discuss it. Ironically, during the June 6 meeting, the secretary of state was the only cabinet member who opposed the compromise. He justified his stance by insisting that "the 54 40 men were the true friends of the administration and he wished no backing out on the subject."[5] Thus, he went from being the most conciliatory to the most aggressive on the Oregon issue and sacrificed his principles on the altar of his ambitions. He intended to run for president in 1848 and assumed that Lewis Cass, a fervent Oregon War

Hawk, would be his toughest rival for the Democratic Party nomination. With most Democrats supporting a hard-line stance, it only made political sense to stand and shrilly shout with them.

Polk was just as careful to appease the Democratic Party's War Hawks. He accepted the British compromise, had a treaty drawn and signed, and then, on June 10, submitted it to the Senate with a curious request. He asked the chamber's advice on whether he should formally submit that treaty for ratification. The Senate agreed by a vote of 38 to 12. He actually submitted the treaty on June 16. The Senate ratified it by 41 to 14 on June 18.

While the Fifty-Four Forty or Fight diehards grumbled, nearly everyone else breathed a deep collective sigh of relief. The nation had just dodged countless bullets. Now the United States could focus on winning its war with Mexico.

The Mexican attack that killed or captured all but one of Captain Thornton's sixty-eight-man company jolted Gen. Zachary Taylor into full awareness of his vulnerability. The enemy army outgunned his by nearly two to one, and a portion had already crossed the Rio Grande. What if General Arista led over the rest of his five thousand troops, severed Taylor's twenty-five-mile supply line back to Port Isabel, and hemmed the Americans against the river? There would be no choice but a humiliating surrender.

Taylor acted decisively on May 1. Leaving Maj. Jacob Brown in command of five hundred troops at Fort Texas, he withdrew his army to Port Isabel. He did so just in time. As Taylor had feared, Arista had ordered General Torrejón to cut him off. Torrejón barely missed Taylor as he marched his men within cannon shot of Fort Texas. Arista joined him with about half of the region's Mexican troops. As his men set up artillery batteries, he demanded that Brown surrender. When Brown defiantly refused, Arista ordered his guns to open fire.

Taylor meanwhile resupplied his army at Port Isabel. Detachments, desertions, and disease had whittled his field force to 2,288 troops. Although he faced a much larger Mexican army, Taylor stoically led his men back to rescue Fort Texas. Learning of his advance, Arista left a skeleton force to continue the siege and led 3,709 troops seven miles up the road to Palo Alto. On May 8, with the Mexican army blocking his path, Taylor quickly scanned the enemy's positions, conferred tersely with his staff, and then ordered an all-out frontal assault. After fierce fighting, the Americans routed the Mexicans, killing 102 and wounding 120, while losing only 5 killed and 48 wounded. Thornton's defeat was sharply avenged.[6]

The Americans reaped further vengeance the following day. Arista withdrew his battered army to Resaca de la Palma, three miles from the Rio Grande. The Americans attacked and routed the Mexicans again, this time inflicting even heavier casualties of 154 dead, 205 wounded, and 156 missing, while losing 33 dead and 89 wounded. Arista retreated his army up the Rio Grande valley to the closest ford and then across to the south bank.[7]

Had Taylor vigorously pursued Arista, he could have turned the Mexican retreat into a rout, bagged many more troops and supplies, and trapped the entire enemy army with an unfordable stretch of river at its back. Instead, Taylor encamped his troops around Fort Texas. It would not be the last time that Taylor failed to convert a limited victory into a decisive one.

The Mexicans were desperately short of troops, supplies, and morale. Arista withdrew his army's remnants, now down to just 2,638 troops, to Monterrey. After scouts brought word that the enemy had vanished, Taylor led his army across the Rio Grande and occupied Matamoros on May 18.[8]

The Americans had decisively trounced the Mexican army in two hard-fought battles and expelled it from the lower Rio Grande valley. Taylor sent back word to the White House of these victories and amassed supplies while awaiting further instructions. In honor of Fort Texas's valiant commander, who was killed during the siege, he renamed the post Fort Brown; this fort would eventually develop into the city of Brownsville.

Taylor's failure to land a knockout blow despite two chances to do so lost him Polk's confidence: "General Taylor . . . is not the man for command of the army. He is brave but does not seem to have resources or grasp of mind to conduct such a campaign."[9] More lay behind Polk's condemnation of Taylor than just his military shortcomings. The president feared even more the victorious general's political ambitions. Some prominent Whigs were already touting Taylor as their party's best potential nominee for the 1848 presidential election. The Whig Party's previous and so far only winning White House candidate had also been a famed general, William Henry Harrison. The hope was that the Whig Party could promote Taylor, as they had Harrison, as their populist answer to Jackson.

So far, no general affiliated with the Democratic Party had won similar fame. Polk could only dream of changing this. But to do so, he would have to conjure up someone to supersede Taylor. The trouble was that the only current alternative lacked Democratic Party credentials.

Polk summoned Maj. Gen. Winfield Scott, the army's highest-ranking general, to the White House on May 13 and offered him command of America's field armies. He did so with mixed feelings, confiding to his diary, "Scott did not impress me favorably as a military man" as he was "rather scientific and visionary in his views."[10] That Scott did not measure up in Polk's mind alongside his idol Andrew Jackson is not surprising. Polk had never served in the military, let alone fought in battle. His notions of war and warriors were formed by listening wide-eyed to the tales of Jackson and the coterie of hard-drinking, hard-bitten officers who had fought alongside him. As such, he was projecting his own inadequacies as the nation's commander in chief when he dismissed Scott as "rather scientific and visionary in his views." Politics also warped Polk's impression. Scott, like Taylor, was a confirmed if lukewarm Whig. Although Polk had pledged to be a one-term president, he did not want to bequeath to the next Democratic Party nominee a Whig military hero for a rival.

Scott was well aware of Polk's views. Upon receiving the president's summons, he feared that he was going to be sidelined to make way for a Democratic political appointee. His eyes filled with tears and his voice choked when Polk explained the reason for their meeting. He eagerly and gratefully accepted the assignment.

The president's reluctant decision would decisively affect the war's outcome. Of the possible field commanders, only Scott could have overcome the logistical, strategic, and tactical challenges in feeding his army and fighting the enemy all the way from the Gulf of Mexico to the Halls of Montezuma. Certainly, his laconic colleague Zachary Taylor was not up to the job. The American army has probably never had a more glaring contrast between its two leading generals, with "Old Fuss and Feathers" Scott alongside "Old Rough and Ready" Taylor.

Their difference was not just one of style. Taylor knew little and cared less about the science and art of war. His favorite tactic was the bayonet charge straight at the enemy. He left to his staff the irksome task of scrounging up enough beans and bullets for his boys.

In contrast, although little known today, Scott is rated among the greatest generals in American history.[11] He first achieved acclaim during the War of 1812 with his brilliant handling of his well-trained regiment at the Battles of Queenston Heights, Fort George, Chippewa, and Lundy's Lane. A bullet in the shoulder at Lundy's Lane sidelined him for months and prevented him from being promoted to an army command. He bolstered his practice of war by studying its theory and practice. Fluent in French, he explored the campaigns of Napoleon and other great European generals by reading their memoirs. His flaws were in his personality. Like many highly intelligent people, he was impatient with those less gifted who blindly followed their prejudices rather than reason. In addition, he was vain, pompous, easily offended, and quick-tempered. He counted more enemies and critics than admirers and followers.

Scott's emotional meeting with the president only briefly dissipated his fears of being set up and trumped politically. Polk worked with congressional Democratic Party leaders to draft and pass a bill that created two more major generals and four brigadier generals, all White House appointees. Scott tried to deter this in a letter to War Secretary Marcy, by expressing his resentment at being placed "in the most perilous of all positions—a fire upon my rear from Washington, and the fire in front from the Mexicans."[12]

Marcy, of course, shared the letter with Polk, who convened the cabinet to discuss it. The president authorized Marcy to rebuke Scott for assuming "the most unworthy motives in the Executive Government—of bad faith toward yourself—of a reckless disregard for the interests of the country—of a design to carry on a war against the public enemy."[13] Both letters were passed to the *Daily Union*, the administration's mouthpiece, for publication.

This attempt to embarrass and discredit Scott backfired. In fact, Marcy presented the most damning criticisms of the Polk White House and failed to refute them. Although Scott's words appeared self-righteous and paranoid, Whigs rallied around their general and blasted Polk and the Democrats for trying to undercut him. Thus did the president and his men sow discord rather than unity in the war's opening stage. These chasms and animosities would steadily worsen.

Taylor meanwhile opened a new campaign on July 6, as his troops began a ninety-mile march up the Rio Grande valley to Camargo. After setting up a supply depot, he sent an advanced guard to occupy Cerralvo, sixty miles south on the road to Monterrey. The only formidable foes that his army encountered along the way and in camp were germs. Diseases debilitated or outright killed fifteen hundred men, or nearly a third of his army. Taylor spent almost two months massing troops and supplies. By late August his army numbered three thousand regulars and seventy-seven hundred volunteers. The lack of supplies forced Taylor to take only his regulars and half his volunteers on the march to Monterrey. He split his troops into three divisions led by Gens. William Worth, David Twiggs, and William Butler. The supplies were packed on fifteen hundred mules and in 180 mule- or ox-drawn wagons. The daunting logistical challenge of moving all those men and supplies to Cerralvo was not finished until early September.[14]

The first regiments began their march on the ninety miles of rutted road to Monterrey on September 11. Eight days later, Taylor's 6,220 troops massed just beyond cannon shot of the city. Awaiting the Americans were Gen. Pedro de Ampudia, 7,303 troops, and 42 cannons.[15] Monterrey lay on the north bank of the Rio San Juan de Monterrey. The road to Camargo ran northeast and the road to Saltillo southwest of the city. A citadel, dubbed the Black Fort by the Americans, guarded the city's northern approach. Redoubts studded the city's outskirts. The Mexicans converted the walled bishop's palace atop Independent Hill, west of the city, into a fort. Two other forts crowned Federation Hill, south of the river.

Taylor convened a council of war and hammered out a plan. On September 20 Gen. William Worth led his division to march north around the city and mass astride the road leading to the enemy's distant supply depot at Saltillo. Two days later, American troops captured the Black Fort, while the rest of the army assaulted and took various points along the city's fringe. At the cost of 120 killed and 368 wounded, the Americans cut off Ampudia, inflicted 367 casualties, and were poised to bag his entire army.[16]

Then, once again, Taylor let the enemy escape. On September 25 he accepted Ampudia's request for an eight-week armistice; he would withdraw his army from Monterrey within the first week. Ampudia said that talks had opened between the United States and Mexico, and this lie cinched the deal by prompting Taylor to yield on humanitarian and diplomatic grounds: "It would be judicious to act with magnanimity towards a prostrate foe, particularly as the president of the United States had offered to settle all differences between the two nations by negotiating."[17] Thus did the Monterrey campaign end with the city's capture and the enemy army's escape.

In contrast, American victories elsewhere were decisive. On May 13 Polk and his cabinet agreed to march an army to conquer first New Mexico and then California. To lead this campaign, Polk tapped Col. Stephen Watts Kearny and promoted him to brevet brigadier general.[18] Kearny was then in his thirty-fourth year in the army and fifty-first year of life. After fighting in the War of 1812, he had spent most of the following decades on the western frontier commanding a succession of posts, including Fort Crawford, Jefferson Barracks, Fort Gibson, Fort Des Moines, and finally, Fort Leavenworth. In 1836 he was promoted to colonel and assigned command of the First Dragoons, which he recruited and drilled into the army's best regiment. He led the dragoons in two peaceful but muscle-flexing expeditions to impress the Indians: one up the Missouri to the Platte River mouth in 1839 and another west along the Oregon Trail to the South Pass in the Rocky Mountains in 1845. He was a highly intelligent, energetic, and strict but just leader respected by his fellow officers and common soldiers alike.

Fort Leavenworth occupied a first-rate strategic site that overlooked the Missouri River and short spurs that led to both the Santa Fe and Oregon Trails. Five hundred and thirty seven miles separated Fort Leavenworth from Santa Fe. Upon receiving his orders on May 26, Kearny immediately began gathering troops, supplies, transport, and draft animals for what was dubbed the Army of the West. A week later, he read new orders. After seizing New Mexico, he was to march to California.

The Army of the West was actually a brigade composed of four companies of the First Dragoons: an artillery company under Capt. Meriwether Lewis Clark, the First Missouri Mounted Regiment led by Col. Alexander Doniphan, the Second Missouri Mounted Regiment led by Col. Sterling Price, and the Mormon Battalion led by Capt. James Allen. The Mormon Battalion remains the only unit in the American army ever raised on the basis of religion; its troops were recruited at the Mormon's Winter Quarters camp near Council Bluff, and they agreed to serve in return for discharge in California, where they could settle. The First Missouri assembled at Fort Leavenworth by early June; the Second Missouri and Mormon Battalion would not arrive until late July.

Kearny sent off his available troops in contingents. The first two dragoon companies rode toward Santa Fe on June 6. Doniphan and his men left on June 16. Kearny parted on June 30 with his last two dragoon companies. Accompanying Kearny was Lt. William Emory of the Topographical Corps; Emory would map the territory through which they journeyed. The Army of the West's first division alone was an impressive assertion of American power. In all, 1,458 troops, a dozen six-pounder cannons, four twelve-pounder howitzers, 156 supply wagons, 3,658 draft mules, 459 riding horses, and 14,904 cattle stretched in a long dusty line across the plains.[19]

The march was tedious rather than dangerous. Although Comanche war parties attacked isolated wagon trains along the stretch of Santa Fe Trail that passed through their land, they stayed clear of such a formidable force. The worst danger was suffering dysentery from drinking foul water along the way. Bent's Fort was a welcome stopping place sited on the Arkansas River's north bank about two-thirds of the way down the trail. The Bent brothers, Charles and William, had entered the Santa Fe trade shortly after the market opened in 1821; they erected their trading post in 1832.[20]

At Bent's Fort Kearny got the latest information about the challenges ahead. It was quite possible that the Army of the West could seize New Mexico without firing a shot. The province was defended by only a couple of hundred regular troops scattered among the towns. The militia was poorly armed and motivated. Their military leaders might just capitulate with Kearny's troops massed before them. Or their civil leaders might be bought off ahead of time. New Mexican officials enriched themselves by shaking down American merchants and trappers, no one more so than Governor Manuel Armijo, who also assumed the post of customs collector.

Accompanying Kearny was someone who could pull off a backroom deal. James Magoffin was a frontier entrepreneur who had trekked the Santa Fe Trail several times, spoke Spanish, and had nurtured many relationships in New Mexico, including one with Governor Armijo. He also had influential friends in Washington City. Senator Thomas Hart Benton summoned him to the capital and asked his assistance in taking over New Mexico. Magoffin readily agreed to travel with the army and act as an envoy.

As the army rested at Bent's Fort several days, Kearny sent Magoffin ahead with an escort of a dozen dragoons commanded by Capt. Philip Cooke and a message from Kearny to Armijo. Kearny's message understandably angered the governor. The general explained that he was coming to occupy Texas's western boundary, which lay on the Rio Grande. This, of course, included Santa Fe and most other New Mexican towns.

Kearny led his column from Bent's Fort on August 2. He and his footsore men shuffled into Las Vegas, New Mexico's easternmost town, on August 14. The general had the mayor gather the population in the plaza. He then climbed a wooden ladder to the top of one of the flat-roofed adobe buildings lining the square and, with an interpreter repeating each sentence, read them a proclamation that he hoped would win their allegiance: "I have come amongst you by the order of my government to take possession of your country. We come amongst you as friends, not as enemies; as protectors, not as conquerors. Henceforth I absolve you of all allegiance to your government."[21] Although the inhabitants can be forgiven if they were skeptical of these promises, Kearny would be true to his word.

Meanwhile, Magoffin's mission appeared to fail. Honor demanded that Armijo reject any capitulation without first an exchange of gunfire. He ordered Col. Manuel Pinto to mobilize all armed men for the province's defense. They would make their stand at Apache Canyon, a dozen miles east of Santa Fe on the trail toward the United States. Nearly four thousand men had gathered there by mid-August.

Word reached Kearny of Armijo's plan, and he braced himself to fight a bloody battle. But as his army approached Apache Canyon, scouts reported that no enemy forces lay ahead. For the Mexicans, survival proved more appealing than honor. When Armijo convened a council of war with Pinto and other ranking officers, they urged him not to resist Kearny. Armijo dismissed his men and fled to Mexico.

Kearny and his troops marched into Santa Fe on August 18. With the mayor beside him, he declared that New Mexico was now part of the United States. He moved into the governor's palace, and he had his men build and garrison Fort Marcy on a hill overlooking the town about six hundred yards from the plaza. He recognized the vital importance of winning hearts and minds. He appointed Charles Bent New Mexico's governor. He asked Doniphan, a lawyer, to draft a set of laws to rule the territory; the result became known as the Kearny Code. He issued regulations setting official business license fees and strictly forbidding bribery. He held a ball for Santa Fe's leading citizens and his officers. Although he was a Protestant, he attended Catholic mass. He was always polite, sensitive, and accessible to New Mexicans.

Having secured the region, Kearny set off with three hundred dragoons for California on September 25. He left behind orders that when Col. Sterling Price and his Second Missouri Mounted Regiment and the Mormon Battalion reached Santa Fe, Doniphan would lead his regiments south to capture El Paso. Meanwhile, Doniphan would send envoys with large military escorts to the Navajo, Apache, and Ute bands to explain the transfer of power and to forge peace treaties with those peoples.

Kearny's peaceful occupation of New Mexico was militarily and diplomatically flawless. Unfortunately, his decisions in California would be marred by bloodshed and controversy.

The Polk administration had sown the seeds for California's conquest the previous year in reaction to belligerent talk by Mexican president Herrera and General Paredes.[22] When Polk convened his cabinet on September 16, 1845, Mexico appeared to teeter at the brink of civil war. The one issue on which all prominent Mexicans agreed was to reject any talks with, let alone concessions to, the United States. Thus, a diplomatic resolution of the conflict was dead for the foreseeable future.

Of all the Mexican territories that the Polk administration sought, California was at once the most distant and potentially lucrative. The president and his secretaries agreed that their only choice was to take this realm if the Mexican government refused to sell. Ideally, they hoped to acquire California much as they had Texas, with an American revolt deposing Mexican rule and then annexation to the United States.

To this end, Secretary of State Buchanan sent instructions to Thomas Larkin, the American consul at Monterey, to inform the British and other foreign powers that the United States would "vigorously interpose" any attempt by them to seize California. He should also assure Californians to expect full American support for "a sister republic" if they declared independence and for a sister state if they sought annexation.[23]

Cdre. Robert Stockton and the frigate USS *Congress* would deliver these instructions to Larkin. Stockton was more than a message bearer. He was to replace the conscientious but cautious Cdre. John Sloat in command of the Pacific flotilla.[24]

President Polk dispatched, on October 30, a messenger with additional instructions to Larkin and Sloat. Although he left months after Stockton, Lt. Archibald Gillespie arrived in California first. Stockton had to sail all the way around the Cape of Good Hope at South America's southernmost tip. Gillespie took a steamer to Veracruz and crossed over to Mazatlan, the Pacific flotilla's base. On February 11, 1846, Gillespie reached Mazatlan and conveyed his orders to Sloat. The commodore authorized a warship to carry Gillespie to Monterey. Sloat would follow with the rest of the flotilla if he heard that war had erupted.

Polk's only known asset in California was Larkin. But he thought he might have another source of power there to wield against the Mexicans. The trouble was that the president had no idea whether the second asset was in place or even en route. After reaching Sloat and Larkin, Gillespie's mission was to track down this elusive force. So, in addition to his official dispatches, the lieutenant carried verbal instructions from Polk and personal letters from Thomas Hart Benton, among the most powerful senators, to his son-in-law, the American army's most famous officer.

Although John Frémont was renowned for being a great "pathfinder," "mapmaker" or, for some, "troublemaker" might be more appropriate sobriquets.[25] He mostly did not so much find new paths as follow and chart existing ones. He did so with great skill and courage, and perhaps even greater ego and hubris. Behind his feats was marriage to a remarkable woman, Jessie Benton, the senator's beguiling and brilliant daughter. His father-in-law had pressured the War Department to send him off on exploring expeditions. His wife vividly wrote up his adventures into official reports and eventually his memoir. Without this formidable backing, Frémont would have been a bit rather than a key actor in the war climaxing the Jackson era.

Frémont entered the army and the West by chance. He was born in Savannah into a ménage à trois among his mother, her aged husband, and her French tutor and lover, his real father. His natural ambitions were spurred as he sought to bury with ever greater achievements the stigma of his scandalous birth and upbringing. As a young man, he changed his name and sought to make his fortune in Charleston. There his proficiency at mathematics and self-promotion garnered the attention of Joel Poinsett, a prominent South Carolina politician who eventually became President Van Buren's secretary of war. Poinsett got Frémont a lieutenant's commission in the Corps of Engineers and an assignment to join Joseph Nicollet's expeditions to map the region between the Mississippi and Missouri Rivers. In Washington City, he met Jessie Benton, then sixteen years old, was smitten, and passionately courted her. Benton had no intention of marrying his daughter to some penniless and, as rumor had it, bastard lieutenant and had him posted to the Des Moines River to map that watershed. Somehow Frémont wrangled a leave, returned to Washington City, and eloped with Jessie in October 1841. Benton was livid when he found out but gradually warmed to their marriage.

Benton's conversion was rooted in more than sentiment. In the senator's hands, Frémont could advance Benton's own vision of American expansion and manifest destiny. In the spring of 1842 he found Frémont a mission leading an expedition that mapped the Oregon Trail as far as South Pass on the Continental Divide. The following year, he put Frémont on an expedition to seek a passage over the southern Rocky Mountains and into the Great Basin all the way to the Sierra Nevada Mountains and over them into California. With mountain man Kit Carson as their guide, Frémont and his men made it through the Rockies easily enough but hit a wall at the Sierra Nevadas. They headed north searching for a pass all the way to the narrow path leading over to Klamath Lake and eventually zigzagged their way down into California's Central Valley. They wintered at Sutter's Fort and pushed south to the valley's end, over Cajon Pass, and then eastward all the way to St. Louis. This second trek lasted seventeen months from March 1843 to August 1844. The expedition's published report made Frémont a national hero.

Frémont had spent far more time on the trail than with his young bride. This may partly have been the senator's intent, but others were far more important. In October 1845 Benton and Frémont met with

President Polk at the White House. There they devised a third expedition destined to become the most vital. Exactly what understanding was reached among the three men will never be known. Polk's diary was as vague as Frémont's later memoir, and both were likely deliberately so. What is clear is the chasm between what Frémont was officially ordered to do and what he did.

Frémont was supposed to map the Arkansas River headwaters and then return to Washington City within the year. Instead, with Carson again guiding, he led his sixty men to California. They sauntered into Fort Sutter on December 9, 1845. Leaving most of his men at the fort, he and a few trusted followers headed on to Monterey, which they reached on January 17, 1846. Frémont reported to Larkin, who gave him credit for buying crucial supplies from Sutter. He received permission from Gen. José Maria Castro to winter his expedition in the San Joaquin Valley before heading north to Oregon in the spring.

As a guest, Frémont proved to be a host's worst nightmare. He committed aggressive acts designed to provoke a fight. Rather than stay in the San Joaquin Valley, he and his sixty heavily armed and hardened men advanced to the coast near Monterey. On March 5, 1846, Castro ordered him to leave. Frémont refused and instead led his men atop Gavilan Peak, where they raised the American flag and fortified their camp. Castro advanced on the position with two hundred men. Larkin intervened before blood was shed and talked a reluctant Frémont into standing down. Frémont and his men headed north on March 9.

If Frémont received secret orders to claim California for the United States, his quixotic behavior appeared to ruin whatever opportunity existed or had been created. Rather than inspire a revolt, he instead was forced into a humiliating retreat. How different the situation might have been had he wintered his men in the San Joaquin Valley while he secretly circulated among the American communities preparing them for a takeover some time later that year.

But then Castro acted in a way that nullified his victory over Frémont. On April 17 he ordered all non-Mexicans to leave California. Rumor had it that he also encouraged the Indians to attack Americans wherever they could be found. This alienated countless American settlers, who might otherwise have sat on the sidelines when fighting eventually broke out.

As fate would have it, Lieutenant Gillespie landed at Monterey the same day Castro expelled Frémont and his men. He delivered his terse written and verbal messages to Larkin. The White House's official word to Larkin was ambiguous. On one hand, the United States would "make no effort and use no influence to induce California to become one of the free and independent states of this union." Yet, "should California assert and maintain her independence, we shall render her all the kind offices in our power as a Sister Republic." For this, "the Californians would be received as brethren, whenever this can be done without affording Mexico just cause of complaint."[26] This last stipulation all but ordained a military resolution of the issue. Mexico would not voluntarily cede California any more than it had Texas; it could be coerced only with overwhelming force.

Frémont's assistance in inciting the Americans living in California could be critical, assuming he was in the region. Gillespie asked his whereabouts. Larkin could only point him to Fort Sutter, where he and his men were last reported seen before they headed north toward Oregon. Gillespie galloped off on a fast horse and caught up to the expedition on Upper Klamath Lake's south shore on May 9. After his epic journey, Gillespie nearly did not make it. Frémont and his men rescued him after he was waylaid by Indians.

After listening to Gillespie's message, Frémont announced to his men a dramatic change in plans. He later wrote, "I saw the way opening clear before me. War with Mexico was inevitable; and a grand opportunity now presented itself to realize in their fullest extent the far-sighted views of Senator Benton, and make the Pacific Ocean the western boundary of the United States. I resolved to move forward on the opportunity."[27]

Yet another armed band of Americans entered the fray. On June 14 thirty-two Sonoma Valley settlers led by Ezekiel Merritt barged into the hacienda of Mariano Vallejo, the region's largest landowner, took him prisoner, and declared the California Republic. To emphasize this act, they sewed up a crude flag with a red grizzly bear above a white star on a brown field and raised it above the hacienda. Their movement was soon dubbed the Bear Flag Revolt. They elected William Ide their commander in chief.

The rebels' decision to incarcerate Vallejo was unfortunate. He was actually a friend of Larkin's and most other Americans'. Had the rebels tried instead to enlist him in their cause, he most likely would have discouraged Mexicans from opposing them and might have openly joined.

Learning of the revolt, Castro sent fifty troops to crush it. On June 23 the rebels scattered the soldiers without losing a man. Frémont linked forces with them and assumed command of the California Battalion. During a Fourth of July party in Sonoma, Frémont declared California's independence. Although war had indeed erupted between the United States and Mexico, no word of this critical event had yet reached California. Nonetheless, Frémont apparently was acting on a verbal message from the president conveyed by Gillespie.

Meanwhile, a couple of thousand miles away, another American commander with standing orders was acting far more cautiously. Cdre. John Sloat sat tight with his flotilla at Mazatlan even though he knew that fighting had broken out along the Rio Grande. He ordered sails set only after receiving, on June 7, official word that Congress had declared war against Mexico. One month later, his flotilla was anchored before Monterey. On July 7 he landed at the head of 225 marines and armed sailors. Before the customs house, Sloat declared America's takeover of California. He called on all Mexicans to submit peacefully to American rule and promised that the Americans would respect Mexican laws and customs. He dispatched a warship to Yerba Buena, as San Francisco was then called, to occupy the town. He sent off an officer to Sonoma to ask the Bear Flag rebels to submit to American rule.

The American force in Monterey soon swelled with reinforcements. On July 14 Stockton arrived and replaced Sloat as the Pacific flotilla's commander. Five days later, Frémont led his California Battalion into Monterey. Stockton mustered the California Battalion into the U.S. Army and promoted Frémont to major. Leaving a small contingent behind, he packed the California Battalion aboard his vessels and sailed south to conquer the rest of California. Off San Pedro, he split his forces. He would land his marines and sailors to take San Pedro and then Los Angeles, while Frémont and his men sailed on to San Diego.

The Americans occupied these towns without bloodshed in early August. Frémont left a small garrison and marched north to join Stockton and his men at Los Angeles. There, on August 17, Stockton declared that California was now annexed to the United States and that he was the territory's acting governor. He sent Kit Carson, Tom Fitzpatrick, and fifteen other men east to carry word of California's largely peaceful takeover to the president at the other end of the continent. With Gillespie and forty-eight men garrisoning Los Angeles, Stockton and Frémont returned to Monterey. Although California appeared subdued, the "shock and awe" of the American conquest would soon wear off.

While adventurous Americans were winning glory and plunder for their country in distant lands, the Polk administration was increasingly entangled in mundane but no less vital pursuits in Washington. Wars are budget busters. As it had during other wars, the United States squared off against Mexico without its leaders considering how to pay for it. The federal government's only significant source of money was tariffs, and these fell far short of covering expenses. There was no income tax, and nobody proposed one. So, the government bridged the widening chasm between spending and revenues with borrowed money. All this new debt was serviced with the old, with the worsening burden passed to future generations.

Polk proposed two measures intended to shore up the federal government's shaky finances. First, he presented a new tariff, which he hoped would at once raise revenues and alleviate southern complaints about protecting northern industries. The 1846 Tariff Act cut the tariff rate so that it no longer nurtured infant industries and broadened it to embrace more imports. That bill passed the House by 114 to 95 on July 3, 1846, and the Senate by 27 to 26 on July 26.

Polk then asked Congress to reconsider an "independent treasury" bill that had passed the House but died in the Senate the previous year. The financial chaos and uncertainty that President Jackson inflicted on the economy with his crusade against the monster bank lingered a decade after his "victory." The 1846 Independent Treasury Act tried to mend some of the damage. Henceforth federal funds would be deposited only in the Treasury, and Washington would accept only specie for payments of tariffs, land sales, license fees, or fines. The House version passed by 122 to 66 on April 2, the Senate version by 28 to 25 on August 1, and the reconciled bill in both houses on August 5. Polk signed it into law that day.

This policy secured and depoliticized federal money. All the coins were in a vault rather than spread among the often shady, volatile, corrupt pet banks of an administration's political allies. The downside was that the money seeped rather than flowed through the economy as the government paid what it owed its employees, contractors, and financiers. This left the private sector all the more reliant on paper certificates of fluctuating and often dubious value, which in turn stymied potential growth as investors feared risking their money in the perilous speculative sea.

Then, on ideological and fiscal grounds, Polk angered Hamiltonians by vetoing a $1,378,450 rivers and harbors internal improvement bill. The House passed the bill by 109 to 90 on March 20 and the Senate by 34 to 16 on July 24. In his veto message of August 3, Polk rejected the bill as unconstitutional and an unnecessary fiscal burden in wartime.[28]

As word of distant victories reached the capital, the debate intensified over exactly what, if anything, to take after winning the war. The spectrum ranged from nothing to all of Mexico. One position became entangled with the $2 million defense appropriation bill that Polk sent to Congress on August 4. That bill passed the Senate by 33 to 19. It took longer to pass the House, and when it did, it came with a string attached that infuriated Polk and all other slavocrats.

The Mexican War enflamed regional animosities over slavery. Most northerners feared that southerners sought to conquer New Mexico and California in order to spread slavery across those lands. The Whigs rallied popular support in the North by playing on those fears. Northern Democrats thought of a way they might win back some of that support. By a vote of 108 to 43, the House had recently passed an administration bill for the Oregon Territory, based on the 1787 Northwest Ordinance and including the clause that "neither slavery nor involuntary servitude shall ever exist in said Territory." Slavocrat senators filibustered this bill to death. Nonetheless, the House's overwhelming backing of the bill inspired a group of northern Democrats led by David Wilmot of Pennsylvania. With what became known as the Wilmot Proviso, he amended the appropriations bill to forbid the introduction of slavery in any territories taken from Mexico.[29]

As if the Mexican War's domestic and international issues were not complex enough, the Wilmot Proviso planted the slavery debate at the heart of them. Slavocrats tried to kill the amendment, but a coalition of Whigs and nearly all free-state Democrats approved it by 83 to 64. The complete bill passed by 87 to 64. The bill moved to the Senate, where slavocrats filibustered it. Polk condemned this "mischievous and foolish amendment. . . . What connection slavery had with making peace with Mexico . . . is difficult to conceive."[30]

Although solid majorities in both congressional chambers had initially voted for war against Mexico, over time more Americans questioned the decision's wisdom. Much of the criticism singled out the president. "Mr. Polk's War" was deliberately uttered to recall an earlier generation's condemnation of the disastrous "Mr. Madison's War." For opponents, this put a despised human face on the war's viler reasons. They argued that Polk was the slave states' front man who provoked and waged an unnecessary and blatant war of imperialism to expand their territory, wealth, and power. Among the most popular proponents of that view was James Russell Lowell, who wrote a series of vivid essays on the topic called the Bigelow Papers. Yet there were no mass protests, let alone riots, in the streets. Henry David Thoreau famously spent a night in jail in protest against a state tax that paid for its volunteer regiments, but this apparently was it. Nonetheless, the 1846 elections reflected the shift in public opinion. The Democratic Party lost thirty-five seats in the House, leaving the Whigs in control with a 115 to 108 majority, but retained a slender majority in the Senate.

Polk was embittered by the loss and the mounting criticism of him and his policies.[31] He struck back in his December address to Congress, insisting that the "war had not been waged with a view to conquest, but having been commenced by Mexico, it has been carried into the enemy's country and will be vigorously prosecuted there with a view to obtain an honorable peace." He then condemned his critics, who portrayed Mexico as the victim as American aggression, as traitors: "A more effectual means could not have been devised to encourage the enemy and protract the war than to advocate and adhere to their cause, and thus give them 'aid and comfort.'" Finally, he called on Congress to appropriate $23 million to prosecute the war through 1848 if need be. Of that, he asked for $2 million to be set aside as a downpayment on a peace treaty, while the rest would finance the army and navy campaigns. He hoped eventually to field 36,400 troops, of which 17,000 would be regulars, 9,400 volunteers in the field, and 10,000 reserve volunteers to be sent to the front if necessary.[32] Polk eventually received this funding but only after the Wilmot Proviso was again inserted and eventually ejected from the appropriation bill. As for the treason charges levied by Polk and other Jacksonians against those who opposed the war, Congressman Daniel King of Massachusetts offered a defiant reply: "If an earnest desire to save my country from ruin and disgrace be treason, then I am a traitor."[33]

Polk made his first attempt to end the war with diplomacy just a couple of months after he entered it. On July 27, 1846, he had Buchanan write his counterpart a letter asking for talks. He did not receive a reply until September 19. What he read was discouraging. Negotiations would not even be considered until Mexico's congress met in December.[34]

This prompted Polk to take a harder line against the Mexicans. He had War Secretary Marcy issue orders for the army to seize rather than pay for provisions from the Mexican people. He had Navy Secretary John Mason, who replaced Bancroft in September, order Commodore Conner to capture Tampico and tighten the blockade elsewhere along the gulf coast.[35]

So far the only deal the White House had cut with a prominent Mexican would prolong rather than end the war. The day the war officially began, Navy Secretary Bancroft ordered the Pacific and gulf flotilla commanders to blockade Mexico's ports. Commodore Conner deployed his flotilla to capture Matamoros and plug six other gulf ports—Veracruz, Tampico, Soto la Marina, Tuxpan, Alvarado, and San Juan Batista. The blockade sought to cut off Mexico from vital sources of men, matériel, and money. However, Conner was instructed to permit one exception: "If Santa Anna endeavors to enter the Mexican ports, you will allow him to pass freely."[36]

To encourage Santa Anna's return, Polk dispatched Capt. Alexander McKenzie to Havana to explain to Santa Anna the White House's terms for ending the war and to guarantee him safe passage. They met on July 6. The offer gratified and tempted Santa Anna, but it was a month before he decided to seize it. He sailed from Havana on August 8. Polk appears to have known when Santa Anna would return from exile. That same day, he asked Congress for a $2 million discretionary fund to "provide for any expenditure which may be necessary to make in advance for the purpose of settling our difficulties with the Mexican Republic."[37]

Upon reaching Mexico City on September 15, Santa Anna received the army's command from President José Mariano Salas. Not surprisingly to anyone who knew his character, the dictator reneged on his understanding with the Polk administration that he would negotiate the war's end. Instead, he issued a proclamation whereby he vowed "to devote myself, until death, to the defense of the liberty and independence of the Republic!"[38]

This betrayal may have actually worked to America's advantage. Santa Anna was as militarily inept as he was morally corrupt. During Mexico's war with the United States, this self-styled "Napoleon of the West" typically lost every battle he fought decisively; vainly killed off tens of thousands of his men through slaughter, disease, or death marches; and left Mexico prostrate to American demands.

Polk, meanwhile, was understandably apoplectic when he learned of Taylor's "great error" at Monterrey. The commander in chief was absolutely correct in castigating Taylor for having "had the enemy in his power and should have taken them prisoners, deprived them of their arms, discharged them on their parole of honor, and preserved the advantage which he had obtained by pushing on without delay further into the country." If he had, this "probably would have ended the war with Mexico."[39] He fired off an order to Taylor to resume his offensive after informing the enemy that the armistice had terminated.

Rather than immediately march south, Taylor sent Gen. John Quitman and a thousand troops southeastward to capture Victoria, Tamaulipas's capital. Victoria was roughly halfway from Monterrey to Tampico on the coast. The American navy occupied Tampico without a fight on November 12. These moves simultaneously opened a shorter supply line to the army at Monterrey, secured most of northeastern Mexico, and gave the United States a significant swath of territory to wield as a bargaining chip or even to keep.

Having secured this route, Taylor marched his army fifty miles south, occupied an undefended Saltillo, and then advanced twenty miles further to Agua Nueva. He ended his advance there for good reasons. The two hundred miles of road from Agua Nueva to San Luis Potosi passed mostly through a barren, waterless desert. His army would arrive before that city depleted of men, supplies, and energy. If the army suffered defeat, it would be forced to retreat over the same merciless landscape. It made more military and diplomatic sense to hold his ground and entice Santa Anna to attack him. Then, Santa Anna and his weakened army would face a fresh, entrenched enemy and a vast desert behind them as their only line of retreat.

News of Taylor's lateral move against Victoria and halt at Agua Nueva enraged Polk. He castigated Taylor as "a weak man . . . made giddy with the idea of the presidency. . . . I am now satisfied that he is a narrow minded, bigoted partisan, without resource and wholly unqualified for the command he holds."[40] In this, the president revealed his ignorance of strategy and clearly projected onto the general the same criticisms leveled by his enemies against himself.

Meanwhile, Kearny and his dragoons headed west to California. The expedition had an astonishing encounter at Socorro on October 6. The famed mountaineers, Kit Carson and Tom Fitzpatrick, along with fifteen other frontiersmen rode up to them with exciting news— the Americans had conquered California! While retaining a hundred dragoons and Carson to lead him to California, Kearny sent the rest of his troops back to Santa Fe, and Fitzpatrick continued on to Washington. If California was subdued, a larger force was unnecessary and would eat up scarce supplies and compete for what few and often foul water holes lay ahead.

Unfortunately, the struggle for California had not ended. The shock and awe of the initial rapid American takeover had worn off. Capt. José María Flores had mobilized several hundred Mexican troops and forced Lieutenant Gillespie to surrender his forty-eight men at Los Angeles on September 28. After releasing Gillespie's troops on parole, Flores dispatched forces to capture the American garrisons at Santa Barbara and San Diego.

Stockton was at Monterey when he learned of these events. Before sailing south with his flotilla, he sent word to Frémont, in the Central Valley, to march to Los Angeles. On October 8 the flotilla anchored off San Pedro. Stockton sent ashore Capt. William Mervine with a mixed force of 285 marines, sailors, and mountain men. The Americans retook San Pedro and marched toward Los Angeles. Flores blocked his way with cavalry and a light cannon. After suffering fourteen casualties, Mervine withdrew with his men to San Pedro. Stockton decided to garrison San Pedro and sail south to take San Diego. Once again, his troops could occupy a port but were not numerous enough to scour enemy horsemen from the surrounding region. The Mexican commander, Capt.

Andrés Pico, adapted the same hit-and-run cavalry tactics Flores had used to the north.

Stockton received an astonishing message on December 3. Kearny and a hundred dragoons were at Warner Ranch, fifty miles east of San Diego, recuperating themselves and their mounts after an exhausting two-month desert trek. The general knew of the revolt and asked for the latest intelligence and advice. Stockton replied by dispatching Gillespie and thirty-nine mounted men to join Kearny and then together attack Pico.

Kearny had no trouble finding the enemy. Pico had learned of Kearny's advance and blocked his route at San Pasqual, twenty miles east of San Diego. Although a rain storm had soaked his men's gunpowder, Kearny led his dragoons against Pico's lancers on December 5, 1846. The result was slaughter as the Mexicans killed twenty-one dragoons and wounded twenty more, including Kearny, before finally being driven off with twenty-seven casualties. Pico and his men then besieged Kearny and the remnants of his command atop Mule Hill. That night, Carson and a companion sneaked through the enemy lines, and two days later, they reached San Diego. Stockton led a hundred sailors and eighty marines to the rescue. Pico and his men withdrew to Los Angeles.[41]

Kearny, Stockton, and their combined forces advanced northward; drove off attacks by Flores, Pico, and 450 troops at the Battles of San Gabriel and Mesa; and recaptured Los Angeles on January 10, 1847. Pico and his men slipped away to the Central Valley but ran into Frémont and his California Battalion marching south. With his command's supplies and morale nearly exhausted, Pico agreed to surrender. On January 14, 1847, Frémont and Pico signed the Treaty of Cahuenga, whereby Mexico yielded California to the United States in return for amnesty for all Mexicans who fought against the Americans and equal rights for both peoples.

Unfortunately a nasty spat of politics marred this triumph. With their common enemy gone, a simmering power struggle erupted among the Americans over who should govern the conquered province. Before sailing away to Mazatlan on January 22, Stockton dubbed Frémont California's governor and commander in chief, even though Kearny as a brevet general far outranked the brevet major. Kearny protested to no avail. For now, Frémont had the prestige, most of the men, and Stockton's authorization to prevail. This changed on February 13, when Kearny received orders from Gen. Winfield Scott granting him the powers that Frémont had asserted.

After setting up a civil government, Kearny appointed Col. Richard Mason the governor and began the journey back to Washington City with his dragoons and Frémont. Upon reaching Fort Leavenworth, Kearny ordered Frémont arrested and shackled. The party reached Washington City on September 11, 1847. Senator Benton exploded in wrath and protested to President Polk when he learned that his son-in-law was to be court-martialed for disobeying orders, conduct prejudicial to the public service, and most alarmingly, the capital offense of mutiny. The court unanimously found Frémont guilty on all counts and ordered him cashiered, although six of the twelve jurors called for clemency.

This posed a dilemma for Polk. Frémont was not just a powerful senator's son-in-law but also a popular hero. The president would outrage an adoring public if he did not pardon Frémont and outrage most of the military establishment if he did. Polk split the difference by remitting rather than dismissing the findings and letting Frémont rejoin his regiment. The denial of an exoneration enraged Frémont, Benton, and their many supporters. Frémont resigned his commission, and Benton broke forever as Polk's friend and ally.

California was not the only Mexican province in which American shock and awe was fleeting. In Santa Fe, rumors of a conspiracy to revolt reached the ears of Governor Charles Bent and Col. Sterling Price. Bent authorized Price to round up the suspects, and the colonel and his men did so on December 15. The suspects were soon released for lack of evidence, and officials reasoned that if a threat ever existed, anyone involved would be too intimidated to resurrect it. The crackdown, however, enflamed the rage against the American conquistadors among New Mexico's displaced political elite, led by Archbishop Antonio Martínez and former lieutenant governor Diego Archuleta. Still, despite living in New Mexico and wrangling with Martínez and Archuleta for many years, Bent saw no danger. In early January, he left Santa Fe to be with his family at Taos.

Rebels attacked and murdered him and six other Americans on January 19, and another thirteen Americans elsewhere in the region over the next week. Price dispatched contingents of the Second Missouri to suppress the rebels and reassert control. The worst fighting was at Mora, Canada, Embudo Pass, and Pueblo de Taos. The Americans defeated the mixed forces of Mexicans and Pueblo Indians in all these battles, inflicting far more casualties than they suffered. The fighting ended on February 3, with the bombardment and storming of Pueblo de Taos, where as many as 150 Indians were killed at the cost of 7 dead and 47 wounded Americans. Price followed up these victories with arrests and trials of some of the leading conspirators. Although charges were not brought against Martínez and Archuleta, several other ringleaders were found guilty and hanged for inciting the mob that murdered Bent and other Americans. The crushing of the revolt restored order, but ani-mosities burned beneath the surface.

As these tragic events occurred, Col. Alexander Doniphan led the 856 men of his First Missouri Mounted Regiment to take first El Paso and then Chihuahua. On Christmas Day five hundred Mexican troops led by Maj. Antonio Ponce de Leon charged them at Brazitos, thirty miles north of El Paso. The American riflemen shot down more than a hun-dred Mexicans before Ponce de Leon withdrew his men. The Americans resumed their march and, two days later, entered El Paso unopposed. There Doniphan and his men tarried for more than a month as they massed supplies and reinforcements. On February 8, 1847, Doniphan led south 924 troops, 6 cannons, 300 merchants and teamsters, and 312 military and civilian wagons.[42]

The army was just fifteen miles from Chihuahua on February 28, when the enemy was spotted ahead. Awaiting them in redoubts were 1,200 cavalry, 1,500 infantry, 1,200 militia, and a dozen cannons manned by 119 gunners commanded by Gen. García Conde. As a lawyer rather than a soldier by profession, Doniphan was uninhibited by military con-vention. He organized his force into four columns of troops, cannons, and wagons and led them straight toward the Mexican line. Then, just beyond cannon shot, he ordered the columns to swing wide and rumble around the enemy's left flank. Conde sent his cavalry after the Ameri-cans, but the riflemen and artillery drove them off with three hundred casualties. Conde ordered his army to retreat to Chihuahua and then abandoned the city as Doniphan's army approached.[43]

The Americans marched into Chihuahua on March 2. After six weeks of rest, Doniphan received orders to march east and join Taylor's army, which had withdrawn from Agua Nueva to a mountain pass at Buena Vista, a dozen miles south of Saltillo. He and his men ended this exhausting 524 mile trek on May 21, three months to the day after Taylor desperately needed them.

Taylor prepared for an expected Mexican offensive by massing troops and supplies at Buena Vista. On December 21 the first contingents of Gen. John Wool and his 1,400 troops and 118 wagons appeared, having trudged all the way from San Antonio, which they left on August 14. Wool's original mission was to capture Chihuahua. Realizing he would lose too many men across the waterless desert on the way, he veered to join Taylor instead. These troops brought Taylor's army up to 4,594 men. He soon needed every one of them.[44]

Santa Anna did exactly as Taylor hoped he would. He led 21,530 troops, 21 cannons, and 100 or so carts filled with supplies from San Luis Potosi on January 28, 1847. He had only 15,142 with him as he neared Buena Vista on February 22, having lost six thousand to death and desertion along the way. Still, his army outnumbered the American army by three to one. This was bad enough, but most of Taylor's troops were fresh volunteers untested by battle. Santa Anna sent a demand under a flag of truce that Taylor surrender. Shortly after receiving Taylor's defiant refusal, Santa Anna ordered his army to attack.[45]

The Battle of Buena Vista was the war's largest in the number of troops involved and causalities. During the two days that the battle raged, the Americans were at times nearly overwhelmed by the sheer masses of Mexicans charging them. At one point, General Wool blurted to Taylor, "General, we are whipped." Taylor grimly replied, "That is for me to decide." Taylor ordered a series of counterattacks that drove off the Mexicans. Santa Anna finally withdrew his army on the night of February 23. The Americans had held their ground at the cost of 272 killed and 387 wounded; among those killed was a son of Henry Clay. Santa Anna's losses were far worse, 591 killed, 1,048 wounded, and 1,894 missing. Another two thousand were lost in the grueling post-battle march back across the desert. He returned to San Luis Potosi with ten thousand men, or only half the number he left with.[46]

Once again, Taylor failed to follow up his tactical victory with a rapid advance that might have captured the enemy's army. This time, he had a good reason. During and after the battle, an astonishing fifteen hundred of his troops deserted. Although he soon received that many in reinforcements, his army was still less than half the size of Santa Anna's. He was also short of supplies as guerrillas had attacked wagon trains along the road from Camargo.[47]

News of Taylor's latest victory only worsened Polk's political myopia. Having previously attacked the general for being too slow to advance, the president now condemned him for advancing too far: "If Gen. Taylor is in any danger . . . it is in consequence of his having, in violation of his orders, advanced beyond Monterrey. The truth is that from the beginning of the War he has been constantly blundering into difficulties, but has fought out of them, but at the cost of many lives."[48]

Polk and his cabinet agreed on November 14, 1846, that only total war would bring Mexico's government to its knees. This meant capturing Veracruz and then marching on the capital, while destroying any Mexican forces along the way. As for who should lead the army, there was only one clear choice. Taylor was too indecisive and unskilled for such a daunting mission, yet seniority forbade one of his subordinates, preferably a Democrat, from being promoted over his head and given the command. Only Gen. Winfield Scott possessed the requisite experience, rank, and skills. The trouble was that Polk despised him for being vainglorious and overbearing. Plus, Polk knew that the more victorious Scott was in the field, the more likely the Whig Party would tap him as their presidential nominee for 1848. So, the president held his nose when he asked Scott to command the Mexico City campaign on November 19, 1846.[49]

Scott massed troops and supplies and worked with the navy to gather enough vessels to transport his army to Mexico. He withdrew nearly all the regular troops from Taylor's army, including eight thousand from the divisions of Gens. William Worth and David Twiggs, two squadrons of dragoons, two artillery batteries, and four thousand troops from volunteer regiments commanded by Robert Patterson. Scott had 141 special surfboats built and stacked aboard the nearly one hundred transport ships, already burdened with hundreds of tons of munitions and provisions packed below deck.

Among the army's officers were some destined to win fame in the next war, including Robert E. Lee, Ulysses S. Grant, William Sherman, George McClellan, Joseph Johnston, Pierre Beauregard, George Meade,

James Longstreet, and George Pickett. The skills and professionalism of these West Point graduates were of incalculable value to the campaign. Unfortunately, their leadership was at times distorted by the political appointees with whom Polk saddled Scott and his army—Gens. William Butler, Robert Patterson, Gideon Pillow, John Quitman, and Franklin Pierce were distinguished for their Democratic Party loyalty rather than military acumen. During the campaign, Scott and many of his officers were inspired and instructed by a popular book published three years earlier. William Prescott's *History of the Conquest of Mexico* vividly explored the epic adventure of Hernando Cortez and his conquistadors three centuries earlier.[50]

Congress helped the fight with a $23 million war appropriation bill in January 1847. A bill to expand the army with ten new volunteer regiments, however, died in the Senate. Although mostly New England senators opposed the bill, they were joined by an unlikely ally. John Calhoun of South Carolina blamed Polk for starting the war and called for ending it by having American troops simply defend what they had taken. He argued that by doing so, the Americans would save lives and money; sooner or later the Mexicans would have to negotiate. Lewis Cass of Michigan denounced this plan as a path to disaster. The Mexicans would build up their forces until they were powerful enough to push back the Americans. They would come to the negotiating table only after they were militarily brought to their knees.[51]

Meanwhile, Col. Alexander Atocha reappeared in Washington on January 11, 1847, with letters from Gens. Santa Anna and Juan Almonte. They proposed a peace with a Rio Grande frontier and California's cession for $20 million. Talks would be held at Havana. As a goodwill gesture, the United States would lift its blockade of Mexican ports. Atocha did not know if they were also willing to part with New Mexico.[52]

Polk and his cabinet decided to express their interest in talks without offering any proposals. For now, they wanted an open diplomatic door that they could walk through several months later. Meanwhile, Scott's army would be ready to sail in mid-February. Assuming the invasion was successful, the Mexicans would be increasingly eager to cut a deal with more concessions the closer Scott got to the capital.

Commodore Daniel Conner commanded the armada packed with twelve thousand troops that dropped anchor off Veracruz's coast on

March 4, 1847. Scott's army hit a beach just beyond cannon shot of the city on March 9. Worth's division led the way, followed by those of Twiggs and Patterson. No Mexican troops sortied to oppose them. Scott arced his army to hem in the city, had batteries erected at key points, and ordered the guns to open fire. Over the next two and a half weeks, the Americans fired sixty-seven hundred rounds against Veracruz. Meanwhile, Scott sent out expeditions to round up draft animals and carts to haul enough supplies for his army on the long march to Mexico City. The Mexicans held out valiantly until March 27, when Gen. José Landero surrendered the city and nearly five thousand troops.

With Veracruz secure, Scott turned his army westward. Two routes led from Veracruz to Mexico City, the National Road taken by Cortez and the road via Orizaba. Either route would be a hard trek that climbed in switchbacks steeply over the Sierra Madre Mountains. Numerous defiles on both roads could be easily fortified and defended. Scott chose to follow in the conquistador's footsteps, more because it was less rugged than because of the allure of emulating history. It was imperative to reach Jalapa, seventy-four miles from the coast, as soon as possible. At 4,680 feet above sea level, the town was a safe haven from yellow fever, which could decimate his army. Scott issued the orders to march on April 4. He led only about eight thousand troops toward the capital. He had to leave behind not just a garrison at Veracruz but another four thousand volunteers whose enlistments either had expired or soon would.

Santa Anna, meanwhile, had retreated with his army's remnants from Buena Vista to San Luis Potosi. Learning of Scott's invasion, he left a contingent behind and quick-marched most of his men toward the threat on the coast. By mid-April, he massed twelve thousand troops and forty-three cannons at Cerro Gordo, a town in a mountain pass on the National Road.

Scott's army approached Cerro Gordo on April 11. The Mexican position appeared impregnable. His troops would be slaughtered if they directly attacked the fortified narrow pass packed with troop and cannons. In a daring reconnaissance, Capt. Robert E. Lee found a narrow mountain path that outflanked the enemy. On April 18 Scott ordered a bombardment followed by a feint up the road, while Twiggs's division filed along the trail that led behind Santa Anna's army. The Americans routed the Mexicans and captured three thousand soldiers and Santa Anna's wooden leg at a cost of 63 killed and 368 wounded.[53]

Unfortunately, Scott was unable to swiftly follow up his victory. His supply line to the coast was tenuous. There were simply not enough carts and draft animals to keep the army adequately supplied. Guerrillas attacked isolated supply trains and detachments.

Scott could have stayed put, awaited more supplies and men as they trickled in over the coming months, and then tried to advance later that summer. Instead, he made a decision that was likely inspired by Hernando Cortez's order to burn his fleet during his conquest of Mexico three centuries earlier. He called up all his detachments guarding his rear and marched on Mexico City. Henceforth, his army would live off the peasants and captured enemy depots.

Worth spearheaded the advance and took Puebla on May 15. Throughout the summer, Scott gathered more troops and supplies for a decisive push against Mexico City. In July Maj. Gen. Gideon Pillow marched into camp at the head of forty-five hundred mostly Tennesseans and Pennsylvanians. On August 6 Brig. Gen. Franklin Pierce appeared with twenty-five hundred troops. Pillow and Pierce were military amateurs handpicked by Polk for their loyalty to him and the Democratic Party. One of them proved to be a Trojan horse. Pillow served as Polk's mole in Scott's army and, like that animal, undermined the general's command with his ill-disguised zeal to seize it for himself. He sent back a stream of letters to Polk, other leading politicians, and prominent newspapers, savaging Scott for anything that went wrong and taking credit for all that went right. Lt. William Sherman described Pillow as "a mass of vanity, conceit, ignorance, ambition, and want of truth."[54]

Polk and his cabinet worried that Scott was incapable of marching his army all the way to Mexico City and defeating any enemy armies in the way. If his campaign stalled, much as Taylor's had in northern Mexico, the result would be a costlier stalemate in lives, money, and thus, political capital. Antiwar voices would multiply in number and volume. The worst case would be a humiliating withdrawal that would make the Mexicans more defiant than ever.

War and diplomacy were inseparable; the success or failure of one was dependent on the other. Polk reasoned that the time was ripe for his latest diplomatic initiative. Even before he learned of Veracruz's capture, he asked Secretary of State Buchanan to draw up a list of diplomatic goals and concessions. Buchanan submitted a draft to the president and his cabinet on April 13, 1847. The goals were simple—Mexico would recognize America's annexation of Texas; Americans would have the right to build a canal and railroad across the Tehuantepec peninsula; the international boundary would extend westward from the Rio Grande along the 32nd parallel to the Pacific Ocean; and the United States would pay up to $15 million and the assumption of Mexican debts to Americans for the transfer of all Mexican lands north of that line. To this, Polk added his willingness to double the asking price if need be, but he and his other secretaries wanted more land, including lower as well as upper California.

With the goals determined, the next step was to find someone who could win all this at the negotiating table. Buchanan recommended Nicholas Trist as the best man for the mission. Trist was the State Department's chief clerk; had practiced law and served as Andrew Jackson's secretary before becoming a diplomat; was for eight years the American consul in Havana, where he became fluent in Spanish; and was a loyal Democrat.[55]

Trist set forth from Washington on April 16 on the long journey to Mexico. His mission was supposed to be secret, but word leaked to the *Daily Union*, which ran the story a few days later. The leak's source was none other than Buchanan. Although discretion is among the key requirements for being a diplomat, Buchanan lacked that essential quality. This lifelong bachelor with presidential aspirations loved to whisper secrets to curry favor and admiration.

The revelation of the Polk administration's goals and strategy nearly destroyed the mission's chance of success. When word got back to Mexico, the elite adamantly rejected any cession of territory at any price. Meanwhile, Congress and public opinion split bitterly over whether the demands were too little, too much, or just right.

As if all this made a diplomatic breakthrough improbable enough, Trist and Scott became estranged even before they met. The reason was an order from War Secretary Marcy to Scott that appeared to give Trist the power to call a halt to military operations if he judged it prudent for his diplomacy to do so. After reaching Veracruz on May 6, Trist forwarded Scott this dispatch along with a letter from Buchanan to Mexico's foreign minister. What Trist did not forward were his own instructions, which clearly stated that the fighting would persist until a treaty was signed. Had he sent on his instructions or, better yet, handed over all the documents in person, he might have quickly assuaged Scott's rage that a clerk could supersede the commanding general's power to wage war as he saw fit. Marcy's instructions fueled Scott's paranoia that the Polk administration was trying to undercut his victorious march for the vilest of political motives. After all, the president had saddled the commander with a slew of Democratic Party generals, and Gideon Pillow lost no chance to backbite and undercut him.

Scott fired off angry letters to Marcy and Trist condemning any interference in his command. Rather than make a conciliatory reply by pledging not to meddle, Trist instead shot off his own angry riposte, and for weeks, those were the last communications between them. Upon learning of the tiff, Polk had Marcy and Buchanan order his respective subordinate to stand down and make up. This failed as each refused to be the first to seek reconciliation with the other. The stalemate broke only after Scott learned that a life-threatening illness afflicted Trist. He sent Trist a jar of guava marmalade and a note wishing him a speedy recovery. The simple gesture filled Trist with gratitude. The diplomat and general swiftly reached an understanding and forged a friendship. The fate of nations is at times determined by such quirks of personality and behavior.[56]

Meanwhile, the letter from Secretary of State Buchanan to Foreign Minister Domingo Ibarra was forwarded via Charles Bankhead and Edward Thornton, Britain's respective minister and consul in Mexico City. Ibarra, however, passed the letter to Mexico's congress, whose War Hawks rejected Buchanan's call for negotiations as long as American troops rested on their nation's soil.

Scott and Trist faced a dilemma shared by anyone who did any kind of business in Mexico. The doors to power opened only after palms had been generously greased. The unofficial word from Santa Anna was that peace could be bought with an under-the-table fee of $1 million; the general wanted a ten thousand dollar payment up front with the rest to follow when the treaty was signed. Scott convened his generals and asked their opinion. They eventually agreed that the deal might save countless lives and money. Indeed, this shakedown was actually a bargain compared to the $2 million that the Polk administration had earlier mulled paying the dictator. Trist sent word to Santa Anna that they were willing to pay his price. Santa Anna replied with regret that Mexico's congress refused to grant him the power to make peace.

This did not end the matter. Gen. Gideon Pillow gleefully informed his boss of the aborted deal. The president and other Democratic Party leaders were eager to find any excuse to discredit or outright fire the Whig generals Scott and Taylor and replace them with loyalists. Polk seized upon this proposed $1 million bribe to justify dismissing Scott, even though no money ever exchanged hands and he himself had been willing to pay Santa Anna and his coterie double the sum in exchange for peace. In the end, cooler heads within the cabinet talked Polk out of cashiering Scott.[57]

This decision became imperative as a scandal threatened the Polk administration in August 1847. Newspapers reported that nearly $6 million dollars of war appropriations had been deposited in Democratic Party pet banks. Little of this sum had been spent on the war. Instead, the banks used the money to speculate in various financial schemes, many highly risky. Rather than deny or vainly try to cover up the revelations, Polk cleverly nipped the scandal in the bud by promptly having Treasury Secretary Walker recall the money and investigate allegations of wrongdoing. Not surprisingly, the subsequent report reassured the public that nothing illegal had transpired. It was all political business, as usual.[58]

By early August, Scott's army had swelled on paper to fourteen thousand troops split among the divisions of Worth, Twiggs, Pillow, and Quitman. The trouble was that more than twenty-five hundred troops were bedridden, and another six hundred were on their feet but still too weak to march. Scott ordered his 10,738 healthy troops to head to Mexico City on August 7.[59]

Santa Anna and about seven thousand troops blocked the American advance at El Peñón Pass. Once again, Capt. Robert E. Lee found a way to outflank what appeared to be a nearly impregnable position. Scott left a division to divert the Mexicans' attention while he led his other three divisions in a long, grueling march to a road leading over into the south end of Mexico Valley. With Scott threatening to cut off his retreat, Santa Anna withdrew his army to a position along the Churubusco River.

Scott unleashed his troops in a double envelopment of twenty thousand Mexican troops on August 20. He had no choice in this tactic because a frontal attack was impossible. South of the river was a vast mass of broken volcanic rock known as the Pedregal, impassable to troops. The divisions of Worth and Pillow struck the Mexican army's left at Contreras; Twigg the enemy's right at Churubusco. The Americans routed the Mexicans and chased them nearly to the gates of the capital, killing or wounding more than 4,000 and capturing 3,000 at a cost of 133 dead and 865 wounded. Ulysses Grant later extolled Scott's "strategy and tactics" at the battle of Churubusco as "faultless."[60]

Scott had Santa Anna on the ropes. He was about to land a knockout blow when Santa Anna sent a plea for a truce and talks. Scott's reply reflected his humanitarianism: "Too much blood has already been shed in this unnatural war between the two great Republics of this Continent. It is time that the differences between them should be amicably and honorably settled. . . . I am willing to sign, on reasonable terms, a short armistice."[61] On August 22 envoys from each side agreed to a cease-fire within seventy-eight miles of the capital, a prisoner exchange, a halt to fortifying and reinforcing positions, American liberty to buy supplies from Mexico City, peace talks, and resumption of hostilities only after forty-eight hours' notice.

Although talks opened between Trist and Mexican officials on August 27, they swiftly deadlocked. The Mexicans were willing to make only two concessions. They would accept America's annexation of Texas with a border on the Nueces River. They would also cede territory from the 42nd parallel boundary set by 1819 Adams-Onís Treaty down to the 37th parallel, which would secure San Francisco Bay for the United States. The envoys insisted that these concessions would come only at a high price, although they did not yet name a number. And this was not all. They demanded that before a treaty could be signed, the United States had to cancel all Mexican debts to Americans and pay for all the damage incurred on Mexican territory since the war began. Trist countered by giving up the demand for Baja California and Tehuantepec peninsula transit rights but continued to press for upper California and New Mexico. A posttreaty joint commission could decide whether the border ended on the Nueces River or Rio Grande. The Mexicans adamantly rejected these proposals. Trist sent Buchanan a full report of this first round of negotiations.[62]

Meanwhile, Santa Anna violated the truce terms by bolstering Mexico City's fortifications, troops, and supplies and cutting off sales of provisions to the Americans. Disgusted by all this, Scott notified Santa Anna that the truce would end on September 7.

Polk was outraged when he learned of the truce. Once again, a Mexican general had snookered a Whig general by playing on his humanitarian instincts. After twice routing Santa Anna, Scott should have administered the coup de grace. The Mexicans would give in diplomatically only after they were crushed militarily. Polk had Marcy fire off an order to Scott to terminate the truce and destroy the Mexican army. This turned out to be unnecessary.[63]

Scott resumed the offensive on September 8, the day after the truce ended, by launching Worth's division against Molino del Rey, a fortified cluster of stone buildings rumored to house a cannon foundry. Santa Anna counterattacked. Scott fed in Twiggs's division. After fierce fighting, the Americans took the position, inflicted 2,000 casualties, and took 685 prisoners at a cost of 116 dead and 665 wounded.[64]

Scott then marched his army and attacked Chapultepec Castle, which guarded the city's western approach, on September 13. After fierce fighting, the Americans took this key position at the cost of 130 killed and 702 wounded; in turn, they killed 655, wounded 823, and captured 823 Mexicans. As he watched his routed troops stream back into the city, Santa Anna angrily blurted, "I believe if we were to plant our batteries in Hell the damned Yankees would take them from us." He ordered a hasty evacuation of the capital and led his army's remnants far north up the valley. The American army marched triumphantly into Mexico City on September 14.[65]

Students of the art of war will forever study Scott's Mexico City campaign. In his fine history of that conflict, Jack Bauer succinctly explains why: "With an army of less than 11,000 troops, Scott had overcome one exceeding 30,000 well dug in and defending its own capital. The Americans inflicted casualties of more than 7,000, took an additional 3,750 prisoners, and seized seventy-five cannon and 20,000 small arms along with large quantities of munitions."[66]

After securing the capital, Scott sent out forces to occupy Cuernavaca, Pachuca, and Toluca, cities on roads leading to Mexico City. He then levied an assessment of $150,000 to underwrite his army's expenses. Part of this paid for a thousand women to sew new uniforms for his men. He set up military commissions to serve as a court system. He had $3.9 million in tax revenues collected and, much to the surprise of Mexico's elite, distributed to the states. He appointed General Quitman to serve as the city's governor.

Although skirmishes occasionally erupted at outposts in the valley and along the long road leading back to Veracruz, the Mexican army was shattered beyond reconstruction. The Gulf and Pacific flotillas continued to blockade enemy-held ports and occasionally take them. Santa Anna's humiliating defeats left him thoroughly disgraced, and he yielded the presidency to Foreign Minister Peña on September 16. Peña dismissed Santa Anna on October 7, with the warning that he would soon face a court-martial. Santa Anna once again fled into exile. Peña did not last long as his willingness to negotiate an end to the war incensed the diehards. On November 11 Gen. Pedro María Anaya forced him to hand over power and returned him to the Foreign Ministry. Yet the Moderados regained the upper hand over the Puros in Congress when they defeated by 46 to 29 a bill that would have forbidden any cession of territory to the United States.[67]

Meanwhile, Polk learned of the first negotiation round not from Trist but from a Mexican newspaper. He erupted in anger when he read the concessions that Trist had made on Baja, Tehuantepec, and the Nueces River. He forged a cabinet consensus to recall the hapless envoy. For now, he would not name a successor. Later, Polk reckoned it was a mistake not to immediately send a diplomat to at once recall and replace Trist. Of course, at the time, he could not have anticipated that Trist would defy his recall and persist in negotiating with the Mexicans. It then made diplomatic sense to abruptly end the talks and play hard to get. Mexican desperation would worsen as the American occupation persisted with no end in sight. Eventually, the Mexicans would crack and concede far more than they would if the Americans appeared too eager for a deal. And what might additional American demands include? Treasury Secretary Walker and Attorney General Nathan Clifford called for taking the entire province of Tamaulipas, which included the port of Tampico. Secretary of State Buchanan insisted on cutting the top price from $30 million to $15 million.[68]

With the enemy routed and the capital secured, some of the American generals turned on each other with backbiting and undermining. It got so bad that on November 22, 1847, Scott ordered courts-martial for Gen. Gideon Pillow, Gen. William Worth, and Col. James Duncan for various acts of insubordination, including getting newspapers articles published that lauded themselves and denigrated their commander.

Polk was incensed when he learned of the courts-martial. On January 3, 1848, he convened his cabinet and swiftly forged a consensus to recall Scott. His replacement would be the newly appointed Maj. Gen. William Butler, whose credentials as a Democratic Party loyalist far outweighed the reality of his limited experience in the War of 1812. Polk would wield Butler like a stone to kill not one but two irritating birds. Butler would wear two hats, one military and the other diplomatic. He would replace Scott as commanding general and Trist as the peace envoy.

Much of the rancor that Polk vented against Trist and Scott was provoked by a swelling antiwar movement and harsh critics in Congress and beyond. The nation split bitterly over what constituted a just peace. The champions of victory without conquest fell into three often overlapping camps: those who opposed any expansion of slavery; those who feared that taking lands inhabited by millions of mestizos, or mixed-race people, would eat away at America's culture, political system, and white majority; and those who believed that imperialism was wrong. Relatively few people fell in the latter category. Most Americans believed that the war was just and that some acquisition of territory was justifiable. Champions of the Wilmot Proviso would take territory only if slavery was forbidden there. Perhaps most people supported the Polk administration's territorial ambitions. Finally, there were those who insisted that the United States should take all of Mexico and reimpose slavery throughout that land. These divisions at once reflected and shaped those in Congress, with Democrats controlling the Senate and Whigs the House.

All the divisiveness and attacks angered Polk. He squared off with his array of critics in his annual address to Congress on December 7, 1847. His primary task was to refute those who called for victory without spoils. He did so with powerful logic: "The doctrine of no territory is the doctrine of no indemnity, and, if sanctioned, would be a public acknowledgement that our country was wrong, and that the war declared by Congress with extraordinary unanimity, was unjust, and should be abandoned; an admission unfounded in fact and degrading to the national character."[69]

Whig opposition peaked on January 3, 1848, with the House's 85 to 81 vote for John Quincy Adams's resolution that the war had been "unnecessarily and unconstitutionally begun by the president of the United States," an allusion to Polk's order for Taylor to march his army into the disputed territory; that American forces should be immediately withdrawn; that the boundary should split the difference between the Nueces River and Rio Grande; and that the president must render all his diplomatic correspondence concerning John Slidell, Santa Anna, and other key figures. The resolution died in the Senate along with other initiatives. Daniel Webster of Massachusetts failed to convince his colleagues to approve his resolution for a victory without territory. John Calhoun of South Carolina also failed to get the votes for his proposal to let states that emerged from the conquered territories decide for themselves whether they would be free or slave. A proposal by Daniel Dickinson of Indiana that the United States take all of Mexico likewise went nowhere. Polk denied the truth of the resolutions against him and refused to submit any diplomatic correspondence on the ground that it would violate executive privilege.[70]

As if all the blistering criticism from politicians and newspapers was not enraging enough for Polk, he soon received word of Trist's defiance. Upon receiving his recall on November 16, Trist promptly informed Peña that he would soon be leaving. This actually worked to America's advantage. Peña and other Moderados recognized that Trist had made key concessions without receiving anything in return. His replacement would undoubtedly not just revoke his concessions but demand much more. And this would likely follow yet another devastating campaign by Scott designed to destroy the remaining Mexican forces around the region. The Moderados talked Anaya into agreeing to formal talks. On November 24 Peña sent word to Trist that he was authorized to begin negotiations.

This inspired Trist to commit a bold act—he would defy his recall and win a peace grounded on his original instructions. In a sixty-five page letter to Buchanan, he justified his decision and castigated him and the president for their myopia and meddling. Upon reading the letter on January 15, Polk exploded in wrath and condemned Trist for being "arrogant, impudent, and very insulting to his Government and even personally offensive to the President." A feeling of impotence greatly fueled his rage. How can one subdue a rogue diplomat several weeks distant? If he were a military officer, he could be arrested for defying orders. But Trist was a civilian—although his behavior was outrageous, it was not strictly illegal. If the law was murky, the politics of trying to remove Trist were clear enough. Congress and public opinion were bitterly split over whether the war was just and what spoils, if any, should be reaped from victory. Making a stink over Trist's defiance would only exacerbate these differences. General Butler could quietly displace Trist after he reached Mexico City.[71]

Yet no breakthrough immediately followed. Instead, during their meetings in December and January, neither Trist nor Peña budged from his position. Time, however, leaned more heavily on the Mexicans than the Americans. Every day that enemy troops occupied the capital and large swaths of the nation beyond was an agony for Mexican patriots. Ever more of the elite reluctantly agreed that the only way to rid Mexico of the gringos was to exchange the territory they demanded for desperately needed cash. But they prevailed on Trist to accept the Gila River rather than the 32nd parallel as part of the frontier. Trist agreed.

Trist and Peña signed the Treaty of Guadeloupe Hidalgo on February 2, 1848. Mexico recognized Texas's annexation and ceded lands above a boundary that ran along the Rio Grande to just below El Paso, then west and up to the Gila River, down it to the mouth of the Colorado River, and south to a westward line that hit the Pacific Ocean just below San Diego. For this, the United States would pay Mexico $15 million and assume the $3.25 million in various debts that Mexicans owed Americans. The $18.25 million was half of what he was authorized to pay under his instructions.[72]

When the treaty reached the White House on February 19, Polk gathered his cabinet to debate it. The reaction was mixed. Although the mutual cessions largely followed Trist's official instructions, the Mexican government's refusal to promptly accept them after Scott's victorious campaign rendered them moot in the minds of Polk and other hard-liners. At the very least, America should have won Baja California and transit rights across the Tehuantepec, which were in Trist's instructions. But the United States should also have taken territory deep into northern Mexico to justify the war's worsening toll in lives and money and to punish the Mexicans for stonewalling long after they were honorably defeated. Yet only Treasury Secretary Walker and Secretary of State Buchanan advocated rejecting the treaty and demanding more territory. In the end, Polk forged a consensus that while "Trist has acted very badly . . . the treaty is one that can be accepted."[73]

The president sent the treaty to the Senate. Powerful voices rose against the document. Some argued that it took too much. Thomas Hart Benton of Missouri would have the Nueces rather than the Rio Grande form Texas's southern frontier with Mexico. Daniel Webster of Massachusetts proposed an amendment that would have returned to Mexico all lands west of the Rio Grande. Others argued that the treaty took too little. Sam Houston of Texas and Jefferson Davis of Mississippi tried to amend the treaty so that the United States took the states of Tamaulipas, Nuevo León, Coahuila, and Chihuahua. Roger Baldwin of Connecticut tried to attach the Wilmot Proviso to the treaty. The only reservation that succeeded was one that removed rights for the Catholic Church and existing landholders. When the final vote came on March 10, 1848, the Senate ratified the Treaty of Guadeloupe Hidalgo on a largely party line vote of 38 to 14. Mexico's Chamber of Deputies ratified the treaty by 51 to 35 on May 19 and its Senate by 33 to 4 on May 24. Polk received Mexico's ratified treaty on July 4, 1848.

The Mexican War won for the United States a vast region of 529,617 square miles at the cost of $58 million to fight and $18.25 million to settle. These were the upfront financial costs. Washington paid over time another $64 million in pensions and disability to veterans. The territory was bought with more than hard cash. Of the 104,556 troops who served during the war, 13,768 died, the highest proportion of any war in American history. Of these deaths, 1,192 died in battle, 529 later from wounds, and 11,155 from disease. In addition, 4,102 men were wounded in battle, 9,754 were discharged for disability, and 9,207 deserted. As for the Mexican financial and human loses, the exact figures will never be known, but as many as fifty thousand troops and civilians may have died.[74]

Were America's gains worth the costs? The answer, of course, depends on one's values. The Mexican War has always troubled humanitarians. Ulysses Grant, then a captain, called it "the most unjust war ever waged by a stronger against a weaker nation." He assailed the Polk administration for trying "to provoke hostilities" by deploying American "troops on the edge of the disputed territory." To this end, "it was essential that Mexico should commence" the war by attacking first. He explained the psychological effect of that act on Congress: "Once initiated there were but few public men who would have the courage to oppose it. Experience proves that the man who obstructs a war in which his nation is engaged, no matter right or wrong, occupies no enviable place in life or history."[75]

Polk was at times reckless, aggressive, and amoral. To win Oregon and the Southwest, he was willing to lead the nation to war against Britain and Mexico separately or even simultaneously. Like a more recent president who pushed the United States into a controversial war, Polk's belligerence was driven by demons lurking in both his psyche and ideology. War was a glorious abstraction to him—he had never served in the army, let alone experienced war's horrors. As commander in chief, he could at once overcompensate for his inadequacies, remain safe, and take credit for all the victories. All this compelled him to unblinkingly send men to kill and maim and be killed and maimed.

Nonetheless, the United States and Mexico had irreconcilable differences that made war all but inevitable. The Mexicans believed that America's annexation of Texas in itself justified war and that any cession of land elsewhere was unthinkable. Most Americans not only believed annexation was justified and nonnegotiable but also supported forcing the Mexicans to sell New Mexico and California to the United States.

Neither the United States nor Mexico was solely responsible for the war between them. Each government committed aggressive acts that made war increasingly likely. It was certainly not America's fault that Mexicans failed decade after decade to form a stable government. Indeed, Mexico's quasi anarchy pressured the United States to take lands deemed essential for its national security before Britain or some other great power did.

There is no question which side first declared war, ordered an attack, and drew blood. President Paredes declared war on March 21, 1846. On April 5 War Minister José María Tornel y Mendívil ordered Gen. Mariano Arista, the army's commander in the lower Rio Grande valley, to cross to the north side and attack any American forces in the vicinity. On April 25 Arista's advanced guard assaulted an American dragoon company, killed sixteen, wounded five, and captured fifty.

Polk made this attack the centerpiece of his war message to Congress. Yet, long before he had hoped to provoke a war when he ordered General Taylor to march his army into the disputed territory between the Nueces River and Rio Grande. Although the Texans claimed the Rio Grande as their border, the claim had no legal grounds. Instead, Spanish and Mexican authorities considered the Nueces River the border. Although Santa Anna signed the Treaty of Velasco granting independence to Texas with a Rio Grande border, he was overthrown and the Mexican government repudiated the treaty. The legitimacy of Texas's claim for independence is supported by Mexico's failure to crush it and international recognition of it. Taylor's march into the disputed territory was a might makes right attempt by the Polk administration to claim legitimacy for owning that territory.

Whether or not the war was just, the United States mostly fought it justly. The Americans warred against Mexico in full accord with the era's international law, morality, and honor. American leaders mostly displayed restraint and sensitivity. Generals Taylor and Scott agreed to truces when they were on the brink of annihilating the Mexican armies before them. Ulysses Grant recalled, "General Taylor was opposed to anything like plundering by the troops, and . . . looked upon the enemy as the aggrieved party and was not willing to injure them further. . . . His orders to the troops enjoined scrupulous regard for the rights of all peaceable persons and the payment of the highest price for all supplies taken for the use of the army."[76]

And the United States was certainly a generous victor. Envoy Trist was perhaps too willing to compromise during his first negotiation round. The Polk administration could have simply taken those lands or even more by claiming them as a victor's rightful reparations from the defeated. Instead, the bill to American taxpayers was at least $18.25 million, atop the war's upfront and long-term costs.

Perhaps the ultimate justification for the war and treaty is the legacy of what happened to that swath of territory annexed to the United States. Today, the people living in those lands are largely prosperous, peaceful, and free. Had those territories remained in Mexican hands, they would be as mired in poverty, corruption, and violence as the rest of that benighted nation.

21

The Legacy

Tyranny is a disregard of the law and the substitution of individual will for legal restraint.

NATIONAL INTELLIGENCER

I confess that in America I saw more than America; I
sought there the image of democracy itself, with its inclina-
tions, its character, its prejudices, and its passions, in order to
learn what we have to fear or to hope from its progress.

ALEXIS DE TOCQUEVILLE

If the Union is once severed, the line of separation will grow
wider and wider, and the controversies which are now debated and settled in the halls of legislation will then be tried
in the fields of battle and determined by the sword.

ANDREW JACKSON

What makes an age? A key challenge, value, leader, or some mélange may
distinguish an expanse of years. Leaders loom large in how Americans
understand their past and present. Not surprisingly, American history
is marked by a series of ages named after dominant men.

Historians debate how vital Andrew Jackson's role was in the age named after him. Would an age of Jackson have existed without its namesake? The author of this era's most exhaustive overview dissents from the notion of an age of Jackson. Daniel Walker Howe tries to "avoid the term because it suggests that Jacksonism describes America as a whole, whereas in fact Andrew Jackson was a controversial figure and his political movement bitterly divided the American people."[1] But this, of course, is the essential argument for an age of Jackson. It was not merely a man who overshadowed those thirty-three years of American history but a political philosophy that the man epitomized and countless others fervently emulated or just as fervently opposed.

The age of Jackson appropriately begins and ends with American victories, one military and the other diplomatic, in controversial wars. Andrew Jackson presided over both victories, in the first as the commanding general and in the second by personifying the ideology that drove the nation into the Mexican War as well as the earlier War of 1812.

The United States declared war against Britain in June 1812 largely by the War Hawks' power to politically stampede most senators and representatives along with a weak-willed president with wild-eyed rhetoric that at once provoked overweening fear, pride, and greed. The result was an utter disaster for American power, wealth, and security. Rather than swiftly rout the redcoats, conquer Canada, and force the British to cede to Washington's demands, the American armies suffered one humiliating defeat after another, while the body count and national debt soared. The Treaty of Ghent ended the war with a draw. Yet Jackson obscured much of this in the popular imagination by his crushing victory over a British army at New Orleans on January 8, 1815, which tragically took place after the peace treaty had been signed.

Three decades later, similar passions carried the United States into war with Mexico but with far different results. American forces routed their foes in nearly every battle. An army led by Gen. Winfield Scott trod in the footsteps of the conquistador Hernando Cortez all the way to the Halls of Montezuma and captured Mexico's capital. Under the Treaty of Guadeloupe Hidalgo, signed on February 2, 1848, Mexico recognized America's earlier acquisition of Texas and yielded New Mexico and California in return for $18.25 million. Although Andrew Jackson was no longer alive to celebrate that national triumph, his aggressive, expansionist spirit lived on through his protégé President James Polk.

The many reasons that explain the very different results of the War of 1812 and Mexican War are ultimately rooted in the art of power. American leaders proved as inept in wielding that art in the first war as they were skilled in the latter war. Over the intervening expanse of decades, how far did Andrew Jackson and his political philosophy transform America's art of power?

The age of Jackson is best known as the era in which the last restraints were removed so that all white men could vote and run for office. Jackson did not initiate that development. What he did do was skillfully personify and lead the democratizing political, economic, and social changes to take and wield national power as president.

Jackson's populism was real. He championed universal white male suffrage and the "common man" against such "evils" as "moneyed interests," nullifiers, and abolitionists. He repeatedly called for eliminating the Electoral College and allowing the direct election of the president as well as electing rather than appointing judges. He best expressed these views in his farewell address:

> The planter, the farmer, the mechanic, and the laborer all know that their success depends upon their own industry and economy, and that they must not expect to become suddenly rich by the fruits of their toil. These classes of society form the great body of the people of the United States; they are the bone and sinew of the country. . . . But . . . they are in constant danger of losing their fair influence in the Government, and with difficulty maintain their just rights against the incessant efforts daily made to encroach upon them . . . [by] the moneyed interests.[2]

So, if Jackson did not initiate a new stage of democracy in America, he certainly accelerated its blossoming.

Yet democracy must be distinguished from demagogy. Jackson personified the latter. Here again, although he did not invent this black art, he excelled in the practice. Tragically, American politics has always been sullied by those who advocate blind ideological belief over reason, smear and obstruct rather than compromise, and sheer might over the law and right. Although politics has been a dirty game from the nation's beginning, the nastiness has oscillated with time. The Era of Good Feelings following the War of 1812 morphed into the acidic age of Jackson. The turning point was the 1824 election and Jackson's shrill condemnation of the corrupt bargain between Adams and Clay, which he insisted robbed him of the White House.

Attributing exaggerated or outright fabricated unsavory views, acts, and intentions to one's political enemies is clearly a source of enormous power to those who wield it. But the politics of the "big lie" or "big smear" is disastrous for America because it corrodes the nation's liberal values. Democracy in America or anywhere else depends on an enlightened rather than ignorant, fearful, and hateful public. When demagogues propagate lies and shout down those trying to engage in a reasoned debate, they attack the nation's most cherished values. Vicious demagoguery hardly originated with Andrew Jackson and his followers. Tragically, it is as old as the nation and may eventually destroy America.

Jackson whipped up these mass emotions not just to get himself elected to two terms as president but to ensure that Jacksonians dominated all three federal government branches long after he left office. The Democrats would hold at least one house of Congress and usually both until the southern states seceded from the United States in early 1861. He helped play kingmaker to three of his protégés, with Martin Van Buren and James Polk following him to the White House and Sam Houston becoming president of the Republic of Texas. As president, Andrew Jackson packed the Supreme Court with seven of his disciples. He gleefully replaced as the chief justice his nemesis John Marshall with his ideological soul mate Roger Taney. Taney devoted his eighteen years on the bench, from 1836 to 1864, to destroying as much of Marshall's Hamiltonian legacy as possible and imposing Jacksonism in the ruins. Taney's campaign culminated with the 1857 Dred Scott decision, which denied not just citizenship but humanity to blacks.[3]

Jackson and his followers understood and exploited a fundamental flaw of human nature—most people would rather follow a charismatic leader who is wrong than a weak leader who is right. This is perhaps the most important reason why Jackson got away with repeated violations of the Constitution and law with only one official Senate censure, which was later rescinded. Of all the controversies Jackson provoked in his lifetime, these were most vital to the fate of America's art of power.

As a general and president, he did not hesitate to violate the spirit and even letter of the Constitution and other laws when they forbade him from asserting his will. This raises crucial questions for those committed to America's liberal democratic system. Should anyone for any reason be allowed to break the law? Is there an inherent conflict between liberty and security, or does the violation of individual rights in the name of security ultimately erode the nation's most cherished values and thus its security?

Jackson's usurpations were hardly the first nor last in American history. President John Adams triggered the first serious constitutional crisis with his 1798 Sedition Act. The most recent crises came from the array of alleged high crimes and misdemeanors committed by the administrations of Ronald Reagan and George W. Bush; few of their underlings were investigated let alone convicted, and both presidents escaped impeachment. The violations that a president and his team can commit without punishment establish precedents that can profoundly warp and stunt the nation's legal and moral development.

Jackson's presidency differed from those of his predecessors in another crucial way—he was the first openly anti-intellectual president. He was no policy wonk who carefully studied the issues and chose the course that appeared to best promote American national interests. His political beliefs and acts originated from deep within his scarred psyche and bile-filled gut. Speechwriters refined his churning emotions into coherent arguments, and mostly able department secretaries and congressional allies translated them into laws and policies. But there was no question of who was in command. Jackson abruptly rejected the views of even his closest advisers if they disputed his prejudices.[4]

One looks in vain at Jackson's policies for philosophical consistency; the only foundation was his indomitable will to assert his power over his foes. To this end, he supported Georgia's nullification of laws and Supreme Court rulings protecting Indian rights and denied South Carolina's nullification of tariff laws. He vetoed the renewal of the second bank's charter, withdrew its federal deposits, and spread them among his state pet banks but also vetoed a bill that would have distributed 10 percent of land-sale revenues to the states for internal improvements. He championed the common man with his rhetoric, while depriving him with policies that demanded hard coin for public land or that thwarted internal improvements and protective tariffs. Alexis de Tocqueville noted the corrosive political and constitutional effects of this abuse of power: "The power of General Jackson constantly increases . . . but that of the president diminishes. In his hands, the federal government is strong; it will pass to his successor enfeebled."[5]

Contrary to Jackson's principles and promises, the federal budget and number of personnel were larger when he left the White House than when he entered eight years earlier. Two reasons account for his failure to live up to his creed: one political and the other administrative. Although Jackson did not invent the spoils system, he carried it to unprecedented heights by shamelessly using federal positions to reward political supporters. Nor, of course, did Jackson invent corruption, yet his administration surpassed its predecessors in the scale and notoriety whereby its officials and political allies shamelessly plundered public resources for private gain. Jackson himself became the corrupter in chief by distributing tens of millions of dollars from the Bank of the United States to his pet banks. Political payback aside, more officials were necessary to regulate the economy as it expanded and diversified. Yet, in accommodating this need, Jackson rebuked his own philosophy.[6]

Jackson diminished American wealth and thus power in critical ways.[7] His worst blow to national security was his malicious and systematic destruction of the Second Bank of the United States. In destroying the bank, he transformed a healthy financial system that nurtured the nation's economic development into a house of cards that collapsed months after he left office. The immediate effect was a prolonged double-dip recession that began in 1837 and did not end until 1843. But over the long term, Jackson may have stunted the nation's development by a generation or more by depriving Washington of the power to regulate the money supply and thus business cycles. And this robbed the nation of the power to uphold his one progressive economic policy— ending the national debt.

Andrew Jackson is given credit for being the only president who eliminated the national debt. But his success on this issue occurred despite, rather than because of, his policies. A boom in trade and land sales garnered enough revenue not just to eliminate the national debt but to run budget surpluses for two years. Unfortunately, Jackson's policies of destroying the Bank of the United States and distributing its assets among his pet banks promoted a speculative financial bubble that popped shortly after he left office and led to the national debt's resurgence.

Tragically for the United States, Jackson was neither the first nor the last president whose ideologically driven policies repeatedly shot America in the economic foot. In this, he joins Thomas Jefferson, James Madison, Herbert Hoover, Ronald Reagan, and George W. Bush, whose policies weakened America by causing financial collapses and depressions or vastly piling up the national debt.

Yet not all of Jackson's policies undermined American power, wealth, and principles. He most clearly preserved American power in the nullification crisis. He did so by condemning nullification as unconstitutional while offering South Carolina's radicals a compromise that gave them a face-saving excuse to rescind their law. Although the compromise resolved the immediate crisis, it gave South Carolina and other slave states a precedent not just for nullification but for outright secession.

To properly assess Jackson's art of power, one must distinguish the Machiavellian and American versions. Jackson was as successful in the former as he was a failure in the latter. An editorial in the *National Intelligencer* on October 2, 1833, offered a succinct definition of a useful analytical tool for the age: "Tyranny is a disregard of the law and the substitution of individual will for legal restraint."[8] Jackson epitomized tyranny in his character and policies. Few administrations that have occupied the White House have matched and none have exceeded the Jackson administration as an "imperial presidency."[9] The net effect of President Andrew Jackson's policies was to weaken America economically, constitutionally, and morally.

If only one Jacksonian unambiguously advanced American national interests, it was James Polk. He won the White House as the dark-horse candidate, but he can also be seen as a dark horse of power. It was easy for Polk's political friends and foes alike to underestimate him. His modest stature and personality tended to fade beside such charismatic powerhouses as Jackson, Adams, Clay, Calhoun, Van Buren, and Webster. Yet he was adept at asserting power first as Speaker of the House and then as president. After he entered the White House, he did what he promised to do. He aggrandized American territory by one-third by taking the Oregon and the Southwest Territories from Britain and

Mexico, respectively, and he signed into law the versions of banking and tariff bills that he wanted. If the art of power is about getting what one wants, then James Polk was a master, especially given the vast expanse of his territorial ambitions and the strength of the two countries who disputed them.

The trouble was that in exercising his will, Polk also got what he did not want. For good reasons, this naturally pessimistic and dour man found little solace in all his astonishing feats. When he wearily left office, the nation was more bitterly divided than ever. The question of whether slavery or freedom should prevail in the new territories was a political tar baby that smeared everyone and threatened to burst into flames. His beloved Democratic Party split bitterly between two presidential candidates, Lewis Cass and Martin Van Buren, and thus, the Whig candidate and war hero Gen. John Taylor won the 1848 election. Exhausted by his disappointments and labors, Polk died on June 15, 1849.

If one of Jackson's disciples excelled in outrageous antics and lasting feats, then surely it was Sam Houston. Under Old Hickory's stern eyes, Houston proved to be a fierce and fearless warrior in the Battle of Horseshoe Bend, when he twice led assaults that left him with an arrow in his leg and bullet in his shoulder. Elsewhere, he was either reviled or admired for his fondness for outlandish dress, excessive drink, and women of easy virtue. With Jackson's patronage, he rose swiftly in Tennessean politics all the way to the governor's mansion. His first wife fled him within a month after they exchanged vows, and Houston's seeping wounds, peculiar sexual tastes, and lingering venereal diseases were whispered as among the causes. He resigned the governorship and spent the next few years in drunken exile among the Cherokees. Jackson got him rehabilitated and elected to the Senate, but this body expelled him for beating up one of his colleagues. Afterward, he went to Texas with Jackson's secret instructions to engineer that Mexican province's independence and then annexation to the United States. He did so by first destroying Santa Anna's army and capturing the dictator at the Battle of San Jacinto and then getting elected as the Republic of Texas's president, whereupon he applied for annexation. Houston was a quintessential Jacksonian in values and temperament.

Although Jacksonism dominated the age, two other political philosophies asserted their own versions of the art of power. Paradoxically,

Jeffersonians can only begin to wield power after setting aside their own creed, that is, "the government that governs least governs best." This is indeed what Thomas Jefferson himself did to win his presidency's greatest coup, the Louisiana Purchase. He vainly searched the Constitution's text for any line that explicitly empowered the federal government to buy land, especially on such a vast scale from a foreign country. But, eventually, he violated his own zealous belief in the Constitution's literal interpretation and sent the treaty to the Senate for approval. He believed that cutting off the nation's trade with foreign belligerents would bring them to their knees, but his 1807 Embargo Act backfired by devastating America's economy. His belief that the nation is best defended by militia and gunboats led to humiliating disasters during the War of 1812.

Jefferson's most devoted protégé was even more inept in the White House. Of the eight men who served as president from 1815 to 1848, none provides a more glaring example of how not to wield power than James Madison. His worst failure was letting the War Hawks stampede him into an unjustified and disastrous war with Britain. He himself spearheaded the elimination of the First Bank of the United States. This would have devastated the economy at any time but proved to be especially destructive on the War of 1812's eve, when the government would ever more desperately need money. After the war, Madison, chastened by the catastrophic results of his policies, embraced the Hamiltonism that he had formerly so viciously attacked. He worked with Congress to set up the Second Bank of the United States, protective tariffs for infant industries, and money for roads, canals, and ports.

As a Jeffersonian in the age of Jackson, no one was a more eloquent firebrand than John Calhoun. When he was first elected to Congress in 1811, he was philosophically a shrill Jacksonian on war with Britain and a sober Hamiltonian on the economy, but during the 1820s he morphed into a zealous Jeffersonian champion of nullification. He elaborated the view that sovereignty lies in the states rather than "the people" in his books *A Disquisition on Government* and *A Discourse on the Constitution*. That South Carolinian patriot received his higher education in the North, first at Yale and then as a law student with Judge Tapping Reeve in Litchfield, Connecticut. These years of sojourn among "Yankees" reinforced his natural melancholy, introversion, and love for his native land. His career included prolonged stints in the House and Senate, interrupted by service as secretary of war, vice president, and secretary of state, respectively, under presidents Monroe, Jackson, and Tyler. Although he ran several times, he never realized his dream of winning the White House.[10]

So, how well did Calhoun wield the art of American power? Despite his dazzling résumé, his legislative and policy achievements were scant. He thrived on ideals rather than deals and so preferred to vent his passions in speeches that celebrated state sovereignty and slavery rather than work with others to craft the minutiae of laws. During his four decades in politics, the two issues for which he most fervently crusaded—the War of 1812 and nullification—led to catastrophes for American power, wealth, and principles.

History reputes the claims of Jeffersonians and Jacksonians that government stymies the economy. Hamiltonians argue that while inept policies can certainly worsen a situation, sensible policies can accelerate the nation's development far beyond what the private sector is capable of on its own. Avoiding the former and pursuing the latter depends on two forces. There must be a lean, muscular state run by worldly, pragmatic, problem-solving, virtuous men who have mastered the art of progressive power. America's Constitution provides all the implied and explicit powers needed to overcome any domestic or foreign challenges. During the age of Jackson, four men personified Hamiltonism.

Henry Clay competed with John Calhoun in a myriad of ways, including who underwent the more startling philosophical transformations. He began his political career as a fervent Jeffersonian, became an even more zealous Jacksonian in the years leading up to and during the War of 1812, and then thereafter matured into a rock-ribbed Hamiltonian. This evolution reveals the suppleness of his mind and psyche. He was man enough to repent, learn, and change from his follies. The War Hawk who helped rush the nation into a disastrous conflagration with Britain became the elder statesman who cautioned against provoking a war with Mexico. He embraced a fervent American nationalism after winning Aaron Burr's acquittal in his first treason trial. The man who cheered the destruction of the First Bank of the United States in 1811 cheered its resurrection as the Second Bank of the United States in 1816. The young politician who vilified protective tariffs and internal improvements championed them from his middle age onward. In a congressional career that spanned four decades and stints in the House and Senate, Clay proved to be a master of the art of legislation by getting scores of bills passed and usually signed into law. For instance, he was able to sidestep or enlist Jacksonians and increase the annual rivers and harbors budget from $129,000 in 1829 to $1,786,000 in 1836, thus implementing a key element of his American System.[11] His greatest acts of statesmanship were crafting the compromises of 1820, 1833, and 1850, which prevented the Union's breakup during crises. He also proved himself to be a canny diplomat at the 1814 peace conference at Ghent and as secretary of state under President John Quincy Adams. Yet, he failed in each of his three attempts to win the White House. His most glaring moral, political, and philosophical contradiction was over slavery; he hated the practice and called for its abolition, but he never liberated any of the slaves who worked his plantation or personally served him. Nonetheless, Henry Clay is a close runner-up to James Polk in the title for the age's greatest master of the art of American power.

John Quincy Adams was the age's only Hamiltonian president. Taking the White House capped an astonishing résumé that included serving as a member of the five-man diplomatic team that negotiated the Treaty of Ghent with Britain, as a congressional representative and senator from Massachusetts, and as the secretary of state. His ability to wield the art of power, however, varied from one position to the next. As the secretary of state, he proved himself a master with his 1819 Adams-Onís Treaty, which annexed Florida to the United States, and his 1823 Monroe Doctrine, which asserted an American sphere of influence over the Western Hemisphere that administrations have tried to uphold ever since. In contrast, he was a miserable president both in temperament and achievement. In his inaugural address, he presented an ambitious Hamiltonian list of things to do and failed in every one.

Daniel Webster remained a pliable Hamiltonian throughout his political career. Born in rural New Hampshire, he turned to books to relieve the tedium of a sickly childhood. His fine mind was honed at Phillips Exeter Academy, Dartmouth College, and Portsmouth's law courts. His reputation for oratory and Federalist principles got him elected to the House of Representatives as a "peace candidate" from New Hampshire in 1813, but he served only two terms before he moved to Boston, where he flourished as a lawyer. He was elected to Massachusetts' assembly in 1823 and the U.S. Senate in 1827. His Senate career lasted until his death in 1852 but was interrupted with stints as the secretary of state first under Presidents Harrison and Tyler and then under President Fillmore. Webster was nicknamed "Black Dan" for his swarthy complexion, disposition, and behavior. Although generally gregarious, he had bouts of melancholy, ate and drank prodigiously, and squired a series of mistresses over the decades. If Henry Clay promoted Hamiltonism through laws, Webster largely did so through court cases. No one in American history has argued more than his 168 cases before the Supreme Court from 1816 to 1852, of which he won about half. With a few words, he expressed his political philosophy: "Government must do for individuals [that] which individuals cannot do for themselves."[12]

John Marshall competes with Polk and Clay as the most vital practitioner of the art of American power during the age of Jackson.[13] In his thirty-four-year tenure as the Supreme Court's chief justice, from 1801 to 1835, he rooted his decisions in such Hamiltonian principles as the Constitution's supremacy as the law of the land, the sovereignty of the federal government and the subordination of the states, the federal government's implicit and explicit "necessary and proper" powers to fulfill its duties, and the Supreme Court's judicial review power to determine the constitutionality of any law. The landmarks included *Marbury v. Madison* (1803), *Fletcher v. Peck* (1810), *McCulloch v. Maryland* (1819), *Dartmouth College v. Woodward* (1819), *Cohen v. Virginia* (1821), *Gibbons v. Ogden* (1823), *Johnson v. McIntosh* (1823), and *Worcester v. Georgia* (1832). In the *McCulloch* case, Marshall expressed the Hamiltonian view that the Constitution was "intended to endure for ages to come, and consequently, to be adapted to the various crises of human affairs."[14]

Waging war is the bluntest tool in the art of power. This art is at times crucial for defending or enhancing national interests. Ambitious officers had few chances to prove their mettle between the War of 1812 and the Mexican War. They found little glory and much ignominy fighting the Arikara, Seminole, and Fox and Sauk Indians. The Second Seminole War in particular tarnished the reputations of a series of commanders, including Winfield Scott and John Taylor, who would win renown in the Mexican War. Fighting a guerrilla war demands abilities that are distinct from those wielded in a conventional war; America's leaders are still trying to master this lesson.

Only Andrew Jackson excelled in the art of Indian warfare during this age. He did so in 1817 and 1818 by employing the same ruthless strategy and tactics of hunting down, surrounding, and annihilating bands of hostile Seminoles and of intimidating their British and Spanish backers that he had used against the Creeks in 1813. As a result, the Seminoles would not war again against the United States until 1835.

Jackson also mastered conventional war against the British. In this he used a strategy opposite that he wielded against Indians. Rather than seek and destroy the invaders, he let them come to him. His defensive strategy, however, was anything but passive. He launched an immediate night attack after the British appeared below New Orleans and thereafter daily dispatched skirmishers to harass and exhaust the enemy. Meanwhile, he had his men erect earthworks behind a canal with one flank anchored on the Mississippi River and the other on a swamp. When the British finally launched their assault on the morning on January 8, 1815, the Americans slaughtered them. Despite this resounding victory, Jackson remained cautious, perhaps unduly so. Had he immediately sent his army surging after the routed redcoats, he might have forced the British army to surrender. On the other hand, he knew the British still outnumbered him and feared that his zealous but ill-disciplined men might dissolve before a massed bayonet counterattack in an open field.

Two other commanders excelled in that age. Gens. Zachary Taylor and Winfield Scott shared a vital distinction—each won every battle that he fought. Yet their styles of command could not have differed more. Ulysses Grant served under and admired both men. He found that

> Scott was precise in language, cultivated a style peculiarly his own; was proud of his rhetoric; not averse to speaking of himself, often in the third person. . . . Taylor was not a conversationalist, but on paper he could put his meaning to the construction of high-sounding sentences. But . . . both were great and successful soldiers . . . patriotic and upright in all their dealings. Both were pleasant to serve under—Taylor was pleasant to serve with. Scott saw more through the eyes of his staff officers than through his own. His plans were deliberately prepared and fully expressed in orders. Taylor saw for himself, and gave orders to meet the emergency without reference to how they would read in history.[15]

Taylor's favorite tactic, the massed bayonet charge straight at the enemy, generally carried the day. It worked best in the field against masses of poorly trained, led, equipped, and motivated Mexicans. It was costly at Monterrey, where he lost one of every ten of his troops in a series of uncoordinated attacks against Mexicans defending forts, redoubts, and stone houses. Scott was the age's greatest general. No less than Arthur Wellesley, Duke of Wellington, believed that Scott as the student of Napoleon had far surpassed that military master and all others: "His campaign was unsurpassed in military annals."[16] Although this assessment may be excessive, Scott was indeed an imaginative strategist and tactician. Students of warfare will forever study his Mexican War campaign as nearly flawless in every dimension.

Yet the generalship of both Taylor and Scott was diminished by their lack of a quality that personified Jackson—utter ruthlessness. During the Mexican War, both Taylor and Scott were on the verge of destroying enemy armies when they agreed to truces that let them escape. With his killer instinct, Jackson would have demanded the Mexicans' immediate surrender and, if refused, would have ordered his men to annihilate them.

Scott and Taylor excelled in two other crucial dimensions of the art of military power—logistics and morale. Each inspired his troops to the greatest exertions and sacrifices, not only by displaying his own bravery, but by doing everything possible to ensure that his army was well fed and equipped. Looking back, Ulysses Grant reckoned that never had "a more efficient army for its number and armament . . . ever fought a battle than the one commanded by General Taylor in his first two engagements." Professionalism explains why. The officers were either West Point graduates or had served for many years, and they inspired extraordinary efforts from "the rank and file composed of men who had enlisted in a time of peace for seven dollars a month and were necessarily inferior . . . to the average volunteers enlisted later in the war expressly to fight."[17]

As for mobilizing the nation's resources for the Mexican War, the Polk administration deserves high marks for being able to raise, train, equip, transport, and supply enough troops on enough far-flung fronts to crush Mexico. The army officially numbered 637 officers and 5,925 men on the war's eve. During the war, recruitment expanded the regular army to 1,016 officers and 35,009 enlisted men, while 73,532 joined volunteer state regiments. The Marines expanded from 42 officers and 986 men to 75 officers and 1,757 men.[18] This achievement largely accrues to the skills and devotion of War Secretary William Marcy and Navy Secretary John Mason.

Nonetheless, President Polk's performance as commander in chief was hardly flawless. He made a grave mistake when he ruled that volunteer enlistments were for twelve months rather than the war's duration. Regiments no sooner entered the field than their ranks thinned as enlistments expired. This atop the attrition from disease, desertion, and battle restricted the ability of Taylor and Scott to act swiftly and decisively at crucial moments. As if this constraint was not troublesome enough, Polk inflicted another. Democratic Party loyalty rather than military competence was the criteria whereby Polk appointed and dispatched a dozen generals to the field. There some of the generals, most notoriously Gideon Pillow, launched political backstabbing attacks on their Whig commanders.

Andrew Jackson's legacy endures. In the early nineteenth century, Jacksonism emerged brawny and bullying into the political arena and has held its own against any rivals ever since. Many reasons explain why Jacksonism has nearly always flourished and often dominated. Perhaps most important have been its "greed is good" and "might makes right" assertions, which justify taking political power and shamelessly wielding it to further enrich and empower oneself.

Ideologically, Jacksonism inspires the Far Right of America's political spectrum, most recently the neoconservative and Tea Party movements. For them, politics is not the "art of compromise," but the continual obstruction and ideally utter annihilation of one's foes. To this end, Jacksonians prefer to shout down, demonize, and bully rather than outreason their opponents. Like most conservatives today, Jackson genuinely believed that he personified the common man even if his policies satisfied the emotional rather than material needs of most people and what few benefits his policies generated almost exclusively went to rich planters and bankers. Paradoxically, Jacksonians among the middle class and poor zealously uphold the philosophy's attitudes, assumptions, and behaviors even when Jacksonian policies tend to make them poorer rather than richer.

Jackson could have written the neoconservative playbook with its crusade in Iraq, disdain for the Constitution or laws, and ability to whip up a mass fear, hate, and hope and to convert this zeal into an outpouring of populist support through votes and money. His views are also in near-perfect accord with the Tea Party movement, which champions balanced budgets; the gutting or outright destruction of all government programs except the Pentagon, whose budget should continue to soar; the expulsion of all illegal aliens; the repeal of any laws and regulations that restrict business, pollution, or campaign finance; majority rule (as long as they are the majority) over minority rights; and the condemnation of Wall Street and other financial giants who exploit the "average American." As important, Jacksonian rage and the need for hated scapegoats to destroy fuel the Tea Party movement.

Yet, had Jackson witnessed the last several decades, he would have harshly criticized his successors and their followers on several key issues. Most notably, the only president who eliminated the national debt would have eviscerated Ronald Reagan for policies that in a mere eight years tripled the national debt and transformed America from the world's largest creditor into the worst debtor country; he would have been only slightly less blistering of George W. Bush for doubling the national debt during his two terms in power. As a warrior, he would have been silently contemptuous that both Reagan and Bush, despite all their flag-waving, had dodged fighting in the wars of their respective eras.

Throughout the nation's history, Jacksonism has been largely a disaster for American power, wealth, security, and honor. By acting on the notion that power ultimately flows out of gun barrels, Jacksonians have repeatedly shot the nation in the foot whenever they have taken over the government. Yet America endures these interludes and generally revives economically when an electorate disillusioned with the inevitable disasters caused by ideological excesses returns pragmatists to power. That tug-of-war between the Jacksonians and Jeffersonians on one side and the Hamiltonians on the other raged fiercely from 1815 to 1848, with the former enjoying the edge nearly all those years. Although Jacksonism and Jeffersonism alike condemned any notion of government helping to develop the economy, their actual policies often departed from this principle.[19]

Overall, the United States was a wealthier, more powerful country in

1848 than in 1815. America's economy tripled, with exports rising from $53 million to $159 million and farm production from $338 million to $904 million. The most valuable product and export was cotton, whose production soared from 209,000 bales in 1815 to 2,615,000 bales in 1847. This domination of commodities obscures the steady rise of manufactured products within the economy. The industrial and transportation revolutions stimulated each other as canals, steamships, and railroads linked ever more remote, rural regions into one vast national economy. Ever more wealth was created and distributed along this market, transportation, and communication web in a dynamic relationship among financiers, merchants, workers, and farmers.[20]

The population tripled from 7.23 million in 1810 to 23.2 million in 1850. Although babies born in the United States accounted for most of that increase, the immigration of more than a million Irish, Germans, and other nationalities during the 1840s also contributed. The center of population and thus political and economic gravity marched steadily westward. The nation's population not only grew, it urbanized—the number of cities with more than twenty-five thousand people soared from five in 1820 to twenty-six in 1850. Although this influx of foreigners tended to suppress wages, American society became steadily more mobile and middle class. The downside was that southern sectionalism and radicalism grew during the Jackson era.[21]

And, yes, America ended the age more democratic than it began it as the last restrictions on voting and running for office for white men were removed. Parties with distinct agendas competed and alternated in power. Newspapers and civic organizations flourished. Statesmen were able to overcome with hard-forged compromises a series of crises that threatened to tear the nation apart.

Alexis de Tocqueville was impressed. He summed up his experience in one line: "I confess that in America I saw more than America; I sought there an image of democracy itself, of its penchants, its character, its prejudices, its passions, I wanted to become acquainted with it if only to know at least what we ought to hope or fear from it."[22] And he found much to fear. He observed in Americans tendencies toward the tyranny of the political majority and religious sects; a want of genuine debate on the issues; the triumph of materialism, conformism, and legalism over humanism and individualism; the evils of slavery and racism; and the power of state over national ties. Presciently, he warned that these flaws could lead to disunion and civil war. What he could not foresee was that America would emerge from that war with its institutions and laws far more closely aligned with its ideals as the age of Jackson yielded to the age of Lincoln.

ABBREVIATIONS

Adams Diary John Quincy Adams, *Memoirs of John Quincy Adams: His Diary from 1795 to 1848*, 12 vols. (Philadelphia: J. B. Lippincott, 1877).

Annals *Debates and Proceedings in the Congress of the United States*, 42 vols. (Washington, DC: Gales and Seaton, 1834–1856), http://memory.loc.gov/ammem/amlaw/lwsp.html.

ASPFA *American State Papers: Foreign Affairs*, 6 vols. (Washington, DC: Gale and Seaton, 1832–1859).

ASPIA *American State Papers: Indian Affairs*, 38 vols. (Washington, DC: Gale and Seaton, 1832–1861).

ASPMA *American State Papers: Military Affairs* (Washington, DC: Gale and Seaton, 1832).

Buchanan Works John Bassett Moore, ed., *The Works of James Buchanan* (New York: Antiquarian Press, 1960).

CAJ Andrew Jackson, *The Correspondence of Andrew Jackson*, ed. John Spencer Bassett, 6 vols. (Washington, DC: Carnegie Institution, 1926–1935).

Calhoun Papers John C. Calhoun, *The Papers of John C. Calhoun*, ed. Robert L. Meriwether et al., 28 vols. (Columbia: University of South Carolina Press, 1959–2003).

Clay Papers   Henry Clay, *The Papers of Henry Clay*, ed. James
F. Hopkins et al., 11 vols. (Lexington: University Press of Kentucky, 1959–1992).

Congressional Globe   *Congressional Globe*, 46 vols. (Washington, DC:
Blair and Rives, 1834–1873), http://memory.loc
.gov/ammem/amlaw/lwcg.html.

Grant Memoir   Ulysses Grant, *The Personal Memoirs of Ulysses
S. Grant* (Princeton, NJ: Collectors Reprints,
1998).

HS   Census Bureau, *Historical Statistics of the United
States, Colonial Times to 1957* (Washington, DC:
Department of Commerce, 1960).

Jefferson Writings   Thomas Jefferson, *The Writings of Thomas Jefferson*, ed. Andrew A. Lipscomb, 20 vols. (Washington, DC: Thomas Jefferson Memorial
Association of the United States, 1905).

LC   Library of Congress, Washington, DC.

Manning, Correspondence   William Ray Manning, ed., *The Diplomatic
Correspondence of the United States: Inter-
American Affairs*, 21 vols. (Washington, DC:
Carnegie Endowment for International Peace,
1932–1939).

Monroe Writings   James Monroe, *The Writings of James Monroe*,
ed. Stanislaus Murray Hamilton, 7 vols. (New
York: Putnam, 1898–1903).

NYPL   New York Public Library, New York.

PAJ   Andrew Jackson, *The Papers of Andrew Jackson*, ed. Samuel B. Smith and Harriet Chappell
Owsley, 8 vols. (Knoxville: University of Tennessee Press, 1980–2010).

Polk Correspondence   James K. Polk, *The Correspondence of James K.
Polk*, ed. Herbert Weaver et al., vols. 1–6 (Nashville: Vanderbilt University Press, 1969–1989);
vols. 7–10 (Knoxville: University of Tennessee
Press, 1993–2004).

Polk Diary   James K. Polk, *The Diary of a President, 1845–
1849*, ed. Allan Nevins, 4 vols. (London: Longmans, Green, 1929).

Register of Debates   *Register of Debates in Congress*, 14 vols. (Washington, DC: Gales and Seaton, 1825–1837), http://memory.loc.gov/ammem/amlaw/lwrd.html.

Richardson Messages   James D. Richardson, ed., *A Compilation of the Messages and Papers of the Presidents*, 20 vols. (New York: Bureau of National Literature, 1897–1922).

NOTES

INTRODUCTION: THE ART OF JACKSONIAN POWER

1. For the best overview of this age, see Daniel Walker Howe, *What Hath God Wrought: The Transformation of America, 1815–1848* (New York: Oxford University Press, 2007). For a classic work on why Jackson personified that age, see John William Ward, *Andrew Jackson: Symbol of an Age* (New York: Oxford University Press, 1962). See also Arthur M. Schlesinger, *The Age of Jackson* (Boston: Little, Brown, 1945); Glyndon G. Van Deusen, *The Jacksonian Era, 1828–1848* (New York: Harper and Brothers, 1966); Edward Pessen, *Jacksonian America: Society, Personality, and Politics* (Homewood, IL: Dorsey Press, 1978); Daniel Feller, *The Jacksonian Promise: America, 1815–1840* (Baltimore: Johns Hopkins University Press, 1995); Charles Sellers, *The Market Revolution: Jacksonian America, 1815–1846* (New York: Oxford University Press, 1996); Harry L. Watson, *Liberty and Power: The Politics of Jacksonian America* (New York: Hill and Wang, 2006).

2. For an excellent analysis, see Walter Russell Mead, *Special Providence* (New York: Routledge, 2002). To Jacksonism, Hamiltonism, and Jeffersonism, Mead adds Wilsonism.

3. William Nester, *The Hamiltonian Vision, 1789–1800: The Art of American Power during the Early Republic* (Washington, DC: Potomac Books, 2012); John Nelson, *Liberty and Property: Political Economy and Policymaking in the New Nation* (Baltimore: Johns Hopkins University Press, 1986).

4. John Quincy Adams, speech, December 6, 1825, Richardson, *Messages*, 2:866–968.

5. William Nester, *The Jeffersonian Vision, 1800–1815: The Art of American Power during the Early Republic* (Washington, DC: Potomac Books, 2012); Lawrence Banning, *The Jeffersonian Persuasion* (Ithaca, NY: Cornell University Press, 1978).

6. Thomas Jefferson, *Notes on the State of Virginia*, ed. William Peden (Chapel Hill: University of North Carolina Press, 1955).

7. Marquis James, *The Life of Andrew Jackson* (Indianapolis: Bobbs-Merrill, 1938); Robert V. Remini, *Andrew Jackson: The Course of the American Empire, 1767–1821* (New York: Harper and Row, 1977); Robert V. Remini, *Andrew Jackson: The Course of American Freedom, 1822–1832* (New York: Harper and Row, 1981); Robert V. Remini, *Andrew Jackson: The Course of American Democracy, 1833–1845* (New York: Harper and Row, 1984); Sellers, *Market Revolution*.

8. Richard Hofstadter, *The American Political Tradition and the Men Who Made It* (New York: Alfred A. Knopf, 1948); Bray Hammond, *Banks and Politics in America from the Revolution to the Civil War* (Princeton, NJ: Princeton University Press, 1957); Michael Paul Rogin, *Fathers and Children: Andrew Jackson and the Subjugation of the American Indian* (New York: Alfred A. Knopf, 1975); James C. Curtis, *Andrew Jackson and the Search for Vindication* (Boston: Little, Brown, 1976); Andrew Burstein, *The Passions of Andrew Jackson* (New York: Alfred A. Knopf, 2003).

9. Grant Memoir, 70.

1. THE MAKING OF THE MAN

1. Sean Wilenz, *Andrew Jackson* (New York: Henry Holt, 2005), 17.

2. Quoted in Augustus Buell, *The History of Andrew Jackson: Pioneer, Patriot, Soldier, Politician, President* (New York: Charles Scribners' Sons, 1904), 1:68–69.

3. For the best account of the early years between Jackson and Rachel, see Remini, *Andrew Jackson*, 1:xviii, 57–69.

4. J. G. M. Ramsey, *Annals of Tennessee to the End of the Eighteenth Century* (Charleston, SC: J. Russell, 1853), 648.

5. Andrew Jackson, letter to Jack Sevier, May 8, 1797, PAJ, 1:136.

6. Remini, *Andrew Jackson*, 1:109–110.

7. For the following possibly exaggerated or even apocryphal story, see James Parton, *The Life of Andrew Jackson* (New York: Mason Brothers, 1860–61), 1:228–29.

8. For the following story, see ibid., 1:165.

9. Remini, *Andrew Jackson*, 1:136–43.

10. Ibid., 1:144–58.

11. Malcolm Rohrbough, *The Trans-Appalachian Frontier: People, Societies, and Institutions, 1775–1850* (Bloomington: University of Indiana Press, 2007).

12. For the two deepest explorations of his psyche, see Rogin, *Fathers and Children*; and Burstein, *Passions of Andrew Jackson*.

13. H. W. Brands, *Andrew Jackson: His Life and Times* (New York: Doubleday, 2005), 294–97.

14. Andrew Jackson, letter to Richard Call, September 9, 1819, PAJ, 4:271.

15. Remini, *Andrew Jackson*, 2:9–10.

16. Notes of an 1824 conversation with Thomas Jefferson, in Daniel Webster, *The Papers of Daniel Webster*, ed. Charles M. Wiltse (Hanover, NH: University Press of New England, 1974–1983), 1:376.

17. Andrew Jackson, letter to James Monroe, January 6, 1817, CAJ, 2:272–73.

18. Andrew Jackson, message to Congress, July 10, 1832, Richardson, Messages, 3:1153.

19. Andrew Jackson, letter to James Monroe, November 12, 1816, CAJ, 2:265.

20. Andrew Jackson, letter to John Overton, January 22, 1798, CAJ, 1:43.

21. Andrew Jackson, letter to James Monroe, March 18, 1817, CAJ, 2:282–83.

22. Andrew Jackson, letter to James Hamilton, June 29, 1829, CAJ, 3:412.

23. Parton, *Andrew Jackson*, 3:490.

24. Andrew Jackson, letter to William Conway, April 4, 1831, CAJ, 4:256; Andrew Jackson, letter to Ellen Hanson, March 25, 1835, CAJ, 5:333.

25. Andrew Jackson, speech to New Orleans citizens and soldiers, December 15, 1814, PAJ, 3:205.

2. THE BATTLE OF NEW ORLEANS

1. The best overview remains that of Donald R. Hickey, *The War of 1812: A Forgotten Conflict* (Urbana: University of Illinois Press, 1990). Other good accounts include John Elting, *Amateurs to Arms: A Military History of the War of 1812* (New York: Da Capo Press, 1995); Walter Borneman, *1812: The War That Forged the Nation* (New York: HarperCollins, 2004).

2. Andrew Jackson, address to the Second Division, PAJ, 2:290–92.

3. Ibid.

4. Charles Nettels, *The Emergence of a National Economy* (New York: Holt, Rinehart, and Winston, 1962), 396.

5. Hickey, *War of 1812*, 29.

6. John Armstrong, letter to Andrew Jackson, February 5, 1813, CAJ, 1:275–76.

7. Thomas Hart Benton, letter to Andrew Jackson, July 25, 1813, PAJ, 2:414.

8. For two good histories of the Red Stick War, see David S. Heidler and Jeanne T. Heidler, *Old Hickory's War: Andrew Jackson and the Quest for Empire* (Mechanicsville, PA: Stackpole Books, 1996); John Buchanan, *Jackson's Way: Andrew Jackson and the People of the Western Waters* (New York: Wiley, 2001). For a good overview of the Indians, see J. Leitch Wright, *Creeks and Seminoles: The Destruction and Regeneration of the Muscogulge People* (Lincoln: University of Nebraska Press, 1986). For the broader historic struggle of the United States for the region, see Thomas Clark and John Guice, *Frontiers in Conflict: The Old Southwest, 1795–1830* (Albuquerque: University of New Mexico Press, 1989).

9. Thomas Holmes account, in Lucille Griffith, *Alabama: A Documentary History* (Tuscaloosa: University of Alabama Press, 1972), 109–10.

10. John Coffee, letter to Andrew Jackson, November 4, 1813, in *The Historical*

Register of the United States, ed. Thomas H. Palmer (Philadelphia: G. Palmer, 1816), 1:333–335.

11. Andrew Jackson, letter to Willie Blount, November 15, 1813; and Andrew Jackson, letter to Thomas Pinckney, December 3, 1813, both in Jackson Papers, LC.

12. John Reid and John Henry Eaton, *The Life of Andrew Jackson, 1817*, ed. Frank Lawrence (Tuscaloosa: University of Alabama Press, 1974), 84–85.

13. For the following account and words, see Parton, *Life of Jackson*, 1:508.

14. Andrew Jackson, letter to John Woods, March 14, 1814, PAJ, 3:48–49.

15. Andrew Jackson, letter to Thomas Pinckney, March 28, 1814, PAJ, 3:52–53; Andrew Jackson, letter to Willie Blount, March 31, 1814, CAJ, 1:491–92.

16. David Crockett, *A Narrative of the Life of Davy Crockett of the State of Tennessee*, ed. James A. Shackford and Stanley J. Folmsbee (1834; repr., Knoxville: University of Tennessee Press, 1973), 90.

17. John Hoyt Williams, *Sam Houston: The Life and Times of the Liberator of Texas, an Authentic American Hero* (New York: Touchstone, 1993); Marshal De Bruhl, *The Sword of San Jacinto: A Life of Sam Houston* (New York: Random House, 1993).

18. Reid and Eaton, *Life of Jackson*, 165–67.

19. John Armstrong, letter to Andrew Jackson, May 22, 28, 1814; and Andrew Jackson, letter to John Armstrong, June 8, 1814, both in Jackson Papers, LC.

20. Andrew Jackson, letter to Mateo González Manrique, July 18, 1814, CAJ, 2:15–16.

21. John Gordon, letter to Andrew Jackson, July 20, 1814, CAJ, 2:17–18.

22. Andrew Jackson, letter to Robert Butler, August 27, 1814, CAJ, 2:31–32.

23. Andrew Jackson, letter to Mateo González Manrique, September 17, 1814, CAJ, 2:45.

24. James Monroe, letter to Andrew Jackson, October 21, 1814, CAJ, 2:79.

25. Andrew Jackson, letter to James Monroe, October 26, 1814, PAJ, 3:173.

26. Andrew Jackson, letter to Mateo González Manrique, November 6, 1814, CAJ, 2:92.

27. Robert V. Remini, *The Battle of New Orleans: Andrew Jackson and America's First Military Victory* (New York: Penguin, 1999); Robin Reilly, *The British at the Gates: The New Orleans Campaign of 1812* (Toronto: Robin Brass Studio, 2002).

28. Andrew Jackson, letter to Rachel Jackson, August 5, 1814, Jackson Papers, LC.

29. Andrew Jackson, letter to New Orleans Citizens and Soldiers, December 15, 1814, PAJ, 3:204–5.

30. Reid and Eaton, *Life of Jackson*, 287.

31. Buell, *History of Jackson*, 1:357–58.

32. Remini, *Andrew Jackson*, 1:263.

33. Reilly, *British at the Gates*, 258.

34. Remini, *Battle of New Orleans*, 114.

35. Remini, *Andrew Jackson*, 1:285.

36. Ibid., 314.

37. Vincent Nolte, *The Memoirs of Vincent Nolte: The Adventures of an Adventurer* (New York: G. Howard Watt, 1934), 238–39.

3. THE FATE OF SPANISH FLORIDA

1. Brands, *Jackson*, 302.

2. Ibid.

3. Alexander Dallas, letter to Andrew Jackson, July 1, 1915, CAJ, 2:212–13.

4. For the most in-depth assessment, see Irving Brant, *James Madison: Commander-in-Chief, 1812–1836* (Indianapolis: Bobbs-Merrill, 1961). See also Frank A. Updyke, *The Diplomacy of the War of 1812* (Baltimore: Johns Hopkins University Press, 1915); Roger H. Brown, "Who Bungled the War of 1812?," *Reviews in American History* 19 (1992): 183–87.

5. John Sugden, *Tecumseh's Last Stand* (Norman: University of Oklahoma Press, 1985); Wright, *Creeks and Seminoles*; Richard White, *The Middle Ground: Indians, Empires, and Republics in the Great Lakes Region, 1650–1815* (New York: Cambridge University Press, 1991).

6. Nettels, *National Economy*, 385, 396, 399; Hickey, *War of 1812*, 303.

7. J. Van Fenstermaker, *The Development of American Commercial Banking, 1782–1837* (Kent, OH: Kent State University Press, 1965), 111; Hammond, *Banks and Politics in America*, 182–83.

8. Hickey, *War of 1812*, 302; Etling, *Amateurs to Arms*, 18.

9. Nettels, *National Economy*, 396.

10. Quote from Allen Johnson and Dumas Malone, eds., "Stephen Decatur," *Dictionary of American Biography* (New York: Charles Scribners' Sons, 1943), 3:189; For the operations, see Frederick Leiner, *The End of Barbary Terror* (New York: Oxford University Press, 2006); Glenn Tucker, *Dawn Like Thunder: The Barbary Wars and the Birth of the U.S. Navy* (Indianapolis: Bobbs-Merrill, 1963).

11. Wright, *Creeks and Seminoles*; James W. Covington, *The Seminoles of Florida* (Gainesville: University of Florida Press, 1993); Kenneth W. Porter, *The Black Seminoles* (Gainesville: University of Florida Press, 1996).

12. Andrew Jackson, letter to Edmund Gaines, April 8, 1816, CAJ, 2:235–37.

13. Andrew Jackson, letter to Mauricio de Zuniga, April 23, 1816, CAJ, 2:241–42.

14. Edmund Gaines, letter to D. C. Clinch, May 23, 1816, ASPFA, 4:558.

15. Andrew Jackson, letter to William Crawford, June 13, 1816, CAJ, 2:248.

16. Rogin, *Fathers and Children*, 165.

17. Noble Cunningham, *The Presidency of James Monroe* (Lawrence: University of Kansas Press, 1990); Harry Ammon, *James Monroe: The Quest for National Identity* (Charlottesville: University of Virginia Press, 1990).

18. Andrew Jackson, letter to James Monroe, March 4, 1817, CAJ, 2:277–81.

19. Andrew Jackson, Division Order, April 22, 1817, PAJ, 4:113–14.

20. Andrew Jackson, letter to Winfield Scott, September 8, 1817, CAJ, 2:325;

Winfield Scott, letter to Andrew Jackson, October 4, 1817, PAJ, 4:142–43; Andrew Jackson, letter to Winfield Scott, December 3, 1817, PAJ, 4:157–58.

21. James Monroe, letter to Andrew Jackson, December 28, 1817, Monroe Papers, NYPL; Andrew Jackson, letter to James Monroe, January 6, 1818, CAJ, 2:345–46.

22. Andrew Jackson, letter to James Monroe, January 6, 1818, CAJ, 2:345–46

23. Andrew Jackson, letter to James Monroe, June 2, 1818, Monroe Papers, NYPL.

24. James Monroe, letters to John Calhoun, May 19, 1830, and January 30, 1818, Calhoun Papers, 11:165, 2:104.

25. "Jackson Exposition, 1831," in Thomas Hart Benton, *The Thirty Years' View: Or, A History of the Working of the American Government for Thirty Years, from 1820 to 1850* (New York: D. Appleton, 1854), 1:170.

26. Andrew Jackson, Letter Book, CAJ, 2:346n.

27. Andrew Jackson, letter to Francisco Caso y Luengo, April 6, 1818, in Parton, *Life of Jackson*, 2:451.

28. Andrew Jackson, letter to William Rabun, May 7, 1818, ASPMA, 1:777.

29. William Rabun, letter to Andrew Jackson, June 1, 1818, Jackson Papers, LC.

30. José Masot, letter to Andrew Jackson, May 22, 1818, Calhoun Papers, 2:371; Andrew Jackson, letter to Luis Piernas, May 24, 1818; Andrew Jackson, letter to José Masot, May 25, 1818, both in PAJ, 4:210, 211.

31. Parton, *Life of Jackson*, 2:492–93.

32. Andrew Jackson, letter to James Monroe, June 2, 1818, Monroe Papers, NYPL.

33. Luis de Onís, letter to John Quincy Adams, July 23, 1818, ASPFA, 4:496–97.

34. Henry Clay, speech, Annals, 15th Cong., 2nd sess., 655, 831–55.

35. James Monroe, letter to Andrew Jackson, July 19, 1818, Monroe Writings, 4:54–61; John Quincy Adams, letter to Luis de Onís, ASPFA, 4:497–99.

36. Andrew Jackson, letter to James Monroe, August 19, 181, CAJ, 2:389–91.

37. Andrew Jackson, letter to George Gibson, February 1, 1820, PAJ, 4:235.

38. Annals, 15th Cong., 2nd sess., 515–38; Merrill Peterson, *The Great Triumvirate: Webster, Clay, and Calhoun* (New York: Oxford University Press, 1988), 55–56.

39. Senate, Report on Jackson Campaign, ASPMA, 1:743.

40. Philip Coolidge Brook, *Diplomacy and the Borderlands: The Adams-Onís Treaty of 1819* (Berkeley: University of California Press, 1939); Charles Carroll Griffin, *The United States and the Disruption of the Spanish Empire, 1810 to 1822* (New York: Hippocrene Books, 1968).

41. Doak's Stand Treaty, ASPIA, 2:225; Andrew Jackson and Thomas Hinds, letters to John Calhoun, October 19, 21, 1820, ASPIA, 2:241–44.

42. James Monroe, letter to Andrew Jackson, January 24, 1821, Jackson Papers, LC; Andrew Jackson, letter to James Monroe, February 11, 1821, Monroe Papers, NYPL.

43. Andrew Jackson, letter to John Coffee, July 18, 1821, CAJ, 3:105.

44. Parton, *Life of Jackson*, 2:630–31.

45. Andrew Jackson, letter to Eligius Fromentin, September 3, 1821, PAJ, 5:100.

46. Brands, *Jackson*, 360.

47. Andrew Jackson, letter to James Monroe, November 14, 1821, CAJ, 3:129.

4. THE FIRE BELL IN THE NIGHT

1. George Dangerfield, *The Era of Good Feelings* (Chicago: Ivan Dee, 1989).

2. Thomas Jefferson, letter to Benjamin Austin, January 9, 1816, Jefferson Writings, 13:71.

3. Dangerfield, *Era of Good Feelings*; Norman Risjord, *The Old Republicans: Southern Conservatism in the Age of Jefferson* (New York: Columbia University Press, 1965); Shaw Livermore, *The Twilight of Federalism: The Disintegration of the Federalist Party, 1815–1830* (New York: Gordian Press, 1972).

4. Richard Timberlake, *The Origins of Central Banking in the United States* (Cambridge, MA: Harvard University Press, 1978).

5. John Larsen, *Internal Improvements: National Public Works and the Promise of Popular Government in the Early United States* (Chapel Hill: University of North Carolina Press, 2001).

6. Steven Siry, *DeWitt Clinton and the American Political Economy: Sectionalism, Politics, and Republican Ideology, 1787–1828* (New York: P. Lang, 1990); Evan Cornog, *The Birth of Empire: DeWitt Clinton and the American Experience* (New York: Oxford University Press, 2000).

7. Carol Sheriff, *The Artificial River: The Erie Canal and the Paradox of Development* (New York: Farrar, Straus and Giroux, 1997); Ronald Shaw, *Erie Water West: A Story of the Erie Canal* (Lexington: University of Kentucky Press, 2007).

8. Mark Killenbeck, *McCulloch v. Maryland: Securing a Nation* (Lawrence: University of Kansas Press, 2006).

9. Sellers, *Market Revolution*, 136.

10. Murray Rothbard, *The Panic of 1819: Reactions and Politics* (New York: AMS Press, 1973); HS, 1:201–2, 209; Daniel Feller, *The Public Lands in Jacksonian Politics* (Madison: University of Wisconsin, 1984), 26–38.

11. Arthur Zilversmit, *The First Emancipation: The Abolition of Slavery in the North* (Chicago: University of Chicago Press, 1967); Donald L. Robinson, *Slavery in the Structure of American Politics, 1765–1820* (New York: W. W. Norton, 1979); Roger Ransom, *Conflict and Compromise: The Political Economy of Slavery* (New York: Cambridge University Press, 1989).

12. Thomas Cobb and James Tallmadge, speeches, February 16, 1819, Annals, 15th Cong., 1st sess., 1203–4.

13. Thomas Jefferson, letter to John Holmes, April 22, 1820, in Thomas Jefferson, *The Selected Writings of Thomas Jefferson*, ed. Adrienne Koch and William Peden (New York: Modern Library, 1944), 698.

14. Andrew Jackson, letter to Andrew Donelson, April 16, 1820, PAJ, 4:367.

15. Glover Moore, *The Missouri Controversy, 1819–1821* (Gloucester, MA: P. Smith, 1967); William W. Freehling, *The Road to Disunion* (New York: Oxford University Press, 2007).

16. Robert Remini, *Henry Clay: Statesman for the Union* (New York: W. W. Norton, 1991).

17. Henry Clay, speech, July 26, 1816, Clay Papers, 2:216–21.

18. Bradford Perkins, Warren Cohen, and Walter Lafeber, eds., *The Creation of the American Empire, 1776–1865* (New York: Cambridge University Press, 1993); William Earl Weeks, *Building the Continental Empire* (Chicago: University of Chicago Press, 1996).

19. Richard Oglesby, *Manuel Lisa and the Opening of the Missouri Fur Trade* (Norman: University of Oklahoma Press, 1984).

20. Axel Madsen, *John Jacob Astor: America's First Multimillionaire* (New York: Wiley, 2001); James Rhoda, *Astoria and Empire* (Lincoln: University of Nebraska Press, 1990).

21. David Dary, *The Santa Fe Trail: Its History, Legends, and Lore* (New York: Penguin, 2002); Stephen Hyslop, *Bound for Santa Fe: The Road to New Mexico and the American Conquest, 1806–1848* (Norman: University of Oklahoma Press, 2002); Dale Morgan, *Jedediah Smith and the Opening of the West* (Lincoln: University of Nebraska Press, 1964); William Goetzmann, *Exploration and Empire: The Explorer and the Scientist in the Winning of the American West* (New York: Vintage Books, 1972); David Wishart, *The Fur Trade of the American West, 1807–1840: A Geographical Synthesis* (Lincoln: University of Nebraska Press, 1979); William Goetzmann, *New Lands, New Men: American and the Second Great Age of Discovery* (Austin: Texas State Historical Association, 1995); Weeks, *Building the Continental Empire*.

22. Francis Paul Prucha, *American Indian Policy in the Formative Years* (Cambridge, MA: Harvard University Press, 1962).

23. William Nester, *The Arikara War: The First Plains Indian War, 1823* (Missoula, MT: Mountain Press, 2001); Richard Chokey, *William H. Ashley: Enterprise and Politics in the Trans-Mississippi West* (Norman: University of Oklahoma Press, 1990).

5. THE MONROE DOCTRINE

1. Alfred Burt, *The United States, Great Britain, and British North America from the Revolution to the Establishment of Peace after the War of 1812* (New York: Russell & Russell, 1940); Bradford Perkins, *Castlereagh and Adams, England and the United States, 1812–1823* (New York: Cambridge University Press, 1965); Kenneth Borne, *Britain and the Balance of Power in North America, 1815–1871* (Berkeley: University of California Press, 1967); Reginald Stuart, *United States Expansionism and British North America, 1775–1871* (Chapel Hill: University of North Carolina Press, 1988); William Earl Weeks, *John Quincy Adams and American Global Empire* (Lexington: University Press of Kentucky, 1992).

2. Henry Clay, speech, March 25, 1818, *Abridgement of the Debates of Congress from 1789 to 1856* (New York: D. Appleton, 1858), 6:139.

3. *National Intelligencer*, July 11, 1821, NYPL.

4. Arthur Whitaker, *The United States and the Independence of Latin America, 1800–1830* (New York: W. W. Norton, 1964); Dexter Perkins, *The Monroe Doctrine, 1867–1907* (Gloucester, MA: P. Smith, 1966); Ernest May, *The Making of the Monroe Doctrine* (Cambridge: Harvard University Press, 1975); John Johnson, *A Hemisphere Apart: The Foundations of United States Policy toward Latin America* (Baltimore: John Hopkins University Press, 1990).

5. Richardson, Messages, 2:209, 217–19.

6. Dangerfield, *Era of Good Feelings*, 3–6.

7. Frederick Merk, *The Monroe Doctrine and American Expansionism, 1843–1849* (New York: Alfred A. Knopf, 1966); Donald Dozer, ed., *The Monroe Doctrine: Its Modern Significance* (Tempe: Arizona State University Press, 1976).

6. THE CORRUPT BARGAIN

1. Andrew Jackson, letter to James Gadsden, December 6, 1821, CAJ, 3:141.

2. Andrew Jackson, letter to James Gadsden, January 29, 1822, PAJ, 5:139.

3. Andrew Jackson, letter to Richard Call, June 29, 1822, PAJ, 5:199.

4. Andrew Jackson, letter to John Quincy Adams, March 15, 1823, CAJ, 3:192–93.

5. Andrew Jackson, letter to Henry Baldwin, May 20, 1824, PAJ, 5:411–12.

6. Andrew Jackson, letter to L. H. Coleman, April 26, 1824, CAJ, 3:249–50.

7. Andrew Jackson, letter to William Lewis, May 7, 1824, Jackson-Lewis Papers, NYPL.

8. [John Eaton], *The Letters of Wyoming, to the People of the United States, on the Presidential Election, and in Favour of Andrew Jackson* (Philadelphia: n.p., 1824). See also Gabriel L. Lowe, "John H. Eaton, Jackson's Campaign Manager," *Tennessee History Quarterly* 11 (1952): 99–147.

9. Remini, *Andrew Jackson*, 2:83.

10. Andrew Jackson, letter to William B. Lewis, February 14, 1825, PAJ, 6:29–30.

11. Andrew Jackson, letter to Samuel Swartwout, February 22, 1825, CAJ, 3:278–79.

12. Remini, *Andrew Jackson*, 2:84.

13. Samuel Flagg Bemis, *John Quincy Adams and the Foundations of American Foreign Policy* (Westport, CT: Greenwood Press, 1981); Samuel Flagg Bemis, *John Quincy Adams and the Union* (Westport, CT: Greenwood Press, 1980); Mary Hargreaves, *The Presidency of John Quincy Adams* (Lawrence: University of Kansas Press, 1985); Paul C. Nagel, *John Quincy Adams: A Public Life, A Private Life* (Cambridge, MA: Harvard University Press, 1999); Robert V. Remini, *John Quincy Adams* (New York: Henry Holt, 2002).

14. John Quincy Adams, speech, December 6, 1825, Richardson, Messages, 2:866–968.

15. Andrew Jackson, letter to John Branch, March 3, 1826, in Remini, *Andrew Jackson*, 1:111.

16. Stuart Bruchey, *Enterprise: The Dynamic Economy of a Free People* (Cambridge: Harvard University Press, 1990), 201.

17. [John Calhoun], South Carolina Exposition, December 19, 1828, Calhoun Papers, 10:445–507.

18. Richard P. McCormick, *The Second American Party System: Party Formation in the Jacksonian Era* (Chapel Hill: University of North Carolina Press, 1966).

19. Remini, *Andrew Jackson*, 2:110.

20. Andrew Jackson, letter to John Coffee, May 12, 1828, in Remini, *Andrew Jackson*, 2:138.

21. Parton, *Life of Jackson*, 3:160–62.

22. Arthur Schlesinger and Fred Israel, eds., *The History of American Presidential Elections, 1789–1968* (New York: Chelsea House Publishers, 1971), 1:492.

23. Andrew Jackson, letter to John Coffee, January 17, 1829, in Remini, *Andrew Jackson*, 2:156.

7. THE SCANDALS

1. Andrew Jackson, letter to Rachel Jackson, February 27, 1824, in Remini, *Andrew Jackson*, 2:161.

2. Nicolas Biddle, the president of the Bank of the United States, appears to have coined those terms when he noted that the Jackson administration's "kitchen . . . predominates over the Parlor." Nicholas Biddle, letter to Robert Gibbes, December 31, 1831, Biddle Papers, LC.

3. Erik McKinley Eriksson, "The Federal Civil Service under President Jackson," *Mississippi Valley Historical Review* 13 (1926–27): 527–28; Adams Diary, 8:148.

4. John Marszalek, *The Petticoat Affair: Manner, Mutiny, and Sex in Andrew Jackson's White House* (Baton Rouge: Louisiana State University Press, 2000).

5. Andrew Jackson, letter to John McLemore, n.d. [April 1829]; Andrew Jackson, letter to Richard Call, July 5, 1829, both in CAJ, 4:21, 31.

6. Sam Houston, letter to Andrew Jackson, May 11, 1829, *The Personal Correspondence of Sam Houston*, ed. Madge Roberts (Denton: University of North Texas Press, 1996), 1:132–33.

7. Andrew Jackson, letter to John McLemore, n.d. [April 1829], Jackson Papers, NYPL.

8. John Calhoun, letter to Andrew Jackson, May 25, 1830, in Remini, *Andrew Jackson*, 2:245.

9. Andrew Jackson, letter to John Calhoun, May 30, 1830, CAJ, 4:141.

10. Remini, *Andrew Jackson*, 2:308–9.

11. Henry Wikoff, *Reminiscences of an Idler* (New York: Ford, Howard, and Hulbert, 1880), 29–31.

12. *National Intelligencer*, June 10, 1834, NYPL.

13. Leonard D. White, *The Jacksonians: A Study in Administrative History, 1829–1861* (New York: Free Press, 1954), 424–30; *Annals*, 22nd Cong., 1st sess., 1325.

8. THE MONSTER BANK

1. Andrew Jackson, Annual Message to Congress, December 8, 1829, Richardson, *Messages*, 3:1005–25.

2. Philip D. Jordan, *The National Road* (Indianapolis: Bobbs-Merrill, 1948).

3. Thomas Govan, *Nicholas Biddle* (Chicago: University of Chicago Press, 1959); Ralph C. H. Catterall, *The Second Bank of the United States* (Chicago: University of Chicago Press, 1960); Jean Wilburn, *Biddle's Bank: The Crucial Years* (New York: Columbia University Press, 1967).

4. Nicholas Biddle, letter to Daniel Webster, October 29, 1822, *The Correspondence of Nicholas Biddle* (Boston: J. S. Canner, 1966), 39.

5. Nicolas Biddle, letter to Thomas Swann, March 17, 1824, *Annals*, 23rd Cong., 2nd sess., 17:297–98; and Robert Remini, *Andrew Jackson and the Bank War* (New York: W. W. Norton, 1967).

6. Andrew Jackson, letter to John Quincy Adams, April 24, 1821, ASPFA, 4:756.

7. Benton, *Thirty Year's View*, 1:235.

8. Amos Kendall, letter to Francis Blair, March 1, 1830, Blair-Lee Papers, Princeton University, Princeton, NJ.

9. Martin Van Buren, *The Autobiography of Martin Van Buren*, ed. John C. Fitzpatrick (Washington, DC: Government Printing Office, 1920), 625.

10. Peterson, *Great Triumvirate*, 208.

11. Andrew Jackson, message to Congress, July 10, 1832, Richardson, Messages, 3:1139–53.

12. *Globe*, September 5, 1832, NYPL.

13. Steven Bullock, *The Revolutionary Brotherhood: Freemasonry and the Transformation of the American Social Order, 1730–1840* (Chapel Hill: University of North Carolina Press, 1995); Paul Goodman, *Towards a Christian Republic: Antimasonry and the Great Transition in New England, 1826–1836* (New York: Oxford University Press, 1988).

14. Svend Peterson, *A Statistical History of the American Presidential Elections* (New York: Ungar, 1963), 20–21.

9. THE NULLIFICATION CRISIS

1. William Freehling, *The Nullification Era: A Documentary Record* (New York: Harper & Row, 1967).

2. Robert Hayne, speech, January 25, 1830, Register of Debates, 21st Cong., 1st sess., Senate, 46–50.

3. Daniel Webster, speech, January 26–27, 1830, Register of Debates, 21st Cong., 1st sess., Senate, 80.

4. Van Buren, *Autobiography*, 415.

5. Parton, *Life of Jackson*, 3:284–85.

6. Andrew Jackson, letter to John Coffee, December 14, 1832, CAJ, 4:499–500.

7. Andrew Jackson, proclamation, December 10, 1832, Richardson, Messages, 2:1203–15.

8. Andrew Jackson, letter to Lewis Cass, December 17, 1832, CAJ, 4:502–3.

9. Andrew Jackson, letter to Joel Poinsett, December 9, 1832, CAJ, 4:498.

10. Andrew Jackson, letter to Lewis Cass, October 29, 1832, CAJ, 4:483.

11. Andrew Jackson, special message to Congress, January 16, 1833, Richardson, Messages, 3:1174–94.

12. Andrew Jackson, letter to Joel Poinsett, January 24, 1833, CAJ, 5:11.

13. Merrill Peterson, *Olive, Branch, and Sword: The Compromise of 1833* (Baton Rouge: Louisiana State University Press, 1982).

14. Andrew Jackson, Second Inaugural Address, March 4, 1833, Richardson, Messages, 3:1222–24.

15. Parton, *Life of Jackson*, 3:447.

16. Manisha Sinha, *The Counterrevolution of Slavery: Politics and Ideology in Antebellum South Carolina* (Chapel Hill: University of North Carolina Press, 2000), 60.

10. THE SPOILS

1. Nicholas Biddle, letter to Daniel Webster, April 8, 1833, Biddle Correspondence, 202.

2. James Hamilton, *Reminiscences of James A. Hamilton* (New York: Charles Scribner, 1869), 253.

3. Andrew Jackson, letter to Martin Van Buren, September 8, 1833, Jackson Papers, LC.

4. Amos Kendall, letter to Andrew Jackson, March 20, 1833, CAJ, 5:41–44.

5. William Duane, *Narrative and Correspondence Concerning the Removal of the Deposites, and Occurrences Connected Therewith* (Philadelphia, 1838), 95–100; William Duane, letter to Andrew Jackson, July 10, 1833; Andrew Jackson, letter to William Duane, July 12, 17, 1833, both in Jackson Papers, LC.

6. Frank Otto Gatell, "Secretary Taney and the Baltimore Pets," *Business History Review* 39 (1965): 205–27; White, *Jacksonians*, 477, 469–79.

7. Andrew Jackson, letter to Martin Van Buren, October 5, 1833, CAJ, 5:216.

8. Nicholas Biddle, letter to Joseph Hopkinson, February 21, 1834, Biddle Papers, LC.

9. Catterall, *Second Bank*, 351–52.

10. Andrew Jackson, letter to James Hamilton, February 2, 1834, CAJ, 5:244.

11. Henry Clay, speech, Register of Debates, 23rd Cong., 1st sess., 84–85.

12. Parton, *Life of Jackson*, 3:542.

13. Andrew Jackson, letter to Andrew Jackson Jr., February 16, 1834, CAJ, 5:249.

14. Andrew Jackson, Protest to the Senate, April 15, 1834, Richardson, Messages, 3:85.

15. Andrew Jackson, letter to John Coffee, April 6, 1834, in Remini, *Andrew Jackson*, 3:167.

16. Sellers, *Market Revolution*, 344.

17. *Globe*, January 12, 1835, NYPL.

18. Remini, *Andrew Jackson*, 3:246, 248.

19. Andrew Jackson, veto message, December 4, 1833, Richardson, Messages, 2:57–68.

20. Register of Debates, 24th Cong., 1st sess., 51.

11. THE MASTER'S NIGHTMARE

1. Parton, *Life of Jackson*, 3:488.

2. For the best firsthand account, see Benton, *Thirty Years' View*, 1:522–23.

3. David Brion Davis, *The Slave Power Conspiracy and the Paranoid Style* (Baton Rouge: Louisiana State University Press, 1969).

4. Thomas Jefferson, letter to John Holmes, April 22, 1820, Jefferson Writings, 1434.

5. John Lofton, *Denmark Vesey's Revolt: The Slave Plot that Lit a Fuse to Fort Sumter* (Kent, OH: Kent State University Press, 1983).

6. Kenneth Greenburg, ed., *Nat Turner: A Slave Rebellion in History and Memory* (New York: Oxford University Press, 2004); Herbert Aptheker, *Nat Turner's Slave Rebellion: Including the 1831 Confessions* (New York: Dover Publications, 2006).

7. Frederick Douglass and Harriet Jacobs, *The Narrative of the Life Frederick Douglass, an American Slave, and Incidents in the Life of a Slave Girl* (New York: Modern Library, 2004).

8. James Wesley Smith, *Sojourners in Search of Freedom: The Settlement of Liberia by Black Americans* (Lanham, MD: University Press of America, 1987); Amos Beyan, *The American Colonization Society and the Creation of the Liberian State* (Lanham, MD: University Press of America, 1991); Antonio McDaniel, *Swing Low, Sweet Chariot: The Morality Cost of Colonizing Liberia* (Chicago: University of Chicago Press, 1995).

9. Henry Mayer, *All on Fire: William Lloyd Garrison and the Abolition of Slavery* (New York: St. Martin's Press, 1998).

10. Bertham Wyatt-Brown, *Lewis Tappan and the Evangelical War against Slavery* (Cleveland: Case Western Reserve University Press, 1969); Julie Keffrey, *The Great Silent Army of Abolitionism* (Chapel Hill: University of North Carolina Press, 1998); Fergus Bordewich, *Bound for Canaan: The Underground Railroad and the War for the Soul of America* (New York: HarperCollins, 2005); Bruce Laurie, *Beyond Garrison: Antislavery and Social Reform* (New York: Cambridge University Press, 2005).

11. David Grimsted, *American Mobbing, 1828–1861: Toward Civil War* (New York: Oxford University Press, 1998), 13.

12. Amos Kendall, letter to postmaster of Charleston, August 4, 1835, *Niles Weekly Register*, August 22, 1835, NYPL.

13. Andrew Jackson, letter to Amos Kendall, August 9, 1835, CAJ, 5:360–61.

14. Dwight Dumond, *Antislavery: The Crusade for Freedom in America* (Ann Arbor: University of Michigan Press, 1961), 245–46.

15. Howard Jones, *Mutiny on the* Amistad*: The Saga of a Slave Revolt and Its Impact on American Abolition, Law, and Diplomacy* (New York: Oxford University Press, 1987).

16. John Marshall, letter to Joseph Story, September 22, 1832, quoted in Kent Newmyer, *John Marshall and the Heroic Age of the Supreme Court* (Baton Rouge: Louisiana State University Press, 2001), 386.

17. Austin Allen, *The Origins of the Dred Scott Case: Jacksonian Jurisprudence and the Supreme Court* (Athens: University of Georgia Press, 2006).

12. THE TRAIL OF TEARS

1. Andrew Jackson, Annual Message, December 6, 1830, Richardson, Messages, 3:1082–86.

2. Paul Prucha, *American Indian Policy in the Formative Years: The Indian Tribes and the Intercourse Acts, 1790–1834* (Cambridge, MA: Harvard University Press, 1962); Paul Prucha, *American Indian Treaties: The History of a Political Anomaly* (Berkeley: University of California Press, 1994); Tim Garrison, *The Legal Ideology of Removal: The Southern Judiciary and the Sovereignty of the Native American Nations* (Athens: University of Georgia Press, 2002); Lindsay Robertson, *Conquest by Law: How the Discovery of America Dispossessed Indigenous Peoples of Their Lands* (New York: Oxford University Press, 2005).

3. For a concise overview, see Francis Paul Prucha, *The Great Father: The United States Government and the American Indian* (Lincoln: University of Nebraska Press, 1986), 64–107. See also Grant Foreman, *Indian Removal: The Emigration of the Five Civilized Tribes* (Norman: University of Oklahoma Press, 1953): Mary E. Young, *Redskins, Ruffleshirts, and Rednecks: Indian Allotments in Alabama and Mississippi, 1830–1860* (Norman: University of Oklahoma Press, 1961); Ronald Satz, *American Indian Policy in the Jackson Era* (Lincoln: University of Nebraska Press, 1975); Tim Alan Garrison, *The Legal Ideology of Removal: The Southern Judiciary and the Sovereignty of Native American Nations* (Athens: University of Georgia Press, 2002).

4. Andrew Jackson, Draft of First Message to Congress, December 7, 1829, Richardson, Messages, 2:1025.

5. Andrew Jackson, Address to the Chickasaw, August 23, 1830, in Remini, *Andrew Jackson*, 2:269–70.

6. John Ehle, *The Trail of Tears: The Rise and Fall of the Cherokee Nation* (New York: Anchor Book, 1988); William G. McLoughlin, *The Cherokee Renaissance in the New Republic* (Princeton, NJ: Princeton University Press, 1992); Frances Patton Statham, *The Trail of Tears* (New York: Fawcett Columbine, 1993); Theda Perdue, Michael Green, and Colin Calloway, eds., *The Cherokee Nation and the Trail of Tears* (New York: Penguin, 2007).

7. Ehle, *Trail of Tears*, 224–25.

8. *Worcester v. State of Georgia*, 31 U.S. 515 (1832).

9. Horace Greely, *The American Conflict: A Story of the Great Rebellion in the United States* (Hartford, CT: O. D. Case, 1879), 1:106.

10. Edwin Miles, "After John Marshall's Decision: *Worcester v. Georgia* and the Nullification Crisis," *Journal of Southern History* 39 (1973): 519–44.

11. Andrew Jackson, letter to John Coffee, April 7, 1832, in Remini, *Andrew Jackson*, 2:277.

12. Andrew Jackson, letter to Cherokee chiefs, March 16, 1835, *Globe*, March 28, 1835, NYPL.

13. Ehle, *Trail of Tears*, 390–91.

14. Cecil Eby, *"That Disgraceful Affair": The Black Hawk War* (New York: W. W. Norton, 1973); Kerry Trask, *Black Hawk: The War for the Heart of America* (New York: Henry Holt, 2006); Patrick Jung, *The Black Hawk War of 1832* (Norman: University of Oklahoma Press, 2007).

15. Andrew Jackson, 1833 Address to Congress, Richardson, Messages, 2:1166.

16. John Quincy, *Figures of the Past from the Leaves of Old Journals* (Boston: Roberts Brothers, 1883), 298.

17. John Mahon, *A History of the Seminole War* (Gainesville: University of Florida Press, 1967); George Buker, *Swamp Sailors: Riverine Warfare in the Everglades, 1835–1842* (Gainesville: University of Florida Press, 1975); John Missall and Mary Lou Missall, *The Seminole Wars: America's Longest Indian Conflict* (Gainesville: University of Florida Press, 2004).

18. Andrew Jackson, letter to Seminole Chiefs, February 16, 1835, in Remini, *Andrew Jackson*, 3:306.

19. Andrew Jackson, letter to Benjamin Butler, November 2, 1836, Benjamin Butler Papers, NYPL.

20. Andrew Jackson, letter to Thomas Jessup, November 5, 1836, in Remini, *Andrew Jackson*, 3:310.

21. Covington, *Seminoles of Florida*, 72.

22. Andrew Jackson, letter to James Gadsden, n.d. [November 1836]; Andrew Jackson, letter to Joel Poinsett, October 1, 1837, both in CAJ, 5:434, 512.

13. THE WORLD BEYOND

1. John Belohlavek, *Let the Eagle Soar! The Foreign Policy of Andrew Jackson* (Lincoln: University of Nebraska Press, 1985).

2. Remini, *Andrew Jackson*, 2:286.

3. Andrew Jackson, letter to Edward Livingston, June 27, 1834, in Remini, *Andrew Jackson*, 3:211.

4. Andrew Jackson, report to Congress, January 15, 1836, Register of Debates, 24th Cong., 1st sess., 163.

5. Andrew Jackson, letter to Edward Livingston, February 27, 1836, in Remini, *Andrew Jackson*, 3:288.

6. Parson, *Life of Jackson*, 3:336–38.

14. THE TEXAS REVOLUTION

1. A. W. Terrell, "Recollections of General Sam Houston," *Southwestern Historical Quarterly* 14 (1912): 126.

2. Andrew Jackson, letter to Anthony Butler, April 19, 1832, CAJ, 4:436.

3. James L. Haley, *Sam Houston* (Norman: University of Oklahoma Press, 2002), 89.

4. Sam Houston, letter to Andrew Jackson, February 13, 1833, Houston Writings, 1:274–76.

5. Andrew Jackson, letter to Anthony Butler, August 24, 1832, CAJ, 4:335.

6. Anthony Butler, letter to Andrew Jackson, October 28, 1833, CAJ, 5:219.

7. Andrew Jackson, letter to Anthony Butler, November 27, 1833, CAJ, 5:228–29.

8. Anthony Butler, letter to Andrew Jackson, February 6, 1834, CAJ, 5:244–46.

9. Andrew Jackson, letter to Anthony Butler, October 1829, CAJ, 4:81.

10. Martha Manchaca, *Recovering History, Constructing Race: The Indian, Black, and White Roots of Mexican Americans* (Austin: University of Texas Press, 2001), 172; Alwyn Barr, *Texans in Revolt: The Battle for San Antonio, 1835* (Austin: University of Texas Press, 1990), 17.

11. David Weber, *The Mexican Frontier, 1821–1846* (Albuquerque: University of New Mexico Press, 1982).

12. Gregg Cantrell, *Stephen Austin* (New Haven, CT: Yale University Press, 1999).

13. For the best recent biography, see Will Fowler, *Santa Anna of Mexico* (Lincoln: University of Nebraska Press, 2007).

14. Paul Lack, *The Texas Revolutionary Experience* (College Station: Texas A & M University Press, 1992); H. W. Brands, *Lone Star Nation: The Epic Story of the Battle for Texas Independence* (New York: Anchor, 2005).

15. For a military history of the Texas war for independence, see Stephen Hardin, *Texas Illiad: A Military History of the Texas Revolution* (Austin: University of Texas Press, 1996). For an excellent first-person account of the campaign from the Mexican perspective, see José de la Peña, *With Santa Anna in Texas* (College Station: Texas A & M University Press, 1997).

16. Randy Robert and James Olsen, *A Line in the Sand: The Alamo in Blood and Memory* (New York: Free Press, 2002); William C. Davis, *Three Roads to the Alamo: The Lives and Fortunes of David Crockett, James Bowie, and William Barret Travis* (New York: HarperCollins, 1998).

17. William Bradle, *Goliad: The Other Alamo* (New York: Pelican Publishing, 2007); Jay A. Stout, *The Slaughter at Goliad: The Mexican Massacre of 400 Texas Volunteers* (Annapolis, MD: Naval Institute Press, 2008).

18. Edmund Gaines, letter to Lewis Cass, March 29, 1836, *Papers of the Texas Revolution*, ed. John H. Jenkins (Austin: Presidial Press, 1973), 5:231–33.

19. Lewis Cass, letter to Edmund Gaines, April 25, 1836, *Papers of the Texas Revolution*, 6:53–54.

20. K. Jack Bauer, "The U.S. Navy and Texas Independence: A Study in Jacksonian Integrity," *Military Affairs* 34 (April 1970): 44–48.

21. Ann Fears Crawford, ed., *The Eagle: The Autobiography of Santa Anna* (Austin: University of Texas Press, 1967), 57; *Globe*, January 21, 1837, NYPL.

22. John Quincy Adams, speech, May 25, 1836, Register of Debates, 24th Cong., 2nd sess., House, 4041–47.

23. Santa Anna, letter to Andrew Jackson, July 4, 1836, CAJ, 5:412.

24. Andrew Jackson, letter to Sam Houston, September 4, 1836, CAJ, 5:425.

25. Andrew Jackson, letter to Santa Anna, September 4, 1836, CAJ, 4:426.

26. Andrew Jackson, message to Congress, December 21, 1836, Richardson, Messages, 2:1488.

27. Andrew Jackson, letter to Edmund Gaines, September 4, 1836, CAJ, 5:424.

28. Sam Houston, letter to Andrew Jackson, September 4, 1836, CAJ, 5:425.

29. Remini, *Andrew Jackson*, 3:365.

30. William Wharton, letter to Samuel Houston, January 24, 1837, Manning, Correspondence, 193–94.

15. THE LITTLE MAGICIAN

1. Daniel Howe, *The Political Culture of the American Whigs* (Chicago: University of Chicago Press, 1979); Michael F. Holt, *The Rise and Fall of the American Whig Party* (New York: Oxford University Press, 2003).

2. Henry R. Stanton, *Random Recollections* (New York: Harper and Brothers, 1886), 205–6.

3. John Niven, *Martin Van Buren: The Romantic Age of American Politics* (New York: Oxford University Press, 1983), 397. See also Major Wilson, *The Presidency of Martin Van Buren* (Lawrence: University of Kansas Press, 1984); Donald Cole, *Martin Van Buren and the American Political System* (Princeton, NJ: Princeton University Press, 1984).

4. Andrew Jackson, address to the nation, March 4, 1837, Richardson, Messages, 4:1511–15.

5. Catterall, *Second Bank*, 508.

6. Peter Rousseau, "Jacksonian Monetary Policy, Specie Flows, and the Panic of 1837," *Journal of Economic History* 62 (2002): 457–88.

7. Dan Monroe, *The Republican Vision of John Tyler* (College Station: Texas A & M Press, 2003); Edward Crapol, *John Tyler, the Accidental President* (Chapel Hill: University of North Carolina Press, 2006).

8. Svend Petersen, *A Statistical History of the American Presidential Elections* (New York: Westport, CT: Greenwood Publishing, 1981), 18–27.

9. Norma Lois Peterson, *The Presidencies of William Henry Harrison and John Tyler* (Lawrence: University of Kansas Press, 1989).

10. Francis Blair, letter to Andrew Jackson, April 4, 1841, CAJ, 6:97–98.

11. Albert Corey, *The Crisis of 1830–1842 in Canadian-American Relations* (New

York: Russell and Russell, 1970); Kenneth Stevens, *Border Diplomacy: The Caroline and McLeod Affairs in Anglo-American-Canadian Relations, 1837–1842* (Tuscaloosa: University of Alabama Press, 1989); Howard Jones, *To the Webster-Ashburton Treaty: A Study in Anglo-American Relations, 1783–1843* (Chapel Hill: University of North Carolina Press, 1977).

16. THE INDUSTRIAL AND CULTURAL REVOLUTIONS

1. Douglass North, *Economic Growth in the United States, 1790–1860* (New York: W. W. Norton, 1966); Thomas Cochran, *Frontiers of Change: Early Industrialization in America* (New York: Oxford University Press, 1983); Walter Licht, *Industrializing America* (Baltimore: Johns Hopkins University Press, 1995).

2. Angela Lakwete, *Inventing the Cotton Gin* (Baltimore: Johns Hopkins University Press, 2003); Gavin Wright, *The Political Economy of the Cotton South: Households, Markets, and Wealth in the Nineteenth Century* (New York: W. W. Norton, 1978); John Hebron Moore, *The Emergence of the Cotton Kingdom in the Old Southwest* (Baton Rouge: Louisiana State University Press, 1988).

3. Bruchey, *Enterprise*, 149.

4. Ibid., 154. See also Roger Burlingame, *March of the Iron Men: A Social History of Union through Invention* (New York: Grosset and Dunlap, 1960); George Daniels, *American Science in the Age of Jackson* (Tuscaloosa: University of Alabama Press, 1994).

5. Paul Gates, *The Farmer's Age: Agriculture, 1815–1860* (Armonk, NY: M. E. Sharpe, 1989); Allan Kulikoff, *The Agrarian Origins of American Capitalism* (Charlottesville: University of Virginia Press, 1992).

6. Robert Dalzell, *Enterprising Elite: The Boston Associates and the World They Made* (Cambridge, MA: Harvard University Press, 1987); Thomas Dublin, *Lowell: The Story of an Industrial City* (Washington, DC: U.S. Department of the Interior, 1992).

7. Bruchey, *Enterprise*, 152; Theodore Steinberg, *Nature Incorporated: Industrialization and the Waters of New England* (New York: Cambridge University Press, 1991).

8. George Rogers Taylor, *The Transportation Revolution, 1815–1860* (New York: Holt, Rinehart, and Winston, 1951).

9. John Stover, *American Railroads* (Chicago: University of Chicago Press, 1961); Albert Fishlow, *American Railroads and the Transformation of the Antebellum Economy* (Cambridge: Harvard University Press, 1965).

10. Albert Fishlow, "Internal Improvements," in Lance Davis et al., *American Economic Growth: An Economist's History of the United States* (New York: Joanna Colter Books, 1972), 473–74. For an excellent overview on canals, see Carter Goodrich et al., *Canals and American Economic Development* (Port Washington, NY: Kennikat Press, 1972).

11. Taylor, *Transportation Revolution*, 63–64.

12. John McCusker, "The Demise of Distance: The Business Press and the Origins of the Information Revolution in the Early Modern Atlantic World," *American History Review* 110 (2005): 295–321.

13. Richard John, *Spreading the News: The American Postal System from Franklin to Morse* (Cambridge, MA: Harvard University Press, 1995).

14. Alexis de Tocqueville, *Democracy in America* (Chicago: University of Chicago Press, 2000), 50.

15. For the best work on this process, see Richard Bushman, *The Refinement of America: Persons, Houses, Cities* (New York: Vintage Books, 1993).

16. Theodore Sizer, ed., *The Age of the Academies* (New York: Columbia University Press, 1970); James McLachlan, *American Boarding Schools: A Historical Study* (New York: Scribners' Sons, 1970); Donald Tewksbury, *The Founding of American Colleges and Universities before the Civil War* (Princeton, NJ: Princeton University Press, 1989), 32–46.

17. Lee Soltow and Edward Stevens, *The Rise of Literacy and the Common School in the United States* (Chicago: University of Chicago Press, 1981), 11–22.

18. Michael Gilmore, *American Romanticism and the Marketplace* (Chicago: University of Chicago Press, 1985); William Gilmore, *Reading Becomes a Necessity of Life: Material and Cultural Life in New England, 1780–1835* (Knoxville: University of Tennessee Press, 1989); William Charvat, *Literary Publishing in America, 1790–1850* (Amherst, MA: University of Massachusetts Press, 1993); Meredith McGill, *American Literature and the Culture of Reprinting, 1834–1853* (Philadelphia: University of Pennsylvania Press, 2003).

19. Nina Burleigh, *The Stranger and the Statesman: James Smithson, John Quincy Adams, and the Making of America's Greatest Museum* (New York: HarperCollins, 2003).

20. Gavin Wright, *The Political Economy of the Cotton South: Households, Markets, and Wealth in the Nineteenth Century* (New York: W. W. Norton, 1978); Charles Bolton, *Poor Whites of the Antebellum South* (Durham, NC: Duke University Press, 1994); Jonathan Wells, *The Origins of the Southern Middle Class* (Chapel Hill: University of North Carolina Press, 2004).

21. Howe, *What Hath God Wrought*, 473.

22. Joseph Rayback, *A History of American Labor* (New York: Free Press, 1966); Walter Hugins, *Jacksonian Democracy and the Working Class* (Palo Alto, CA: Stanford University Press, 1960).

23. *Globe*, August 21, 1835, NYPL.

24. Richard B. Morris, "Andrew Jackson, Strikebreaker," *American History Review* 55 (1949): 66.

25. Irwin Wyllie, *The Self-Made Man in America: The Myth of Rags to Riches* (New York: Rutgers University Press, 1954).

26. Quoted by David M. Kennedy, introduction to Howe, *What Hath God Wrought*, xiii.

17. THE TRANSCENDENTALISTS

1. O. B. Frothingham, *Transcendentalism in New England* (Boston: American Unitarian Association, 1903); Perry Miller, ed., *The Transcendentalists* (Cambridge, MA: Harvard University Press, 1950); Francis O. Matthiessen, *American Renaissance: Art and Expression in the Age of Emerson and Whitman* (New York: Oxford University Press, 1968); Lawrence Buell, *Literary Transcendentalism: Style and Vision in the American Renaissance* (Ithaca, NY: Cornell University Press, 1973); Anne Rose, *Transcendentalism as a Social Movement* (New Haven, CT: Yale University Press, 1981); Lawrence Buell, *New England Literary Culture from the Revolution through the Renaissance* (New York: Cambridge University Press, 1986).

2. Ralph Waldo Emerson, "Nature," in *The Essential Writings of Ralph Waldo Emerson*, ed. Mary Oliver (New York: Modern Library, 2000), 6.

3. For the classic work on the relationship between Americans and nature, see Roderick Nash, *Wilderness and the American Mind* (New Haven, CT: Yale University Press, 1967).

4. Robert Hughes, *American Visions: The Epic History of Art in America* (New York: Alfred A. Knopf, 1997), 147.

5. David Henry Thoreau, *Walden Pond* (New York: Barnes and Noble, 1993), 75.

6. Richard Stotkin, *Regeneration through Violence: The Mythology of the American Frontier, 1600–1860* (Norman: University of Oklahoma Press, 2000), 466–513.

7. Andrew Delbanco, *Melville* (New York: Alfred A. Knopf, 2005); Brenda Wineapple, *Hawthorne: A Life* (New York: Alfred A. Knopf, 2003); Kenneth Silverman, *Edgar A. Poe: Mournful and Never-Ending Remembrance* (New York: HarperCollins, 1991); Jerome Loving, *Walt Whitman: The Song of Himself* (Berkeley: University of California Press, 1999).

8. Edward L. Widmer, *Young America: The Flowering of Democracy in New York City* (New York: Oxford University Press, 1999), 22.

9. Bushman, *Refinement of America*, 243.

18. THE ANNEXATION

1. Justin H. Smith, *The Annexation of Texas* (New York: AMS Press, 1971); Frederick Merk, *Slavery and the Annexation of Texas* (New York: Alfred A. Knopf, 1972); David Pletcher, *The Diplomacy of Annexation* (Columbia: University of Missouri Press, 1973).

2. Andrew Jackson, letter to William Lewis, September 18, 1843, CAJ, 6:229–30.

3. Andrew Jackson, letter to Nashville Union, May 13, 1844, CAJ, 6:290–91.

4. Ephraim Douglas Adams, *British Interests and Activities in Texas, 1838–1846* (Baltimore: Johns Hopkins University Press, 1910); Frederick Merk, *The Monroe Doctrine and American Expanisionism, 1843–1846* (New York: Alfred A. Knopf, 1966).

5. Henry Clay, letter to Willie Mangum, April 17, 1844, reprinted in the *National Intelligencer*, April 27, 1844; Henry Clay, letter to Stephen Miller, July 1, 1844, Clay

Papers, 4:490–91; Henry Clay, letter to Thomas Peters and John Jackson, July 27, 1844, reprinted in the *North Alabamian*, August 16, 1844; Martin Van Buren, letter to William Hammett, April 20, 1844, reprinted in the *Globe*, April 27, 1844, both in NYPL.

6. Andrew Jackson, letter to William Lewis, May 7, 1844, Jackson-Lewis Letters, NYPL; Andrew Jackson, letter to Francis Blair, May 11, 1844, Jackson Papers, LC; James Polk, letter to Salmon Chase, April 23, 1844, Polk Correspondence, 7:105–6.

7. John Calhoun, letter to Richard Pakenham, April 18, 1844, Calhoun Papers, 18:273–78.

8. Andrew Jackson Donelson, letter to John Calhoun, November 23, 1844, Calhoun Papers, 20:350.

9. Holt, *Rise and Fall of the Whig Party*.

10. Henry Hubbard et al., letter to James Polk, May 29, 1844; James Polk, letter to Henry Hubbard et al., June 12, 1844, both in Polk Correspondence, 7:241–42, 276.

11. John L. Moore, Jon P. Preimesberger, and David R. Tarr, eds., *The Congressional Quarterly's Guide to U.S. Elections* (Washington, DC: Congressional Quarterly, 2001), 1:649, 732.

12. John Tyler, message to Congress, December 2, 1844, Richardson, Messages, 5:2197–98.

13. Juan Almonte, letter to John Calhoun, March 6, 1844, Manning, Correspondence, 8:163.

14. Pletcher, *Diplomacy of Annexation*, 184–85.

15. Luis Cuevas, letter to Wilson Shannon, March 28, 1845; Wilson Shannon, letter to Luis Cuevas, March 31, 1845; Luis Cuevas, letter to Wilson Shannon, April 2, 1845, *National Intelligencer*, April 28, 1845, NYPL.

16. James Polk, inaugural address, March 4, 1845, Richardson, Messages, 5:2231.

17. Charles G. Sellers, *James K. Polk, Jacksonian, 1795–1842* (Princeton, NJ: Princeton University Press, 1957); Eugene Irving McCormac, *James K. Polk: A Political Biography*, 2 vols. (New York: Russell & Russell, 1965); Charles G. Sellers, *James K. Polk, Continentalist, 1843–1846* (Princeton, NJ: Princeton University Press, 1966); William Dusinberre, *Slavemaster President: The Double Career of James Polk* (New York: Oxford University Press, 2003); Walter R. Borneman, *Polk: The Man Who Transformed the Presidency and America* (New York: Random House, 2009); Robert Merry, *A Country of Vast Designs: James K. Polk, the Mexican War, and the Conquest of the American Southwest* (New York: Simon & Schuster, 2009).

18. Merry, *Country of Vast Designs*, 131.

19. James, *Life of Jackson*, 624.

20. Richard R. Stenberg, "President Polk and California: Additional Documents," *Pacific Historical Review* 10, no. 2 (June 1941): 219.

21. James Polk, December 29, 1848, in Polk Diary.

22. Jean Baker, *James Buchanan* (New York: Times Books, 2004), 25–26, 31.

23. Sellers, *Continentalist*, 213.

24. Smith, *Annexation of Texas*, 410.

25. George Bancroft, letter to Robert Stockton, April 22, 1845, in *The Origins of the War with Mexico: The Polk-Stockton Intrigue* by Glenn W. Price (Austin: University of Texas Press, 1967), 48.

26. Price, *Origins of the War with Mexico*, 76; Richard R. Stenberg, "The Failure of Polk's Mexican War Intrigue of 1845," *Pacific Historical Review* 4 (March 1935): 36–68.

27. Archibald Yell, letter to James Polk, September 10, 1845, Polk Correspondence, 10:220.

28. Stephen Douglas, letter to James Polk, August 25, 1845, Polk Correspondence, 10:183.

29. *National Intelligencer*, June 17, 1845, NYPL.

19. THE MANIFEST DESTINY

1. John O'Sullivan, "Annexation," *United States Magazine and Democratic Review* 17, no. 85 (July–August 1845): 5; Robert Sampson, *John L. O'Sullivan and His Times* (Kent, OH: Kent State University Press, 2003).

2. Albert K. Weinberg, *Manifest Destiny: A Study of Nationalist Expansion in American History* (Chicago: Quadrangle Press, 1963); Frederick Merk, *Manifest Destiny and the Mission in American History* (New York: Alfred A. Knopf, 1963); Thomas Hietala, *Manifest Destiny: Anxious Aggrandizement in Late Jacksonian America* (Ithaca, NY: Cornell University Press, 1985); Amy Greenberg, *Manifest Destiny and the Antebellum American Empire* (New York: Cambridge University Press, 2005); Thomas Jefferson, letter to James Madison, April 27, 1809, Jefferson Writings, 12:274–77; George Bancroft, *A History* (Boston: C. Bowen, 1837); William Ellery Channing, letter to the Hon. Henry Clay on the Annexation of Texas, August 1, 1737, *The Works of William Ellery Channing* (Boston: J. Monroe, 1847), 2:181–261; Annals, 16th Cong., 1st sess., 1719–31.

3. Richard M. Clokey, *William H. Ashley: Enterprise and Politics in the Trans-Mississippi West* (Norman: University of Oklahoma Press, 1990); Harrison Clifford Dale, *The Explorations of William H. Ashley and Jedediah Smith, 1822–1829* (Lincoln: University of Nebraska Press, 1991).

4. Morgan, *Jedediah Smith*; Barton Barbour, *Jedediah Smith: No Ordinary Mountain Man* (Berkeley: University of California Press, 2009).

5. Madsen, *John Jacob Astor*.

6. John D. Unruh, *The Plains Across: The Overland Emigrants and the Trans-Mississippi West, 1840–1860* (Urbana: University of Illinois Press, 1993).

7. Richard Bushman, *Joseph Smith and the Beginning of Mormonism* (Urbana: University of Illinois Press, 1984).

8. Leonard Arrington and Davis Britton, *The Mormon Experience: A History of the Latter-Day Saints* (Urbana: University of Illinois Press, 1992), 101; Leonard Arrington, *Brigham Young: American Moses* (Urbana: University of Illinois Press, 1986).

9. Nathaniel Philbrick, *Sea of Glory: America's Voyage of Discovery, The U.S. Exploring Expedition, 1838–1842* (New York: Penguin, 2004); Charles Wilkes, *Narrative of the United States Exploring Expedition* (Upper Saddle River, NJ: Gregg Press, 1970).

10. Oscar Whither, *The Great Northwest: A History* (Westport, CT: Greenwood Press, 1981), 121, 124.

11. James Polk, inaugural address, March 4, 1845, Richardson, Messages, 5:2231.

12. Henry Clay, letter to Worthington, June 24, 1843, Clay Papers, 9:828.

13. *Tribune*, May 9, 1845; *National Intelligencer*, May 5, 1845; *Daily Union*, May 9, November 6, 1845, NYPL.

14. James Buchanan, letter to Richard Pakenham, July 1845; Richard Pakenham, letter to James Buchanan, July 29, 1845, Buchanan Works, 6:203, 220.

15. Polk Diary, 1:2–5, 62–64.

16. For a classic account of that era, see Richard Henry Dana, *Two Years before the Mast* (New York: New American Library, 2009).

17. "The Californians," *Daily Union*, September 9, 1846, NYPL; John S. D. Eisenhower, *So Far from God: The U.S. War with Mexico, 1846–1848* (New York: Doubleday, 1989), 203.

18. McCormac, *Polk*, 386–87.

19. Andrew Jackson, address to Congress, February 6, 1837, Report no. 752, House of Representatives, 29th Cong., 1st sess.; Report of Senate Committee of Foreign Relations, February 19, 1837, May 16, 1845; Report of House Committee on Foreign Relations, February 24, 1837, *Daily Union*, NYPL.

20. James Buchanan, letter to William Parrot, March 28, 1845, Buchanan Works, 6:133; William Parrot, letter to James Buchanan, April 26, 1848, Manning, Correspondence, 8:712

21. William Marcy, letters to Zachary Taylor, May 28, June 15, July 30, 1845, quoted in Pletcher, *Diplomacy of Annexation*, 255–56.

22. George Bancroft, letter to David Conner, July 11, 1845, in McCormac, *Polk*, 2:375.

23. Polk Diary, 1:1–11.

24. William Parrot, letter to James Buchanan, August 24, 1845, Manning, Correspondence, 746–47.

25. James Polk, letter to John Slidell, November 10, 1845, Polk Correspondence, 10:362–63; James Buchanan, letter to John Slidell, November 10, 1845, Buchanan Works, 6:294–306.

26. James Polk, message to Congress, December 2, 1845, Richardson, Messages, 5:2242–49.

27. Lewis Cass, Senate speech, December 15, 1845, *Daily Union*, December 15, 1845, NYPL.

28. *Daily Union*, April 23, 1846, NYPL.

29. John Slidell, letter to James Buchanan, December 17, 1845, printed in *Daily Union*, May 18, 1846, NYPL.

30. John Slidell, letter to James Polk, December 29, 1845, Polk Correspondence, 10:362–63.

31. Eisenhower, *So Far from God*, 49.

32. James Buchanan, letter to John Slidell, January 20, 1846, *Daily Union*, May 19, 1846, NYPL.

33. Polk Diary, 1:223–25, 226, 233–34.

34. John Slidell, letter to James Buchanan, March 12, 1846, Borneman, *Polk*, 199.

35. K. Jack Bauer, *Zachary Taylor: Soldier, Planter, Statesman of the Old Southwest* (Baton Rouge: Louisiana State University Press, 1958); Brainerd Dyer, *Zachary Taylor* (Baton Rouge: Louisiana State University Press, 1946).

36. Eisenhower, *So Far from God*, 52.

37. Minutes of a meeting between Gen. William Worth and Gen. Rómulo Díaz de la Vega, March 28, 1846, *Daily Union*, May 11, 1846, NYPL.

38. Joseph Wheelan, *Invading Mexico: America's Continental Dream and the Mexican War, 1846–1848* (New York: Carol & Graf, 2007), 89.

39. Ibid., 90.

40. Bauer, *Zachary Taylor*, 149.

41. Polk Diary, 1:382–90.

42. James Polk, war message to Congress, May 11, 1846, Richardson, Messages, 5:2287–93.

43. John Calhoun, speech, Congressional Globe, 29th Cong., 1st sess., 302; *Daily Union*, May 12, 1846, NYPL.

44. For the origins of the war, see Price, *Origins of the War with Mexico*; Thomas Benjamin, "Recent Historiography of the Origins of the Mexican War," *New Mexico Historical Review* 54 (July 1979): 169–81; Norman A. Graebner, "The Mexican War: A Study in Causation," *Pacific Historical Review* 49 (August 1980): 405–46; John Edward Weems, *To Conquer a Peace: The War between the United States and Mexico* (College Station: Texas A & M University Press, 1974). For overviews of the war, see Justin Harvey Smith, *The War with Mexico* (Gloucester, MA: P. Smith, 1963); Eisenhower, *So Far from God*; K. Jack Bauer, *The Mexican War, 1846–1848* (Lincoln: University of Nebraska Press, 1992); and Wheelan, *Invading Mexico*. For naval operations, see K. Jack Bauer, *Surfboats and Horse Marines: U.S. Naval Operations in the Mexican War* (Annapolis: U.S. Naval Institute, 1969). For opposition to the war, see John Schroeder, *Mr. Polk's War: American Opposition and Dissent, 1846–1848* (Madison: University of Wisconsin Press, 1973); Robert W. Johannsen, *To the Halls of Montezuma: The Mexican War in the American Imagination* (New York: Oxford University Press, 1987).

20. THE MEXICAN WAR

1. Donald Houston, "The Superiority of American Artillery," *The Mexican War*, ed. Odie Faulk and Joseph Stout (Chicago: University of Chicago Press, 1973), 101–9; William DePalo, *The Mexican National Army, 1822–1852* (College Station: Texas A & M University Press, 1997); Richard Winders, *Mr. Polk's Army: The American Military Experience in the Mexican War* (College Station: Texas A & M University Press, 1997).

2. Sellers, *Continentalist*, 376.

3. Louis McLane, letter to James Buchanan, February 3, 1846, Buchanan Works, 6:334–35.

4. Polk Diary, 1:397–98.

5. Ibid., 452–53.

6. Bauer, *Mexican War*, 57.

7. Ibid., 62.

8. Ibid., 82.

9. Polk Diary, 2:119.

10. Ibid., 1:402.

11. John S. D. Eisenhower, *Agent of Destiny: The Life and Times of General Winfield Scott* (New York: Free Press, 1997); Allen Peskin, *Winfield Scott and the Profession of Arms* (Kent, OH: Kent State University Press, 2003).

12. Winfield Scott, letter to William Marcy, May 21, 1846, *Daily Union*, June 8, 1846, NYPL.

13. William Marcy, letter to Winfield Scott, May 23, 1846, *Daily Union*, June 8, 1846, NYPL.

14. Bauer, *Mexican War*, 89; Eisenhower, *So Far from God*, 111.

15. Bauer, *Mexican War*, 100.

16. Ibid.

17. Borneman, *Polk*, 245.

18. Dwight L. Clarke, *Stephen Watts Kearny, Soldier of the West* (Norman: University of Oklahoma Press, 1961).

19. Bauer, *Mexican War*, 130.

20. David Lavender, *Bent's Fort* (Lincoln: University of Nebraska Press, 1954).

21. William Emory, *Lieutenant Emory Reports*, ed. Ross Calvin (Albuquerque: University of New Mexico Press, 1951), 49–51.

22. Neal Harlow, *California Conquered: The Annexation of a Mexican Province, 1846–1848* (Berkeley: University of California Press, 1982).

23. James Buchanan, letter to Thomas Larkin, October 17, 1845, Buchanan Works, 6:275–76.

24. George Bancroft, letter to John Sloat, June 24, 1845, in Bornemann, *Polk*, 180–81.

25. Ferol Egan, *Frémont: Explorer for a Restless Nation* (Garden City, NY: Doubleday, 1977); Andrew Rolle, *John Charles Frémont: Character as Destiny* (Norman: University of Oklahoma Press, 1991); Tom Chaffin, *Pathfinder: John Charles Frémont and the Course of American Empire* (New York: Hill and Wang, 2002).

26. James Buchanan, letter to Thomas Larkin, n.d., in Merry, *Country of Vast Designs*, 295–96.

27. John Charles Frémont, *Memoirs of My Life* (New York: Cooper Square Press, 2001), 490.

28. James Polk, veto messages, August 3, 1846, Richardson, Messages, 5:2252.

29. Charles Going, *David Wilmot, Free-Soiler: A Biography of the Great Advocate of the Wilmot Proviso* (Gloucester, MA: P. Smith, 1966).

30. Polk Diary, 2:75–77.

31. Schroeder, *Mr. Polk's War*; Johannsen, *To the Halls of Montezuma*.

32. James Polk, annual message to Congress, December 8, 1846, Richardson, Messages, 8:2321–56.

33. Schroeder, *Mr. Polk's War*, 79.

34. James Buchanan, letter to the Mexican foreign minister, July 27, 1846, *Daily Union*, August 13, 1846, NYPL; Polk Diary, 2:144.

35. Polk Diary, 2:145.

36. George Bancroft, letter to David Conner, May 13, 1846, in Eisenhower, *So Far from God*, 91.

37. James Polk, message to Congress, August 8, 1846, Richardson, Messages, 5:2309–10.

38. Eisenhower, *So Far from God*, 116.

39. Polk Diary, 2:156.

40. Ibid., 249–50.

41. Eisenhower, *So Far from God*, 222–26.

42. Bauer, *Mexican War*, 153, Eisenhower, *So Far from God*, 241–44.

43. Bauer, *Mexican War*, 154; Eisenhower, *So Far from God*, 244–47.

44. Bauer, *Mexican War*, 146–51.

45. Ibid., 206–9.

46. Ibid., 209–18; Eisenhower, *So Far from God*, 188, 190.

47. Eisenhower, *So Far from God*, 190.

48. Polk Diary, 2:444.

49. Ibid., 244–45.

50. Alfred Bill, *Rehearsal for Conflict: The War with Mexico, 1846–1848* (New York: Cooper Square, 1969).

51. John Calhoun, speech, February 9, 1847; *Congressional Globe*, February 11, 1847; Lewis Cass, speech, February 10, 1847; *Daily Union*, February 11, 1847, NYPL.

52. *Congressional Globe*, January 12, 1847, NYPL.

53. Bauer, *Mexican War*, 259–68.

54. Wallace Ohrt, *Defiant Peacemaker: Nicholas Trist in the Mexican War* (College Station: Texas A & M University Press, 1997), 131.

55. Robert W. Drexler, *Guilty of Making Peace: A Biography of Nicholas P. Trist* (Lanham, MD: University Press of America, 1991).

56. William Marcy, letter to Winfield Scott, April 14, 1847; Winfield Scott, letter to Nicholas Trist, May 7, 1847; Winfield Scott, letter to William Marcy, May 7, 1847; Nicholas Trist to Winfield Scott, May 9, 1847, *Daily Union*, April 9, 1848, NYPL.

57. Polk Diary, 3:245, 253.

58. Ibid., 130, 153.

59. Smith, *War with Mexico*, 2:87.

60. Bauer, *Mexican War*, 301; Grant Memoir, 60.

61. Winfield Scott, letter to Santa Anna, August 21, 1847, Manning, Correspondence, 8:922–23.

62. Nicholas Trist, letter to James Buchanan, September 4, 1847, with insert, *Daily Union*, February 3, 1848, NYPL.

63. Polk Diary, 2:519, 3:185.

64. Bauer, *Mexican War*, 322.

65. Ibid., 310–18.

66. Ibid., 322.

67. Ohrt, *Defiant Peacemaker*, 133.

68. Polk Diary, 3:196–97, 199, 345–50; James Buchanan, letter to Nicholas Trist, October 25, 27, 1847, Buchanan Works, 7:442–43, 444.

69. James Polk, annual address to Congress, December 6, 1847, *Daily Union*, December 7, 1847, NYPL.

70. Polk Diary, 3:291–92.

71. Nicholas Trist, letter to James Buchanan, December 6, 1847, in McCormac, *Polk*, 2:525–27; Polk Diary, 3:245–46.

72. Robert Brent, "Nicholas P. Trist and the Treaty of Guadeloupe Hidalgo," *Southwestern Historical Quarterly* 57 (1954): 454–74; Jack Northrup, "Nicholas Trist's Mission to Mexico," *Southwestern Historical Quarterly* 71 (1968): 321–46; Richard Griswold de Castillo, *The Treaty of Guadeloupe Hidalgo* (Norman: University of Oklahoma Press, 1990).

73. Polk Diary, 3:345, 346–47.

74. Emory Upton, *The Military Policy of the United States* (Washington, DC: Government Printing Office, 1917), 216–18; Bauer, *Mexican War*, 397–98.

75. Grant Memoir, 18.

76. Ibid., 33.

21. THE LEGACY

1. Howe, *What Hath God Wrought*, 4.

2. Andrew Jackson, address to the nation, March 4, 1837, Richardson, Messages, 4:1511–15.

3. R. Kent Newmyer, *The Supreme Court under Marshall and Taney* (New York: Davidson Harlan, 2006).

4. Richard Hofstadter, *Anti-Intellectualism in America Life* (New York: Alfred A. Knopf, 1963).

5. Tocqueville, *Democracy in America*, 378.

6. Matthew A. Crenson, *The Federal Machine: The Beginnings of Bureaucracy in Jacksonian America* (Baltimore: Johns Hopkins University Press, 1975).

7. Peter Temin, *The Jacksonian Economy* (New York: W. W. Norton, 1969); John McPaul, *The Politics of Jacksonian Finance* (Ithaca, NY: Cornell University Press, 1972).

8. *National Intelligencer*, October 2, 1833, NYPL.

9. Arthur Schlesinger, *The Imperial Presidency* (Boston: Houghton Mifflin, 2004).

10. August O. Spain, *The Political Theory of John Calhoun* (New York: Octagon Books, 1968); Irving Bartlett, *John C. Calhoun: A Biography* (New York: W. W. Norton, 1980); John Niven, *John C. Calhoun and the Price of Union* (Baton Rouge: Louisiana State University Press, 1993).

11. House Report 175, *Annals*, 24th Cong., 2nd sess., 1–2, January 31, 1837.

12. Peterson, *Great Triumvirate*, 98; Maurice C. Baxter, *Daniel Webster and the Supreme Court* (Amherst: University of Massachusetts Press, 1966). Quote from Daniel Webster, *The Writings of Daniel Webster*, ed. James McIntyre (Boston: Little, Brown, 1903), 8:256.

13. G. Edward White, *The Marshall Court and Cultural Change, 1815–1835* (New York: Oxford University Press, 1992); Jean Edward Smith, *John Marshall: Definer of a Nation* (New York: Henry Holt, 1998); Charles F. Hobson, *The Great Chief Justice: John Marshall and the Rule of Law* (Lawrence: University of Kansas Press, 1996).

14. Peter Irons, *A People's History of the Supreme Court* (New York: Penguin, 1999), 137.

15. Grant Memoir, 57.

16. Arthur D. Howden Smith, *Old Fuss and Feathers* (New York: Greystone Press, 1937), 250n.

17. Grant Memoir, 24.

18. Bauer, *Mexican War*, 397–98.

19. Sellers, *Market Revolution*.

20. Robert Gallman and John Wallis, eds., *American Economic Growth and Statistics before the Civil War* (Chicago: University of Chicago Press, 2004); Cathy Matson, ed., *The Economy of Early America: Historical Perspectives and New Directions* (University Park: Pennsylvania State University Press, 2006); Robert Wright, *The Wealth of Nation Rediscovered: The Integration and Expansion in American Financial Markets, 1780–1850* (New York: Cambridge University Press, 2002); Christopher Clark, *The Roots of Rural Capitalism* (Ithaca, NY: Cornell University Press, 1999).

21. Peter McClelland and Richard Zeckhauser, *Demographic Dimensions of the New Republic* (New York: Cambridge University Press, 2004); HS, 1:11–15; Richard Wade, *The Urban Frontier: The Rise of Western Cities, 1790–1830* (Cambridge, MA: Harvard University Press, 1959); David Gilchrist, ed., *The Growth of Seaport Cities, 1790–1825* (Charlottesville: University of Virginia Press, 1967); Sam Bass Warner, *The Urban Wilderness: A History of the American City* (Berkeley: University of California Press, 1995); Charles S. Snyder, *Developments in Southern Sectionalism, 1819–1848* (Baton Rouge: Louisiana State University Press, 1948).

22. Tocqueville, *Democracy in America*, 13.

INDEX

ABOUT THE AUTHOR

Dr. William Nester is a professor in the Department of Government and Politics at St. John's University in New York. He is the author of more than thirty books on different aspects of international relations, miliary history, and the nature of power. He lives in New York.

www.ingramcontent.com/pod-product-compliance
Lightning Source LLC
Chambersburg PA
CBHW030421100426
42812CB00028B/3056/J